Humanism
and the
Rhetoric
of Toleration

Gary Remer

Humanism and the Rhetoric of Toleration

The Pennsylvania State University Press
University Park, Pennsylvania

Library of Congress Cataloging-in-Publication Data

Remer, Gary, 1957–
    Humanism and the rhetoric of toleration / Gary Remer.

        p.   cm.
    Includes bibliographical references and index.
    ISBN 0-271-01480-6
    1. Christian literature, Latin (Medieval and modern)—Europe
—History and criticism.   2. Latin prose literature, Medieval and
modern—Europe—History and criticism.   3. Authors, Latin (Medieval
and modern)—Europe—Political and social views.   4. Latin prose
literature, Medieval and modern—Classical influences.   5. Rhetoric
—Religious apsects—Christianity.   6. Religious tolerance—Europe
—History.   7. Christianity and literature.   8. Toleration in
literature.   9. Rhetoric—1500–1800.   10. Humanists—Europe.
11. Renaissance.   I. Title.
    PA8030.C47R46   1996
    261.7′2′09409031—dc20   95-9739
                                                                  CIP

Copyright © 1996 The Pennsylvania State University
All rights reserved
Printed in the United States of America
Published by The Pennsylvania State University Press,
University Park, PA 16802-1003

It is the policy of The Pennsylvania State University Press to use acid-free paper for
the first printing of all clothbound books. Publications on uncoated stock satisfy the
minimum requirements of American National Standard for Information Sciences—
Permanence of Paper for Printed Library Materials, ANSI Z39.48–1992.

To Karen

אשת חיל מי ימצא ורחק מפנינים מכרה.

Contents

Acknowledgments   ix

Introduction   1

1. Erasmus: The Paradigm of Humanist Toleration   43

2. Acontius and the Revision of the Humanist Defense   103

3. Chillingworth: Humanism in the Seventeenth Century   137

4. Hobbes: Humanism Turned Against Itself   169

5. Bodin: A Different Kind of Humanist Toleration   203

6. Conclusion: The Aftermath of Humanism   231

Selected Bibliography   279

Index   303

Acknowledgments

Without realizing it at the time, I began working on this book more than sixteen years ago, when I wrote a graduate seminar paper on Acontius and religious toleration. The seminar paper evolved into a study of the Northern humanists and religious toleration, later expanding to include an analysis of the influence of rhetorical concepts on humanist theories of toleration, and, in its final form, focusing on the influence of one particular type of rhetoric, *sermo* or conversation, on the humanist defense of religious toleration. To those that have helped me along this tortuous path, I owe a debt of gratitude.

I am grateful to Julian Franklin, who aided me during the earliest phase of my study of humanism and religious toleration. I am deeply indebted to those who made the transition from seminar paper to book-length manuscript easier than it might otherwise have been: David Rapoport, Amos Funkenstein, Richard Ashcraft, Robert Gerstein, Robert Elstad, Craig Thompson, and Karen Mathews. I am grateful to Debora Shuger, Lawrence Green, John Tinkler, Eric Gorham, Thomas Langston, Martyn Thompson, Gerard Hauser, Larry Arnhart, Keith Werhan, Eldon Eisenach, Michael Zuckert, Kate Langdon Forhan, and Walter Nicgorski for their constructive criticisms of the successive drafts of the manuscript. I am indebted to the readers for Penn State Press, Gordon Schochet and Marion Kuntz, for their help in improving my manuscript. I also owe a debt of gratitude to Dennis Kehoe, Charles Witke, Rush Anne Johnson, and Sister Fidelis Harl for their assistance in translating many of the primary sources.

Thanks are due the UCLA's Clark Memorial Library not only for the fellowships I received in 1986–87 and in the summer of 1991, but for providing me with an intellectual home during my dissertation years. I am also grateful to the Huntington Library for giving me a summer fellowship in 1990.

I am grateful to the editors of the journals that published portions of some of my chapters for permission to reprint these materials. My initial ideas on Erasmus, the focus of Chapter 1, appeared in "Rhetoric and the Erasmian Defence of Religious Toleration," published in *History of Political Thought* 10 (1989): 377–403. Portions of Chapters 1, 3, and 6 appeared in "Humanism, Liberalism, and the Skeptical Case for Religious Toleration," published in *Polity* 25 (1992): 21–43. Chapter 4 is a revised and expanded version of "Hobbes, the Rhetorical Tradition, and Toleration," published in

The Review of Politics 54 (1992): 5–33. Portions of Chapters 1 and 5 appeared in "Dialogues of Toleration: Erasmus and Bodin," published in *The Review of Politics* 56 (1994): 305–36. For Chapter 4 and portions of Chapters 1 and 5, permission is granted by the editors of *The Review of Politics* at The University of Notre Dame.

I am most indebted to friends and family, whose support was more moral than academic. I am grateful for the encouragement I received from Ruth O'Brien, Carol Plunkett, Grace Tiffany, and Rebecca and Sammy Alexander. I offer my sincerest thanks to my parents for their patience, endurance, and support. Finally, I wish to single out my wife, for unfailing love, devotion, and much more, and our infant son, for the joy he unwittingly provided by simply being himself.

Introduction

What Is Humanist Toleration?

The close of the Renaissance was a time of religious intolerance. The French Wars of Religion (1562–93), the Thirty Years' War (1618–48) in Germany, the English Civil War (1642–49), the mass persecution of Anabaptists (1525–1618), and the intensification of witch-hunting (1580–1650) are all examples of the religious violence of that era.[1] True, the persecution of heretics was not new. There already existed a long-standing tradition within the Roman Catholic Church that justified the persecution of the doctrinally deviant.[2] Unlike pagans and Jews, who were tolerated in theory,[3] heretics,

---

1. See Claus-Peter Clasen, *Anabaptism: A Social History, 1525–1618* (Ithaca: Cornell University Press, 1972), 358–422, and Brian P. Levack, *The Witch-Hunt in Early Modern Europe* (London: Longman, 1987), 170–75.

2. It was in the second century that heresy took on the meaning of doctrinal deviation. St. Paul used heresy to connote "discordant," not theological, error. See Edward Peters, ed., *Heresy and Authority in Medieval Europe* (Philadelphia: University of Pennsylvania Press, 1980), 14–17.

3. Christian authorities from St. Augustine to St. Thomas Aquinas supported the limited toleration of non-Christians with the axiom that no person can believe against his will, *credere non potest homo nisi volens.* Joseph Lecler, *Toleration and the Reformation,* trans. T. L. Westow (New York: Association Press, 1960), 1:72; St. Thomas Aquinas, *Summa theologiae,* trans. Thomas Gilby (New York: McGraw-Hill, 1974), 2.2.q10.a8. Erasmus notes the traditional protection of non-Christians in his *De bello turcico* (*On the War against the Turks*), published in about 1530: "The mass of Christians are wrong . . . in thinking that anyone is allowed to kill a Turk, as one would a mad dog, for no better reason than he is a Turk. If this were true then anyone would be allowed to kill a Jew; but if he dared to do so he would not escape punishment by the civil authorities. The Christian magistrate punishes Jews who break the state's laws, to which they are subject, but they are not put to death because of their religion;

having accepted the faith at one time, were considered as having willfully denied it.[4] Moreover, since they still claimed to be Christians, heretics were viewed as an insidious, corrupting force within the body of the faithful.[5] Nevertheless, although the sixteenth and seventeenth centuries had no monopoly on religious persecution and warfare, the proliferation of sects brought on by the Reformation produced a unique situation: a multiplicity of confessions, living side by side, each convinced that it alone possessed the truth and that the others were heretics. The Roman Catholics were not alone in considering heresy a capital crime. Luther, Zwingli, and Calvin all sanctioned the death penalty for heretics.[6]

The sixteenth and seventeenth centuries, however, were not monolithically intolerant. There were also voices of moderation at this time, foremost among them, the Renaissance humanists. They developed their arguments in northern Europe, where the Reformation took hold, in response to the proponents of religious intolerance.[7] Presented with the fact of confessional pluralism, these humanists rejected the attempts of their more dogmatic

---

Christianity is spread by persuasion, not by force; by careful cultivation, not destruction." Erika Rummel, ed., *The Erasmus Reader* (Toronto: University of Toronto Press, 1990), 321–22.

4. *The Political Writings of St. Augustine*, ed. Henry Paolucci (South Bend, Ind.: Regnery/Gateway, 1962), 190–240; David A. J. Richards, *Toleration and the Constitution* (New York: Oxford University Press, 1986), 87–88. For a full discussion of Augustine's views on heresy, see Herbert Deane, *The Political and Social Ideas of St. Augustine* (New York: Columbia University Press, 1963), 172–220.

5. Comparing heresy to forgery, which was then a capital offense, St. Thomas Aquinas argued that the heretic's crime was worse than the forger's: "It is, indeed, far more serious to pervert the faith which ensures the life of the soul than to counterfeit money which is only necessary for our temporal needs." *Summa theologiae* 2.2.q11.a3.

6. Luther justified the execution of heretics by defining them as blasphemers. See Roland Bainton, *Studies on the Reformation* (Boston: Beacon Press, 1963), 39–40.

7. Although toleration drew its advocates from throughout Western Christendom, including the Catholic South, the Roman Catholic Church's reconstitution of the Holy Office of the Inquisition in 1542 prevented much open discussion of toleration in Italy and Spain. See, for example, Silvana Seidel Menchi, *Erasmo in Italia: 1520–1580* (Turin: Bollati Boringhieri, 1987), 288, on the increased repression of persons possessing prohibited books in mid-sixteenth-century Italy. Thus, although Italy — more religiously diverse than is commonly assumed — produced some of the leading evangelical humanist defenders of toleration in the sixteenth century, the Catholic Inquisition forced these champions of toleration into Switzerland, England, and Poland, where they could write and publish against both Catholic and Protestant intolerance. On religious dissent in sixteenth-century Italy, see Delio Cantimori, *Eretici italiani del Cinquecento: Ricerche storiche* (1939; rpt., Florence: Sansoni, 1967); Anne Jacobson Schutte, "Periodization of Sixteenth-Century Italian Religious History: The Post-Cantimori Paradigm Shift," *The Journal of Modern History* 61 (1989): 269–84; and John Martin, *Venice's Hidden Enemies: Italian Heretics in a Renaissance City* (Berkeley and Los Angeles: University of California Press, 1993). Among the prominent Italian humanist cham-

contemporaries to reimpose religious unity through force. Christian concord, these humanists believed, must be achieved through other, nonviolent means.

There is broad agreement among scholars on the general characteristics of the humanist defense of religious toleration.[8] The humanists emphasized persuasion over force as a means to resolve religious disagreements. Their goal of peaceful resolution was aided by the distinction they made between the fundamentals of faith, which were few in number, and the nonessentials, or adiaphora. Although the fundamentals of faith had to be accepted, Christians were permitted to adopt a skeptical outlook toward the adiaphora. By requiring adherence to only a few essential doctrines, the humanists could be tolerant on the rest. This strategy, they hoped, would reunite Christians divided by the Reformation. Finally, the humanists emphasized ethics, which they believed to be the core of Christianity, over dogma. Consequently, they were more concerned with trespasses against morality than with offenses against doctrine. This attitude further reinforced the humanists' reluctance to condemn others for heresy.

Although scholars have capably described the humanists' views on toleration, they have not adequately explained the intellectual setting that gave rise to the humanists' arguments. Two main accounts are offered of the conceptual milieu that engendered humanist toleration; both are flawed. The first contends that the humanists' arguments reflected the values of the Enlightenment or of nascent liberalism.[9] J. W. Allen, for example, believes that the

---

pions of toleration that converted to Protestantism were Bernardino Ochino, Jacobus Acontius (the focus of Chapter 3), Mino Celsi, Celio Secundo Curione, and Lelio Sozzini.

8. See Lecler, *Toleration and the Reformation*, 1:105, 121–32; Henry Kamen, *The Rise of Toleration* (London: World University Library, 1967), 28 and 86–87; Wallace K. Ferguson, "The Attitude of Erasmus Toward Toleration," in *Persecution and Liberty: Essays in Honor of George Lincoln Burr* (New York: Century, 1931), 171–81; Willson H. Coates, Hayden V. White, and J. Salwyn Schapiro, *The Emergence of Liberal Humanism: An Intellectual History of Western Europe* (New York: McGraw-Hill, 1966), 39–44; *The Encyclopedia of Philosophy*, 1972 ed., s. v. "humanism"; Hugh Trevor-Roper, *Catholics, Anglicans and Puritans: Seventeenth-Century Essays* (Chicago: University of Chicago Press, 1988), 189 and 193–95; Hans R. Guggisberg, "The Defense of Religious Toleration and Religious Liberty in Early Modern Europe: Arguments, Pressures, and Some Consequences," *History of European Ideas* 4 (1983): 35–50; and Gustav Mensching, *Tolerance and Truth in Religion*, trans. Hans-J. Klimkeit (University: University of Alabama Press, 1971), 84–87.

9. See John Tulloch, *Rational Theology and Christian Philosophy in England in the Seventeenth Century* (Edinburgh: William Blackwood, 1874), 2–3; J. B. Bury, *A History of Freedom of Thought* (Oxford: Oxford University Press, 1952), 55–57, 73–74; Mensching, *Tolerance and Truth in Religion*, 84–87; Joseph Lecler, S.J., "Religious Freedom: An Historical Survey," trans. Theodore L. Westow, in *Religious Freedom, Canon Law*, ed. Neophytos Edelby

Renaissance thinkers implicitly claimed "for the individual a right to form and to express what conclusions he could about religion."[10] Similarly, W. K. Jordan credits the humanists with laying "the groundwork for a rational and liberal system of thought," and Thomas Lyon asserts that they "sowed the seeds of a rational skepticism."[11] As I shall demonstrate, such claims, left unqualified, go too far. The humanists did not accept the rationalism of the Enlightenment; they were deeply religious men who believed in divinely revealed truths. Nor were the humanists religious individualists, à la liberalism. Unlike liberal advocates of religious liberty, the humanists did not place the right to conscience at the center of their defense of religious toleration.

The second account identifies the characteristics of the humanists' toleration with humanism itself. It is argued that the humanists were moderate, skeptical, that they desired Christian unity, emphasized ethics over dogma, and so on, because these attitudes define them as humanists.[12] This explanation, however, relies on a circular argument that defines humanism in terms of a certain set of values, and those values in terms of their humanism.

---

and Teodoro Jiménez-Urresti (New York: Paulist Press, 1966), 18:14; Richards, *Toleration and the Constitution*, 88–89; E. R. Briggs, "An Apostle of the Incomplete Reformation: Jacopo Aconcio (1500–1567)," *Proceedings of the Huguenot Society of London* 22 (1976): 493–94. On how one humanist, Erasmus, was perceived by nineteenth-century liberals as one of their own, see Bruce E. Mansfield, "Erasmus in the Nineteenth Century: The Liberal Tradition," *Studies in the Renaissance* 15 (1968): 193–219. Also Augustin Renaudet, *Etudes Erasmiennes* (Paris: Libraire E. Droz, 1939), 122–89, who devotes a chapter to Erasmus's theological modernism. The tendency to see the humanists as precursors of the Enlightenment was even accepted by the Enlightenment itself, which regarded the humanists as "prophets of the free human spirit, working toward their emancipation from the narrow confines of the world of medieval religion." See Alister McGrath, *The Intellectual Origins of the European Reformation* (Oxford: Basil Blackwell, 1987), 36.

10. J. W. Allen, *A History of Political Thought in the Sixteenth Century* (London: Methuen, 1928), 79.

11. W. K. Jordan, *The Development of Religious Toleration in England* (London: George Allen & Unwin, 1932–1940; rpt., Gloucester, Mass.: Peter Smith, 1965), 1:29–30; T. Lyon, *The Theory of Religious Liberty in England: 1603–39* (Cambridge: Cambridge University Press, 1937), 18.

12. This explanation is assumed by most writers on humanist toleration. See, for example, Lecler, *Toleration and the Reformation*, 1:105, 121–32, and Ferguson, "Attitude," 172–73. There is no necessary contradiction between explaining the humanists' toleration as a consequence of their modernity and defining it as an inherent part of their humanism. As Manfred Hoffmann has argued in his article "Erasmus and Religious Toleration," many interpreters of Erasmus have equated his humanism with modern values. See *Erasmus of Rotterdam Society Yearbook Two* (1982): 80.

If the humanist defense of toleration is to have any actual connection to the historical tradition called "humanism," then it must be linked to the Renaissance revival of the *studia humanitatis*: grammar, rhetoric, history, poetry, and moral philosophy.[13] It is not to be equated with secular humanism or with a philosophy emphasizing humane values. More particularly, humanist toleration must be explicated with reference to the most distinctively humanistic of these studies: rhetoric. As Paul Oskar Kristeller has observed, Renaissance humanism "must be understood as a characteristic phase in what may be called the rhetorical tradition in Western culture."[14] But Kristeller himself has viewed rhetoric more as it relates narrowly to the humanists' professional concerns than in terms of its broader effect on the humanists' ideas.[15] More common today is the belief that rhetoric's preeminence did have philosophical implications for the humanists.[16] Hanna H. Gray exemplifies this position when she argues that "certain basic presuppositions and attitudes . . . identify the [humanist] movement as a whole," attitudes derived from classical rhetoric "or classical rhetoric as interpreted and adapted in the Renaissance."[17]

Like Gray, I entertain a more expansive view of rhetoric and its influence on the humanists, and I contend that rhetoric was for the humanists almost a weltanschauung, with its own values and outlook. The tradition of classical rhetoric, I argue, best explains the humanist defense of toleration: the humanists' preference for persuasion over force; their skepticism and

13. On defining Renaissance humanism, see Paul Oskar Kristeller, *Renaissance Thought: The Classic, Scholastic, and Humanist Strains* (New York: Harper & Row, 1961), 9–10, and Craig R. Thompson, "The Humanism of More Reappraised," *Thought* 52 (1977): 233.

14. Kristeller, *Renaissance Thought*, 11–13.

15. Thomas O. Sloane, *Donne, Milton, and the End of Humanist Rhetoric* (Berkeley and Los Angeles: University of California Press, 1985), 90; William J. Bouwsma, review of *Renaissance Humanism: Foundations, Forms, and Legacy*, ed. Albert Tabil Jr., *Church History* 59 (1990): 68.

16. Noteworthy among those who affirm the philosophical, or ideological, implications of rhetoric for the humanists are Hanna H. Gray, "Renaissance Humanism: The Pursuit of Eloquence," *Journal of the History of Ideas* 24 (1963): 497–514; William J. Bouwsma, *The Culture of Renaissance Humanism* (Washington, D.C.: AHA, 1973) and "Changing Assumptions in Later Renaissance Culture," *Viator* 7 (1976): 421–40; Nancy S. Struever, *The Language of History in the Renaissance: Rhetoric and Historical Consciousness in Florentine Humanism* (Princeton: Princeton University Press, 1970); Jerrold E. Seigel, *Rhetoric and Philosophy in Renaissance Humanism: The Union of Eloquence and Wisdom, Petrarch to Valla* (Princeton: Princeton University Press, 1968); Charles Trinkaus, *In Our Image and Likeness: Humanity and Divinity in Italian Humanist Thought*, 2 vols. (Chicago: University of Chicago Press, 1970); and Sloane, *Humanist Rhetoric*, particularly 90–99.

17. Gray, "Renaissance Humanism," 497–98.

toleration in nonessentials; and their emphasis on ethical living over dogma. The rhetorician's commitment to *decorum*, his ability to argue both sides of an issue, and his search for an acceptable epistemological standard in probability and consensus influenced the humanists' arguments. Classical rhetoric was not, of course, the sole source of the humanists' toleration. Other principles, such as the inviolability of conscience—especially important to Protestant humanists—may partly explain their support for toleration. Nevertheless, classical rhetoric is both the primary influence on and common denominator to the different humanist justifications for greater religious freedom.

Since I explain humanist toleration primarily through the influence of rhetorical concepts, my work can be classified as a study in the history of ideas, yet I do not see this development as occurring in some relatively autonomous world of ideas. The humanists' ideas were shaped by the historical events of their period, like the English Civil War, and new historical events, like the Reformation, forced the humanists to reconsider the earlier medieval consensus against religious toleration. Nevertheless, in this work I focus on the humanists' ideas and not on the political and social events that surrounded those ideas.

The religious toleration defended by the humanists came in two basic forms. In its minimal form, humanist toleration was sufferance for prudential reasons. For example, humanists counseled toleration of heretics, temporarily, so that the heretics might be persuaded of the truth or so that the bloodshed that would ensue from trying to suppress them might be avoided. Here, toleration does not connote acceptance. Consistent with the Latin root of the word "toleration"—*tolerare*: to bear, to endure, to put up with—the humanists' toleration of heretics suggested moral disapproval. The second form of humanist toleration, however, connotes acceptance of the suspect individual or group by granting him or it full membership in the Church. In this case, the humanists argued that religious dissenters who disagree on nonessentials, but accept the fundamentals of faith, should be allowed to retain their differences and remain within the Church. In late seventeenth-century England, this type of toleration was termed "comprehension" because it sought to include, or "comprehend," Nonconformists within the Established Church. Although during the late seventeenth century, comprehension was distinguished from toleration, the former applying to denominations inside the Established Church and the latter to Christian denominations outside, the humanists of the sixteenth and early seventeenth century would not have accepted this post-Restoration distinction. Because the humanists refused to recognize the permanent fragmentation of Christian unity, they would have regarded all bona fide Christian denominations as inside the Church. Toleration of Christian denominations outside the Church, such as was considered toward the end of the seventeenth century, would have meant the breakup of the universal Church, a concession humanists were unwilling to make.[18]

Regardless of its different forms, the humanists saw toleration as a grant or privilege bestowed by a legitimate granting agency, usually the state with the participation of the Church. Toleration so understood is distinct from religious liberty. Under a regime of toleration dissenters depend on the approval of, or at least the voluntary inaction of, superior authority. By contrast, liberty is not granted but *held* independently of any granting agency.[19] The humanists did not call for religious liberty, the very concept of which first appeared at the end of the seventeenth century.

Desiderius Erasmus (1466–1536), the leading humanist and rhetorician of his age, first established the basic structure of the humanist defense of religious toleration and revealed its origin in rhetoric, to be precise in two rhetorical genres, preaching and conversation. Each genre became a model for a different type of toleration, corresponding, generally, to the earlier division between the basic forms of humanist toleration. Erasmus's first type of toleration, patterned after the genre of preaching, represents toleration in its minimal form. The character of this toleration is reflected in the *decorum* of preaching, which obliges the preacher to accommodate himself to his listeners, even to those who err. The burden, for Erasmus, was on the orthodox speaker to find a more effective way of presenting his message. When the heretic rejects the truth, Erasmus argued, the preacher must be patient with him. *Decorum* itself enjoins moderation, since according to Erasmus, moderate speech is a more effective means of persuasion than

18. Another, less common form of toleration advanced by the humanists was toleration of non-Christians. For most humanists, the toleration of non-Christians was of the kind traditionally permitted by the Church: no forcible conversion to Christianity, but maintenance in a subservient position. Humanism, however, did give rise, on its margins, to a call for a fuller toleration of non-Christians on the ground that non-Christians possessed elements of religious truth. I discuss this more fully in Chapter 6.

19. Gordon J. Schochet, "John Locke and Religious Toleration," in *The Revolution of 1688–1689: Changing Perspectives*, ed. Lois G. Schwoerer (Cambridge: Cambridge University Press, 1992), 150–51; Gordon J. Schochet, "From Persecution to 'Toleration,'" in *Liberty Secured? Britain before and after 1688*, ed. J. R. Jones, vol. 2 of *The Making of Modern Freedom* (Stanford: Stanford University Press, 1992), 127–28; Jordan, *Religious Toleration in England*, 1:19–20.

either abusive speech or action. Nevertheless, preaching could not provide Erasmus with a model of full toleration. Since he believed that preaching concerns matters that should be known with certainty—the fundamentals of faith and the principles of Christian living—the preacher cannot genuinely enter into a debate with his audience. The preacher cannot value a heretic's opinion. Rather, he can only tolerate the heretic in order to change him.

By contrast, Erasmus's second type of toleration, modeled after the genre of conversation represents the broader form of humanist toleration. Conversation concerns a speaker who is engaged in a discussion with one or more others with the goal of arriving at the truth. No one claims certainty. Thus the relationship between interlocutors in conversation, unlike the speaker-auditor relationship in preaching, is nonhierarchical. The *decorum* of conversation, to further the discovery of truth, demands that each participant in the conversation be treated respectfully and allowed to contribute to the discussion. Because no consensus has been reached on the matters being debated, the participants decide for themselves where probability lies. But Erasmus does not apply this "maximal" toleration to all matters or to all people. He does not permit discussion of the fundamentals of faith, defined by Church consensus; only nonessential beliefs are open to debate. And he restricts doctrinal discussion, primarily, to the scholarly elite, excluding the common people. Erasmus may tolerate dissenters from the mass of the people by including them in the Church, but he does not permit them to engage in theological debate regarding adiaphora.

Broader conceptions of toleration arose after Erasmus. Jacobus Acontius (c. 1500–c. 1567), Protestant convert and methodological reformer, expanded Erasmus's *sermo*-based defense of toleration. Instead of restricting conversation to the nonessentials, Acontius argues that all beliefs should be discussed, at least initially. He also disposes of Erasmus's distinction between the learned, who may engage in doctrinal conversation, and the masses, who may not. Every person, according to Acontius, must be given a chance to offer an opinion. In Acontius, preaching ceases, in any way, to be a model of toleration; conversation becomes the sole genre for treating all doctrinal matters, essential and nonessential.

Acontius's innovations were carried forward by William Chillingworth (1602–44), who continues to justify toleration based on the model of conversation. Chillingworth, the most systematic of the seventeenth-century English humanists, uses arguments from probability and accommodation to extend the traditional humanist defense of toleration, applying the rhetorical standard of probability to the fundamentals of faith.[20] Because he believes that certainty is impossible in religious matters, Chillingworth cannot as easily preclude debate on any doctrine, including dogma traditionally considered essential to salvation. Chillingworth also surpasses his humanist predecessors in his explication of accommodation. Rather than define any specific beliefs as fundamental, he implies that the fundamentals must be accommodated to the individual. This willingness to accommodate fundamentals to circumstance weakened the humanist conception of a discrete body of fundamentals. More immediately destructive of the humanist defense of toleration, however, was Chillingworth's emphasis on political obedience. In his later years, Chillingworth allowed political exigencies to overshadow his concern for religious toleration. Although he never completely subordinated toleration to political order, he paved the way for those, like Hobbes, who did.

Erasmus, Acontius, and Chillingworth remained committed humanists throughout their lives. The political philosopher Thomas Hobbes (1588–1679), however, began his scholarly career as a humanist, only to reject humanism later. Motivated by the fear of civil war, Hobbes abandoned the humanists' rhetorically influenced epistemological presuppositions in favor of the authority of science. Geometry, not humanist rhetoric, was Hobbes's model. His rejection of humanist premises also entailed his rejection of the humanist defense of toleration. Although Hobbes retained many of the terms of the humanist defense, like the "fundamentals of faith," he emptied them of their tolerant implications. Thus he exploited the term "fundamentals of faith," not to broaden the area of toleration, but to neutralize any religious claims against the sovereign. For Hobbes, an internal belief that Jesus is Christ is the only prerequisite for salvation. Because it is impossible for the ruler to infringe upon this single fundamental, no subject can raise a religious objection to the ruler's exercise of power. Nevertheless, Hobbesian political theory is, in principle, neutral on the question of toleration. The sovereign must look to the interest of the commonwealth to decide whether or not to be tolerant. Although Hobbes himself did not believe that religious pluralism was conducive to the well-being of the state, there is nothing in Hobbes's theory that rules out toleration, if the sovereign believes the policy to be beneficial.

20. Jordan, *Religious Toleration in England*, 2:377; Barbara Shapiro, *Probability and Certainty in Seventeenth-Century England: A Study of the Relationships Between Natural Science, Religion, History, Law, and Literature* (Princeton: Princeton University Press, 1983), 80.

Hobbes's critique of humanism did not end humanist toleration since his conclusions were too radical to gain widespread acceptance. But Hobbes's criticism of humanist toleration did express a truth about the emerging world. The ideal of conversation, on which the humanists based their defense of toleration, presupposed a discursive community intent on discovering truth. Western culture, however, was moving away from the traditional organic community toward a more atomistic society, that is, from *Gemeinschaft* to *Gesellschaft*. Exemplifying this change was the continuing disintegration of Christendom. Christian unity, which the humanists simultaneously asserted and sought to recapture, was superseded by ever greater religious diversity. In place of the single Body of Christ, of which every person was a part, the new society was composed of as many bodies as there were persons. The individualism of Hobbes's social contract theory, in which the state is created for and legitimated by self-interest, symbolizes this evolution well. There is no "common good" in the Hobbesian Commonwealth, only private goods.

Hobbes pointed to another change in Western thought. The humanists' skepticism was tempered by their belief that some truths, the fundamentals of faith, could be known with at least a high degree of certainty. With the rise of modernity, religious uncertainty increasingly prevailed. Modern writers were no longer willing to "take refuge in the opinion of the Skeptics," as did Erasmus, only "wherever this is allowed by the inviolable authority of the Holy Scriptures and by the decrees of the Church."[21] The humanists could not stop the process of questioning and doubting that they had begun. Hobbes expressed the modern form of skepticism by denying the objective existence of all religious and moral beliefs, excluding the existence of God. For Hobbes, these beliefs are as idiosyncratic as gustatory preferences, and, therefore, in the absence of a sovereign power to coerce external uniformity, religious and moral consensus is unattainable.

The critique Hobbes leveled against humanism and the humanist defense of religious toleration was anticipated by at least one humanist: Jean Bodin (1530–96). He, like Hobbes, feared the anarchic consequences of religious rhetoric and debate. But instead of abandoning humanist toleration, as Hobbes later did, Bodin upheld religious conversation and its rules of *decorum*, which formed the heart of his and other humanist arguments for

---

21. Erasmus, Desiderius, *De libero arbitrio*, in *Luther and Erasmus: Free Will and Salvation* (English translations of Erasmus's De libero arbitrio and Luther's De servo arbitrio), edited by E. Gordon Rupp and Philip S. Watson (Philadelphia: Westminster Press, 1969), 37.

religious toleration. Unlike other humanists, though, Bodin could offer a humanist response to what later became the Hobbesian critique by changing the purpose of conversation. Humanists such as Erasmus, Acontius, and Chillingworth had used conversation to move the interlocutors closer to truth. They believed that the different denominations would agree on the fundamentals of faith and then peacefully disagree on the rest. Hobbes, however, thought that religious disputants, necessarily failing to agree, would eventually resort to force. Hobbes concluded, therefore, that without a single authority to decide in favor of one version of truth, civil war was likely. Bodin broke with the other humanists and agreed with Hobbes's position that religious discussions are potentially dangerous. But Bodin understood that such conversations threatened civil order only when they were intended to undermine the original beliefs of the interlocutors. As Bodin saw it, religious conversation could also be used to reinforce the interlocutors' original beliefs, so that none of the participants would feel threatened in retaining their initial views. Bodin could accept each speaker persisting in his or her original beliefs, including non-Christian participants in the conversation, because he believed that different religions express only parts of a more complex truth. Thus, the advocates for each religion could claim the right to be tolerated because they represented separate aspects of a greater truth.

As Hobbes's criticism of humanist toleration signaled the rise of modernity through its individualism and skepticism, Bodin's revision of humanist toleration pointed to another side of modernity: the extension of full toleration to non-Christians. Whereas early sixteenth-century supporters of religious toleration concerned themselves almost solely with toleration of other Christians, later advocates of religious liberty, in the seventeenth century and beyond, broadened their arguments to include non-Christians. Bodin heralded the modern approach to toleration not only in approving the expansion of toleration, but also in one of the justifications he used to support this expansion: the argument from conscience. Although this argument, which figures prominently in later theories of toleration, was not Bodin's principal justification of toleration, he makes use of this argument more than most other humanists. Thus, in addition to his primary justification of toleration for non-Christians—that non-Christians, like Christians, were partners in truth—Bodin also relied, secondarily, on the argument from conscience, the argument that sincere belief must not be violated. The only exception Bodin made in his defense of conscience is atheism. Bodin deemed the atheist a threat to society, as well as someone incapable of sincere conscience.

Although Bodin made some use of the argument from conscience, it was John Locke (1632–1704) who advanced a full-fledged theory of toleration grounded on conscience. Locke respects even non-Christian claims to conscience and excludes atheists from protection, claiming that they (and most Roman Catholics) endanger civil society. Locke differs from Bodin and other humanists, however, in framing his discussion of conscience in terms of individual, prepolitical rights. Locke thereby places the right to conscience firmly beyond the grasp of the state. Although Locke's theory of toleration laid the foundation for later liberal, rights-based arguments for religious liberty, he did not abandon the humanists' communitarian arguments for toleration. Rather, humanist and liberal, communitarian and individualist, arguments coexist in Locke, who continued to accept the humanists' religious probabilism and belief in consensus. This is not the case with Pierre Bayle (1647–1706). Unlike Locke, but like Hobbes, Bayle argues that nothing can be known of religion. Nevertheless, whereas Hobbes uses skepticism to justify the sovereign's control over religion, Bayle uses his skepticism to defend religious toleration. Bayle's radical skepticism, however, leads him to reject the humanist defense of toleration *in toto*. Bayle's toleration, unlike Locke's, is based solely on the individual's right to conscience. Because no belief can be shown to be objectively more valid than another, Bayle supports anyone's right to conscience, so long as that individual is not an atheist.

Bayle's religious skepticism and individualism ultimately triumphed in Western liberal societies, but the humanists' arguments have not disappeared. Rather, the humanists' arguments from religion have been transformed into the secular theory of free speech known as the marketplace of ideas. The beginnings of that transformation are visible in John Milton's *Areopagitica* and reach their latest stage in the contemporary decisions of the U.S. Supreme Court. In the Supreme Court's free speech opinions, humanist and nonhumanist assumptions coexist, making present-day First Amendment theory multifarious and often contradictory: the humanists' belief in objective truth coexists with an opposing tradition of radical skepticism; and the humanists' conviction that conversation must be civil coexists with the principle of neutrality toward the speaker's rhetorical medium. Ultimately, I argue, humanism's legacy is a belief in the state's affirmative responsibility to foster the discovery of truth. Against the libertarian position that opposes any regulation of speech, the humanist stance is to fashion an environment conducive to rational discussion. For some, rational discussion is promoted by a ban on pornography and hate speech; for others, by the Fairness

Doctrine and campaign finance reform legislation. Despite their differences, these policies share the humanist viewpoint that truth is not the product of a laissez-faire marketplace.

Classical Rhetoric

Decorum

Although the humanist defense of religious toleration was developed during the sixteenth and seventeenth centuries, the intellectual roots of humanist toleration date back to the ancient tradition of classical rhetoric. By "classical rhetoric" I mean the art of persuasion developed by the Greeks and Romans of the classical period. The standard ancient texts of classical rhetoric are Aristotle's *Rhetoric* (composed circa 330 B.C.E.), the anonymous *Rhetorica ad Caius Herennium* (c. 84 B.C.E.), Cicero's *De inventione* (c. 87 B.C.E.), and *De oratore* (54 B.C.E.), and Quintilian's *Institutio oratoria* (c. 94 C.E.). Classical rhetoric remained a separate tradition and a central element in education through antiquity, the Middle Ages, the Renaissance, and the early modern period, only to disappear in the nineteenth century.[22]

Clearly, however, there are different strains of classical rhetoric: Sophistic, Aristotelian, Hellenistic, Ciceronian, Christian, among others. Classical rhetoric's trends inclined in several directions, some more philosophical and others more technical. Rhetoricians have also differed among themselves on the preferred oratorical style, for example, Asiatic or Attic, grand or plain. These and other divisions within classical rhetoric demonstrate that it is a complex tradition, replete with divergent tendencies. I speak, therefore, not of a unitary classical rhetoric that influenced the humanists, but rather of the characteristics and varieties of classical rhetoric that shaped the humanists' defense of religious toleration.[23]

22. For a basic outline of classical rhetoric, see George Kennedy, *Classical Rhetoric and Its Christian and Secular Tradition from Ancient to Modern Times* (Chapel Hill: University of North Carolina Press, 1980), 3–17; Brian Vickers, *In Defence of Rhetoric* (Oxford: Clarendon Press, 1988), 1–82; and Thomas M. Conley, *Rhetoric in the European Tradition* (New York: Longman, 1990). On the disappearance of rhetoric, see Tzvetan Todorov's review of *In Defence of Rhetoric*, in *The New Republic*, 23 January 1989, 35–38, and Samuel Ijsseling, *Rhetoric and Philosophy in Conflict: An Historical Survey* (The Hague: Martinus Nijhoff, 1976), 1.

23. I pay particular attention in this book to the writings of Cicero and Quintilian, who were the main authorities of classical rhetoric during the Renaissance. John Monfasani, "Humanism

Common to all rhetorical approaches is the understanding that content (*res*) cannot be separated from form (*verba*), which is to say that human communication always occurs within a given context.[24] Because ideas once spoken are indissolubly linked to the conditions of their transmission, that is, to language, tone, organization, time, place, and the like, the classical rhetoricians taught that the successful orator must be mindful of propriety. "I shall begin by approving of one who can observe what is fitting," Cicero writes. "This, indeed, is the form of wisdom that the orator must especially employ—to adapt himself to occasions and persons."[25] And roughly two thousand years after Cicero, Chaim Perelman and Lucie Olbrechts-Tyteca write in *The New Rhetoric*, their magisterial work in the revival of rhetoric in the twentieth century, that "the essential consideration for the speaker who has set himself the task of persuading concrete individuals is that his construction of the audience should be adequate to the occasion."[26] The Greeks termed this rhetorical accommodation to occasion *kairos* and *to prepon*. The Romans, who influenced the humanists more substantially, spoke of *decorum* and *apte dicere*.[27] Regardless of nomenclature, the ancient rhetoricians recognized that how orators express themselves is as important as the ideas they express. Hence, Cicero states that "although a word has no force apart from the thing, yet the same thing is often either approved or rejected [that is, seems plausible or not to the listener] according as it is expressed in one way or another."[28] The expression does not change the truth expressed, but truth badly expressed does not persuade. To ensure success, therefore, the classical orators tried to encapsulate *decorum* in a variety of rules that govern the speaker's choice of words and style, even dress and facial expressions.

---

and Rhetoric," in *Renaissance Humanism: Foundations, Forms, and Legacy*, ed. Albert Rabil Jr. (Philadelphia: University of Pennsylvania Press, 1988), 3:185–86.

24. Ijsseling, *Rhetoric and Philosophy in Conflict*, 35; Peter France, *Rhetoric and Truth in France: Descartes to Diderot* (Oxford: Clarendon Press, 1972), 32.

25. *Orator* 35.123. All quotations from Cicero, unless otherwise indicated, are from the Loeb Classical Library editions.

26. *The New Rhetoric: A Treatise on Argumentation*, trans. John Wilkinson and Purcell Weaver (Notre Dame: University of Notre Dame Press, 1969), 19.

27. George Kennedy, *The Art of Persuasion in Greece* (Princeton: Princeton University Press, 1974), 66–67; Richard A. Lanham, *A Handlist of Rhetorical Terms: A Guide for Students of English Literature* (Berkeley and Los Angeles: University of California Press, 1968), 29–30; Cicero *De oratore* 3.10.37; and M. Fabius Quintilian *Institutio oratoria* 2.13.1–8. All quotations from Quintilian, unless otherwise indicated, are from the Loeb Classical Library edition.

28. *Orator* 22.72.

The rules of rhetoric are dictated by prudential knowledge. As Cicero explains, "The knowledge of what is appropriate to a particular occasion is a matter of prudence."[29] But prudence requires more than mere knowledge of technique; it calls for an understanding of human nature. As Perelman and Olbrechts-Tyteca have observed, "Concern with the audience transforms certain chapters in the classical treatises on rhetoric into veritable studies in psychology."[30] The specific precepts of rhetoric, as the rhetoricians themselves allow, are only "the children of expediency," "liable to be altered by the nature of the case, circumstances of time and place, and by hard necessity itself."[31] Rules should be followed only if they work. When they do not, the orator must ignore the rules and instead conform to the general demands of *decorum* and expediency (ibid. 11.1.8–14).

The rhetorical precept of *decorum* obliges orators to familiarize themselves with the multiplicity of human personalities. Thus Cicero observes that it is the orator's responsibility to gain "profound insight into the character of men, and the whole range of human nature."[32] Cicero's observation is preceded by Plato's belief that the orator must "know what types of soul there are" to match the soul-types with the appropriate forms of discourse.[33] Speakers, Plato writes in *Phaedrus*, must "order and arrange [their] discourse accordingly, addressing a variegated soul in a variegated style . . . and a simple soul in a simple style" (277b–c). It is this acceptance

29. *De oratore* 3.55.212.

30. "For instance, in the passage in the *Rhetoric* dealing with the factors of age and fortune in audiences, Aristotle includes many shrewd descriptions of a differential-psychological nature that are still valid today. Cicero shows the necessity of speaking differently to the class of men which is 'coarse and ignorant, always preferring immediate advantage to what is honorable' and to 'that other, enlightened and cultivated, which puts moral dignity above all else [*Partitiones oratoriae* 90].' Later, Quintilian dwells on character differences, which are important to the orator." Perelman and Olbrechts-Tyteca, *New Rhetoric*, 20.

31. Quintilian *Institutio oratoria* 2.13.1–8.

32. *De oratore* 1.12.53. Likewise, Aristotle writes that in addition to being able to reason logically, the orator must be able to "understand human characters and excellences, and to understand their emotions—that is, to know what they are, their nature, their causes and the way in which they are excited." *Rhetoric* 1358a22–25. All quotations from Aristotle, unless otherwise indicated, are from *The Complete Works of Aristotle*, ed. Jonathan Barnes, 2 vols. (Princeton: Princeton University Press, 1984).

33. Plato *Phaedrus* 271c–d. All quotations from Plato, unless otherwise indicated, are from *The Collected Dialogues of Plato*, ed. Edith Hamilton and Huntington Cairns (Princeton: Princeton University Press, 1985). On the relationship between rhetoric and knowledge of the emotions, see Donald C. Bryant, "Aspects of the Rhetorical Tradition: The Intellectual Foundation," *Quarterly Journal of Speech* 36 (1950): 172.

of *decorum* that defines Plato's *Phaedrus* as rhetorical in contrast to his *Gorgias*, notwithstanding the two works' philosophical similarities.[34]

The principle of appropriateness, as conceived by the classical orators, extends beyond speech into the realm of action. Noting the analogy between *decorum* in oratory and prudence in life, Cicero writes: "The universal rule . . . [in both] is to consider propriety."[35] Speech and action should be suited to one's goals. Thus, both Cicero and Quintilian demonstrate that artists, poets, and military generals must all adapt themselves to the demands of propriety.[36] In so doing, these rhetoricians foster a general recommendation of expediency and concern for the current circumstances, endorsing the prudent man, not only the prudent orator, as an exemplar. The humanists, following the ancients' precedent, argued that religious persecution is wrong, in part, because it is imprudent.[37]

Dominant Characteristics: The Main *Genera*

Decorum is a universal characteristic of classical rhetoric; however, we can discern other dominant, though not universal, characteristics from the main genres of oratory. Beginning with Aristotle, the principal exponents of classical rhetoric have identified three basic categories of speech: deliberative, judicial or forensic, and epideictic or demonstrative.[38] Deliberative oratory has its origins in the political assembly, where the deliberative orator seeks to persuade his audience to take or refrain from taking some specific action, such as going to war. Judicial oratory is used in the courtroom, where the speaker tries to persuade the jury of his (or his client's) innocence or guilt.[39]

34. *Phaedrus* 277b–c.
35. *Orator* 21.71. Cf. Isocrates *Panegyricus* 9–10: "For the deeds of the past are, indeed, an inheritance common to us all; but the ability to make proper use of them at the appropriate time, to conceive the right sentiments about them in each instance, and to set them forth in finished phrase, is the peculiar gift of the wise." All quotations from Isocrates, unless otherwise indicated, are from the Loeb Classical Library editions.
36. Examples of the propriety of poets, artists, and military generals are found in *Orator* 22.73–74 and *Institutio oratoria* 2.13.3–14.
37. For a discussion of the Renaissance humanists' adoption of *decorum* as a model of behavior, see Gray, "Renaissance Humanism," 506.
38. See Aristotle *Rhetoric*, bk. 1, chap. 3; Cicero *De inventione* 1.5.7; and Quintilian *Institutio oratoria* 3.4.12–15. For a general discussion of the three genres of oratory, see Vickers, *In Defence of Rhetoric*, 53–62.
39. In ancient Greece, the accused normally pleaded their own cases. By contrast, in Rome most major cases were pleaded by professional orators, called patrons. See George Kennedy, *The Art of Rhetoric in the Roman World* (Princeton: Princeton University Press, 1972), 12–13.

Epideictic oratory is the genre concerned with praise and blame, intended, most often, for ceremonial occasions like funerals. Each form of oratory also has its distinct end:[40] For Aristotle, deliberative oratory has as its end expediency, and for Cicero and Quintilian, expediency and honor;[41] judicial oratory aims at justice; and epideictic oratory aims at honor. Taken as a whole, however, the three oratorical *genera*, or at least deliberative and judicial, which are discussed most in the major classical rhetoric texts, possess some common characteristics: they are directed to the concrete; they are popularly oriented; they appeal to emotions; they are agonistic; and they are skeptical.[42]

The main tendency of classical rhetoric is directed to the concrete, which means, first, that the orator attempts to lead his audience to action: "It is with action that [rhetoric's] practice is chiefly and most frequently concerned."[43] The staples of classical rhetoric, deliberative and judicial oratory, are particularly aimed at action, but even epideictic can lead to action by inspiring the listeners to emulation.[44] Cicero gives voice to the orator's goal

40. Aristotle *Rhetoric* 1358b20–30.

41. Cicero *De inventione* 2.51.155–56. Cicero argues here that all three branches of oratory have honor, in one form or another, as their end. Judicial oratory has equity, "a subdivision of the larger topic of 'honor.'" Deliberative speech has both honor and expediency. And in epideictic, "It is honor alone." Quintilian agrees with Cicero that honor is an end of deliberative oratory: "If it should be necessary to assign one single aim to deliberative I should prefer Cicero's view that this kind of oratory is primarily concerned with the honorable." *Institutio oratoria* 3.8.1.

42. Vickers, *In Defence of Rhetoric*, 53–54. I do not intend this list to be exhaustive. I only list those characteristics relevant to my argument.

43. Quintilian *Institutio oratoria* 2.18.2–5. This relationship between rhetoric and action is explicit in the traditional three *officia oratoris*, or duties of an orator. As stated by Cicero, and restated by Quintilian and St. Augustine, the man of eloquence is to prove (*probare*) or instruct (*docere*), to please (*delectare*), and to stir (*movere*). See *Orator* 21.69–70; Quintilian *Institutio oratoria* 3.5.2 and 12.10.59; and Augustine of Hippo, *On Christian Doctrine*, trans. D. W. Robertson Jr. (Indianapolis: Bobbs-Merrill, 1958), 136–37. All citations from *On Christian Doctrine*, unless otherwise indicated, are from this edition. Of the three *officia*, it is the last duty, focused on action, that receives Cicero's highest praise: "It is the one thing of all that avails most in winning verdicts," and in it "is summed up the entire virtue of the orator." *Orator* 21.69. Quintilian has a similar view of *movere*'s primacy. See *Institutio oratoria* 4.5.6 and 5.8.3.

44. "To praise a man is in one respect akin to urging a course of action. The suggestions which would be made in the latter case become encomiums when differently expressed. . . . Consequently, whenever you want to praise anyone, think of what you would urge people to do." Aristotle *Rhetoric* 1367b35–1368a10. Quintilian argues more forthrightly the practical side of epideictic. "Roman usage," in contrast to Greek, "has given it a place in the practical tasks of life." *Institutio oratoria* 3.7.1–2. Similarly Cicero writes that "there is no class of oratory capable of producing more copious rhetoric or of doing more service to the state, nor any in which the speaker is more occupied in recognizing the virtues and vices" than epideictic. *De partitione oratoria* 20.69. See Vickers, *In Defence of Rhetoric*, 55 and 59; John O'Malley,

of persuading to action: "Service is better than mere theoretical knowledge, for the study and knowledge of the universe would somehow be lame and defective, were no practical results to follow."[45]

To say that the main genres of oratory are concrete indicates, second, that the orator concerns himself with specific and immediate matters, not abstract questions.[46] The distinction between the specific and immediate, on the one hand, and the abstract, on the other, is captured by the rhetorical division between the *definite* and the *indefinite* question. Quintilian explains the difference between the two as follows: "*Indefinite* questions are those which may be maintained or impugned without reference to persons, time or place and the like. The Greeks call them *theses*, Cicero *propositions*, others *general questions relating to civil life.* . . . *Definite* questions involve facts, persons, time and the like. The Greeks call them *hypotheses*, while we call them *causes*. In these the whole question turns on persons and facts."[47] The rhetorician has traditionally involved himself with the *definite* question, the philosopher with the *indefinite* question. Thus the young Cicero excludes the latter from oratory. "I think that everyone understands perfectly," he writes, "that these [abstract] questions are far removed from the business of an orator."[48] And although Cicero in his mature writings eventually does include the *indefinite* question in the orator's repertoire—at least in the "outstanding orator's"—in the main *genera* abstract arguments are still subordinated to the specific and immediate issues.[49]

Along with their concrete subject matter, the three chief types of oratory are also characterized by a popular audience: political assemblies, juries, and

---

S.J., *Praise and Blame in Renaissance Rome: Rhetoric, Doctrine, and Reform in the Sacred Orators of the Papal Court, c. 1450–1521* (Durham: Duke University Press, 1979), 41.

45. Cicero *De officiis* 1.43.153. In arguing for the ideal of action over speculative knowledge, Cicero reflects traditional Roman values. See his statement in *De republica* 1.2.2, that "it is not enough to possess virtue, as if it were an art of some sort, unless you make use of it. . . . [T]he existence of virtue depends entirely upon its use; and its noblest use is the government of the State." See also *De officiis* 1.44.156 and 158.

46. O'Malley, *Praise and Blame,* 41.

47. *Institutio oratoria,* 3.5.5–7.

48. *De inventione* 1.6.8. Aristotle thinks that rhetoric (as opposed to dialectic) "deals in its conclusions rather with individual cases than with general principles or universal rules, maxims and axioms." Edward Meredith Cope, *The Rhetoric of Aristotle with a Commentary,* rev. and ed. John Edwin Sandys (Cambridge: Cambridge University Press, 1877), 1:3. "The duty of rhetoric," Aristotle writes, "is to deal with such matters as we deliberate upon without arts or systems to guide us." *Rhetoric* 1357a2–3.

49. See *Orator* 14.45–46 and *De oratore* 3.30.120–21. Quintilian notes Cicero's change of heart in *Institutio oratoria* 3.5.14–15.

crowds gathered for special occasions.[50] Rhetoricians note this fact by counseling the orator to accommodate himself to the language and assumptions of the masses. The orator, Aristotle advises, "must use . . . notions possessed by everybody."[51] Similarly, Cicero observes that "the whole art of oratory," as opposed to the arcane subject matter of other arts, "lies open to the view, and is concerned in some measure with the common practice, custom, and speech of mankind, so that, whereas in all other arts that is most excellent which is farthest removed from the understanding and mental capacity of the untrained, in oratory the very cardinal sin is to depart from the language of everyday life, and the usage approved by the sense of the community."[52]

As a consequence of oratory's popular character, rhetoricians have traditionally viewed emotional appeals as necessary. They are required, Quintilian maintains, in all three types of oratory.[53] Aristotle accedes to the necessity of emotional appeals only reluctantly, asserting initially that "the arousing of prejudice, pity, anger, and similar emotions has nothing to do with the essential facts," but conceding soon that, given Athens' large juries and assemblies, the orator must appeal to emotions.[54] Accordingly, Aristotle devotes a significant portion of book 2 of *Rhetoric* to an account of arguing from the emotions. Quintilian less ambivalently notes that oratory, because it is practiced before the people-at-large, must make use of emotions. Speaking of orators, he writes: "We on the other hand have to compose our speeches for others to judge, and have frequently to speak before an audience of men who, if not thoroughly ill-educated, are certainly ignorant of such

---

50. An exception is the deliberative oratory appropriate to a smaller audience, such as the Senate.

51. *Rhetoric* 1355a25–30. The orator's audience is composed of "persons who cannot take in at a glance a complicated argument." *Rhetoric* 1357a2–5.

52. *De oratore* 1.3.12. This identification of rhetoric with the public is accepted by opponents of rhetoric too, like Plato in *Gorgias*. There, Plato distinguishes between dialectic (philosophy) and rhetoric: dialectic is between individuals; rhetoric, by contrast, reaches out to the masses. For Plato, however, this numeric difference in audience (that is, the individual versus the many) only points to a more fundamental distinction. Plato believes that the one-on-one dialectic is designed to effect moral reform; public communication aims solely at pleasing the audience: "For I know how to produce one witness to the truth of what I say, the man with whom I am debating, but the others I ignore. I know how to secure one man's vote, but with the many I will not even enter into discussion." *Gorgias* 474a. See also Vickers, *In Defence of Rhetoric*, 107, and George Klosko, "Rational Persuasion in Plato's Political Theory," *History of Political Thought* 7 (1986): 15–31.

53. *Institutio oratoria* 3.4.15. See France, *Rhetoric and Truth*, 28–32.

54. *Rhetoric* 1354a15–20, 1377b21–25; Vickers, *In Defence of Rhetoric*, 72–73.

arts as dialectic: and unless we force, and occasionally throw them off their balance by an appeal to their emotions, we shall be unable to vindicate the claims of truth and justice."[55] Both Aristotle and Quintilian betray a similar view of the common man and human nature. Reason may be sufficient for philosophers, but the masses do not decide on reason alone. The average person's nature necessitates extrarational appeals. And, as Quintilian argues, a prudent use of emotions will not only benefit the orator personally, but, if he is a good orator (a *vir bonus dicendi peritus*) truth and justice as well (ibid. 12.1.1).

The importance of emotional appeals to classical rhetoric is indicated by their status as modes of persuasion or proofs. Aristotle established, and subsequent rhetoricians have accepted, three modes of persuasion: *ethos, pathos,* and logical explanation.[56] Only the last is directed to the listener's reason; the first two, as Quintilian points out, appeal to emotions.[57] And of the three rhetorical proofs, it is *pathos,* the most emotionally charged, that is most highly valued. *Pathos* is depicted as the quintessential rhetorical talent. Cicero writes that "every one must acknowledge that of all the resources of an orator far the greatest is his ability to inflame the minds of his hearers and to turn them in whatever direction the case demands. If the orator lacks that ability, he lacks the one thing most essential."[58] Cicero even advises the orator to prefer emotion to reason. Thus, the hearer should be "so affected as to be swayed by something resembling a mental impulse or emotion,

---

55. *Institutio oratoria* 5.14.29.

56. "Of the modes of persuasion furnished by the spoken word there are three kinds. The first kind [*ethos*] depends on the personal character of the speaker; the second [*pathos*] on putting the audience into a certain frame of mind; the third on the proof, or apparent proof, provided by the words of the speech itself." *Rhetoric* 1356a1–4. *Ethos* persuades when "the speech is so spoken as to make us think [the speaker] more credible, [since] we believe good men more fully and more readily than others." *Rhetoric* 1358a3–13. *Pathos* succeeds "when the speech stirs the emotions," for "our judgments when we are pleased and friendly are not the same as when we are pained and hostile." *Rhetoric* 1356a13–19. Logical explanation works "through the speech itself when we have proved a truth or an apparent truth by means of the persuasive arguments suitable to the case in question." *Rhetoric* 1356a19–21. The original Aristotelian sense of *ethos,* however, changes under the Romans, and it comes to mean a gentler form of the emotions roused by *pathos.* Cicero contrasts *ethos,* which is "courteous and agreeable, adapted to win good will," with *pathos,* which is violent, hot, and impassioned. *Orator* 36.128. See Vickers, *In Defence of Rhetoric,* 74. I am following the noted scholar of Aristotelian rhetoric William M.A. Grimaldi, S.J., in translating the third mode of persuasion as "logical" explanation, instead of using the traditional term *logos.* See his *Aristotle, Rhetoric I: A Commentary* (New York: Fordham University Press, 1980), 40.

57. *Institutio oratoria* 6.2.8.

58. *Brutus* 80.279. See also *Brutus* 93.22 and *Orator* 36.127.

rather than by judgment or deliberation. For men decide far more problems by hate, or love, or fear, or illusion, or some other inward emotion, than by reality."[59] Quintilian adopts Cicero's preference for *pathos* to logical explanation. In a passage that seems to justify the most damning critiques of rhetoric, Quintilian recommends emotional appeals for their unique ability to deceive, when judges "and their thoughts have actually to be led away from the contemplation of the truth . . . and just as lovers are incapable of forming a reasoned judgment on the beauty of an object of their affections, because passion forestalls the sense of sight, so the judge, when overcome by his emotions, abandons all attempts to enquire into the truth of the arguments, is swept along by the tide of passion, and yields himself unquestioning to the torrent."[60] Quintilian's use of *pathos* to pervert the truth contradicts Christian morality. Nonetheless, Augustine and his Christian successors do not abandon emotional appeals. Because orthodox Christian theology posits a radical disjunction between reason and volition, brought on by the Fall, Christian rhetoricians, such as Augustine, can justify *pathos* for "moving the minds of listeners, not that they may know what is done, but that they may do what they already know should be done."[61]

The manner in which the orator appeals to passions alludes to rhetoric's agonistic ("fighting") nature. The orator uses passions purposefully. He excites the audience's passions both to persuade them of his position and, in deliberative and judicial oratory, to defeat his opponent: "To prove one's own case and demolish the adversary's."[62] The contentious character of political speech is suggested by the fact that the Greek word *agon* means not only "contest" or "struggle," but also denotes the "public assembly" and "assembly place."[63] (Although epideictic oratory is mainly celebratory, not contentious, it has also been used agonistically in both legal and political settings.)[64] We can, therefore, characterize classical oratory as agonistic. People use rhetoric, as Aristotle states in the first few sentences of *Rhetoric*,

59. *De oratore* 2.42.178.
60. *Institutio oratoria* 6.2.5–6. See also Vickers, *In Defence of Rhetoric*, 76–78.
61. Augustine *On Christian Doctrine* 4.27.
62. Cicero *Orator* 25.122.
63. Paul A. Rahe, *Republics Ancient and Modern: Classical Republicanism and the American Revolution* (Chapel Hill: University of North Carolina Press, 1992), 43.
64. "The award of praise or blame to a witness may carry weight in the courts, while it is also a recognized practice to produce persons to praise the character of the accused. Further the published speeches of Cicero directed against his rivals in the election to the consulship . . . are full of denunciation." Quintilian *Institutio oratoria* 3.7.2.

"to defend themselves and attack [others]."[65] Rhetoric's combative character is illustrated by its metaphors. In Isocrates, the orator becomes the athlete struggling against his opponent in the gymnasium.[66] In this imagery is reflected the "feeling that oratory is a contest in which man exhibits something of his manliness."[67] Later, Cicero and Quintilian reject the ideal of orator as athlete, adopting instead the metaphor of the orator as soldier, vanquishing his enemies on the battlefield.[68] For them, the athlete was too pampered, unable to compete in the real world. The "athletic" orator would succumb under pressure, "like bodies accustomed to the oil of the training school, which for all the imposing robustness which they display in their own contests, yet, if ordered to make a day's march with the troops, to carry burdens and mount guard at night, would faint beneath the task and long for their trainers to rub them down with oil and for the free perspiration of the naked limbs."[69] Regardless of the metaphor chosen, athletic or military, rhetoric is represented as a struggle in which one side wins and the other side loses.

Rhetoric's agonistic structure, which pits orator against orator, signals the final characteristic of the main *genera*, which is skepticism, or the denial of (certain) knowledge.[70] Contentiousness indicates a controversial subject matter, since without controversy, orators would have no need (or justification) to compete with each other; and controversy betokens uncertainty, since there can be no controversy where there is certainty.[71] The orator's inability to demonstrate his argument with certainty is evident in the

---

65. *Rhetoric* 1354a5–6. See George Kennedy's translation, *On Rhetoric: A Theory of Civic Discourse* (New York: Oxford University Press, 1991), 29.

66. See, for example, Isocrates *Panegyricus* 45–46.

67. Kennedy, *Art of Persuasion*, 189.

68. Cicero, *De oratore* 1.24.157 and 2.20.84, *Orator* 13.42; and Quintilian *Institutio oratoria* 10.5.17–20. See Debora K. Shuger, *Sacred Rhetoric: The Christian Grand Style in the English Renaissance* (Princeton: Princeton University Press, 1988), 21–23.

69. Quintilian *Institutio oratoria* 11.3.26–27.

70. The rhetorician's skepticism derives from the nature of his subject matter, which is not "outside the control of mere opinion, and within the grasp of exact knowledge." Cicero *De oratore* 1.23.108.

71. "The very nature of deliberation and argumentation is opposed to necessity and self-evidence, since no one deliberates where the solution is necessary or argues against what is self-evident. The domain of argumentation is that of the credible, the plausible, the probable to the degree that the latter eludes the certainty of calculations." Perelman and Olbrechts-Tyteca, *New Rhetoric*, 1. To the extent that epideictic oratory is not contentious, but celebratory (or condemnatory) it is not characterized by skepticism. O'Malley acknowledges this difference in epideictic, referring to the genre as "dogmatic" versus "disputatious." See *Praise and Blame*, 43 and 159–62. Epideictic, however, was sometimes applied to contentious situations, as noted earlier.

deliberative genre, where the orator deliberates about a future action, in which there is rarely only a single option. Aristotle perceives the indeterminacy of deliberative issues when he states: "The subjects of our deliberation are such as seem to present us with alternative possibilities: about things that could not have been, and cannot now or in the future be, other than they are, nobody who takes them to be of this nature wastes his time in deliberation."[72] Quintilian concludes, similarly, that "deliberation is always concerned with questions where some doubt exists."[73]

Judicial oratory, unlike deliberative oratory, concerns facts, which are, in theory, ascertainable and immutable. Nevertheless, the judicial genre also pertains to matters that are, at least in the present, under contention. For although an action in the past either did or did not occur, conclusive proof that it occurred might not be available. Evidence, termed "inartificial proofs" in the rhetorical treatises, can be refuted: witnesses, documents, confessions extracted by torture, and so on are impeachable.[74] And the arguments that the orator himself invents, the so-called "artificial proofs," rarely prove a case with certainty.[75] In addition to the uncertainty of legal proofs is the ambiguity of the law itself. Cicero states that "those cases which are such that the law involved in them is beyond dispute, do not as a rule come to a hearing at all." Therefore, the ambiguity of the law allows the orator "to find some authority in favor of whichever side he is supporting."[76]

Without the possibility of certainty in most deliberative or judicial proceedings, rhetoricians have relied on probability as their standard of knowledge. Plato attributes argument from probability to the fifth-century rhetoricians, Tisias and Gorgias, although, in fact, it was used in Athens before Gorgias's arrival in 427.[77] Plato is not sanguine about the rhetori-

---

72. *Rhetoric* 1357a4–7. See also 1357a23–27: "Most of the things about which we make decisions, and into which we inquire, present us with alternative possibilities. For it is about our actions that we deliberate and inquire, and all our actions have a contingent character; hardly any of them are determined by necessity." Cf. Isocrates *Antidosis* 256: "With this faculty [that is, rhetoric] we both contend against others on matters which are open to dispute and seek light for ourselves on things which are unknown."

73. "It appears to me . . . that where necessity exists, there is no room for deliberation, any more than where it is clear that a thing is not feasible." Quintilian *Institutio oratoria* 3.8.25.

74. Quintilian *Institutio oratoria*, bk. 5, chaps. 1–7.

75. There does exist a category of irrefutable arguments or "those which cannot be otherwise." See Cicero *De inventione* 1.29.44–45 and Quintilian *Institutio oratoria* 5.9.3–7. If these arguments predominated, however, there would be no dispute between parties.

76. *De oratore* 1.57.241–42.

77. *Phaedrus* 267a–b. My discussion of probability in ancient Greece is based on Kennedy, *Art of Persuasion*, 30–31 and 40. The first known use of argument from probability occurred

cian's use of probability. For Plato, probability is sham truth, which orators have substituted for the genuine article.[78] Aristotle, however, vindicates probability against Plato's charge by concluding that it is impossible to impose a standard of certainty on material that does not permit it. The knowledge that Plato demands is simply not applicable to rhetoric, according to Aristotle, because the orator addresses issues in which necessary and certain knowledge cannot be attained. Aristotle validates argument from probability, explicitly, by identifying the enthymeme (the rhetorical syllogism in which the speaker begins from probable premises) and example (rhetorical induction in which a proposition is proved probable on the basis of previous examples) as the fundamental tools of logical explanation in rhetoric.[79] Implicit in Aristotle's delineation of two distinct rhetorical modes of demonstration is the conviction that, notwithstanding their probabilistic assumptions, these types of argument are as legitimate for rhetoric as the syllogism is for logic. Probability was also central to Roman rhetoric. Cicero makes use of probability both personally, in his speeches, and in his rhetorical writings, even equating rhetorical argument with probability.[80] Quintilian also links rhetoric to probability when he writes that rhetoric "always [aims] at stating what is probable."[81]

---

in the sixth century B.C.E. Homeric *Hymn to Hermes*, in which Hermes, seeking to dissuade Apollo from harming him, argued that it was unlikely that he was a cattle thief, seeing that he was only a day-old babe. Sophocles' *Oedipus the King*, 583–615, provides another example of argument from probability, this time from the fifth century. In *Oedipus*, Creon attempted to prove that he had no motive to kill the king by arguing that such an action was improbable on his part: would he kill the king, he asked, when he had all the benefits but none of the hardships of office?

78. "In the law courts nobody cares a rap for the truth. . . . Even actual facts [he writes mockingly] ought sometimes not be stated if they don't tally with probability; they should be replaced by what is probable, whether in prosecution or defense; whatever you say, you simply must pursue this probability they talk of, and can say good-by to the truth forever." *Phaedrus* 272d–273e.

79. *Rhetoric* 1357a14–15. What Aristotle says of the dialectical syllogism, in the *Topics* 100b20, is true of the rhetorical syllogism, since both take the probable as their point of departure. *Rhetoric* 1354a–1358a; *Topics* 1.1 and 1.12; *Prior Analytics* 2.27. See also William M.A. Grimaldi S.J., *Studies in the Philosophy of Aristotle's Rhetoric*, in *Hermes: Zeitschrift für Klassische Philologie* (Weisbaden: Franz Steiner, 1972), and Victoria Kahn, *Rhetoric, Prudence, and Skepticism in the Renaissance* (Ithaca: Cornell University Press, 1985), 33.

80. "Cicero makes considerable use of argument from probability, built on the evidence of documents and witnesses," in *Pro Quinctio*. See Kennedy, *Art of Rhetoric*, 143. Cicero classifies the types of argument from probability in *De inventione* 1.29.44ff. In *Partitiones oratoriae* 2.5, Cicero writes that an argument is "a plausible device [*probabile inventum*] to obtain belief."

81. *Institutio oratoria* 2.17.39.

The description of rhetoric as concerned with the nondemonstrable and, consequently, with the probable parallels the principles of Academic skepticism, the philosophical school with which Cicero identified.[82] This form of skepticism was formulated first by Arcesilas of Pitane (c. 315–241 B.C.E.) and elaborated, a century or so later, by Carneades (c. 213–129 B.C.E.).[83] Academic skepticism, as articulated by Carneades, denied the existence of epistemological certainty. The impossibility of knowledge could be displayed, the Academics believed, by their exercise of arguing *in utramque partem*, on either side of a question, as well as against every opinion forwarded.[84] This method of argumentation was perfected by Carneades who, according to Cicero, would argue in favor of justice one day, only to refute his arguments the next day.[85] Unlike the Pyrrhonian skeptics, however, the Academic skeptics did not believe that skepticism should degenerate into total doubt and suspension of judgment.[86] In the absence of certainty, the Academics were willing to accept probability as the closest approximation of the truth, and they, who had previously employed argument *in utramque partem* to deny the possibility of knowledge, now used the same procedure to arrive at verisimilitude.[87] By arguing the strengths and weaknesses of each position, the skeptic could then compare the different opinions and decide which one is most probable.[88] Recognizing the compatibility

82. Cicero *Tusculan Disputations* 2.3.9, 4.21.47; *De officiis* 2.2.7–8; *De natura deorum* 1.5.11.

83. Both Arcesilas and Carneades were heads of the Academy founded by Plato, which, in its shift to skepticism, came to be known as the "New Academy." For Cicero's account of the development of Academic skepticism, see *Academica* 1.12.43–46. Recent discussions of the Academic skeptics include Charlotte Stough, *Greek Skepticism: A Study in Epistemology* (Berkeley and Los Angeles: University of California Press, 1969), chap. 3; *The Encyclopedia of Philosophy*, 1972 ed., s.v. "skepticism"; Marjorie O'Rourke Boyle, *Rhetoric and Reform: Erasmus' Civil Dispute with Luther* (Cambridge: Harvard University Press, 1983), 17–20; and Peter Green, *Alexander to Actium: The Historical Evolution of the Hellenistic Age* (Berkeley and Los Angeles: University of California Press, 1990), 607–8.

84. Cicero *Academica* 1.12.45, 1.18.60; *De natura deorum* 1.5.11.

85. *De republica* 3.5.9.

86. Pyrrhonian skepticism, named for its reputed founder, Pyrrho of Ellis (c. 360–c. 270 B.C.E.), received its fullest expression in Sextus Empiricus's *Outlines of Pyrrhonism* (written in the latter part of the third century C.E.). The Pyrrhonians believed that the Academics, by asserting that nothing could be known, were, in effect, asserting something. Instead, the Pyrrhonians proposed to assert nothing, not even whether or not knowledge was possible. This suspension of judgment, they thought, would lead to a state of mental calm (*ataraxia*), in which social conventions would be followed undogmatically.

87. Cicero *De officiis* 2.2.7; *Academica* 2.3.7–9, 2.31.99–100.

88. As Cicero explains: "And as to the fact that our school argues against everything, that is only because we could not get a clear view of what is 'probable,' unless a comparative

between rhetoric and skepticism, Cicero advised orators to turn to the Academic skeptics, as he himself had done, particularly to their argument *in utramque partem*. He declares his preference for the Academy's rule of "discussing both sides of every question, not only for the reason that in no other way did I think it possible for the probable truth to be discovered in each particular problem, but also because I found it gave the best practice in oratory."[89] Only an orator who could argue both sides of any issue "would be the one and only true and perfect orator."[90]

Conversation

In addition to the three main oratorical genres, there exists another kind of rhetoric identified by the classical rhetoricians: conversation (*sermo*). Although this genre has received scant attention from ancients and moderns, Cicero does describe it. He contrasts it with public judicial or deliberative speech, which he refers to, collectively, as "oratory," *contentio*: "Speech also has great power, and that in two areas: in oratory and in conversation. Oratory [*contentio*] should be employed for speeches in law-courts, to public assemblies or in the senate, while conversation [*sermo*] should be found in social groups, in philosophical discussions and among gatherings of friends—and it may also attend dinners!"[91] Although Cicero acknowledges

---

estimate were made of all the arguments on both sides." *De officiis* 2.2.8. See also *Tusculan Disputations* 2.3.9 and *Academica* 2.3.7–8. Cf. Aristotle *Topics* 101a35–37, where Aristotle writes that "the ability to puzzle on both sides of a subject will make us detect more easily the truth and error about the several points that arise." See also Alain Michel, *Rhétorique et philosophie chez Cicéron: Essai sur les fondements philosophique de l'art de persuader* (Paris: Presses Universitaires de France, 1960), 158–73.

89. *Tusculan Disputations* 2.3.9.

90. *De oratore* 3.21.80. A variation of argument *in utramque partem*, as Cicero observes, was developed by Aristotle and the Peripatetics. See Aristotle *Rhetoric* 1355a29–35; and Cicero *De oratore* 3.19.71, 3.27.107; *Orator* 14.46; *De finibus* 5.4.10; and *De oratore* 1.34.157–59. Plato also observes, disparagingly, the orator's ability to argue both sides of an issue: "Then he whose speaking is an art will make the same thing appear to the same persons at one time just and at another, if he wishes unjust. . . . And in political thinking he will make the same things seem to the State at one time good and at another the opposite." *Phaedrus* 261c–d. That type of rhetoric which follows the Academic skeptic's pattern of debating both sides of an issue to arrive at a decision has been termed "controversial rhetoric" by some contemporary scholars. See Conley, *European Tradition*, chap. 1 and 2, and Sloane, *Humanist Rhetoric*, 115 and 296 n. 33.

91. *De officiis* 1.37.132. Translation from Cicero, *On Duties*, Cambridge Texts in the History of Political Thought, ed. M. T. Griffin and E. M. Atkins (Cambridge: Cambridge University Press, 1991), 51. See also *De officiis* 2.14.48–49. Cicero's distinction was preceded

that conversation is a distinct type of rhetoric, he admits that it is not adequately treated by the rhetoricians: "Guidance about oratory is available, provided by the rhetoricians, but none about conversation, although I do not see why that could not also exist." Not systematically analyzed by the ancient rhetoricians, conversation has been easy to overlook. It is, however, the single most important rhetorical genre for understanding the humanist defense of religious toleration.

Because conversation is a form of rhetoric, Cicero believes that rhetorical precepts are pertinent: "Such advice as there is about words and opinions will be relevant also to conversation."[92] Cicero's belief that conversation should be treated rhetorically would suggest that he formulated an appropriate rhetoric for his own conversational writings, that is, his dialogues, which include most of his rhetorical and philosophical works.[93] Cicero attests to his use of rhetoric in the dialogues, when he differentiates in *De finibus* between the rhetoric he employs there, "the rhetoric of the philosophers," and "the sort which we use in the law-courts."[94]

Sermo embraces the gamut of conversations, but in this book I will focus on a subset of *sermo*: the dialogue. The dialogue, like conversations in general, is distinguished stylistically from the basic kinds of oratory by its form. Unlike common oratory, which a single active speaker delivers to a passive audience, dialogue is conversation between two or more interlocu-

---

by Plato's twofold division of rhetoric: "But the art of the lawyer, of the popular orator, and the art of conversation may be called in one word the art of persuasion. True. And of persuasion, there may be said to be two kinds? What are they? One is private and the other public." *Sophist* 222c–d. In *Phaedrus* 261a, Plato speaks of the art of rhetoric as "a kind of influencing of the mind by means of words, not only in courts of law and other public gatherings, but in private places also." Quintilian cites Plato's category of private rhetoric, designating it "conversational [*sermocinatrix*]" and "adapted for private discussions [*accommodata privatis disputationibus*]." *Institutio oratoria* 3.4.10. Quintilian himself, however, did not accept conversation as a separate category of rhetoric. Epideictic oratory, which cannot be categorized as either *contentio* or *sermo*, possesses attributes of both. Later, the Roman rhetorician C. Julius Victor (fourth century C.E.) distinguished *sermo* from oratory, near the end of his summary of rhetorical theory, *Ars rhetorica*. Victor writes there that an account of *sermo* is necessary because "*sermo* is used more frequently than oration." *C. Iulii Victoris ars rhetorica*, in *Rhetores latini minores*, ed. Charles Halm (Leipzig: B. G. Teubner, 1863; rpt., Frankfurt am Main: Minerva, 1964), 446.

92. *De officiis* 1.37.132. Translation from Cicero, *On Duties*, 51.

93. Cicero's rhetorical dialogues are *De oratore*, *De partitione oratoria*, and *Brutus*, and his philosophical dialogues include *De republica*, *De legibus*, *Academica*, *De finibus*, *Tusculan Disputations*, *De natura deorum*, *De senectute*, *De amicitia*, and *De divinatione*.

94. Cicero *De finibus* 2.6.17, *Tusculan Disputations* 1.47.112.

tors, reflecting, ideally, the give-and-take of their discussion.[95] Although the dialogue is a type of conversation, it is set apart from other varieties of conversation in that it is an inquiry into problems of some importance, in which different positions are explored. Simple, nonpurposive conversations and those that concern "lighter issues" are not dialogue. Diogenes Laertius, in *Life of Plato*, defines dialogue as "a discourse [*logos*] consisting of question and answer on some philosophical or political subject, with due regard to the characters of the persons introduced and the choice of diction."[96] And Cicero, though he describes the particular conversations in his dialogues as *sermones*,[97] nevertheless distinguishes his dialogues from simple conversations by referring to them as *disputationes*, that is, discussions.[98]

A variety of specific forms are consistent with this general characterization of dialogue. For example, the Socratic dialogues of Plato take the form of brief questions and answers between interlocutors.[99] Aristotle's dialogues, which are not extant, were distinguished by a principal speaker, whose continuous speech was occasionally interrupted by other speakers.[100] The Ciceronian dialogue, which most influenced the Renaissance humanists,[101]

95. Of intermediate status, between oratory and pure dialogue, are didactic dialogues, like Cicero's *De partitione oratoria*, which possess dialogue's conversational form, but are not truly interactive because the student is a passive consumer of the teacher's knowledge. Aristotle distinguishes between didactic and examinational arguments on the grounds that in the former the learner does not yet know the appropriate principles of the subject, but that in the latter the answerer is sufficiently knowledgeable of the subject's basic premises: "Didactic arguments are those that deduce from the principles appropriate to each subject and not from the opinions held by the answerer (for the learner must be convinced). . . . Examinational arguments are those that deduce from premises which are accepted by the answerer and which any one who claims to possess knowledge of the subject is bound to know" *De sophisticis elenchis* 165 61–7.

96. Diogenes Laertius *Life of Plato* 3.48, 1:319, in *Lives of Eminent Philosophers*, trans. R. D. Hicks (Cambridge: Harvard University Press, 1972). See also David Marsh, *The Quattrocento Dialogue: Classical Tradition and Humanist Innovation* (Cambridge: Harvard University Press, 1980), 2; Rudolf Hirzel, *Der Dialog: Ein literarhistorischer Versuch* (Leipzig, 1895; rpt., Hildesheim: Georg Olms, 1963), 1:2–7; and the Loeb Classical Library, introduction, to *Brutus*, by Cicero, 8–9.

97. *De oratore* 1.7.27, 1.8.29.

98. Ibid. 1.6.23. *Disputatio* does not mean dispute or disputation. By not equating dialogue with *sermo*, Cicero is presumably alluding to the artificial, mimetic character of his dialogues that stands in contrast to the naturalness and lack of artifice of genuine conversations. I thank Elaine Fantham for this observation.

99. Cicero *De finibus* 2.1.2; Hirzel, *Dialog*, 1:174–271.

100. Cicero *Letters to Atticus* 13.19; Hirzel, *Dialog*, 1:272–308.

101. On Cicero as the primary influence on the humanists, see Marsh, *Quattrocento Dialogue*, 8; Hirzel, *Dialog*, 1:388–89.

usually tended toward the Aristotelian model, insofar as Cicero generally allowed his speakers to carry on for longer, uninterrupted periods[102] (a trait that he identified with rhetoric, as opposed to dialectic).[103] Yet another form of dialogue, initially identified by the ancients and later recognized by the humanists, is the letter.[104]

Ultimately, it is the fundamental principle of *decorum*, not formal or stylistic diversity, that makes a dialogue, or any conversation, rhetorical. *Decorum* is a distinguishing feature of rhetoric, common to *sermo* and *contentio*. And it is with conversational *decorum* in mind that Cicero counsels, "Above all, let [the speaker] have regard for the subject of discussion" and for the other interlocutors ("the company"), "for we do not all at all times enjoy the same subjects in the same way."[105] *Decorum* in conversation, as in oratory (*contentio*), is premised on an awareness that *res* cannot

102. In addition, Cicero employed a variety of characteristic rhetorical devices in his dialogues, such as casting historically important Roman figures as the interlocutors or setting the dialogue in the past, thereby distancing it from his own personal viewpoint or abstracting it from present political conditions.

103. In *De finibus* Cicero cites the view of Zeno the Stoic, who "used to say that the faculty of speech in general falls into two departments . . . and that Rhetoric was like the palm of the hand, Dialectic like the closed fist; because rhetoricians employ an expansive style, and dialecticians one that is more compressed." *De finibus* 2.6.17. See also the Loeb edition's introduction to *Brutus*, 9. Some Ciceronian dialogues, however, are more dialectical, in that they are characterized by more interchange between interlocutors—for example, *De legibus* and *De oratore*. See Hirzel, *Dialog*, 1:463, and Michel, *Rhétorique*, 80–81.

104. As the post-Aristotelian writer Demetrius states in *On Style*: "Artemon, who edited the letters of Aristotle, says that . . . a letter is like one side of a dialogue." Demetrius recommends a simple and informal style as appropriate to the letter and criticizes those who choose an overly dignified or didactic style for turning a letter into a treatise or a conversation into a lecture. G.M.A. Grube, *A Greek Critic: Demetrius on Style* (Toronto: University of Toronto Press, 1961), 29, 111–12. Similarly, the Latin comic poet Sextus Turpilius (died 103 B.C.E.), later cited by Erasmus, termed the letter "a mutual conversation [*mutuus sermo*] between absent friends." Desiderius Erasmus, *De conscribendis epistolis* (1522), in *Collected Works of Erasmus* (hereafter cited as *CWE*) (Toronto: University of Toronto Press, 1974–   ), 25:20, and *Opera omnia Desiderii Erasmi Roterodami* (hereafter cited as ASD) (Amsterdam: North Holland Publishing, 1969–   ), 1.2.225. On an earlier account of Turpilius's definition of the letter, see also Saint Jerome, *Letters of St. Jerome*, letter 8, trans. Charles Christopher Mierow (Westminster, Md.: The Newman Press, 1963), 1:46. The rhetorician Libanius (fl. fourth century C.E.), also quoted by Erasmus, defined the letter as "a certain written conversation [*homilia*] that takes place between one absent person and another . . . ; someone speaks in it as if he were present [speaking] to someone else present." Libanius, *Libanii opera*, ed. Richard Foerster (Leipzig: B. G. Teubner, 1903–27), 9:27. See also *CWE* 25:258 (*Conficiendarum epistolarum formula*, 1520).

105. *De officiis* 1.37.134–35. Translation from Cicero, *On Duties*, 52. See also *De oratore* 2.4.17–2.5.20, where Cicero's interlocutors recognize the need to adhere to "the demands of the occasion" in *sermo*. Those who fail to speak or act with *decorum* are labeled *inepti*.

be abstracted from *verba*, that is, an awareness of the human element in communication. This linking of ideas to actual people and their circumstances is what, most fundamentally, separates *sermo* from dialectic. Although both are investigative arts in which opposing views are considered, dialectic deals with ideas without regard to the emotional state of those involved;[106] from the dialectician's perspective, a valid syllogism is all the proof that is necessary. In *sermo*, by contrast, there is the recognition that even the best proofs do not persuade, unless they are accompanied by rhetorical propriety; each speaker must first accommodate himself to the conditions of the other speakers.[107] Accordingly, Diogenes Laertius defines both dialogue and dialectic as kinds of discourse, but adds to his definition of dialogue the proviso that it must pay "due regard to the characters of the persons introduced and the choice of diction." Dialectic, he continues, is used to "refute or establish some proposition"; it does not demand *decorum* of its practitioner.[108]

Because *sermo* differs from *contentio*, it possesses its own *decorum*: the speaker in a conversation must operate by a set of precepts different from those adhered to by the conventional orator. But what are the relevant differences between the two types of rhetoric? The answer is complicated by the absence of a systematic theory of *sermo*. It is possible, however, to arrive at a better picture of *sermo* by piecing together the relevant sections of Cicero's writings. The humanists, who were thoroughly versed in Cicero's works, did so implicitly. A comparison of relevant passages in Cicero with the known characteristics of the major genres of *contentio* will reveal *sermo*'s distinct rules of *decorum*.

---

106. Although the dialectician is not expected to accommodate himself to the emotional state of the interlocutor, Aristotle believes that the questioner, in dialectic, should not use premises that are either confusing to or unlikely to be accepted by the answerer, since, then, the questioner will be unable to gain agreement for his argument: "In argument with another deduction *per impossibile* should be avoided. For where one has deduced without the *reductio per impossibile*, no dispute can arise; if, on the other hand, one deduces an impossible conclusion, unless its falsehood is too plainly manifest, people deny that it is impossible, so that the questioners do not get what they want." *Topics* 157b34–158a3.

107. See Grimaldi, *Studies*, 3, on the difference, more generally, between dialectic and rhetoric. According to Grimaldi, rhetoric, unlike dialectic, "approaches the subject under the formality of communication, that is to say with the intention of presenting the matter to another in such a way as to make accessible to the other the possibility of reasonable judgment. As the art of language among the Greeks rhetoric recognized the fact that language originates from people and is destined for persons." See also Sloane's comparison of rhetoric with logic or dialectic, in *Humanist Rhetoric*, 62.

108. See note 96.

As already seen, one of the characteristics of *contentio* is its concreteness. Inasmuch as concreteness implies a concern with action, then conversation must also be characterized as concrete. So Cicero states: "Conversations are for the most part about domestic business or public affairs or else the study and teaching of the arts."[109] These subjects are to be treated, in conversation, with an eye to how they will eventually be put into practice. Thus, concerning a dialogue about the Supreme Good, Cicero writes that "the argument ought to amend our lives, purposes and wills, not just correct our terminology."[110]

But even though conversation is action oriented, it is not directed toward a specific action, as is oratory. Conversation, then, is not concrete in the sense that it is directed toward specific and immediate matters. Instead of the *definite* question, *sermo* examines the *indefinite* question. Another way to describe this difference is to say that conversation is philosophical and oratory is not. Conversation's philosophical subject matter is illustrated by Cicero's list of *indefinite* questions, or "propositions of an abstract character." The "indeterminate, unrestricted and far-extending sort of investigation" includes discussions of the following: "good and evil, things to be preferred and things to be shunned, fair repute and infamy, the useful and the unuseful, besides moral perfection, righteousness, self-control, discretion, greatness of soul, generosity, loyalty, friendship, good faith, sense of duty and the rest of the virtues and their corresponding vices, as well as the State, sovereignty, warlike operations, political science and the ways of mankind."[111] These are the sorts of questions, Cicero explains, that fall outside the three main kinds of oratory, and although they are "spoken of by nearly every writer, [they are] explained by none." True, the orator may want to "weave [these questions] skilfully into his discourse, and moreover to speak of these very things in the same way as founders of rules of law, statutes, and civil communities spoke," but it is not his duty "to advise on these matters one by one, as the philosophers do." In other words, the orator can use abstract questions to support his arguments, but such issues are not the focus of his speeches.

The affinity between conversation and philosophical issues is apparent from Cicero's own conversational writings. All Cicero's philosophical works

---

109. *De officiis* 1.37.135. Translation from Cicero, *On Duties*, 52.
110. *De finibus* 4.19.52.
111. *De oratore* 2.15.65–16.68. See also 2.10.41–43 and 3.28.109, and Michel, *Rhétorique*, 219.

were composed in the form of *sermo*, and even those dialogues that are not, strictly speaking, philosophical, reflect a philosophical tendency. For example, Cicero's most important rhetorical work, *De oratore*, is a philosophical treatment of rhetoric, not a technical manual for orators. His goal, there, is to heal the breach between philosophy and rhetoric, for which he blames Socrates, "the source from whom has sprung the undoubtedly absurd and unprofitable and reprehensible severance between the tongue and brain."[112] To philosophers who maintain that the *indefinite question* and philosophy are in the domain of dialectic, not rhetoric,[113] Cicero replies that such matters can be addressed rhetorically by *sermo*. Thus, Cicero speaks of the "rhetoric of the philosophers," an oxymoron to those who accept an unbridgeable gap between philosophy and rhetoric.[114]

Conversation is well-suited to philosophy because conversation can accommodate the absence of consensus in philosophical debate, a condition I explain later. But conversation is also appropriate for philosophical matters because of the unhurried fashion with which its interlocutors and readers can consider the subject. They can mull over the issues and are under no pressure to make an immediate decision. In contrast to *contentio*, which addresses the world of *negotium* (the fact of being occupied), *sermo* is tied to the condition of *otium* (leisure).[115] It is not that *sermo* eschews matters of business or public affairs—we have already seen that it does not—but that

112. *De oratore* 3.16.59–61. See also Vickers, *In Defence of Rhetoric*, 163–64. Conversation's philosophical subject matter, however, was accompanied by rhetoric's practical orientation, so that discussion of philosophy, for Cicero, was supposed to concern real human experience, not irrelevant abstractions; conversation, as discussed above, ought to be directed toward action. Cicero attributes the introduction of this belief to Socrates, who, in his dialogues, "was the first to call philosophy down from the heavens and set her in the cities of men and bring her also into their homes and compel her to ask questions about life and morality and things good and evil." *Tusculan Disputations* 5.4.10.

113. For example, Boethius, in the beginning of book 4 of *De topicis differentiis*, distinguishes between rhetoric and dialectic on the grounds that rhetoric deals with the *definite* question and dialectic deals with the *indefinite* question. "The dialectical discipline," he writes, "examines the thesis [that is, *indefinite* question] only. . . . The rhetorical discipline, on the other hand, investigates and discusses hypotheses [that is, *definite* questions]." Eleanore Stump, *Boethius's De topicis differentiis* (Ithaca: Cornell University Press, 1978), 79. Cicero, however, does not write that rhetoric eschews *indefinite* questions, but that the orator avoids such general questions. *De inventione* 1.6.8.

114. Cicero *De finibus* 2.6.17.

115. Cicero *De natura deorum* 2.1.3, *De officiis* 1.4.13, and *De oratore* 2.5.19; John F. Tinkler, "Renaissance Humanism and the *genera eloquentiae*," *Rhetorica: A Journal of the History of Rhetoric* 5 (1987): 287–88; Michel, *Rhétorique*, 365; Michel Ruch, *Le Préamble dans les oeuvres philosophiques de Cicéron: Essai sur la genèse et l'art du dialogue* (Paris: Belles Lettres, 1958), 83–85.

it approaches them with greater detachment. For example, rather than deciding on a specific question of war and peace, *sermo* considers the preliminary question of when war is justified. Cicero's own period of philosophical activity, when he composed most of his dialogues, took place during his period of *otium*, the years 45 and 44.[116] So long as he "was held entangled and fettered by the multifarious duties of ambition, office, litigation, political interests and even some political responsibility," he did not have the leisure to engage in philosophical reflection, the kind portrayed in his dialogues.[117]

The differences between conversation and the dominant genres of oratory in subject matter point to their distinct forums. Deliberative, judicial, and epideictic oratory are addressed to a popular audience because they concern matters that the public at large can understand and decide: political issues that touch the people directly; the innocence or guilt of the accused; and an individual's personal character. Conversation, however, deals with philosophical questions that are considered beyond the grasp of the common man. The appropriate context for *sermo*, therefore, is not the large audience, but the smaller, elite group. As Cicero put it, "The precision of speech we employ, when abstract truth is critically investigated in philosophical discussion, is one thing; and that employed, when we are adapting our language entirely to popular thinking, is another."[118] Echoing Plato of the *Republic*, Cicero contends that it is not simply that the masses are intellectually incapable of being philosophical, but that the masses are naturally antiphilosophical: "For philosophy is content with few judges, and of set purpose on her side avoids the multitude and is in her turn an object of suspicion and dislike to them, with the result that if anyone should be disposed to revile all philosophy he could count on popular support."[119] The people's bias against abstract thinking absolutely precludes a popular setting for philosophical discussion.

Just as the popular character of the main genres impelled the orator toward emotional appeals, conversation's exclusivity militated against using

116. *De republica* and *De legibus* were his only philosophical dialogues written earlier.

117. Cicero's *otium* was not sought; it came as a consequence of his forced political retirement, his being "released from taking part in the government of the country." *Academica* 1.3.11. Cicero still preferred the life of the statesman to that of the philosopher, and it was his reentry into political life in 44, with his attack on Mark Antony, that led to his proscription and death in December 43.

118. *De officiis* 2.10.35; *De finibus* 2.6.17, 2.25.80–81. Cf. Perelman and Olbrechts-Tyteca, *New Rhetoric*, 7.

119. *Tusculan Disputations* 2.1.4; Plato *Republic* 494a.

the passions. For the philosopher or wise man, unlike the multitude, can deliberate rationally. As Cicero explains: "For it is expedient for the man who cannot resort to reason, to resort to an emotion of the soul: we on the other hand are asking . . . about the wise man."[120] Therefore, whereas *contentio*, that is, speech to the masses, is marked by "extreme energy and passion," and a "vigorous style," *sermo*, which is speech among the select, is serene and restrained.[121] In the fourth century C.E., the Roman rhetorician C. Julius Victor reaffirmed Cicero's opposition to emotional persuasion in *sermo*. According to Victor, conversations should not be like those "disputes [*contentiones*] that carry many persons away to madness"; instead, "quiet is best" for *sermo*.[122]

Classical rhetoric's two nonrational proofs, *ethos* and *pathos*, are excluded from conversation. *Ethos*, when understood as the appeal to the speaker's authority, is eliminated because, as Cicero argues, relying on someone else's opinion—Cicero includes himself—substitutes blind faith for reason: "In discussion it is not so much weight of authority as force of argument that should be demanded. Indeed the authority of those who profess to teach is often a positive hindrance to those who desire to learn; they cease to employ their own judgement, and take what they perceive to be the verdict of their chosen master as settling the question."[123] Cicero cites the Pythagoreans as examples of this uncritical acceptance of authority. In lieu of rational argument, the Pythagoreans replied to their opponents with the words "Ipse dixit," or "He himself said so," referring to their master Pythagoras. The Pythagoreans' error was not that they appealed to authority, since *ethos* was a legitimate rhetorical proof. Their error was that, in using such appeals in philosophical discussion, they transgressed rhetorical *decorum*, which limits *sermo* to rational proof.

Pathos, the eliciting of the audience's passions, is rejected in conversation because the passions, whether "distress and fear," on one extreme, or

---

120. *Tusculan Disputations* 4.25.55.
121. *De oratore* 1.59.255; *De officiis* 1.1.3.
122. *Rhetores latini minores*, 446.
123. *De natura deorum* 1.5.10. See also *Tusculan Disputations* 2.26.63. I concede that the meaning of *ethos* is widely debated. For example, Nan Johnson, in her essay "Ethos and the Aims of Rhetoric," distinguishes between how a variety of rhetoricians—including Plato, Aristotle, Cicero, Quintilian, and Augustine—defined the term differently. According to Johnson, my view of *ethos* as a strategy of manipulating the listener fits best with Cicero's conception. See Nan Johnson, "Ethos and the Aims of Rhetoric," in *Essays on Classical Rhetoric and Modern Discourse*, ed. Robert J. Connors, Lisa S. Ede, and Andrea A. Lunsford (Carbondale: Southern Illinois University Press, 1984), 98–114.

"extravagant joy and lust," on the other, "conflict with deliberation and reason."[124] Passions, "the agitations of the soul alien to right reason," cause an unsoundness of mind in the interlocutors, which prevents them from arriving at the truth, or its closest approximation (ibid. 4.28.61, 4.21.47–48). In the interests of rational discourse and greater truth, Cicero advises the speaker to shun the passions and to avoid actions that will excite them. Consequently, he proposes rules of civility for conversation: the conversation should not be "in the least dogmatic"; no speaker should monopolize the conversation, but all should share in the opportunity to speak; "We must also take the greatest care to show courtesy and consideration toward those with whom we converse"; we should be very sparing in our rebuke of others; and, finally, we should do nothing out of anger.[125] Of all the passions, it is anger, in particular, that Cicero singles out for opprobrium. He does so because anger, more than any other emotion, undermines rational reflection: "Nothing can be done rightly or thoughtfully when done in anger."[126] That anger is inappropriate to conversation, however, does not exclude it from conventional oratory. Anger and allied "negative" emotions, such as hatred, ill-will, fear, and so on, are acceptable tools for the orator in persuading his mass audience.[127] Their exclusion from conversation, like the ban on appeals to authority, is the result of conversation's separate rules of *decorum*.

But if *decorum* is the speaker's accommodation to the listeners' particular circumstances, including their natures or "soul-types," then what kind of *decorum* can there be in conversation that neglects emotions natural to every human being? And how does *sermo* differ from dialectic, if both are restricted to logical argumentation? It is possible to speak of the *decorum* of conversation because conversation does not neglect the emotions; it simply does not exploit them. And conversation differs from dialectic because it attends to the emotions by actively neutralizing their effects on the other

124. Cicero *Tusculan Disputations* 5.15.43.

125. *De officiis* 1.37.134–37. Cf C. Julius Victor, who writes that, in *sermo*, the speaker "should always be honorable, but not inept and quarrelsome"; that he beware whom he injures by speech; that he should "never interrupt, nor make only demands"; and that "brevity is good, but especially in learned conversations, for it is fitting not to waste another's time." *Rhetores latini minores*, 446–47.

126. *De officiis* 1.38.136. Translation from Cicero, *On Duties*. In *Tusculan Disputations* 4.23.52, Cicero asks the question, "Is there anything more like unsoundness of mind than anger?"

127. Cicero *De oratore* 2.44.185, 189–90. Quintilian states that "*pathos* is almost entirely concerned with anger, dislike, fear, hatred, and pity." *Institutio oratoria* 6.2.20.

participants. The speakers in a conversation accommodate themselves to the listeners by being sensitive to the negative impact of emotions. An example of this sensitivity, or *decorum*, is the speaker's handling of *ethos*. Although it would not be permissible for speakers in a conversation to use authority to win the other interlocutors' favor (that is, to use *ethos* to influence others), it would be appropriate for them to ensure that their ideas are not hurt by their character (that is, to safeguard their credibility so that their messages will not be harmed).[128] The *decorum* of conversation, which does not permit emotional manipulation, impels speakers, instead, to seek an emotional equilibrium in the conversation, that is, to produce a condition of tranquillity that would permit reason to come to the fore.

The chief means of achieving tranquillity in conversation is to control the relationship between the interlocutors: Cicero's rules of civility, for example, are intended to effect tranquillity. In addition to the internal regulation of conversation, Cicero tries to control a conversation's external environment. Thus, the setting for Cicero's dialogues is almost always a relaxed milieu, distant from the agitation of the city.[129] The conversation's ambience reflects not only the need for *otium*, but also the rhetorician's awareness that a conversation's surroundings will affect the likelihood of achieving the requisite serenity.

Cicero's objective of tranquillity, however, is not tantamount to the Stoic goal of apathy, described by the Academic philosopher Crantor, and quoted by Cicero, as "'that sort of insensibility which neither can nor ought to exist. . . . For this state of apathy is not attained except at the cost of brutishness in the soul and callousness in the body.'"[130] Rather, Cicero

128. My description of how emotions are to be handled in conversation is similar to William W. Fortenbaugh's description of Aristotelian rhetoric, in "*Benevolentiam conciliare* and *animos permovere*: Some remarks on Cicero's De oratore 2.178–216," *Rhetorica: A Journal of the History of Rhetoric* 6 (1988): 266–67. Aristotle, whose ambivalence about emotional appeals I noted earlier, describes an ideal rhetoric that, like Cicero's model of conversation, consciously seeks to avoid the influence of passions: "The right thing in speaking really is that we should be satisfied not to annoy our hearers, without trying to delight them: we ought in fairness to fight our case with no help beyond the bare facts." Consistent with this view of rhetoric, Aristotle conceives of remedial measures designed to remove prejudice—though he does not limit himself to removing prejudice, but also includes measures to excite prejudice. *Rhetoric* 1404a1–13, 1415a25–28.

129. *Academica* 2.3.9; *De natura deorum* 1.6.15; Ruch, *Préamble*, 80–82; introduction, in *De finibus*, by Cicero, Loeb Classical Library, xvi. It is also possible to control the setting through the arrangement of interlocutors. In *Academica* the participants are seated in full view of one another—ensuring a nonhierarchical environment.

130. *Tusculan Disputations* 3.6.12–13.

wants to rid conversation of destructive passions only, what he terms "mental excitement that is excessive and uncontrolled by reason."[131] Not included in these prohibited passions are constructive emotions, such as devotion, the desire for truth, or the impulse toward fellowship.[132] This last, the urge for fellowship, is the impetus for friendship, and it is friendship that is the paradigmatic association for *sermo*.[133]

"Conversations [*sermones*]," Cicero writes, "flourish best in friendships" (ibid. 1.17.58). The relationship between interlocutors should resemble a community of friends. This stands in stark contrast to oratory's agonistic ideal, where orators confront one another as adversaries. The orator's purpose in *contentio* is to beat his opponent; the speaker's purpose in *sermo* is to seek out the truth, collectively, with the other interlocutors. Cicero, therefore, explains his own mission in *De finibus*, a dialogue on ethics, as follows: "For our object is to discover the truth, not to refute someone as an opponent."[134] Like Ciceronian *sermo*, the Socratic *elenchus*, "the method of scrutiny-by-cross-examination," presupposes friendship, or at least good will, between interlocutors. The inquiry, Plato writes, must be "benevolent" and conducted "without jealousy."[135] Both Socrates and Cicero use the dialogic method toward the same end of finding the truth. For them, the search for philosophical truth is better enhanced by the interlocutors' common bonds than by their antagonistic posturings.

The absence of contentiousness in *sermo*, as should be obvious, does not imply agreement among the interlocutors. Conversations involve disagreements in which each speaker represents a different point of view: in Cicero's dialogues, for example, the view of the New Academy, the Old Academy, the Stoic, the Epicurean, and so on. Reflecting the uncertainty of conversation's subject matter, Cicero adopts the skepticism of the New Academy, as he did

131. *De officiis* 1.38.136.
132. *Tusculan Disputations* 4.25.55; *De officiis* 1.4.13.
133. *De officiis* 1.16.50–17.56.
134. *De finibus* 1.5.13. See also *Tusculan Disputations* 4.21.47. Aristotle distinguishes between "those engaged in competition" and "those who discuss things together in the spirit of inquiry." *Topics* 159a27–38. The interlocutors in Ciceronian *sermo* belong to the latter. Similarly, Perelman and Olbrechts-Tyteca, though they personally minimize the usefulness of this distinction, present the conventional contrast between debate, "in which the partisans of opposed settled convictions defend their respective views," and dialogue or discussion, "in which the interlocutors search honestly and without bias for the best solution to a controversial problem." See *New Rhetoric*, 37–38.
135. Plato Letters: VII 344b. See also *Gorgias* 487a; Klosko, "Rational Persuasion," 18–19; and Martha C. Nussbaum's review of *Socrates, Ironist and Moral Philosopher*, by Gregory Vlastos, *The New Republic*, 16 and 23 September 1991, 34–40.

in oratory. In conversation, as in the dominant genres, Cicero accepts the Academic principle that probability is the best that can be gained. "Further than this," he acknowledges, "the mind of man cannot advance," but is "for a divine being to determine."[136] Again, as in oratory, Cicero turns to argument *in utramque partem* to determine probability. Although he identifies this technique with the Academics, Cicero locates its origins with Socrates, who used his conversational mode, "the negative dialectic," to discover the probable truth.[137] In Cicero's account, arguments pro and con in philosophical conversation and practical oratory function similarly, insofar as they provide the probable truth. Argument *in utramque partem*, however, is distinguished in practical oratory because such argumentation serves the additional purpose of aiding the orator in defeating his competitor. Like the modern-day attorney, who is simultaneously committed to winning his case and furthering justice, the Ciceronian orator trains himself not only, or perhaps not so much, to promote that which is right, but to win any case he might argue.[138] The situation differs with conversation, where the pursuit of truth remains the speaker's sole end. Because it is not the speaker's objective in *sermo* to beat his opponent, he will seek probable truth with moderation: "We . . . whose guide is probability . . . are prepared both to refute without obstinacy and be refuted without anger."[139]

Although the speakers in both *contentio* and *sermo* are skeptical in their debate of the issues, their skepticisms are not identical. First, the skepticism of the orator in *contentio* is ended by resolution of the controversy in question: the decision of the political assembly or jury. The philosophical debates of *sermo*, however, have no resolution, since they have no authoritative arbiter to settle the question.[140] Second, in comparing specifically judicial oratory with *sermo*, the subject matter of judicial oratory (as I have

---

136. *Tusculan Disputations* 4.21.47; 1.11.23; 1.9.17; 5.4.11.
137. *De natura deorum* 1.5.11; *Tusculan Disputations* 1.4.7–8; *Academica* 1.4.16–17.
138. Cicero, *De oratore* 1.34.157–59, 3.21.80; 3.27.107; *Tusculan Disputations* 2.3.9.
139. *Tusculan Disputations* 2.2.5.
140. Tinkler also observes that whereas Academic skepticism is generally characteristic of rhetoric, in *contentio* (unlike *sermo*) the orator is not, himself, permitted to speak skeptically. In public, he is expected to argue, unambivalently, either for or against a position. See "Renaissance Humanism," 295. Cf. Isocrates *Antidosis* 255–56: with the art of discourse "we both contend against others on matters which are open to dispute and seek light for ourselves on things unknown." See also Perelman and Olbrechts-Tyteca, *New Rhetoric*, 38: "In a judicial settlement, for example, we know that the lawyer for each party will tend to develop arguments in favor of a thesis rather than to shed light on some question. The law, by determining the issues to be discussed, favors this one-sided attitude and the adoption of a definite standpoint by the advocate, who then has merely to press this point steadfastly against his opponent."

previously argued) concerns real facts that have occurred, most likely, in the not-too-distant past. So that even if orators, in judicial matters, can usually present credible arguments on both sides of the case, they are limited in their arguments by evidence. The link between conversation's subject matter, which concerns abstract ideas, and the facts, however, is far more tenuous. Therefore, there are fewer restraints on what position a speaker can take in conversation.[141] Questions surrounding the fundamental question of the nature of the gods, such as "what opinions are we to hold about religion, piety, and holiness, about ritual, about honor and loyalty to oaths, about temples, shrines, and solemn sacrifices," exemplify the irresolvable subject matter of conversation. Of these questions, Cicero writes: "Surely such wide diversity of opinion among men of the greatest learning . . . must affect even those who think that they possess certain knowledge with a feeling of doubt."[142] Skepticism, Cicero concludes, is a persistent attribute of *sermo*.[143]

True to the dictates of Academic skepticism, the uncertainty of conversation does not result in indecision, since the criterion of probability is applied. So that when Cicero speaks of "boundless uncertainty" in conversation's issues, it is not the lack of a standard that he refers to, but the absence of any common agreement on which position is most probable. Without the possibility of consensus, Cicero argues that individuals are free to decide probability for themselves: "But let everyone defend his views, for judgment is free: I shall cling to my rule and without being tied to the laws of any single school of thought which I feel bound to obey, shall always search for the most probable solution in every problem."[144] Cicero, however, does exclude some beliefs from his rule of philosophical disagreement: "All men think

141. It is this second distinction, I believe, that Antonius had in mind when he, in *De oratore*, cited (disapprovingly) the rhetorical division between concrete and abstract problems: the concrete problem, which is equated with judicial subject matter, involves "a question in debate and dispute between litigants"; the abstract problem, the subject matter of conversation, is "something involved in boundless uncertainty." Cicero *De oratore* 2.19.78.

142. *De natura deorum* 1.6.14. See also Hirzel, *Dialog*, 1:531.

143. Cicero, despite his disdain for Epicureanism, concedes that he may be in error: "'Many men, many minds'—so it is possible that I am mistaken." *De finibus* 1.5.15.

144. *Tusculan Disputations* 4.4.7. See also *De natura deorum* 1.7.17; *Tusculan Disputations* 2.26.63, 5.29.83; and *De finibus* 5.26.76. At the close of the dialogue *De natura deorum* the interlocutors depart, each with his own view of probability: "Here the conversation ended, and we parted, Velleius thinking Cotta's discourse to be truer, while I felt that that of Balbus approximated more nearly to a semblance of the truth." Cf. *Academica* 2.48.147–48, where the interlocutors return home with consensus. See Hirzel, *Dialog*, 1:511.

that a divine power and divine nature exist,"[145] and "all men throughout the world agree that there is something appertaining to those who have passed away." On such an issue where there is universal agreement, which is "the voice of nature," then "we too are bound to hold the same opinion."[146]

Although many of the debated issues, for which Cicero affirms freedom of judgment, would commonly be considered religious in nature,[147] he does not call for religious toleration.[148] Hellenistic philosophies and Roman religion were distinct, the former concerning opinions, the latter focusing on rites and worship. Thus, Cotta, Cicero's spokesman for the Academic skeptics in *De natura deorum*, distinguishes between his philosophical skepticism, which allows him to question all traditional religious beliefs, and his religion, whose practices he upholds, as pontiff, based on ancestral authority.[149] Similarly, the Roman scholar and Skeptic Varro (116–27 B.C.E.)

145. *Tusculan Disputations* 1.13.30.
146. Ibid. 1.15.35. Cf. Aristotle *Topics*. 105ª1–10: "Not every problem, nor every thesis, should be examined, but only one which might puzzle one of those who need argument, not punishment or perception. For people who are puzzled to know whether one ought to honour the gods and love one's parents or not need punishment, while those who are puzzled to know whether snow is white or not need perception." Perelman and Olbrechts-Tyteca concede that the above statement is "just [Aristotle's] advice addressed to dialecticians, but it reflects the commonsense attitude. Common sense admits the existence of unquestioned and unquestionable truths; it admits that certain rules are 'beyond discussion,' and that certain suggestions 'do not deserve discussion'. An established fact, a self-evident truth, an absolute rule, carry in themselves the affirmation of their unquestionable character, excluding the possibility of pro and con argumentation. Unanimous agreement on particular propositions can make it very difficult to question them." *New Rhetoric*, 56–57.
147. See, for example, the discussions in *De natura deorum*.
148. In addition, Cicero did not intend his call for free philosophical debate as a general defense of free speech. The debates in which he calls for freedom of judgment concerned philosophical issues, not other matters like politics. There is, however, a similarity between the restrictions placed on participation in Ciceronian philosophical debate and in ancient Roman political speech: both were limited to the elite. Unlike ancient Athens, the people of Republican Rome, to say nothing of Imperial Rome, had no general right to free speech. See R. K. Sinclair, *Democracy and Participation in Athens* (Cambridge: Cambridge University Press, 1988), 32, and Josiah Ober, *Mass and Elite in Democratic Athens: Rhetoric, Ideology, and the Power of the People* (Princeton: Princeton University Press, 1989), 78–79, 296. Only the Roman elite possessed this prerogative. "The plain fact, from a political point of view, is that the Roman People went to the Assemblies to listen and to vote, not to speak. Magistrates, leading senators and barristers enjoyed freedom of speech and made the most of it; but they cannot be identified with the Roman People." C. Wirszubski, *Libertas as a Political Idea at Rome during the Late Republic and Early Principate* (Cambridge: Cambridge University Press, 1968), 18–19 n. 2. See also Aulus Gellius on the senator's right—once called upon—to speak on any subject he wished and as long as he wished. *The Attic Nights of Aulus Gellius*, trans. John C. Rolfe (London: William Heinemann, 1927), 1:347.
149. *De natura deorum* 3.2.5–3.4.9. Cotta affirms not only "the rites and ceremonies and

does not view his philosophy as antagonistic to traditional Roman religion.[150] In ancient Rome, religion involved the cult service of the community and the household, not correct doctrine. Therefore, religious toleration would have meant tolerating devotion to a religion other than the state-sanctioned religion, not tolerating the profession of heterodox opinions.[151]

In contrast to the cultic Roman religion, Christianity was a doctrine-based religion, whose theological debates could be compared with the philosophical debates of Cicero and his friends. Both the Hellenistic and Christian debates dealt with speculative opinions about God (or the gods), divine providence, the ends of life, the nature of the soul, and so on. Erasmus applied Cicero's argument for philosophical freedom to the case of religious toleration. Cicero had believed that the *decorum* of *sermo*, determined by *sermo*'s goal of truth, required that the participants be allowed to debate their ideas freely. Erasmus thought that the same *decorum*, with its attendant respect and civility for all participants, demanded toleration for many of the period's theological debates. Erasmus also invoked the *decorum* of *contentio*, which requires the speaker to accommodate himself to the audience, to justify toleration of persons deceived by religious error. Relying on the example of the orator, Erasmus maintained that toleration was a more effective means of leading nonbelievers to religious truth than was persecution.

---

duties of a religion," but also "the beliefs about the immortal gods which have come down to us from our ancestors." It seems clear, however, that except for belief in the divine existence, Cotta's emphasis is on religious practice: "The religion of the Roman people comprises ritual, auspices, and the third additional division consisting of all such prophetic warnings as the interpreters of the Sybil or the soothsayers have derived from portents and prodigies. Well, I have always thought that none of these departments of religion was to be despised" *De natura deorum* 3.2.5.

150. J.H.W.G. Liebeschuetz, *Continuity and Change in Roman Religion* (Oxford: Oxford University Press, 1979), 36–37.

151. According to Peter Garnsey, while the ancient Romans introduced many new gods, this "openness" does not signify Roman toleration of other religions: "Roman-style polytheism was disposed to expand and absorb or at least neutralize other gods, not to tolerate them." Religious organizations that were unauthorized were permitted to exist because there was no way to exclude or eliminate them. See Peter Garnsey, "Religious Toleration in Classical Antiquity," *Persecution and Toleration*, ed. W. J. Shiels (Oxford: Basil Blackwell, 1984), 8–9. Similarly, John North denies the existence of any principled defense of religious toleration during the period of Republican Rome. See J. A. North, "Religious Toleration in Republican Rome," *Proceedings of the Cambridge Philosophical Society* 25 (1979): 86.

1

Erasmus: The Paradigm of Humanist Toleration

Life as a Humanist

Erasmus's reputation as "prince of the humanists" is rightly deserved, for both his life choices and his vast corpus bespeak an intense interest in the endeavors and studies characteristic of Renaissance humanism. Erasmus was educated in Holland, first in Gouda and then, some years later, in the school of St. Lebuinus in Deventer, which came under the influence of the *devotio moderna*, a religious movement that was at best ambivalent about the value of classical studies.[1] Erasmus observed years later that he became a humanist, despite what he learned in school: "In my boyhood the humanities were banished from our schools . . . in spite of this, a sort of inspiration fired me with devotion to the Muses, sprung not from judgment (for I was too young to judge) but from a kind of natural feeling. I developed a hatred for anyone I knew to be an enemy of humane studies and a love for

1. The best known expression of the *devotio moderna* is Thomas à Kempis's *Imitation of Christ*. Marjorie O'Rourke Boyle argues against à Kempis's supposed influence on Erasmus, in *Erasmus on Language and Method in Theology* (Toronto: University of Toronto Press, 1977), 101, 233 n. 244. On Erasmus as a humanist, see Brendan Bradshaw, "The Christian Humanism of Erasmus," *Journal of Theological Studies* 33 (1982): 411–47; James D. Tracy, "Erasmus the Humanist," in *Erasmus of Rotterdam: A Quincentennial Symposium*, ed. Richard L. DeMolen (New York: Twayne Publishers, 1971), 29–47; and Albert Rabil Jr., "Desiderius Erasmus," in *Renaissance Humanism: Foundations, Forms, and Legacy*, ed. Albert Rabil Jr. (Philadelphia: University of Pennsylvania Press, 1988), 2: 216–64. For a more general biography of Erasmus, including his humanism, see Cornelis Augustijn, *Erasmus: His Life, Works, and Influence*, trans. J. C. Grayson (Toronto: University of Toronto Press, 1991), and Roland H. Bainton, *Erasmus of Christendom* (New York: Crossroad Publishing, 1969).

those who delighted in them."[2] After his parents' death in 1485, Erasmus again found himself in an environment that, superficially at least, was less-than-conducive to his development as a humanist: the Augustinian Canons' monastery at Steyn, near Gouda. But Erasmus made use of his six years at the monastery to pursue his humanistic studies. He wrote at this time: "My authorities in poetry are Virgil, Horace, Ovid, Juvenal, Statius, Martial, Claudian, Persius, Lucan, Tibullus, and Propertius; in prose, Cicero, Quintilian, Sallust, Terence." Then, signaling his links to contemporary humanism, Erasmus continued: "Again, in the niceties of style I rely on Lorenzo Valla above all. He has no equal for intelligence and good memory."[3]

In 1493, Erasmus left the monastery to become secretary of the bishop of Cambrai, a post he held for two years. In accepting this position, Erasmus opted for one of the two vocations that Paul Oskar Kristeller describes as characteristically humanistic, that of secretary to a man of rank. In order to sustain himself, Erasmus became a private tutor a few years later, thereby practicing the second distinctively humanistic profession, teaching.[4] Teaching was crucial to Erasmus's self-definition as a humanist.[5] Thus his particular attraction to Quintilian must be due, in part, to the ancient rhetorician's concern with pedagogy. But Erasmus's own role as a teacher and disseminator of the *studia humanitatis* was primarily as a writer, not a personal instructor.

Erasmus's writings embody the humanists' ideals. He manifests the humanist's literary and philological preoccupations in his many translations and critical editions of classical and Christian writings, and he defends the basic premise underlying these works—that classical studies are inherently valuable.[6] But above all, Erasmus demonstrates the humanist's concern with rhetoric. All his writings, including those not specifically devoted to rhetoric, were composed with an eye to their persuasiveness. It is with this attention to oratory that he writes of himself: "Erasmus taught nothing except eloquence."[7] The truth of Erasmus's self-assessment is particularly apparent

---

2. CWE 23:16 (Dedicatory Letter to the *Antibarbari*, 1520).

3. CWE 1:31.97–101 (Letter to Cornelis Gerard, May 1489).

4. Kristeller, *Renaissance Thought*, 11. Erasmus also taught at Cambridge University from 1511 to 1514.

5. Rabil, "Desiderius Erasmus," 223.

6. CWE 23:1–122 (*Antibarbari*, 1520).

7. Erasmus, letter to John Botzheim (30 January 1523), in *Opus Epistolarum Des. Erasmi Roterodami* (hereafter cited as *EE*), ed. P. S. Allen, H. M. Allen, and H. W. Garrod (Oxford: Clarendon Press, 1906–57), 1:30.

in his treatment of religion. In his *Paraphrases* of the New Testament, Erasmus rewrites Scripture in a style designed to appeal to the masses, like "the farmer, the tailor, the mason," and even the disreputable, such as "prostitutes, pimps, and Turks."[8] Similarly, Erasmus writes his *Ecclesiastes* as a manual to instruct preachers in how to proclaim the word of God persuasively.[9] Erasmus's rhetorical sensibility derives most fundamentally from his belief that speech is an essential characteristic of our humanity and godliness. It is to this axiological premise, the source of Erasmus's visceral aversion to force, that I turn.

Rhetorical Predisposition to Persuasion over Force

Classical Roots

In vesting speech with moral import, Erasmus looked to the example of the ancient rhetoricians. For them, the faculty of speech was uniquely human, which also made it, they thought, singularly ethical. Isocrates, Aristotle, Cicero, and Quintilian identify speech as that natural faculty that sets humanity apart from the lower animals.[10] The power of speech, the ancients note, made civilization possible. Isocrates expresses the constructive character of the art of discourse as follows:

> Because there has been implanted in us the power to persuade each other and to make clear to each other whatever we desire, not only have we escaped the life of wild beasts, but we have come together and founded cities and made laws and invented arts; and generally

8. Erasmus, preface to the *paraphrase of St. Matthew* (1520), in *Desiderii Erasmi Roterodami Opera Omnia* (hereafter cited as LB), ed. J. Clericus (Leyden, 1703–6), 7. See also Marjorie O'Rourke Boyle, "Weavers, farmers, tailors, travellers, masons, prostitutes, pimps, Turks, little women, and Other Theologians," *Erasmus in English: A Newsletter Published by University of Toronto Press* 3 (1971): 1–7.

9. LB 5:767–1100 (*Ecclesiastes, sive de ratione concionandi*, 1535).

10. Isocrates *Panegyricus* 48 and *Antidosis* 253–57; Aristotle *Politics* 1253a7–18; Cicero *De oratore* 1.8.32–33; Quintilian *Institutio oratoria* 2.16.12–17.

speaking, there is no institution devised by man which the power of speech has not helped us to establish.[11]

Speech is a tool for technological advancement—a fact the ancient rhetoricians laud. But more important to them, and more praiseworthy, is the power of speech to seek out and create justice. Aristotle writes, with the Greek *polis* in mind, that "the power of speech is intended to set forth the expedient and the inexpedient, and therefore likewise the just and the unjust. And it is characteristic of man that he alone has any sense of good and evil, of just and unjust, and the like."[12] The faculty of speech, the rhetoricians point out, permits the use of reason to create laws "concerning things just and unjust, and things honorable and base."[13] Even after the creation of laws, it is only eloquent speech that makes human beings "learn to keep faith and observe justice and become accustomed to obey others voluntarily."[14] Fundamentally, the rhetoricians are saying that human beings can use speech to transform themselves into moral beings; brutes cannot. As Cicero puts it: "To [other animals] we often impute courage, as with horses or lions, but we do not impute to them justice, fairness or goodness. For they have no share in reason and speech."[15]

As speech is associated with humanity and ethical action, force, its antithesis, is identified by the classical rhetoricians with brutishness and the absence of justice. Cicero opposes the verbal and the violent in his consideration of the justice of warfare. "There are two types of conflict," he writes: "the one proceeds by debate [*disceptatio*], the other by force [*vis*]. Since the former is the proper concern of a man, but the latter of beasts, one should only resort to the latter if one may not employ the former."[16] Because force is characteristic of lower animals, it can never be the source of ethical action; it is, therefore, impossible to compel people to act justly. Cicero illustrates this point with his criticism of Plato's philosopher king. In the *Republic*, Plato had argued that since the philosopher king aspires to a life of

---

11. Isocrates *Antidosis* 254–55. Cicero offers a mythical account, in *De inventione* 1.2.2–3, of the creation of civilization. Initially, human beings lived in a brutish state of nature. They were led out of this primitive condition, however, by a great orator who persuaded his neighbors to abandon their lowly existence. It was this earliest of rhetoricians, Cicero posits, that transformed human beings "from wild savages into a kind of gentle folk."
12. *Politics* 1253a7–18.
13. *Antidosis* 255.
14. *De inventione* 1.2.3.
15. *De officiis*, 1.16.50. Translation from Cicero, *On Duties*.
16. Ibid. 1.11.34.

contemplation, he would have to be constrained to rule. But Cicero responds that Plato is mistaken to think that his philosopher kings rule justly when they are forced to act. Their assumption of a public life, Cicero states, "is something done more fairly when done voluntarily; for something that is done rightly is only just if it is voluntary."[17] Cicero raises this issue of force when discussing matters relevant to the classical state. Neither he nor the other classical rhetoricians address the matter of religious persecution.[18] It was Erasmus who adapted rhetoric's regard for speech to the sphere of religion.

The Divinity of the Word

The ancient rhetoricians established the ethical value of speech by arguing that the capacity to speak distinguishes human beings from lower animals. Erasmus does the same, even offering a physiological account of why speech is peculiar to humans.[19] But Erasmus also interprets verbal capability in religious terms, by making speech as much an expression of the divinity within the person as a line of division between human and beast. Speech, Erasmus observes, is a faculty shared with God. As God's word, most notably incarnated in the person of Jesus, mirrors God's Self, human discourse mirrors the human soul. It is by virtue of our mind and speech that we most resemble God, and that is why we have "nothing more wonderful or more powerful" than speech.[20] The implication here is that speech's prominence follows from its special connection with the divine.

17. "Observe, then Glaucon, said I, that we shall not be wronging . . . the philosophers who arise among us, but that we can justify our action when we constrain them to take charge of the other citizens and be their guardians." *Republic* 519c–521b; *De officiis* 1.9.28.

18. One could argue that Roman religion, polytheistic and ecclectic, provided no heretics to persecute. Peter Garnsey, however, in "Religious Toleration in Classical Antiquity," argues that the ancients were religiously intolerant. Even those who had a ready philosophical basis for toleration, like the Skeptics, were intolerant.

19. *CWE* 29:267 (*Lingua*, 1525). See also LB 5:922C (*Ecclesiastes*), and *CWE* 26:369 (*De recta latini graecique sermonis pronuntiatione dialogus*, 1528). Boyle demonstrates how Erasmus echoed the classical rhetors in viewing speech as a civilizing element, in *Erasmus on Language and Method*, 53–55, and *Rhetoric and Reform* 117–18.

20. LB 5:772E–773A (*Ecclesiastes*). Reflecting the Johannine prologue ("In the beginning was the Word . . ."), Erasmus writes: "*Sermo Patris vivus Christus est*—The Father's Word is the Living Christ—that is, the divine word is incarnated in the person of His son." *EE* 5:316.141 (Letter to Henry VIII, August 1523). See also LB 5:771E–772E (*Ecclesiastes*). The first passage of John, which the Vulgate translated as *In principio erat Verbum*, Erasmus translated as *In principio erat Sermo*. On Erasmus's reasoning and the controversy that ensued, see Boyle's *Erasmus on Language and Method*. Cf. Isocrates *Antidosis* 255–56: "Discourse which is true and lawful and just is the outward image of a good and faithful soul."

Yet if speech is linked to godliness, why do so many churchmen advocate the use of force, its opposite, to bring men to God? Erasmus acknowledges the contradiction inherent in the use of violence to achieve religious ends. Christ, Erasmus states, never resorted to violence: "Christ, as he preached to all, coaxed no one to himself with flatteries or human promises, nor did he compel anyone with force, although he was omnipotent."[21] Similarly, Erasmus writes: "Compulsion is incompatible with sincerity, and nothing is pleasing to Christ unless it is voluntary."[22] Therefore, Erasmus restricts the true preacher to the use of his "tongue, furnished with the word of God."[23] Like Cicero, Erasmus assigns force to a lower ethical plane. The secular realm, which is subordinate to the sacred or ecclesiastical realm, is permitted to compel evildoers; the king has an army, prisons, and various forms of execution at his disposal. The preacher, however, can only persuade men to goodness. He cannot coerce them because force does not engender goodness.[24] In reality, neither magistrates nor preachers can compel someone to righteousness. But for the secular authorities, it is sufficient that the sinner not act on his inclinations. By contrast, the preacher is interested in the person's spiritual condition, not his outward conformity. Since physical duress will not convert the reprobate into believer, the preacher cannot justify using force. Although this limitation makes the preacher's job more difficult than the king's, it also elevates the role of the preacher above any other.[25]

Erasmus's apotheosis of speech, and consequent degradation of force, colored the attitudes of subsequent humanists. His rhetorically influenced views about speech and violence, however, are by themselves insufficient to undermine the argument for persecution. Although we might say that these attitudes were particularly powerful in Erasmus and his humanist successors, there were nonetheless other thinkers who sang the praises of speech while justifying coercion. St. Augustine provides an excellent example. Though Augustine in his early period (391–c. 398) rejected religious coer-

---

21. Erasmus, *Ausgewählte Werke*, ed. Hajo Holborn with Annemarie Holborn (Munich: C. H. Beck, 1933), 254, lines 7–9. See also 223; Boyle, *Rhetoric and Reform*, 159; and Jacques Chomarat, *Grammaire et rhetorique chez Erasme* (Paris: Société d'Edition "Les Belles Lettres," 1981), 2:1138–39.

22. *CWE* 9:257.405–7 (Letter to Jean de Carondelet, "Preface to the Edition of St. Hilary," 5 January 1523).

23. LB 5:789F (*Ecclesiastes*).

24. Erasmus explains that "bodies may be forced, but souls are to be persuaded because they cannot be forced." Ibid. 822B. See also 789F and 805F.

25. Ibid. 821F–822F.

cion altogether, by his later years (after 406), he came to argue that Christian kings were obligated to protect and support the Church against heresy and schism.[26] This obligation meant, in practice, that the state was permitted to persecute the heterodox, short of killing them. Augustine, though, saw no contradiction between his willingness to compel heretics and his faith in the power of the word. The bishop of Hippo, thoroughly trained in rhetoric while still a pagan, never abandoned his belief in the ideal of persuasion even after his conversion to Christianity. His *De doctrina christiana* is a rhetorical classic, establishing the legitimacy of a Christian rhetoric. And in his "Letter to Boniface," Augustine writes: "Does anyone doubt that it is better for man to be led to the worship of God by teaching rather than forced to it by fear of suffering?" That persuasion is more desirable, however, does not invalidate the less desirable method of force. Thus Augustine continues: "Because the former group [that is, persuasion] is preferable it does not follow that those of the latter [that is, force] . . . should be neglected. We have proved by experience and do still prove that it has been a blessing to many to be driven first by fear of bodily pain, in order afterward to be instructed, or to follow up in act what they have learned in word."[27] The intolerant Augustine does not believe that compulsion can, in and of itself, make the heretic a true believer or a good man; faith, he concedes, can never be forced. But coercion can sometimes make the heretic reconsider his errors. When the state forcibly exposes the sinner to godly preaching and removes him from his sinful surroundings, it may help him discover the truth that has so far eluded him. Force, by itself, is neutral, for Augustine. What matters is the ends toward which it is used and the spirit with which it is applied. Used toward godly ends and applied with a spirit of charity, coercion becomes just.[28]

The coexistence, in Augustine, of a Ciceronian appreciation of speech and a legitimation of religious coercion indicates that Erasmus must ground his theory of toleration on more than an amorphous regard for persuasion. Erasmus, therefore, turns to the rhetorical *genera* of preaching and conversation as the bases of his defense of religious toleration. Each rhetorical *genus* treats a different subject matter. Preaching deals with the fundamentals of faith; conversation discusses the nonessentials. Because of their

26. For a good discussion of Augustine's changing views on the coercion of heretics, see Deane, *Ideas of St. Augustine*, 172–220.

27. St. Augustine, *Letters*, in *The Fathers of the Church: A New Translation*, trans. Sister Wilfrid Parsons (New York: Fathers of the Church, 1955), 4:161–62.

28. Deane, *Ideas of St. Augustine*, 204, 217, 197.

different subject matters, each *genus* possesses its own distinct *decorum* and its own form of toleration based on that *decorum*.

Fundamentals of Faith and Nonessentials

Conceptual Division

Erasmus distinguishes the fundamental doctrines necessary for salvation from other, nonessential doctrines or "adiaphora," literally, "things that make no difference."[29] "Adiaphora," as it was used by sixteenth-century reformers, refers to the indifference of rituals neither commanded nor forbidden by the divine law of the New Testament. Thus, the reformers employed the idea of indifferent rituals to condemn Roman Catholicism for burdening the Christian conscience with man-made ceremonies.[30] The

29. Classically, adiaphora—literally, "things that make no difference"—referred to all external things and actions that were not decisive in the moral life of the wise man, but were (at least for the Stoics) to be judged by the end toward which they were directed. So that the adiaphoron (the indifferent thing or act) could become either good or bad, depending on the person's inner disposition. The Christians adopted the term and applied it to externals—such as food, drink, marriage, wealth, and so on—regulated under the Old Law, but morally indifferent under the New, in the sense that the ethical status of these externals was to be determined by the actor's intentions. On the historical development of the concept "adiaphora," see Bernard J. Verkamp, *The Indifferent Mean: Adiaphorism in the English Reformation to 1554* (Athens, Ohio, and Detroit, Mich.: Ohio University Press and Wayne State University Press, 1977), 20–25.

30. Adiaphora, the reformers argued, were to be distinguished from godly directives, like the Decalogue and the precepts of Christ and his Apostles. The latter, although incapable of effecting salvation, were obligatory; the former were a matter of choice (Verkamp, *Indifferent Mean*, 27–28). Admittedly, the reformers recognized that the Christian must sometimes restrain his adiaphoristic liberty out of respect for his weaker brother's conscience. See, for example, Martin Luther, *Commentary on Paul's Epistle to Galatians* (1519), in *Martin Luthers Werke. Kritische Gesamtausgabe* (hereafter cited as WA) (Weimar: Hermann Böhlaus, 1883–1908; rpt, Graz: Akademische Druck-u. Verlagsanstalt, 1964–), 2:478; John Calvin, *Institutes of the Christian Religion* 3.19.10–12; Verkamp, *Indifferent Mean*, 121–25. Nonetheless, the reformers never wavered from their conviction that adiaphora themselves have no inherent religious significance.

The reformers' position that ceremonies are adiaphoral is attacked by Catholics, like Thomas More, on the ground that what was permitted in New Testament times is not necessarily permitted today. "As if the apostle [Paul] did not at times permit certain things," More writes to Luther, "which shortly after even he himself prohibited; unless you now permit

Catholic Erasmus, like the reformers, considered much Catholic ritual to be adiaphora. He viewed pilgrimages, "prostrations before statues and saints," restrictions on food and clothing, which were especially prevalent among the monastic orders, as externals that are sometimes beneficial to those who are weak in their faith, but are all too often mistaken for the essence of Christianity.[31] Unlike most early reformers, however, who focus on ceremonial adiaphora, Erasmus also developed the idea of doctrinal adiaphora; doctrines are indifferent, according to Erasmus, when they are not obligatory.[32] Thus, doctrines that might be philosophically important are nevertheless indifferent to the extent that they are nonessential.

Erasmus's list of doctrinal adiaphora is lengthy; his list of articles of faith is short: "The sum and substance of our religion is peace and concord. This can hardly remain the case unless we define as few matters as possible and leave each individual's judgment free on many questions."[33] For example, although Erasmus declares the doctrine of the Trinity to be essential, many issues surrounding this doctrine are adiaphoral, including the following:

> How person differs from person, and why the bringing forth of the Holy Spirit from the Father is called procession not generation; and whether the divine essence generates or is generated; and whether the divine essence has the same identity in connection with no matter which person of the Trinity, as the divine essence has in connection

---

circumcision to all because Paul once circumcised Timothy." Roman Catholic rites and rituals are not indifferent, More argues, but necessary. *Responsio ad Lutherum, in The Complete Works of St. Thomas More*, ed. John M. Headley (New Haven: Yale University Press, 1969), vol. 5, part 1, p. 421. See also Verkamp, *Indifferent Mean*, 77–78, 115–16.

31. *CWE* 6:84–90 (Letter to Paul Volz, 14 August 1581); *CWE* 7:124.163–125.209 (Letter to Jan Šlechta, 1 November 1519); *CWE* 27:120–35 (*Praise of Folly*, 1514); Erasmus, "The Seraphic Funeral," in *The Colloquies of Erasmus*, trans. Craig R. Thompson (Chicago: University of Chicago Press, 1965), 500–516; Verkamp, *Indifferent Mean*, 24, 36–37. Erasmus also tried to introduce his own new adiaphoral ritual for which he was criticized by the Catholic theologian Nöel Béda: a religious ceremony for adolescents in which they renew their baptismal vows. See Erika Rummel, *Erasmus and His Catholic Critics* (Nieuwkoop: De Graaf Publishers, 1989), 2:40–41.

32. An example of how adiaphora is applied almost solely to ceremony, versus doctrine, is the post-Erasmian Lutheran "Formula of Concord" (1577). See Theodore G. Tappert, trans. and ed., *The Book of Concord: The Confessions of the Evangelical Lutheran Church* (Philadelphia: Muhlenberg Press, 1959), 610–16. See also Clyde L. Manschreck, "The Role of Melanchthon in the Adiaphora Controversy," *Archiv für Reformationsgeschichte* 48 (1957): 165–81, and Verkamp, *Indifferent Mean*, 94–96.

33. *CWE* 9:252.232–234 (Letter to Jean de Carondelet, 5 January 1523). See also *CWE* 250.172–251.188 and 253.244–46.

with the divine being Itself. And whether the power of generating in
the Father be absolute or relative; and whether the power of generating can be imparted to the Son by the Father. Moreover, if it is
conceded that God generates God, whether God generates the self-
same God or another God.[34]

Likewise, according to Erasmus, the doctrine of the Immaculate Conception,
the claims of the Church hierarchy to authority by divine right, and most
questions about the sacraments are adiaphoral.[35]

To doctrinal essentials, Erasmus adds the precepts of Christian living as
fundamental to the faith. He asserts the centrality of ethical behavior to
Christianity in his concept "the philosophy of Christ," which is the essence
of Christ's teaching in the gospels. This philosophy, as explicated by Erasmus, stands in contrast both to ritual and doctrinal adiaphora. For Erasmus,
the philosophy of Christ is found "not in ceremonies alone and syllogistic
propositions but in the heart itself and in the whole life." "In this kind of
philosophy," he writes, "life means more than debate, . . . transformation

34. LB 10:1259F–1260A (*Hyperaspistes* I, 1526).
35. LB 6:696C–D (Note on 1 Cor. 7:39, *Novum Testamentum*, 1519); CWE 9:264.649–51
(Letter to Jean de Carondelet, 5 January 1523); LB 10:1663A–B (*Spongia adversus adspergines
Hutteni*, 1523); LB 6:926–28 (*In Epistolam ad Timotheum I*); *Ausgewählte Werke*, 193, lines
9–28 (*Ratio verae theologiae*); LB 5:1079B (*Ecclesiastes*); CWE 66:11, cited in Augustijn,
Erasmus, 78–79.
In a letter (1 November 1519) to his friend Jan Šlechta, Erasmus summarizes what he
believed to be the fundamentals:

> A few truths are enough, and the multitude are more easily persuaded of their truth if
> they are few. As things are, we make six hundred articles out of one, some of them of
> such a kind that one can be ignorant of them, or unconvinced, without peril to one's
> religion. . . . Besides which the whole of the Christian philosophy lies in this, our
> understanding that all our hope is placed in God, who freely gives us all things through
> Jesus his son, that we were redeemed by his death and engrafted through baptism with
> his body, that we might be dead to the desires of this world and live by his teaching and
> example, not merely harboring no evil but deserving well of all men. . . .
> These above all are the things that must be implanted in the hearts of men until they
> become second nature. If any man wishes to pursue more abstruse questions touching
> the divine nature or the substance of Christ or the sacraments . . . he is welcome to do
> so with this restriction, that to believe what commends itself to this man or that should
> not at once become compulsory for everybody. CWE 7:126.235–127.260 (Letter to Jan
> Šlechta, 1 November 1519).

See also Bainton, *Erasmus of Christendom*, 185–86; Lecler, *Toleration and the Reformation*,
1:126–27; and Erasmus *Inquisitio de Fide: A Colloquy by Desiderius Erasmus Roterodamus
1524*, ed. Craig R. Thompson (Hamden, Conn.: Archon Books, 1975), 39–48.

is a more important matter than intellectual comprehension."[36] Although Erasmus never compromises on doctrinal essentials, he consistently laments doctrine's overshadowing of Christian morality: "You will not be damned if you do not know whether the Spirit proceeding from the Father and the Son has a single or a double principle, but you will not escape perdition unless you see to it in the mean time that you have the fruits of the Spirit, which are charity, joy, peace, patience, kindness, goodness, forbearance, gentleness, faith, moderation, self-control, and chastity."[37] Much of Erasmus's criticism of the scholastics derives from their preference for theological dexterity over piety. More important than scholastic subtleties, Erasmus argues, is a "pure and simple life."[38]

Because ethical action, for Erasmus, is so significant to Christianity, he is able to describe the pagan classics as manuals in the philosophy of Christ. By instructing their disciples in the virtues, philosophers like Socrates, Aristotle, Diogenes, Epictetus, even Epicurus, have unwittingly presented Christ's teachings.[39] Reflecting Erasmus's own reverence for the classics, the interlocutors in Erasmus's colloquy "The Godly Feast" affirm the sanctity of virtuous pagans and their texts. Eusebius, the host in the colloquy, states that "whatever is devout and contributes to good morals should not be called profane," including pagan writings. "Speaking frankly among friends," he continues, "I can't read Cicero's *De senectute, De amicitia, De officiis, De Tusculanis quaestionibus* without sometimes kissing the book and blessing that pure heart, divinely inspired as it was." And of Socrates, who tried his utmost to live righteously without knowing Christ and the Sacred Scriptures,

---

36. From Erasmus's *Paracelsis* (1516), translated by John Olin, in *Christian Humanism and the Reformation*, ed. John C. Olin (Gloucester, Mass.: Peter Smith, 1973), 99–100. See also Thompson, "More Reappraised," 238, and *Inquisitio de fide*, 42–43.

37. CWE 9:252.220–25 (Letter to Jean de Carondelet, 5 January 1523). For a similar statement, see *In Epistolam ad Timotheum*: "In all ages we argue whether the grace by which God loves us and draws us to him and the grace by which we in turn love him is the same grace and whether it is something created or not created. Rather let us act with pure prayers, with innocence of life, with pious deeds, so that God makes us worthy of that gift." LB 6:926–28. See also Erasmus, *Paracelsis*, in Olin, *Christian Humanism*, 98.

38. CWE 6:74.55–76.138 (Letter to Paul Volz, written as the preface to a new edition of the *Enchiridion militis christiani* and printed in August 1518). See also *Praise of Folly* (1511): "Such is the erudition and complexity" of the scholastics ('realists, nominalists, Thomists, Albertists, Ockhamists, and Scotists—and I've not mentioned all the sects, only the main ones'), observes Erasmus, "that I fancy the apostles themselves would need the help of another Holy Spirit if they were obliged to join issue on these topics with our new breed of theologian." But the apostles taught not by syllogism, but "by the example of their way of life and their miracles." CWE 27:127–29.

39. Olin, *Christian Humanism*, 100–101.

Nephalius, one of the interlocutors, exclaims: "'Saint Socrates, pray for us.'"[40] Given his attitude toward ethical pagans, it is little wonder that Erasmus considers it likely that these pre-Christians, notwithstanding their ignorance of Christ, will be saved.[41]

Free Will: Erasmus the Skeptic

For Erasmus, to determine whether a doctrine is essential or not is also to decide the epistemological stance permitted toward that doctrine. In fundamental articles, there must be certainty; in nonessentials, skepticism is allowed.[42] These opposites, "fundamentals" and "nonessentials," "certainty" and "skepticism," frame Erasmus's debate with Luther on free will. Erasmus explicates his own position on free will, vis-à-vis Luther's, in *De libero arbitrio, diatribe sive collatio* (*On Free Will: A Disputation or Comparison*), published in 1524. Luther responded with *De servo arbitrio* (*On the Enslaved Will*), published in 1525. Erasmus then answered Luther with his two-part *Hyperaspistes diatribae adversus servum arbitrium* (*Hyperaspistes: A Warrior Shielding a Discussion Against the Enslaved Will by Martin Luther*),[43] the first part appearing in 1526 and the second in 1527.

The theological point in question in their debate is whether or not our will can affect our salvation. Luther denies that it can. No matter how much we desire to, Luther argues, we cannot will ourselves to fulfill God's law perfectly. Therefore, all our actions are worthless in God's eyes. Justification proceeds from faith alone, which is itself the result of God's grace; salvation is unmerited. Erasmus disagrees. Though acknowledging that faith, not works, is the key to salvation, he nevertheless finds scriptural support for the position that free will plays a role in our redemption. Why would God have

---

40. *Colloquies*, 65–68. On the identity of the interlocutors, see Preserved Smith, *A Key to the Colloquies of Erasmus* (Cambridge: Harvard University Press, 1927), 10–11.

41. Erasmus, in his preface to his edition of Cicero's *Tusculan Disputations* (Paris, 1549), writes: "If a certain crude and confused belief about divine matters was sufficient for salvation for Jews before the gospel was proclaimed, what prevents a cruder knowledge from being good enough for salvation for a pagan to whom even the law of Moses was unknown, especially when his life was upright, and not only upright but even holy?" Erasmus, however, considered this question of salvation for righteous pagans to be adiaphoral. Thus, after expressing his own opinion, he notes that "each person is free to make his judgment." For a discussion of how Erasmus's views on the fate of virtuous pagans compare with other Christian writers and of how Erasmus reconciles his views with the principle of *Nulla salus extra Ecclesiam*, see Thompson, *Inquisitio de fide*, 103–21.

42. LB 10:1305A–B (*Hyperaspistes* I). See also LB 5:1079B (*Ecclesiastes*).

43. The English title is that used in the forthcoming translation in *CWE*.

commanded us to choose good over evil, if there were no choice? Erasmus proceeds to offer biblical examples:

<Joel 2:12> "Return to me with all your heart." <Jonah 3:8> "Let everyone turn from his evil way."
<Isa. 46:8> "Recall it to mind, you transgressors" [Prevaricatores reddite ad cor].
<Jer. 26:3> "Let everyone turn from his evil way, that I may repent of the evil which I intend to do to them because of their evil doings."
<Jer. 26:4> "If you will not listen to me, to walk in my law."

Holy Scriptures are replete with such exhortations. "Almost the whole of Scripture speaks of nothing but conversion, application, and striving after better things. All these go for nothing if once you admit that doing good or bad comes by necessity." Erasmus refuses to accept Luther's explanation that these commandments only serve to demonstrate our unworthiness. Erasmus believes that God would not mislead us in that way.[44] Rather, our virtuous endeavors and righteous deeds, though insufficient to secure God's mercy, unite with His grace, thereby leading us to greater perfection. Human will acts as the apprentice; God's grace, the architect. Will is certainly subordinate to grace, as the apprentice is inferior to the architect, yet, like the apprentice, the will also shares in the work. Or, in another analogy, Erasmus compares our desire for eternal salvation to the wish of "a child who has fallen and has not yet strength to walk" for an apple that the unaided child cannot reach. The child, however, is supported and guided by his father, who willingly places the fruit in the child's hand, "as a reward for running." "The child could not have stood up if the father had not lifted it, could not have seen the apple had the father not shown it, could not advance unless the father had all the time assisted its feeble steps, could not grasp the apple had the father not put it into his hand."[45] God, our Father, extends this same hand to us, through His grace. And like the child's father, God recognizes and rewards us for our attempts, despite our inability to effect our own salvation.[46]

---

44. *Luther and Erasmus*, 56, 59–61.
45. Ibid., 84–85, 91.
46. Trying to avoid the Scylla and Charybdis of either attributing too much or too little to grace, Erasmus sought a compromise. He agreed with those who posit a three-part division of grace—"beginning, progress, and end"—and "attribute the first and last to grace, and only in progress say that free choice achieves anything, yet in such wise that in each individual action two causes come together, the grace of God and the will of man." From this perspective,

In debating free will, Erasmus and Luther do not only disagree on the reality of free will; they also disagree about (1) whether it is essential to take a position on free will and (2) what degree of knowledge is necessary (and possible) in the matter. Luther contends that belief in the nullity of free will is a necessary doctrine: "It is . . . essentially salutary and necessary for a Christian to find out whether the will does anything or nothing in matters pertaining to salvation. . . . If we do not know these things, we shall know nothing at all of things Christian, and shall be worse than any heathen."[47] And Luther asserts that certainty, not skepticism, is required of the believer in an essential doctrine like free will: "The Holy Spirit is no Skeptic, and it is not doubts or mere opinions that he has written on our hearts, but assertions more sure and certain than life itself and all experience."[48]

Erasmus maintains that free will is adiaphoral. The best advice for most of us, he writes, is that we "not waste [our] time or talents on labyrinths of this kind."[49] Implicit in this statement is the belief that it is unnecessary to determine the status of free will. True to his rhetorical bent, Erasmus assumes the role of Skeptic in this debate: "So far am I from delighting in 'assertions' that I would readily take refuge in the opinion of the Skeptics, wherever this is allowed by the inviolable authority of the Holy Scriptures and by the decrees of the Church."[50] To which Luther responds: "Let

---

will—once aroused by grace—can work together with grace. Similarly, will can refuse grace too. Thus, "grace is the principal cause and the will secondary, which can do nothing apart from the principal cause, since the principal is sufficient in itself." Ibid., 90. See also Manfred Hoffmann, "Erasmus on Free Will: An Issue Revisited," *Erasmus of Rotterdam Society Yearbook Ten* (1990): 117–21.

47. Hoffmann, "Erasmus on Free Will," 116–17.

48. Ibid., 109. See Boyle, *Rhetoric and Reform*, particularly 43–66.

49. LB 9:1218B–C (*De libero arbitrio*). In LB 10:1663B (*Spongia adversus aspergines Hutteni*), Erasmus maintains that knowing "whether free will is important to salvation or whether faith alone contributes to salvation" is not an article of faith. See also *CWE* 8:280.358–60 (Letter to Pierre Barbier, 13 August 1521).

50. *Luther and Erasmus*, 37. Cf. *Praise of Folly*: "For human affairs are so complex and obscure that nothing can be known of them for certain, as has been rightly stated by my Academicians [Academic Skeptics], the least assuming of the philosophers." CWE 27:118. Erasmus explains that his skepticism does not signal his indifference to the truth, but that he "will consider matters for a long while and will not rashly make a pronouncement. Therefore he is not a skeptic who cares not to know what is true and what is false, inasmuch as skeptics take their name from attentive observation. But rather a skeptic is he who does not make facile definitions, and does not engage in mortal combat for his opinion, but what another follows as a certain thing he instead pursues as a probable matter." LB 10:1262C–D (*Hyperaspistes* I). Erasmus's explanation of skepticism is etymologically correct, since the word "skeptic," literally "inquirer," derives from the verb σκέπτεσθαι, which means "to observe carefully," "to examine," and "to consider." See Stough, *Greek Skepticism*, 3. Cf. Erasmus's statement on

Skeptics and Academics keep well away from us Christians, but let there be among us 'assertors' twice as unyielding as the Stoics themselves."[51]

Erasmus classifies free will as adiaphoral and as a doctrine that can be debated skeptically because Scripture, for him, defines what is fundamental and must be known with certainty, and Scripture is unclear about free will; some passages seem to argue for its existence and others against it. Where the Bible speaks plainly about dogmas, according to Erasmus, we are bound to believe them with certainty. "I do not put less faith in the divine scriptures," he pronounces, "than if I heard Christ Himself speaking them to me with His own voice; and . . . I doubt less about the things I read there than I do about what I hear with my ears, see with my eyes, and clutch with my hands."[52] Principally, this certitude in Scripture stems from the Divine Spirit, which engenders in us an unshakable conviction that the biblical canon is divinely inspired. What the Spirit effects in us, Erasmus explains, "no human persuasion can produce in our hearts, which is the most certain argument that all these [scriptural] things are done divinely." In addition to his supernatural argument, Erasmus offers other, more mundane, reasons why there can be no question about Scripture's divine origins: Scripture's agreement with natural reason; the miracles by which it was proclaimed; its internal consistency; the consonance between the prophecies of the Old and New Testaments; and Scripture's power to gain acceptance in all ages and by all nations, despite all the worldly forces arrayed against it.[53]

Lacking biblical certitude on the question of free will, Erasmus adopts Academic skepticism and relies on probability as the highest level of knowledge attainable in the matter.[54] Like the Academics, he considers both sides (*in utramque partem*) of the issue to arrive at the most probable conclusion.

---

skepticism with a similar declaration made by the father of humanism, Petrarch, in a letter to Francesco Bruni (25 October 1362): "So much do I fear to become entangled in errors that I throw myself into the embrace of doubt instead of truth. Thus I have gradually become a proselyte of the Academy as one of the big crowd, as the very last of this humble flock: I do not believe in my faculties, do not affirm anything, and doubt every single thing, with the single exception of what I believe is a sacrilege to doubt." Cited in Ernst Cassirer, Paul Oskar Kristeller, and John Herman Randal Jr., eds., *The Renaissance Philosophy of Man* (Chicago: University of Chicago Press, 1948), 34–35.

51. *Luther and Erasmus*, 106.

52. LB 10:1335C (*Hyperaspistes* I). See also CWE 7:126.235–45 (Letter to Jan Šlechta, 1 November 1519).

53. LB 5:1136C (*Symbolum sive catechismus personae catechumenus & catechista*, 1533); LB 5:1135E–1136B. See also LB 5:1078B–D (*Ecclesiastes*), and John B. Payne, *Erasmus: His Theology of Sacraments* (Richmond, Va.: John Knox Press, 1970), 15–17.

54. See, for example, LB 5:1079B (*Ecclesiastes*), where Erasmus writes that "many decrees

Because the biblical texts are ambiguous, Erasmus hopes that he will arrive at probability through a "comparison of Scriptures [*collatione Scripturarum*]"; as M. O. Boyle notes, Erasmus refers to his *De libero arbitrio* as a *collatio*, a comparison.[55] Erasmus's method of *collatio* finds its classical precedent in Cicero, who defines comparison as one of the subdivisions of probability. "A parallel [*collatio*]," Cicero writes, "is a passage putting one thing beside another on the basis of their resemblances."[56] Since Scripture has only a single author, Erasmus's form of *collatio* must ultimately end with textual reconciliation.[57] Thus he harmonizes the texts in favor of the existence of free will, which he finds the more probable opinion. In particular, Erasmus finds "highly probable" (*satis probabilis*) the opinion of those who "attribute most to grace and almost nothing to free will, yet do not deny it altogether," since this view "allows man to study and strive, but does not permit him to make any claims for his own powers."[58]

In *Hyperaspistes*, Erasmus claims that he argues his case, in *De libero arbitrio*, solely by comparing scriptural texts, since Luther will only accept textual proofs.[59] Similarly, in the introduction to *De libero arbitrio* itself, Erasmus points out that he can avoid citing the opinions of "innumerable Greek and Latin writers" on free will, "since Luther does not acknowledge the authority of any writer, of however distinguished a reputation, but only listens to canonical scriptures."[60] Notwithstanding these statements, however, Erasmus does try to persuade his readers, in *De libero arbitrio*, by comparing human authorities. Immediately after declaring his joy at having avoided the great labor of assembling what each author had to say for or

---

of the scholastic theologians" are merely probable because "they cannot be proved clearly through Scripture."

55. *Luther and Erasmus*, 47; LB 9:1220F (*De libero arbitrio*); Boyle, *Rhetoric and Reform*, 20–21, 43–46. Comparison, according to Erasmus, is what enables church councils to arrive at the truth: "Indeed in the church councils what is obscure for some the Spirit reveals to others, so that from a comparison of separate elements nothing remains obscure when each person brings forth what has been disclosed to him." LB 10:1312C–D (*Hyperaspistes* I).

56. *De inventione* 1.30.47–49.

57. "So far we have compared those scriptural passages which establish free will and those, on the other hand, which seem to take it away completely. But since the Holy Spirit, who is their author, cannot contradict himself, we are forced, whether we like it or not, to seek a moderate judgment." LB 9:1241D (*De libero arbitrio*).

58. LB 9:1224C (*De libero arbitrio*); see also LB 9:1241C and LB 10:1327B–C (*Hyperaspistes* I).

59. For example, Erasmus states in *Hyperaspistes* I (LB 10:1295A–B) that he argues, in *De libero arbitrio*, only from Scripture; also LB 10:1314D.

60. *Luther and Erasmus*, 42.

against free will, he proceeds to remind the reader that "if we shall seem to give equal weight with Luther to the testimonies and solid arguments of Holy Scripture, [the reader] should also bear constantly in mind so numerous a body of most learned men who have found approval in so many centuries down to our own day." A large list of Church Fathers and scholastics, "not to mention the authority of so many universities, councils, and supreme pontiffs" affirm the reality of free will. But from the time of the apostles to the present, Erasmus observes that, besides Luther, only Manichaeus, John Wycliffe, and Lorenzo Valla have denied free will.[61]

Free Will: Doctrinal Consensus

Comparing the number, learning, and holiness of the authorities for and against free will, Erasmus finds that the proponents of free will are greater than its detractors. He uses this comparison, like his textual *collatio*, to argue for the probability of free will.[62] Erasmus's probable argument from human authority, however, is not based so much on a weighing of opposing "authorities," as it is grounded on one side's possession of "consensus." Erasmus identifies consensus as a standard of truth: "The decrees of the Catholic Church, especially those set forth by general councils and sanctioned by the agreement of the Christian people [*Christiani populi consensu comprobata*], have so much weight with me that even if my weak mind does not comprehend on the grounds of human reason what is ordained, still I will embrace it as if an oracle coming from God." Therefore, Erasmus excludes from his skepticism only "sacred texts, as long as the sense is quite clear" and the consensual decrees of the Catholic Church. "But in other matters, concerning which the proponents fight to death with great strife, I say that I will easily pass over to the position of the skeptics."[63]

61. Ibid., 42–44. Also LB 10:1314F–1315A.
62. *Luther and Erasmus*, 42–46.
63. LB 10:1262A–C (*Hyperaspistes* I). See also LB 9:1112D (*Responsio ad epistolam paraeneticam Alberti Pii*, 1529); Hoffmann, "Erasmus and Religious Toleration," 104. On Erasmus's conception of the *consensus omnium*, see J. K. McConica, "Erasmus and the Grammar of Consent," in *Scrinium Erasmianum*, ed. J. Coppens (Leiden: E. J. Brill, 1969), 2:77–99; Payne, *Erasmus*, 17–33; and Brian Gogan, *The Common Corps of Christendom: Ecclesiological Themes in the Writings of Sir Thomas More* (Leiden: E. J. Brill, 1982), 365–70. Victoria Kahn discusses Erasmus's view of the *consensus omnium*, as it relates to biblical hermeneutics, in "Authority and Interpretation in the Renaissance: Erasmus, Sidney, and Montaigne" (Ph.D. diss., Yale University, 1979), 46–52. While Erasmus gave greater emphasis to "consensus" after Luther's break with Rome (Gogan, *Common Corps*, 365), Erasmus used

Erasmus finds a classical antecedent for consensus, as he did for comparison, in Cicero's subdivision of probability: Cicero assigns consensus to the category of judgment (*iudicatum*), which is "the approval of an act by the assent or authority or judicial decision of some person or persons."[64] More generally, however, Erasmian consensus derives from the basic assumptions built into the art of classical rhetoric. It was only natural for rhetoricians to view consensus as the criterion of truth, since orators must rely on consensus to persuade. They take as their starting points the assumptions common to all because it is the common people they address.[65] Not only do orators begin with the community's common assumptions, but, notwithstanding their own attempts to influence the views of the community in the end they accept the community's decision, its consensus, as the truth. Be it in the court for legal cases or in the political assembly for political deliberations, it is the relevant community's agreement that defines the truth. An orator's practical reliance on consensus to determine the truth finds theoretical expression in Aristotle's observations that "what all believe to be true is actually true," and "that men have a sufficient natural instinct for what is true, and usually do arrive at the truth."[66] In line with the dominant rhetorical view that oratory deals with probable, not certain, truths, consensus is accepted as prima facie evidence of probability: a fact implicit in the Greek language, which uses the same word, *endoxa*, to denote "probability" as well as "resting on opinion" and "generally accepted," and explicit in Aristotle's statement that consensus corresponds to the probable truth.[67]

Although "consensus" has an established classical tradition, Erasmus's inconstant use of the term shows that he assigns various characteristics to the concept. For example, he seems to contradict himself about the degree of knowledge that consensus provides: certainty or probability. On the one

the concept before the Reformation: for example, when he called, in 1516, for Christian teachers and preachers to concentrate on those matters on which there exists a broad consensus. See LB 6:64F–65D (*Novum Instrumentum*) and McConica, "Grammar of Consent," 81.

64. *De inventione* 1.30.48.

65. *De oratore* 1.3.12.

66. Aristotle *Nichomachean Ethics* 1173a, ed. Martin Ostwald (Indianapolis: Bobbs-Merrill, 1962); *Rhetoric* 1355a15–16; *Topics* 100b20; Klaus Oehler, "Der Consensus omnium als Kriterium der Wahrheit in der antiken Philosophie und der Patristik," *Antike und Abendland* 10 (1961): 106; Kahn, "Authority and Interpretation," 32.

67. Oehler, "Consensus," 106. Aristotle's belief that consensus corresponds to probability influenced Aquinas. Thus, Aquinas sometimes referred to an opinion as "probable among all" or as "probably held by many." See Edmund F. Byrne, *Probability and Opinion: A Study in the Medieval Presuppositions of Post-Medieval Theories of Probability* (The Hague: Martinus Nijhoff, 1968), 106–7.

hand, by forswearing skepticism when there is Church consensus and embracing that consensus "as if an oracle coming from God," Erasmus implies that agreement offers certainty.[68] On the other hand, he accepts the rhetorical standpoint that consensus is proof of probability, not certainty, and therefore fallible.[69] The confusion about the epistemological status of consensus, and whether or not it is permissible to question what the Church has agreed upon, is apparent in Erasmus's discussion of free will. For although Erasmus consistently states that there is a consensus on free will, which he does not doubt, he presents his position as only the most probable, and he allows that Luther may debate the point, albeit moderately and in the appropriate audience.[70] Even the structure of *De libero arbitrio*, with its unresolved argument *in utramque partem*, implicitly signals that free will is a debatable doctrine.[71]

Erasmus is not only ambiguous about the implications of consensus, but also about who or what constitutes consensus. Thus he speaks of the following types of consensus without specifying the differences between them: "the authority of councils and of popes, the consensus of so many centuries and of the whole Christian people"; "that which has been handed down with the authority of the ancients"; and "that which has been handed down with great consensus by all the orthodox."[72] Erasmus, at times, adduces particular forms of consensus like the agreement among the doctors

---

68. LB 10:1262 (*Hyperaspistes* I); *Luther and Erasmus*, 37. Based on these passages, Boyle rejects Richard Popkin's view that Erasmus relied on the Church because of his uncertainty. See Popkin, *The History of Skepticism from Erasmus to Spinoza* (Berkeley and Los Angeles: University of California Press, 1979), 7–8. For Boyle, Church consensus gave Erasmus certainty. See Boyle, *Rhetoric and Reform*, 21 and 171 n. 83, and Marjorie O'Rourke Boyle, "Erasmus and the 'Modern' Question: Was He Semi-Pelagian?" *Archiv für Reformationsgeschichte* 75 (1984): 75–77.

69. *Luther and Erasmus*, 44–46; LB 10:1297D–E; LB 10:1306C–D (*Hyperaspistes* I).

70. *Luther and Erasmus*, 42–44, 97; LB 10:1259D, 1285F, 1293B, 1304F (*Hyperaspistes* I). For other examples of how frequently Erasmus reiterated the consensus on free will, see Boyle, *Rhetoric and Reform*, 136 and 201 n. 13. Erasmus describes his position on free will as "much more probable" than Luther's in *Luther and Erasmus*, 85. See also 41–42, and LB 10:1290B–E (*Hyperaspistes* I), where Erasmus explains the conditions under which questions like free will—which are inexpedient to discuss before the masses—should be debated.

71. Erasmus took an increasingly negative stance toward Luther after the reformer's publication of *De servo arbitrio*. Thus, in *Hyperaspistes*, Erasmus denies that he really treated free will as a debatable doctrine. Rather, he writes, "for the sake of civility I pretended that the investigation of both parties was dubious, so that, with matters thus made even, you might show us something which would incline us, wavering between two views, to your side." LB 10:1304F. See Boyle, *Rhetoric and Reform*, 26.

72. LB 10:1319B–C (*Hyperaspistes* I); LB 5:500B (*De amabili Ecclesiae Concordia*); LB 10:1259D (*Hyperaspistes* I).

or interpreters of Scripture, the Church Fathers, the scholastics, popes, and general councils. Yet he also speaks more generally about the consensus of all Christians, represented by the Church: "I call the Church the consensus of the Christian people."[73] Moreover, Erasmus is not explicit about how long these agreements must persist to be considered bona fide consensus. Some of Erasmus's phrases imply enduring agreements: "the perpetual consensus of the Church," "a perpetual consensus of so many ages and so many nations," or "the consensus of so many centuries."[74] But Erasmus also declares that after the Church "has spoken definitively," even on doctrines that have recently been disputed, he ceases to be a skeptic, which suggests that consensus does not presuppose long-term agreement.[75]

Although Erasmus never explains his variable use of consensus, he applies the term to several kinds of agreement that run along a continuum from the

73. *EE* 7:216.56–60 (Letter to Willibald Pirckheimer, 19 October 1527). Similarly, *EE* 6:351.52–352.56 (Letter to Pirckheimer, 6 June 1526) and *EE* 6:372.26–29 (Letter to Pirckheimer, 30 July 1526). See also Payne, *Erasmus*, 18–33, and McConica, "Grammar of Consent," 85–87.

Erasmus's differentiation between types of consensus, like his concept of consensus itself, is rooted in classical rhetoric. Cicero, for example, distinguishes between three classes of judgment. Each is a discrete kind of agreement that the orator can cite, in legal cases, to argue for probability: (1) "religious sanction," which Cicero defines as a judgment that "has been rendered by judges under oath in accordance with law"; (2) the "common practice of mankind," which is judgment that "all men in general have approved of . . . or have followed"; and (3) a "special act of approval," which "is a case in which there was doubt as to how an event was to be regarded and men have settled it by an authoritative vote." *De inventione* 1.30.48–49. As Alain Michel observes, these three divisions of judgment are linked to different sections of society, with the first and third involving the decisions of the upper classes and the second reflecting popular opinion. *Rhétorique*, 486. Even the most basic and comprehensive category of consensus—from the perspective of the classical rhetorician—is applied to a variety of consensuses. Thus Aristotle defines generally accepted opinions (*endoxa*) as "those that seem right to all people or most people or the wise—and in the latter case all the wise or most of them or those best known and generally accepted [as authorities]." *Topics* 100b18. Translation from Kennedy, *On Rhetoric*, 290. Erasmus retains the classical idea that there are different kinds of consensus, but adapts classical categories to Christian circumstances.

74. LB 10:1318B (*Hyperaspistes* I); LB 5:1171F (*Symbolum*); LB 10:1319B (*Hyperaspistes* I); LB 5:500B (*De amabili Ecclesiae concordia*). Cf. Vincent of Lérins' statement that "in the Catholic Church itself, all possible care must be taken, that we hold that faith which has been believed everywhere, always, by all. For that is truly and in the strictest sense 'Catholic,' which, as the name itself and the reason of the thing declare, comprehends all universally." *The Commonitory of Vincent of Lérins, for the Antiquity and Universality of the Catholic Faith Against the Profane Novelties of All Heresies*, 2.6, trans. Rev. C. A. Heurtley, in *A Select Library of Nicene and Post-Nicene Fathers of the Christian Church*, 2d ser., vol. 11 (New York: The Christian Literature Company, 1894), 132.

75. LB 10:1258D–1259A (*Hyperaspistes* I).

limited to the general and from the probable to the certain. And he considers those forms of consensus that are broader (or more representative) and of longer standing to be more authoritative because they indicate greater scriptural clarity. Accordingly, in ascending order of authority, Erasmus, first, respects the consensus of the *doctores Ecclesiae* (the interpreters of Scripture), especially the consensus of the early Church Fathers, who were closest to the sources.[76] Second, and of still higher status, is the consensus of the Church's general councils. As the fishmonger in Erasmus's colloquy "A Fish Diet" says: "But what proceeds from the authority of a universal council is a heavenly oracle and carries weight equal to that of the Gospels, or surely almost equal."[77] Erasmus, however, establishes preconditions before he submits himself to the councils' decisions. Thus the fishmonger explains that councils must be "solemnly convened and conducted" and their acts must be "proclaimed and received under the guidance of the Holy Spirit."[78] Most important, for Erasmus, is that a council's decree must be approved by the consensus of the Christian people. Only after a council's decree has received such universal consensus is it described, by Erasmus, as "an oracle coming from God," which cannot be doubted.[79]

Third, and of greatest authority, are the doctrines approved by the fullest consensus, which are contained in the Apostles' Creed. Erasmus demonstrates the universal agreement on, and the doctrinal sufficiency of, the

76. Payne, *Erasmus*, 18–23. Cf. More's defense against Luther's charge that More raised the opinions of Church Fathers into articles of faith: "Who ever presented to you as a necessary article of faith, Luther, a single statement of any father whatever? Certainly we present it as probable, and much more probable than your statement, especially because piety opened their eyes while impiety closes yours. . . . But if it is certain that on any point all the ancient fathers long ago agreed, we do not hesitate to oppose such thorough agreement of good men to a single dull-witted scoundrel, when it is clear that they reached agreement through that Spirit who makes those who dwell in a house to be of one mind." *Responsio ad Lutherum*, in *Complete Works of St. Thomas More*, vol. 5, part 1, p. 213, lines 7–21.

77. In Erasmus's colloquy "A Fish Diet" (1526), in *Colloquies*, 327. Although the two characters in the colloquy, the fishmonger and the butcher, are commoners and laymen, "the perceptive reader familiar with Erasmus' other writings has no difficulty in recognizing the main propositions in the dialogue as characteristically Erasmian ones." See also Payne, *Erasmus*, 23–26; McConica, "Grammar of Consent," 87–89.

78. "A Fish Diet," in *Colloquies*, 327. See also LB 10:1569F (*Praestigiarum libelli cujusdam detectio*, 1526).

79. LB 10:1262A–B (*Hyperaspistes* I). See also "A Fish Diet," in Erasmus, *Colloquies*, 338–39, where the fishmonger denies that "it is possible to doubt concerning councils . . . after they have been accepted and approved by the judgment and consent of Christian peoples." Based on his preconditions for a proper council, Erasmus questions the authority of the Councils of Basel (1431–47) and Constance (1414–17), and, particularly, the Lateran Council (1512–17). See "A Fish Diet," in *Colloquies*, 327, and Payne, *Erasmus*, 24.

Apostles' Creed in *Inquisitio de fide* ("An Examination Concerning Faith"). In this colloquy between a Catholic and a Lutheran, the Catholic discovers that the Lutheran, though reputed to be a heretic, adheres to the doctrines of the Apostles' Creed. That both Catholic and Lutheran, despite their serious differences, can agree on the Apostles' Creed, indicates the breadth of the Creed's consensus. Its consensus is also long-lived inasmuch as the Creed's doctrines reflect the apostles' spirit and are, almost without exception, derived from explicit Scripture.[80]

The universal and perpetual consensus on the Creed establishes it as the minimal doctrinal standard required for salvation. Thus the Catholic in *Inquisitio de fide* concludes that the Lutheran, since he accepts the Apostles' Creed, is doctrinally orthodox on the essentials of faith. And Erasmus confirms this conclusion as his own when, elsewhere, he identifies himself as the Catholic interlocutor of the colloquy.[81] Because Erasmus links a doctrine's epistemological status to its degree of consensus, it follows that the Apostles' Creed, with its complete consensus, will be the most certain. Its articles of faith "are so self-evident that it is unthinkable to dispute about them." For Erasmus, full doctrinal consensus is tantamount to doctrines that are clearly stated in Scripture. Lower in the hierarchy are those doctrines that were approved by public authority only after prolonged inquiry: the consensus of Church councils and of *doctores Ecclesiae*, mentioned above. Beneath these are doctrines about which "not even now is there sufficient agreement."[82]

Erasmus affirms the certainty of universally accepted beliefs as an orthodox Christian. But he can also rely on Cicero to justify his present departure from skepticism. For although Cicero, by and large, acknowledges consen-

---

80. Erasmus, however, questions the Apostolic origin of the Creed—surmising instead that it was written at the Council of Nicaea. LB 9:870F (*Declarationes ad censuras lutetiae vulgatas sub nomine Facultatis Theologiae Parisiensis*, 1532), and *Ratio verae theologiae*, in *Ausgewählte Werke*, 211, lines 20–24. Only the article concerning the descent into hell is not expressly stated in Scripture. LB 10:1162A–B (*Symbolum*).

81. LB 9:1060C–D (*Apologia adversus articulos aliquot, per monachos quosdam in Hispaniis exhibitos*, 1528); Hoffmann, "Erasmus and Religious Toleration," 103. Erasmus identifies the two characters of *Inquisitio de fide*—the Catholic Aulus and the Lutheran Barbatius—with himself and Luther. See Thompson, *Inquisitio de fide*, 2 n. 6. Erasmus, in *Spongia* (LB 10:1654A–B), claims that he never called Luther a heretic. Even late in his life, Erasmus reiterates that "nowhere in my writings do I call Luther's doctrine heretical." LB 10:1537D (*Desiderius Erasmus adversus calmumniosissimam epistolam Martini Lutheri*, 1534). See also Thompson's introduction to *Inquisitio de fide*, 1–49.

82. LB 10:1305A–B (*Hyperaspistes* I). Cf. LB 10:1569F–1570A (*Praestigiarum libelli cujusdam detectio*).

sus as the criterion of probability, he too suggests that universal consensus can provide certainty. Such certainty is possible, according to Cicero, because human beings are born with "innate seeds of virtue," which means that they have an innate knowledge of basic moral and religious truths. And though inborn truths are usually corrupted by the "influence of bad habits and beliefs," there are still some truths that remain untouched.[83] Only those beliefs which are universally held, however, should be considered uncorrupted and, therefore, certain: "The unanimity of the races of the world [consensio omnium gentium] must be regarded as a law of nature."[84] Thus Cicero states that belief in the existence of the gods or in the immortality of the soul, which all agree to, cannot be doubted.[85] In effect, Cicero becomes a Stoic on some beliefs, embracing the Stoic standard of certainty. He denies, however, that his Stoic certainty contradicts his Academic skepticism. Both positions can be reconciled within a Skeptical framework, he argues, given that "our Academy grants us great freedom, so that we may be justified in defending whatever seems most persuasive."[86] Since he finds the Stoic outlook most persuasive when there is universal consensus, he defends his Academic right to adopt it.

Erasmus's Stoic certainty, like Cicero's, is restricted. Only beliefs that can command a universal and perpetual consensus are certain; these are the fundamentals of faith. All other beliefs, such as free will, are only probable and not essential.[87] Because the essentials require a perpetual and universal consensus, they will, of necessity, be very few in number.[88] The consequence

---

83. *Tusculan Disputations* 3.1.2. Although Aristotle believes that human beings are naturally predisposed to virtue and the truth, he maintains that this predisposition must also be developed intellectually. Consensus is probable, for Aristotle, because the many are likelier to perceive the truth than the few. Cicero, however, contends that human beings possess innate concepts prior to, and independent of, the development and use of their rational faculties. See Oehler, "Consensus," 105–11. See also Aristotle *Politics* 1286a25–31.

84. *Tusculan Disputations* 3.1.2, 1.13.30. Also 1.15.35, where Cicero writes that "universal agreement [*omnium consensus*] is the voice of nature." See Oehler, "Consensus," 110–11.

85. See Introduction, notes 145 and 146.

86. *De officiis* 3.4.20. Translation from Cicero, *On Duties*, 108. See also *De officiis* 1.2.6, 2.2.7–8.

87. See LB 5:1079B (*Ecclesiastes*): "It is probable that baptizing infants was instituted by the apostles, nevertheless whoever doubts this is not condemned." That a doctrine is merely probable, however, does not automatically imply that this doctrine may be freely questioned. Erasmus thinks that dogmas with a broad and long-standing consensus, even if not universal and perpetual, are highly probable and, normally, should not be debated—especially among the common people.

88. See note 33. Cf. *EE* 4:486.9–10 (Letter to Justus Jonas, 10 May 1521), and *EE* 5:288.104–7 (Letter to Albert of Brandenburg, 1 June 1523). See also Thompson, *Inquisitio de*

of Erasmus's strict standard for fundamentals of faith is greater toleration. The fewer the articles of faith, the greater latitude there is for religious diversity, and the fewer people there are to be labeled heretics. Not only is Erasmus unwilling to label Luther a heretic, he even intimates that the followers of the heresiarch Arius (d. 335) were not heretics.[89]

For Erasmus, however, heresy requires more than fundamental doctrinal error. He defines heresy as not simply error, "but the obstinate malice which for the sake of any advantage is disturbing the tranquillity of the Church by perverted doctrine."[90] Thus besides (1) the perversion of doctrine, heresy presupposes (2) persistence in error, (3) the search for personal advantage, (4) the presence of "malice," that is, the intention to do evil (as opposed to the lesser sin of *stultitia*, foolishness), and, finally, (5) disturbance of the Church's tranquillity. Erasmus deems only persons guilty of all five sins full-fledged heretics.

In addition to fundamental doctrines, Erasmus, like Cicero, declares the certainty of the basic principles of ethical living. Here, Erasmus deems himself, and all other Christians, capable of finding the truth. Although God has not endowed us with the capacity to know all His secrets, Erasmus argues that He has enabled us to know some things, such as "the precepts for the good life."[91] Certain knowledge of morals is reached by studying the Holy Scripture, which, despite its ambiguities on dogmatic matters, is unequivocal on moral precepts.[92] There is no debate over what constitutes the essentials of Christian living as there is, for example, over free will. The clarity of Scripture on ethical living results in a consensus, similar to the complete agreement on doctrinal essentials. Certainty on the principles of morality, however, is not limited to Christians. Besides Scripture, this

---

fide, 10–11; Gogan, *Common Corps*, 369; Bainton, *Erasmus of Christendom*, 185–87; McConica, "Grammar of Consent," 97–98; and Manfred Hoffmann, "Erasmus and Religious Toleration," 103.

89. As Erasmus writes: "The more dogma there is, the more material for heresy." *EE* 5:465.1–468.155 (Letter to William Warham, 1 June 1524). See also Bainton, *Erasmus of Christendom*, 185. On the Arians, Erasmus writes: "Some passages in Holy Scripture gave the appearance of supporting [the Arian position], and rational arguments were not lacking which displayed some semblance of truth." *CWE* 9:261.526–36 (Letter to Jean de Carondelet, 5 January 1523). The Nicene Creed was formed to exclude Arianism, since the earlier Apostles' Creed did not.

90. LB 5:1081B (*Ecclesiastes*). See also Chomarat, *Grammaire et rhetorique*, 2:1132; Hoffmann, "Erasmus and Religious Toleration," 93–100; Rummel, *Catholic Critics*, 2:54, 151.

91. *Luther and Erasmus*, 39–40.

92. LB 10:1300D–E (*Hyperaspistes* I).

knowledge is attained by consulting the natural law, which is "thoroughly engraved in the minds of all men."[93] Both Christians and pagans, therefore, can discern the basics of moral law by natural reason, creating not only a *consensus fidelium* but a *consensus omnium* on the fundamentals of the good life.

To Erasmus the certainty possible in moral matters, which is unattainable in most doctrines, argues for greater emphasis on living an ethical life over living a dogmatically correct life. By directing his condemnations less at heterodoxy than at immoral practice, Erasmus supports, albeit indirectly, religious toleration. Thus, he decries heresy qua immoral behavior more vociferously than heresy as erroneous dogma. The former, although not heresy in the strict sense of the term, "does the greatest harm to our human life and is a major obstacle to the authority of the Gospel."[94] "What does it matter if the tongue does not blaspheme, if the whole life speaks nothing but blasphemy against God? . . . if the Beatitudes which bless the meek and the persecuted are called a lie? What blasphemy could be more detestable than this?"[95] Such heresy manifests itself in the iniquitous deeds of those leaders of the Church who, while preaching the philosophy of Christ, teach nothing by their example but avarice, eagerness for pleasures, passion for war—all things "which are an abomination to Holy Scripture and are rejected even by the philosophers of paganism."[96] We must especially beware, Erasmus writes, of those wicked churchmen who "hide human lusts under the authority of God's law and under the appearance of piety."[97]

One particular form of the heresy of immoral behavior is the disturbing of the Church's tranquillity, which is the fifth element of Erasmus's definition of heresy. For Erasmus, this sin more than any other, accounts for the reputation of Luther and his followers as heretics. Their "heresy," if it is to be termed such, is sedition and schism. Accordingly, Erasmus refers to them as seditious, encouraging the people to oppose the commonwealth in both its divisions, secular and religious. In opposition to the spiritual realm, they have undertaken their beliefs individually, without reference to the com-

93. *Luther and Erasmus*, 49. See also LB 10:1324E–F (*Hyperaspistes* I). Compare Erasmus's conception of human beings as born with "germinal concepts of the ethical good" with Cicero's view of humanity's innate disposition to the good. *Tusculan Disputations* 3.1.2.

94. CWE 8:292.99–293.108 (Letter to Nicholas van Broeckhoven, 31 August 1521).

95. LB 5:560A–B (*De magnitudine misericordiarum Domini Concio*, 1523).

96. CWE 8:293.105–7 (Letter to Nicholas van Broeckhoven, 31 August 1521).

97. LB 5:818F–819A (*Ecclesiastes*). Chomarat explains that this passage refers to the reformers, "who spread their religious concepts by means of violence." *Grammaire et rhetorique*, 2:1137.

monly accepted views of the Church; and against the temporal order, they have caused "tumults" and political mischief.[98] Erasmus does not believe, however, that these acts are exceptional. Rather, the Lutheran rebellion against constituted authority, although egregious, reflects a wider tendency to immoral action. "I know of no one who has become better on account of [the reformers'] Gospel," Erasmus writes, "but I know of many who have become worse."[99] Although Luther and his comrades expected that restoring true doctrine would eventually effect a moral renewal, Erasmus understood that it would not.

Free Will: Rhetorical Choices

We have seen that Erasmus's debate with Luther over free will concerns such theological and epistemological issues as the reality of free will, the need to take a position on the doctrine, and the degree of certainty possible in the

---

98. By "tranquillity of the Church," Erasmus means the peace of the whole Christian commonwealth—including the secular order—since Erasmus defines the *ecclesia* as "the people assembled to listen to the affairs of the republic." LB 5:769A (*Ecclesiastes*). See also LB 10:1576B (*Epistola contra quosdam qui se falso jactant evangelicos*, 1529): "Again, heresy is that which has clear blasphemy such as the doctrine that denies the divine nature of Christ or [doctrine] that accuses Scripture of lying. Heresy also includes the doctrine that seeks riches by evil arts, by civil unrest; heresy seeks political power and civil confusion." Erasmus condemns Lutherans as seditious in *EE* 4:345.40–46, 399.97–99, 459.30–32, and 461.91–93 and 5:34.43–44, 127.47–50, 259.66–68, 387.39–44, and 426.17–19. See Thompson, *Inquisitio de fide*, 16.

99. *EE* 9:456.435–38 (Letter to Martin Bucer, 2 March 1532). Erasmus found the Reformation's inability to usher in a moral transformation to be damning. Thus he explicitly links both his initial defense and his subsequent condemnation of Luther to the reformer's conduct. Until 1520, Erasmus—though pleading ignorance of Luther's writings—defends Luther on the ground that everyone attests to his good life. Concerning those who would have Luther executed, Erasmus writes, "let them convert to Christ those who are now far from him, let them mend the standard of morality among Christians, which is as corrupt as anything even the Turks can show." *CWE* 7:112.120–23. The implication here is that Christians, including those who are considered heretics, suffer a moral problem, not a doctrinal one. Next, when at the end of 1520 Erasmus begins to criticize Luther, he scores Luther, above all else, for his actions, that is, his organizing a separate sect and his abuse of others. Finally, when formally breaking with Luther in 1524 over the matter of the free will, Erasmus ties his rejection of Luther's doctrine of the bondage of the will to the practical effects of Luther's dogma: greater wickedness among men. With respect to Luther's good actions, see *CWE* 6:297.69–73 (Letter to Elector Frederick of Saxony, 14 April 1519), 6:309.40–43 (Letter to Phillipus Melanchthon, 22 April 1519), 6:368.93–96 (Letter to Thomas Wolsey, 18 May 1519), and *CWE* 8:112.138–52 (Letter to Lorenzo Campeggi, 6 December 1520). For a discussion of Erasmus's negative assessment of Luther's behavior, see Chomarat, *Grammaire et rhetorique*, 2:1134. See also *Luther and Erasmus*, 41–42.

matter. But the debate on free will also relates to the issue of rhetorical strategy, that is, to the question of "how and among whom is the doctrine of free will to be discussed?" Erasmus offers a rhetorical strategy situated between silence and openness. At one end, Erasmus argues, are those doctrinal matters that should never be discussed either because they cannot be known, "such as the hour of death or the Day of Judgment," or because they are entirely useless, such as "questions concerning what is present and what is past for God, and whether it is a possible proposition that the Father hates God the Son, and whether the soul of Christ can be deceived or lie." At the opposite end are those religious truths that should be taught and discussed openly: doctrinal essentials and the precepts of the morally good life.[100] Between these two poles stands free will, and similar doctrines, which may be discussed, yet only with restraint and moderation, and exclusively among the learned.

Erasmus limits discussion on free will, in part, because it is an area "into which God has not wished us to penetrate more deeply." But a more important reason why Erasmus restricts discussion on free will is that such discourse may endanger piety, especially if Luther's denial of free will is publicized in the debate. If everything is the result of necessity, Erasmus asks, "what could be more useless than to publish this paradox to the world?" If God rewards and punishes us for actions beyond our control, for which He alone is responsible, then "what a window to impiety would the public avowal of such an opinion open to countless mortals!" People would not better their conduct, arguing instead that they were not responsible for their wrongdoings. They would stop loving a God who moves them to evil, only to punish them later. Most people, only too willing to sin, would use Luther's views to justify their own evil inclinations.[101]

Luther rejects Erasmus's restrictions on discussing free will and contends that the absence of free will must be asserted, irrespective of the consequences. "God . . . has enjoined that his gospel, which is necessary for all,

---

100. *Luther and Erasmus*, 39–40; LB 10:1260C, 1278A (*Hyperaspistes* I). See also Erasmus, *Ratio*, in *Ausgewählte Werke*, 297–98, and LB 10:1278A (*Hyperaspistes* I). Although I speak here of three basic rhetorical strategies, Erasmus himself distinguished them further—and in different ways—depending on his discussion. Cf. Perelman and Olbrechts-Tyteca, *New Rhetoric*, 58: "We must also add that in social life there is rarely a clear line of demarcation to indicate when resumption of debate is allowable and when forbidden. There is a large intermediate zone between absolute prohibition of renewed discussion and its unconditional allowance: this zone is mostly governed by extremely complex traditions and customs. This is a non-negligible aspect of the life of a community."

101. *Luther and Erasmus*, 38–42; LB 10:1283E, 1304F–1305A (*Hyperaspistes* I).

should know no limit of place or time, but should be preached to all in every time and place." For Luther, there is no intermediate strategy between silence and openness. "Truth and doctrine," he states, "must be preached always, openly, and constantly."[102]

The previous comparison suggests that Erasmus seeks a rhetoric for discussing free will that is distinct from the public rhetoric used to declare the fundamentals, whereas Luther does not. The apparent source of this difference is their debate over the doctrinal significance of free will: Luther, who believes that free will is an essential doctrine, argues that it should be preached like an essential doctrine; but Erasmus, who thinks that free will is adiaphoral, envisions a separate rhetoric to discuss it. Their difference in rhetorical choice, however, is more basic than their debate on how to classify free will. Their differing rhetorical strategies reflect their respective attitudes toward the very possibility of beneficial doctrinal adiaphora. Erasmus believes that there exists a category of adiaphoral doctrine that, while not essential to salvation, may, nevertheless, be useful to discuss. These he describes as questions that are "advantageous and necessary, provided they are moderate and gone into as far as is right."[103] Therefore, he can conceive of a rhetoric to treat such nonessential issues, independent of the rhetoric of fundamentals. Luther, in contrast, denies the existence of beneficial, but unessential, doctrine. Because Luther believes that, first, all doctrines are scripturally based and, second, that Scripture is not obscure about doctrine, he defines indifferent doctrine as useless.[104] And since he does not

---

102. *Luther and Erasmus*, 132–33.

103. LB 10:1265A–B (*Hyperaspistes* I). Erasmus writes similarly of "advantageous questions" concerning doctrinal adiaphora that should not be disputed so "that we rend Christian harmony"; in such questions "it is more satisfactory to allow each person to abound in his own interpretation." LB 10:1260C–D.

104. *Luther and Erasmus*, 105, 110–11, 163. Erasmus notes this characteristic of Luther when he states: "Nor on this question am I of your opinion that all the articles of faith [that is, doctrines] are equal." LB 10:1305A (*Hyperaspistes* I). Since Luther does not acknowledge any worth in nonessential doctrine, it is difficult to argue, as B. J. Verkamp does, that the reformer evaluates Christian doctrine hierarchically. See Verkamp, *Indifferent Mean*, 96. Other reformers, however, speak of a genuine hierarchy of doctrine. For example, the humanistically inclined Melanchthon, reacting to the "Interim" of Charles V—which aimed to harmonize Catholic and Protestant doctrines until a council could address the points in dispute—wrote: "But as different as the articles in the book may be, some are right and some are wrong, some speak of the chief articles of belief which all men must know and understand, and some of other matters which are not so necessary to be known." From *Thoughts on the Interim* (*Bedencken auffs Interim*, 1548), quoted in *A Melanchthon Reader*, trans. Ralph Keen (New York: Peter Lang, 1988), 156. Calvin also writes: "For all the articles of true doctrine are not of the same description. Some are so necessary to be known, that they ought to be universally received as

recognize the concept of beneficial adiaphora, he recognizes only a rhetoric of fundamentals. I argue that Erasmus's distinction between two rhetorics, a rhetoric of fundamentals and a rhetoric of nonessentials, forms the basis for two different types of toleration.

The Rhetoric of Fundamentals

Preaching

Preaching, for Erasmus, is the primary rhetoric of the fundamentals of faith, designed to communicate both doctrinal and ethical principles. Preaching has two main functions: instruction, that is, inculcating Christians with the essentials of their faith; and persuasion, that is, leading them to virtue.[105] That preaching is the preeminent means to achieve these ends is implied by Erasmus's glorification of preaching above all other ecclesiastical responsibilities. The preacher, to Erasmus, is the herald of God's word and Christ's ambassador, fulfilling the most dignified of human duties: the gaining of as many souls as possible for his Master. So exalted is the role of preacher that the son of God himself, Erasmus writes, is known as the "Supreme Preacher."[106] Erasmus is not alone in emphasizing the instructive and persuasive functions of preaching and its hallowed position. Luther is remarkably similar to him on these matters: the reformer defines preaching as "teaching and exhortation," pointing up its doctrinal and ethical purposes; and, for Luther, the highest priestly duty, incumbent on all Christians, is preaching God's word.[107]

---

fixed and indubitable principles, as the peculiar maxims of religion; such as, that there is one God; that Christ is God and the Son of God; that our salvation depends on the mercy of God; and the like. There are others, which are controverted among the churches, yet without destroying the unity of faith." *Institutes* 4.1.12.

105. Chomarat, *Grammaire et rhétorique*, 1096–1103; James Michael Weiss, "*Ecclesiastes* and Erasmus: The Mirror and the Image," *Archiv für Reformationsgeschichte* 65 (1974): 99. The preacher, Erasmus explains, teaches sound doctrine, advises, rebukes, comforts, and opposes those who defame the word of the Gospel. LB 5:831C (*Ecclesiastes*).

106. The preacher's office is also the most "excellent for its dignity" in the ecclesiastical hierarchy and certainly more dignified than the king's. LB 5:771C–D, 772B, 802A, 820C–D (*Ecclesiastes*).

107. Luther, *Tischreden* 2199a, cited in John W. O'Malley, S.J., "Luther the Preacher," in *The Martin Luther Quincentennial*, ed. Gerhard Dünnhaupt (Detroit: Wayne State University

Erasmus links preaching to the *genus* of classical oratory known as deliberation. He enumerates five categories of preaching, four of which are derived explicitly from the deliberative genre: the persuasive, the exhortative, the admonitory, and the consolatory. And while the fifth, the laudatory, is ostensibly derived from the demonstrative *genus*, it is refashioned along deliberative lines.[108] Like its classical analogue, Erasmus's sacred oratory is concrete because it is directed toward action. It is the preacher's duty not only to teach, but to delight and to move the audience to act.[109] The preacher persuades, "so that the hearer will want to embrace that which is honorable or useful"; he exhorts, so that people will dare to act; he admonishes, so that the sinner will "reform and amend his life"; he consoles to help people bear the troubles of this life; and he praises or blames so that by using the example of another, the "people should be led to virtue."[110] And though the preacher, while teaching doctrine, does not persuade his audience toward a specific and immediate action, as does the deliberative

---

Press, 1985), 9 and 15 n. 22; Paul Althaus, *The Theology of Martin Luther*, trans. Robert J. Schultz (Philadelphia: Fortress Press, 1966), 315–16. Both Erasmus's and Luther's definitions reflect the view of preaching that had already dominated for almost three centuries. The late twelfth-century scholastic Alan of Lille, in his *Summa de arte praedicatoria*, defines preaching as "an open and public instruction in faith and behavior." Alan of Lille, *The Art of Preaching* (Kalamazoo: Cistercian Publications, 1981), 16–17. See John W. O'Malley, S.J., "Erasmus and the History of Sacred Rhetoric: The *Ecclesiastes* of 1535," *Erasmus of Rotterdam Society Yearbook Five* (1985): 5.

108. Erasmus lists a sixth category—the instructive—but does not develop the concept separately. LB 5:858E–859A, 870D–881C (*Ecclesiastes*). See Weiss, "*Ecclesiastes* and Erasmus," 100–101; John W. O'Malley, S.J., "Content and Rhetorical Forms in Sixteenth-Century Treatises on Preaching," in *Renaissance Eloquence: Studies in the Theory and Practice of Renaissance Rhetoric*, ed. James J. Murphy (Berkeley and Los Angeles: University of California Press, 1983), 244. O'Malley's "Content and Rhetorical Forms" also provides a useful overview of how other humanists related preaching to the classical rhetorical genres. See 238–52. Philip Melanchthon, the humanist of Lutheranism, divided preaching between three basic *genera*: the *genus epitrepticum*, which exhorts to faith; the *genus paraeneticum*, which exhorts to morality; and the *genus didascalium*, which instructs true doctrine. The first two *genera* are adaptations of the deliberative genre. See Philip Melanchthon, *Elementa rhetorices*, in *Corpus Reformatorum*, ed. Carolus Gottlieb Bretschneider (Halle, Germany: C. A. Schwetschke & Sons, 1846; rpt., New York, 1963), 13:421–28, and *De officiis concionatoris*, in *De arte concionandi formulae, ut breves ita doctae & piae* (London, 1570, Henry Bynneman), and O'Malley, "Content and Rhetorical Forms," 242–43. John O'Malley, in his *Praise and Blame in Renaissance Rome*, discusses another group of humanists, who situated sacred rhetoric in the epideictic genre or *genus demonstrativum*.

109. LB 5:859F (*Ecclesiastes*).

110. LB 5:858E–859A; LB 5:877E–F; LB 5:878D–E (*Ecclesiastes*). Cicero places exhortation, reproach, and consolation under the class of questions that deal with proper conduct. *De oratore* 3.30.118.

orator, Erasmus stresses that doctrinal truths should never be divorced from moral action.[111]

Preaching, for Erasmus, shares other similarities with classical deliberation, which are also shared with the two other basic genres of oratory. Like all three main classical genres, preaching addresses a popular audience and, consequently, it appeals to the emotions.[112] Echoing the ancient rhetoricians, Erasmus concedes the sacred orator's reliance on emotional appeals: "Rhetoricians give laurels to this aspect that the power of speaking has influence on judges and snatches them away from [their rational] selves. . . . [T]his faculty is almost a necessity for the one who is speaking to the crude and unskilled multitude . . . because you can inflame the thick and sluggish crowd sooner than you can teach them, and you can drag them sooner than you can lead them."[113] Emotional appeals, however, are not only a substitute for reason. Erasmus thinks that they complement and lay the groundwork for the rational faculties. The preacher's use of *pathos* complements reason because *pathos* arouses the will to follow what reason has already demonstrated. As Erasmus explains: "A good part of the common people sin more by corrupt emotion than by ignorance of the truth. As, for example, no one is ignorant that drunkenness, adultery, and profit obtained through fraud are crimes, but wicked desires snatch people to things which they do not approve." Therefore, he concludes, "it will be convenient here to drive out passions with passions, as a nail is driven out by a nail." According to Erasmus, the preacher, even before he instructs, should use emotions to make his listeners more tractable and attentive: "Hence it is that we teach children virtue first by sorrow, joy, shame, praise, hope, and fear," and only afterward do we reach their intellects. Such preparation is especially necessary given the crowd that the preacher must address, which is "composed of the mixture of children, old men, maidens, and harlots, sailors, drivers, and cobblers, among whom are those who are not far removed from beasts as far as ability to learn is concerned."[114] But perhaps

---

111. The nexus between doctrine and ethical action is key to Erasmus's "philosophy of Christ."

112. Erasmus refers to sermons as *conciones*, echoing the classical *concio* (or *contio*) — "a specific type of deliberative oratory in which a leader addressed not sophisticated statesmen gathered in the Senate, but a popular and perhaps unruly audience of ordinary people." See O'Malley, "Sacred Rhetoric," 14–16.

113. LB 5:976E–F (*Ecclesiastes*). See also *CWE* 27:104–5 (*Praise of Folly*); Albert Rabil Jr., "Cicero and Erasmus' Moral Philosophy," *Erasmus of Rotterdam Society Yearbook Eight* (1988): 79–82.

114. LB 5:976F–977C; LB 5:951B–952C (*Ecclesiastes*). Cf. Augustine's argument, in

the most fundamental reason why Erasmus sanctions pathetic appeals in preaching is because he believes that emotions, rather than merely ancillary to reason, are essential to faith. Erasmus expresses this insight in his "philosophy of Christ," which is more a matter of the heart than of intellectual comprehension, accessible to all, even to a child. Thus the preacher must make his listeners do more than think; he must also make them feel.[115]

Another similarity between preaching and the classical oratorical *genera* is that they are agonistic. Like the classical orator, Erasmus's preacher attempts to elicit negative passions against an adversary. Unlike the classical orator, however, the preacher's adversary is almost never another orator speaking to the same assembly. Rather, the sacred orator's adversaries are, most commonly, sins and Satan: "Anger, hatred, and indignation should not be stirred up against men as against the sins themselves and against Satan, the father of sins."[116] These adversaries, unlike their classical counterparts, lack credibility. Thus, though there is combat in sacred oratory, there is rarely controversy. Controversy requires that both sides be considered, and inasmuch as the preacher's opponents are sin and Satan, the preacher cannot provide a platform to the other side.[117]

Without controversy, skepticism atrophies; people do not doubt matters that are beyond dispute. Indubitable matters are the mainstay of sacred oratory. Book 4 of *Ecclesiastes*, in which Erasmus lists possible topics for

---

the Introduction, note 61, on the need for emotional appeals in sacred oratory. See also Chomarat, *Grammaire et Rhetorique*, 2:1053–59, 1122–23. Cf. Aristotle *Politics* 1334b17–27.

115. Olin, *Christian Humanism*, 96–100; Chomarat, *Grammaire et rhetorique*, 1124–26. Cf. Shuger's discussion of Augustine and emotions, *Sacred Rhetoric*, 46–48. See also John Francis Tinkler, "Humanism as Discourse: Studies in the Rhetorical Culture of Renaissance Humanism, Petrarch to Bacon" (Ph.D. diss., Queen's University, Kingston, Ont., 1983), 126, 219.

116. LB 5:981B–C (*Ecclesiastes*). Toward the end of *Ecclesiastes*, Erasmus constructs a series of antitheses—topics from which the preacher may choose—between God and Satan, virtue and vice, piety and that which opposes piety, and so on. LB 5:1083–87.

117. "*Controversia* requires that both sides of any question be heard, thus creating the conditions necessary for arriving at decisions and negotiating differences in a reasonable way in both politics and philosophy." Conley, *European Tradition*, 37. The classical genres, especially the deliberative and the judicial, were controversial and, therefore, skeptically inclined. But sacred rhetoric was designed to impart the Christian truth and to exhort believers to follow that truth. Rather than being the norm, controversy, from the perspective of Christian orthodoxy, was pathological, and skepticism was anathema. See St. Augustine's authoritative rejection of Academic skepticism in *Contra academicos*, which includes the argument that skepticism leads to moral disorder (3.16.35–36). St. Augustine, *Against the Academicians*, trans. Sister Mary Patricia Garvey (Milwaukee: Marquette University Press, 1957).

preaching, confirms this fact. Erasmus's topics consist almost solely of what he deems to be fundamental doctrines (for example, basic concepts about God, the Church, and Satan) and moral principles (which include divine law, sin, and faith, hope, and charity), that is, things known with certainty.[118] The preacher, Erasmus writes, should speak on "those things which contribute to the commendation of virtues and the detestation of vices [and] on those things which pertain to theological dogmas, that is, what one must feel about God and the divine persons, what one must feel about Christ incarnate, what one must feel about the Church, and the remaining articles of faith." In addition, the preacher should speak about practical matters, such as how to contract marriage and when it may be annulled, when it is right to initiate a war, how magistrates are appointed and the limits of political authority, and how to handle heretics. But Erasmus thinks that preachers should avoid addressing the public on other, less central issues. In fact, Erasmus names one of his topics "Against Curious Questions and Rash Definitions." Speculative questions ("the subtleties of scholastic theologians"), for example, arguments about the hypostatic nature of the Trinity, "are not to be presented to the people." Instead, Erasmus counsels the sacred orator to teach doctrine simply and straightforwardly, as with preaching the Trinity, where "it is enough to profess that there is one God, three persons, all of whom have the same nature, the same divinity, power, wisdom, and goodness."[119]

The certainty implicit in sacred oratory distinguishes this genre from the classical genres, particularly the deliberative, which are characteristically skeptical. I have shown previously how the ancient rhetoricians agreed that deliberation is about doubtful matters. But Erasmus, who derives preaching from the deliberative *genus*, connects only one of his five categories of preaching, that is, the persuasive, to debatable issues. Exhortation is about "devout things that are noncontroversial." Similarly, the admonitory, consolatory, and laudatory classes of preaching are not intended to persuade listeners of doubtful beliefs. As for persuasive preaching, which deals with

118. Erasmus believed that preaching should especially address moral issues. See O'Malley, "Sacred Rhetoric," 24–26.

119. LB 5:1083E–1087F; LB 5:1097C–D; LB 5:1091C–D (*Ecclesiastes*); *Ratio*, in *Ausgewählte Werke*, 300–305. Erasmus does admit that the preacher may look to scholastic debates as source material for his sermons, but only "if they are pursued soberly and if they are based on the fundamentals of Scripture." LB 5:1097D (*Ecclesiastes*). But see O'Malley, "Sacred Rhetoric," on how *Ecclesiastes*, "more than any other single factor, seems to have destroyed, almost at a blow," the scholastic tradition of thematic preaching.

controversial issues, Erasmus acknowledges that even this genre is some-times concerned with the noncontroversial, as when the audience is so ignorant that it doubts things that should not be doubted. In addition, Erasmus identifies the persuasive sermon with *controversia* more out of deference to the classical linkage of persuasion (or deliberation) with skep-ticism than out of a conviction that persuasive preaching should address a host of controversial topics.[120]

As the rhetoric designed to communicate the fundamentals, preaching must be able to address those who deny the fundamentals, that is, heretics. But how should heretics be handled? Erasmus determines the appropriate treatment by following the dictates of *decorum*. Before discussing Erasmus's specific application of *decorum* to heretics, however, I shall first show how Erasmus conceives of *decorum*, more generally, as a Christian precept.

The Consecration of Classical *Decorum*

Decorum, the idea that orators must accommodate themselves to circum-stance, is a defining principle of classical rhetoric. To Erasmus this principle is also central to Christian rhetoric. But Erasmus does not leave *decorum* in its original, classical form. Instead, he Christianizes the concept by endowing Christ with its qualities. And because the Christian orator is bidden to follow the example of "that most excellent preacher, who is called the Word," he must, consequently, follow Christ's *decorum* and prudence, that is, that faculty which, according to Erasmus, teaches adaptation "to the circum-stances of time, place, and person."[121] While this obligation to emulate the "Supreme Preacher" accords with the ancient rhetoricians' insistence upon the "imitation" of excellent orators, it more importantly makes sense within the context of Christianity as an instance of "imitatio Dei," the believer's, and especially the preacher's, duty to imitate Christ.[122]

---

120. LB 5:878A–B (*Ecclesiastes*). See also Chomarat, *Grammaire et rhetorique*, 1:523.

121. LB 5:771D, 773D; LB 5:781B (*Ecclesiastes*); LB 10:1290E (*Hyperaspistes* I). Erasmus not only saw *decorum* and prudence as Christian principles, but implies in his *Ciceronianus* (1528) that they are the essence of classical rhetoric. There he criticizes those preachers who slavishly copied Cicero's Latin, while ignoring Cicero's method, accommodation to circum-stance: "It may well be that the most Ciceronian person is the one least like Cicero, the person, that is, who expresses himself in the best and most appropriate way, even though he does so in a manner very different from Cicero." CWE 28:399.

122. On the influence of the rhetorical conception of "imitation" on humanism, see Gray, "Renaissance Humanism," 506: "The terms *decorum* and *imitatio*, for example, are central in both rhetoric and moral philosophy, and the humanists often appear to fuse their meanings

Christ's *decorum* and prudence, in word and deed, can be discerned from his accommodations to the Jews. Erasmus writes: "That evangelical spirit of Christ has its own prudence, it has its own courtesy and gentleness. Thus Christ accommodated himself to the temperaments of the Jews."[123] He also did not reveal himself at once to them, but *paulatim*, "little by little."[124] Christ obeyed the Mosaic Law for a while; he concealed his divinity, allowing the Jews instead to think him only a prophet; and he instructed his disciples to do the same. He did all these things "in order to lead the Jews to something more perfect, rather than . . . to alienate their minds from himself." He tolerated their ignorance *ad tempus*, temporarily, until they were able to comprehend.[125] Christ's accommodation, however, is not limited to the Jews. Christ prudently came down to the level of any audience, so that they might understand him. He spoke in parables, explaining them to his disciples but not to the masses, who were unprepared to comprehend their meaning. Other times, he deceived his apostles "in order that all their desire for vengeance may be more thoroughly destroyed." After his resurrection, he commanded that the gospel be preached first at Jerusalem, then at Samaria, and only last to the gentiles, this sequence being dictated by the peoples' different circumstances.[126]

Christ realized that only by adapting his style, the genre of his message, would he be able to influence others: "In order to win more people by being amenable he does not hide in the desert, or wear extremely coarse clothes, or eat extremely bitter food (like John the Baptist), but rather he adapts himself to everybody; and, rejecting no company, he eats and drinks anything which is supplied to him."[127] He even became mortal in order to lead other mortals

---

whatever the context. Thus, the imitation of stylistic and of ethical models are spoken of in identical terms." The author of *Ad Herennium*, presumed to be Cicero until the late fifteenth century, considered imitation, theory, and practice to be the foundations of rhetorical education. [Cicero] *Ad Herennium* 1.2.3. See Marc Fumaroli's summary of the first book of *Ecclesiastes*: "The essence of Christian eloquence is in the piety that renders the heart docile to the imitation of Jesus Christ." *L'Âge de l'éloquence: Rhétorique et 'res literaria' de la Renaissance au seuil de l'époque classique* (Geneva: Librarie Droz, 1980), 107.

123. CWE 8:203.70–75 (Letter to Justus Jonas, May 1521).

124. Jacques Chomarat, "Grammar and Rhetoric in the *Paraphrases of the Gospels* by Erasmus," *Erasmus of Rotterdam Society Yearbook One* (1981): 60.

125. LB 7:12E (*Paraphrase of St. Matthew*). See Chomarat, "Grammar and Rhetoric in the *Paraphrases*," 59–60. Cf. Quintilian *Institutio oratoria* 2.13.11–14 on when concealment is justified.

126. LB 7:453D (*Paraphrase of St. Luke*, 1523); LB 5:781F (*Ecclesiastes*).

127. LB 7:68A (*Paraphrase of St. Matthew*), translated by Chomarat in "Grammar and Rhetoric in the *Paraphrases*," 59.

to him. Thus God was incarnated into the person of Christ, lived a life "according to the flesh," and was ultimately crucified to bring greater spirituality to humanity.[128]

Christ's prudence, like the classical orator's, manifested itself in his expediency.[129] He conformed himself to the spiritually immature because it was the expedient means of converting them. He further dissimulated, concealing his divinity from the Jews, for the sake of expediency. But Erasmus points to Paul, not Christ, as the best model of expediency.[130] Paul, who embodied both innocence and wisdom, "became all things to all men, not always doing what was permitted but what was expedient."[131] To those who overemphasized the Mosaic law, he praised faith and grace, "seeming to neglect the works of charity." To those who believed their baptism and their professions of faith sufficient, he commended charity over faith. Preaching to the Athenians in the Areopagus, Paul did not condemn them personally for the crime of idolatry; he cast "responsibility for their sins on the age in which they lived."[132] He did not call the Athenian gods "wood and stone . . . for it would not be expedient."[133] Nor did he speak of the testimony of the Hebrew prophets; they would have very little weight among the Athenians.[134] Rather, he called God the creator of the world and everything in it and Christ a man, mentioning nothing of Christ's divine nature. To bolster his arguments for faith, he adverted to the crowd's authorities, citing an inscription from one of the Athenian altars and the words of their heathen poets.[135] Adapting his speech to the crowd, he was the Christian chameleon, doing and saying what was expedient for the faith.

The imitation of Christ and his disciples, Erasmus argues, requires the

128. LB 7:838E–839B (*Paraphrase of Romans*, 1517).

129. Expediency, as noted in the Introduction, note 41, is the purpose of deliberative oratory.

130. Chomarat, *Grammaire et Rhetorique*, 2:1110. In a description of Paul that could have easily been applied to himself, Erasmus writes that "while he adapts himself to all, he is so variable, that he sometimes seems to contradict himself and to speak inconsistencies, when he is everywhere consistent with himself expedient." LB 5:781E–F (*Ecclesiastes*).

131. LB 5:781B–C (*Ecclesiastes*). In *De libero arbitrio*, Erasmus states: "Paul knew the difference between what things are lawful and what are expedient. It is lawful to speak the truth; it is not expedient to speak the truth to everybody at every time and in every way." *Luther and Erasmus*, 40–41.

132. "'And the times of this ignorance,' Paul writes, 'God winked at.'" Acts 17:30. *CWE* 8:204.101–10 (Letter to Justus Jonas, May 1521). Cf. LB 10:1290E–1281C (*Hyperaspistes* I).

133. LB 5:1065A (*Ecclesiastes*).

134. *CWE* 8:204.115–20 (Letter to Justus Jonas, May 1521).

135. LB 5:1065D–1066 (*Ecclesiastes*).

preacher to say and do those things that will gain the most souls. Like them, he must understand and adapt himself to the nature of that most "crafty and changing creature, . . . more mutable than Proteus himself."[136] He must approach his listeners with calm and gentle words, which will not anger them;[137] engaging in violent debates will only repel those whom he wishes to persuade. The preacher must attend to his congregation's feelings, to capture their emotions.[138] He should not lecture his audience about theological abstractions as dialecticians do; although he may prove his argument, he will not persuade.[139] Certainly, "if instruction does not occur, all else is useless. No one is pleased or moved by what he does not understand or does not believe." Yet any attempt to instruct while ignoring the sentiments of the listeners will only come to naught.[140] The preacher must also sense when to speak and when to remain silent "and to whom, at what time, [and] in what manner to temper his speech." He must recognize the audience's intellectual and spiritual levels. Consequently, when the audience is not sufficiently mature, concealment is sometimes necessary, as when the "listener is either unworthy or is not yet ready to understand a mystery."[141] Like Paul, he must know "how to change his voice and become all things to all men."[142]

Decorum and Toleration

If the imitation of Christ and his Apostle legitimates rhetorical expediency, Erasmus argues, then religious persecution should be condemned as inexpedient. Compelling heretics to the right beliefs does not work. Suppression failed to extirpate Wycliffe's followers in England, and it will not be any more effective against the Lutherans or the Turks; if anything the conditions for extirpating Wycliffe's followers were more favorable.[143] Erasmus realizes that persecuting heretics does not change them; it only makes them more

136. LB 5:823A–B (*Ecclesiastes*).

137. Raymond Himelick, *The Enchiridion of Erasmus* (Gloucester, Mass.: Peter Smith, 1970), 160; LB 10:1282C (*Hyperaspistes* I).

138. LB 5:859F–861E (*Ecclesiastes*).

139. Erasmus criticized dialectic, arguing that since dialectic does not move the "affectus," then dialectic cannot change the heart. Chomarat, *Grammaire et rhetorique*, 2:1122–23.

140. LB 5:859F (*Ecclesiastes*).

141. LB 5:803E (*Ecclesiastes*); cf. LB 5:781F; CWE 8:205.145–50 (Letter to Justus Jonas, May 1521); LB 10:1280E–1281B (*Hyperaspistes* I).

142. LB 5:783B (*Ecclesiastes*).

143. EE 5:260.149–261.160; Thompson, *Inquisitio de fide*, 25–26; CWE 6:75.85–77.165 (Letter to Paul Volz, August 1518).

stubborn and encourages others to their cause. After two Lutherans were burned at Brussels, the whole city was inclined toward Luther. The "recantations, imprisonments and burnings, do nothing but exasperate." The papal and imperial edicts against Luther and the brute force that accompany them "accomplish nothing except to make the evil more wide-spread."[144] Those who believe that they can end heresy through intimidation are mistaken. Souls cannot be forced; they must be persuaded.[145] Religious intolerance is to be opposed because it is senseless. It does not do what it sets out to achieve.

So too Erasmus condemns verbal coercion, maintaining that immoderate language does not persuade, regardless of whether or not it contains the truth. "Attacking the opinions of everyone else, superciliously damning everything, hatefully railing at everyone else, viciously slurring every kind of life," will only cause you to be hated, and "being hated you would be of no good to anyone."[146] Like physical duress, verbal bullying prevents your opponents from considering your ideas, instead, confirming them in their mistaken beliefs. No one will listen to a message couched as harassment, physical or verbal. Persuasion is the means to convert heretics. Therefore, Erasmus urges preachers to conduct themselves, even toward heretics, in a manner that will persuade, following the *decorum* of both Christ and the classical orators.

Decorum demands that preachers deal patiently with persons in error. They cannot expect to change their listeners immediately. Erasmus understands that religious maturity is the product of evolution and is not instantaneous, which is why people cannot be measured by the highest standard of perfection. Like Christ, preachers must be willing to accommodate themselves temporarily to the impious, in order to lead them slowly to piety.[147] Erasmus's rhetorical strategy of accommodation finds its parallel in his willingness to tolerate public imperfections provided such toleration will effect better results: "The people in their weakness must be tolerated and fostered with paternal indulgence, following the example of Christ, who so gently tolerated and fostered his disciples, until by degrees they grow to maturity in Christ. For piety like other things has its infancy, it has its periods

144. *EE* 5:606.165–67 (Letter to Duke George of Saxony, 1 December 1524); *EE* 5:604.104–5.
145. LB 5:822B (*Ecclesiastes*).
146. Himelick, *Enchiridion*, 60. See also Thompson, *Inquisitio de fide*, 15–16, and *CWE* 9:258.419–22 (Letter to Jean de Carondelet, 5 January 1523).
147. Hoffmann, "Erasmus and Religious Toleration," 100; Chomarat, "Grammar and Rhetoric in the *Paraphrases of the Gospels*," 59–66.

of growth, it has its full and vigorous adult strength. But every man according to the measure that is given to him must strive upwards towards Christ."[148] Erasmus applies this toleration to indifferent ceremonies; these practices are, he explains, a first step to a more spiritual Christianity.[149] Erasmus also calls for the toleration of heretics, in the hope that they will be brought back to the truth. "Diligent and faithful workmen," Erasmus suggests, should be dispatched to "sow good seed" among heretics and schismatics, as well as among Jews, Moslems, and pagans. Only as a last resort, when they are too obstinate to be persuaded, are heretics to be shunned.[150] Even then, Erasmus does not surrender hope. Thus he writes on the parable of the tares (Matthew 13:24–30): "The servants who wished to gather up the tares before it was time are those who think that pseudo-apostles and heretics should be destroyed by the sword and put to death; whereas the Master did not wish them destroyed, but rather tolerated so that perchance they might repent and from tares become wheat."[151] So long as the heretic lives, he may abandon his heresy; once dead, he cannot.

The Rejection of Accommodation: Luther

The importance of *decorum* to the argument for toleration is illustrated, negatively, by the example of Luther, who unlike Erasmus, rejects the principle of accommodation in essential doctrine. Luther's opposing stand on *decorum* explains, in large part, his divergent attitude to religious toleration. Where Luther disagrees with Erasmus is not whether the fundamentals of faith should themselves be accommodated, since both Erasmus and Luther affirm that the essentials of faith must not be changed,[152] but whether the preacher should accommodate himself, or his presentation of

148. *CWE* 6:82.318–24 (Letter to Paul Volz, 14 August 1518). Cf. LB 5:500B (*De amabili Ecclesiae concordia*): "The weakness of the people should be tolerated so that gradually they are led to greater perfection."

149. "Some things have been set up by Law, not that they are in themselves good or bad, but because they lead to some extent to piety. . . . Therefore, sometimes, traditional ceremonies may be tolerated, if their suppression would cause a worse evil in still half-carnal men for whom piety, although spiritual in itself, remains intimately linked to this indifferent practice." Chomarat, "Grammar and Rhetoric in the *Paraphrases*," 58; cf. Himelick, *Enchiridion*, 101–30.

150. LB 5:813B–814A (*Ecclesiastes*); LB 5:1086D–E; LB 9:582B–C (*Supputatio errorum in censuris Beddae*).

151. LB 7:79–80 (*Paraphrase of St. Matthew*), translated by Ferguson in "Attitude," 179. See also LB 5:797C (*Ecclesiastes*) and Hoffmann, "Erasmus and Religious Toleration," 105–6.

152. LB 5:500B (*De amabili Ecclesiae concordia*).

doctrine, to the listener. For Luther, the preacher should never accommodate *how* he instructs or rebukes his listeners; nor should he conceal truth or doctrine from them. Rather, he should preach the gospel straightforwardly and not be controlled by the techniques of the orators.[153] In contrast to Erasmus's God, who accommodates Himself to humanity, Luther's God "is no respecter of persons." And unlike Erasmus's Paul, who "became all things to all men," Luther's Paul "wishes the truth to be spoken everywhere at every time and in every way." Luther accuses Erasmus of compromising the fundamental doctrine of the nullity of the will: "Christ says: 'Go into all the world' (Mark 16:15). He does not say, 'Go to one place and not another,' as Erasmus does. And he says, 'Preach the gospel to every creature' (ibid.), not 'to some and not others.'" Instead of accommodation of doctrine, Luther demands unrestricted proclamation.[154]

Luther justifies his rejection of accommodation theologically, by taking responsibility for conversion away from the preacher and vesting it with the Holy Spirit. True, Luther admits that "God gives no one his Spirit or grace except through or with the external Word" of preaching. Nevertheless, Luther denies the preacher's human role in effecting the listener's transformation, which contrasts with Erasmus's affirmation of the preacher's personal role in the conversion process.[155] God, according to Luther, has ordained that preaching must precede the working of the Spirit, but the preacher has no control over how the Word will affect people. "It is easy enough for someone to preach the Word to me," Luther writes, "but only God can put it in my heart. He must speak it in my heart, or nothing at all

---

153. See Luther's letter of 28 May 1522 to Borner or Cubito. In it he criticizes Erasmus, stating, "Truth is more powerful than eloquence." WA *Briefwechsel* 2:544. Luther's opposition to rhetorical *decorum* was not necessarily shared by all his fellow reformers. See, for example, William J. Bouwsma, *John Calvin: A Sixteenth-Century Portrait* (New York: Oxford University Press, 1988), 126–27, for an argument emphasizing Calvin's humanism and accommodation.

154. *Luther and Erasmus*, 132–33; Boyle, *Rhetoric and Reform*, 112–14. In a letter to George Spalatin, dated 9 September 1521, Luther writes: "The kingdom of God consists in power, says Paul. . . . [Erasmus and the Strasbourg reformer Wolfgang Capito's] writings accomplish nothing because they refrain from chiding, biting, and giving offense. For when the popes and bishops are admonished in a civil manner they think it is flattering and keep on as if they possessed the right to remain uncorrected and incorrigible, content that they are feared and that no one dares reproach them." *Luther's Works: American Edition*, vol. 48, ed. Hermann Böhlaus (Philadelphia: Fortress Press, 1963), 306–7.

155. WA 50:245 (*Smalcald Articles*); Althaus, *Theology*, 36–37; L. W. Spitz, "Luther, Humanism, and the Word," *Lutheran Theological Seminary Bulletin* 65 (1985): 12. On Erasmus's view of the preacher's influence, see Boyle, *Rhetoric and Reform*, 113. Erasmus, however, also acknowledges that the preacher will not persuade unless he has the Spirit of Christ in his heart. See O'Malley, "Sacred Rhetoric," 19.

will come of it. If God remains silent, the final effect is as though nothing has been said." God determines when and if the sermon will persuade. The Holy Spirit may first empower the Word buried in one's heart only years after it has been preached. Or for those whom He does not wish to save, God withholds his Spirit, depriving the sermon of any efficacy.[156] Because the preacher's rhetoric does not convert, accommodation is irrelevant. The preacher should not fear the consequences of asserting the unadulterated truth. God will be sure to save His elect, "while the rest perish in unbelief."[157]

Luther's rejection of accommodation evinces itself in his intolerance. His belief in a single truth, which cannot be rhetorically adapted to time, place, and audience, leads him to the conclusion that doctrinal error must always be confronted.[158] Luther, though, was not always the enemy of toleration. In his early period, his intolerant spirit was held in check by the conviction that secular authorities have no power over heresy. Luther sanctioned the use of immoderate or inflammatory language in preaching, but did not yet permit physical coercion.[159] Beginning in 1525, however, Luther, desiring to consolidate his gains, begins to call for state intervention in religion; he is now willing to see the prince "suppress manifest blasphemies of God's name."[160] The God-fearing prince, Luther proposes, should emulate David, who "always checked any public inroads of heresy."[161] At this point, the intolerance that was once implicit in Luther now becomes manifest. He refuses heretics freedom of conscience, asserting that they act out of error. He

156. WA 10.3:260. WA 17[II] (Sermons of 1522): 174; Althaus, Theology, 39–40; Luther and Erasmus, 20.

157. Luther and Erasmus, 136.

158. Bainton, Studies, 32.

159. On Luther's toleration, see his "Eight Sermons at Wittenberg, 1522," in Luther's Works: American Edition, 51:76, 90; The Freedom of a Christian (1520), in Luther's Works: American Edition, vol. 31, 368–69; Luther and Erasmus, 163–64; Boyle, Rhetoric and Reform, 112–13; Bainton, Studies, 22–33; Lecler, Toleration and the Reformation, 1:147–54. Although the early Luther opposed persecution, his rhetoric, rather than merely being nonaccommodating, was even intentionally humiliating. The preacher, according to Luther, should follow God's course of first presenting the Law—bringing the sinner a sense of powerlessness and self-despair over his inability to fulfill the Law—and only then preaching grace, which frees the sinner of his despair. See Lectures on Galatians (1535), in Luther's Works: American Edition, vols. 26–27, ed. Jaroslav Pelikan (St. Louis: Concordia Press, 1963–64); Against the Antinomians (1539), in Luther's Works: American Edition, vol. 47, especially 114; Luther and Erasmus, 137–38. Luther's style of initially humbling the listener runs counter to the dominant tradition of classical rhetoric, which advises the orator to first placate his audience.

160. WA Briefwechsel 3:616 (Letter to Spalatin, 11 November 1525).

161. Robert H. Murray, Erasmus and Luther: Their Attitude to Toleration (New York: Burt Franklin, 1972), 361.

supports the abolition of the Mass, calling it open blasphemy. He argues that everyone must be compelled to attend true Christian services and public preaching, be they believers or not, and he approves the suppression of all public displays of non-Lutheran religion. Luther moreover assents to the expulsion of Catholics, Zwinglians, and Jews from Lutheran territories and to the death penalty for Anabaptists.[162]

Opposing the rhetorical principle of accommodation, Luther defends consistency and an absolute devotion to the truth. Refusing to countenance different denominations in the same territory, he proposes a state free of dissent—an ideal the Lutherans eventually realize in the Peace of Augsburg (1555), which accepted the principle of one religion, one state.[163] Erasmus, however, when faced with the dilemma of Lutherans in Catholic lands, calls for coexistence. He does this, although he also desires unity of worship within each state. Nevertheless, he concludes that under existing conditions, such uniformity is impracticable. Erasmus addresses himself in 1530 to this issue in a letter to Cardinal Campeggi, papal legate in Germany: "I know and detest the insolence of those who lead the sects or favor them, but in the present state of affairs it is more important to look at what the peace of the whole world demands, than what those evil-doers deserve. . . . Occasionally time itself brings a remedy to irremediable wrongs. If on certain conditions the sects could be tolerated . . . it would no doubt be an evil, and a grave evil; I admit it, but in any case a lesser evil than war, and what a war."[164] To Erasmus, the question of whether religious dissenters ought to be tolerated cannot be answered in the abstract, as it can for Luther. Adhering to the rhetorical precept that speech and action should be adapted to the particulars of time, place, and circumstance, Erasmus advocates the legal toleration of Lutherans, *ad tempus*. This is not his ideal, but he is willing to accommodate himself to, and thus tolerate, less-than-ideal conditions.

The Limits of Toleration

Erasmus enjoins the Church from ever using force; the most extreme punishment at its disposal is excommunication.[165] But while Erasmus

---

162. Bainton, *Studies*, 31–44; Roland H. Bainton, *Concerning Heretics* (New York: Columbia University Press, 1935), 45–49; Murray, *Erasmus and Luther*, 360–67; Lecler, *Toleration and the Reformation*, 1:154–64; Kamen, *Rise of Toleration*, 32–42.
163. Bainton, *Studies*, 35; Murray, *Erasmus and Luther*, 259.
164. *EE* 9:15.37–55 (1530), translated by Lecler, *Toleration and the Reformation*, 1:120.
165. LB 9:582A–C (*Supputatio errorum in censuris Beddae*); LB 5:789E–F, 805F, 821F–

expects the prince, "the chief and supreme orator," to use restraint and choose persuasion over coercion whenever possible, he permits him to use capital punishment against heretics only "in the most necessary cases."[166] The State, Erasmus concedes, can execute heretics who pose a threat to civil order: "Even if it is not permitted to kill [simple] heretics, it is certainly lawful to kill blasphemers and rebels, since [killing them] is necessary to protect the state."[167] But Erasmus does not support capital punishment as a common recourse to heresy, since, in practice, he never condones a single heretic's execution.[168]

Erasmus's reluctance to coerce the heterodox does not imply his commitment to religious pluralism. Erasmus entertains no doubt that heretics, because they deny the fundamentals, are wrong. He tolerates them minimally, for reasons of expediency, but he does not respect them or their beliefs. Moreover, he allows for physical coercion against them when they are viewed as seditious. But, unlike the limited toleration patterned after the rhetoric of fundamentals, Erasmus also develops a maximal defense of religious toleration based on the rhetoric of nonessentials. This broad toleration implies a respect for persons and their positions even when they disagree.

The Rhetoric of Nonessentials

Conversation

Conversation, for Erasmus, is the paradigmatic rhetoric of nonessentials. His ancient source for the genre was the classical *sermo*, used most promi-

---

822A, 822C (*Ecclesiastes*); Hoffmann, "Erasmus and Religious Toleration," 105; Ferguson, "Attitude," 179–81.

166. LB 9:1059E (*Apologia adversus Monachos quosdam Hispanos*, 1528). See also Ferguson, "Attitude," 177–79; Hoffmann, "Erasmus and Religious Toleration," 105–6.

167. "Like those people who drag others to the flames for any error at all, those who think that the civil power lacks any right to kill heretics are wrong." LB 10:1576B–C (*Epistola contra quosdam qui se falso jactant evangelicos*). See also *EE* 5:604–6. Although Erasmus never explicitly calls for the execution of any specific heretic, he writes that "the Anabaptists should in no way be endured," implying that he agrees with imperial legislation that prescribed the death penalty for Anabaptists. *Epistolarum Des. Erasmi libri xxxi* (London, 1642), Ep. 77, col. 1963D.

168. Bainton, *Erasmus of Christendom*, 257.

nently by Cicero to discuss philosophical issues on which there was no consensus. But Erasmus also had more immediate examples of conversation before him. The Renaissance humanists, from Petrarch on, had favored the dialogue as a literary genre, and many of them had composed dialogues that resembled the Ciceronian model.[169] These humanist dialogues can be distinguished from the dominant oratorical genres by (some or all) of the characteristics that differentiate *sermo* from *contentio*. Humanist dialogues often deal with an indefinite subject matter, as in the case of Valla's *De voluptate*, a dialogue on the subject of the true good, which was patterned after Cicero's *De finibus*.[170] Like the participants in a Ciceronian dialogue, interlocutors in a humanist dialogue are frequently members of the learned

169. Among the modern works on the humanist dialogue is David Marsh's *Quattrocento Dialogue: Classical Tradition and Humanist Innovation*, a study of the revival of the Ciceronian dialogue in fifteenth-century Italy. Marsh's book, however, does not examine conversation's influence on the sixteenth-century Northern humanists, the focus of this book; nor does he single out religious dialogue for investigation. John Tinkler's theoretical article "Humanism and Dialogue" also examines the humanist dialogue. Tinkler first contrasts the Renaissance humanist dialogue with the medieval scholastic dialogues and then explicates the social milieu in which the humanist dialogue developed. J. F. Tinkler, "Humanism and Dialogue," *Parergon: Bulletin of the Australian and New Zealand Association for Medieval and Renaissance Studies* 6 (1988): 197–214. Tinkler's examples, like Marsh's, are primarily culled from Quattrocento Italy; and, like Marsh, Tinkler does not address the specifically religious uses of dialogue. Different from both is K. J. Wilson's *Incomplete Fictions: The Formation of English Renaissance Dialogue*, which examines Northern humanist dialogues (those of Tudor England) and even includes a discussion of Thomas More's *Dialogue Concerning Heresies*—"a dialogue for theological argument." K. J. Wilson, *Incomplete Fictions: The Formation of English Renaissance Dialogue* (Washington, D.C.: The Catholic University of America Press, 1985), 153. Wilson's book, however, does not bear any more directly on the relationship between the humanist dialogue and toleration than the previous two analyses. More's *Dialogue Concerning Heresies*, although a conversation about religious truth, is not an investigative dialogue between peers, but a didactic, authoritarian dialogue between More and a youth in danger of being lost to the Lutheran heresy. Because there is no question of conducting a genuine conversation with heresy here, this particular dialogue's relevance to toleration is dubious. See Rainer Pineas, "Thomas More's Use of the Dialogue Form as a Weapon of Religious Controversy," *Studies in the Renaissance* 7 (1960): 200–201: "It is established right at the beginning of the work that . . . More is a respected scholar whose opinion will be recognized as the final arbiter of the religious questions in dispute. . . . [More] is not so much arguing with his interlocutor as teaching him by the method of question and answer." See also R. R. McCutcheon, "The *Responsio ad Lutherum*: Thomas More's Inchoate Dialogue with Heresy," *Sixteenth Century Journal* 22 (1991): 77–80, and *The Complete Works of St. Thomas More*, ed. Thomas M. C. Lawler, Germain Marc'hadour, and Richard C. Marius (New Haven: Yale University Press, 1981), vol. 6, part 2, pp. 440–41. Other authors who discuss dialogue as a humanist genre, albeit briefly, are Gray, "Renaissance Humanism," 512–13, and Hirzel, *Dialog*, 2:385–91.

170. Lorenzo Valla, *On Pleasure: De voluptate*, trans. A. Kent Hieatt and Maristella Lorch (New York: Abaris Books, 1977); Tinkler, "Humanism as Discourse," 101. Despite their similar subject matter, Cicero's *De finibus* and Valla's *De voluptate* differ in structure. *De finibus*

elite, as are the characters in Poggio Bracciolini's dialogues or in Giovanni Pontano's dialogue *Aegidius*.[171] And, in contrast to the public orator, these scholarly interlocutors eschew violent emotions and do not aim to persuade by appeal to authority; nor do they engage in the agon characteristic of classical oratory.[172] Rather, the humanists' interlocutors acknowledge the inherent uncertainty of their subject matter and accord the other speakers the freedom to expound their opinions and arrive at their own, different, conclusions. This skeptical tolerance, associated with the Ciceronian dialogue, is visible in Petrarch's *Secretum*, Leonardo Bruni's *Dialogus I*, Poggio's dialogues, and Valla's *De voluptate*, among others.[173]

Like his humanist predecessors, Erasmus also recognizes the distinctive characteristics of *sermo*. He distinguishes *sermo* from *contentio* in his essay on letter writing, *De conscribendis epistolis* or *On the Writing of Letters* (1522), in which he defines the letter as "a mutual conversation between absent friends," and he follows Cicero's belief that conversation, unlike oratory, is private and familiar (fit for social groups, philosophical discussions, and gatherings of friends). Thus Erasmus writes: "If there is something that can be said to be characteristic of this genre [of letter writing], I think that I cannot define it more concisely than by saying that the wording of a letter should resemble a conversation between friends."[174] Nevertheless, when Erasmus divides letters into four different classes, he aligns three of the classes, which he refers to as persuasive, encomiastic, and judicial, with the three main genres of oratory, that is, the deliberative, the forensic, and

---

examines its subject in separate discussions, whereas *De voluptate* places the interlocutors in a common discussion that seeks a synthetic judgment. See Marsh, *Quattrocento Dialogue*, 56.

171. Marsh, *Quattrocento Dialogue*, 54, 101.

172. Ibid., 34–35; Tinkler, "Humanism and Dialogue," 204–7; Marsh, *Quattrocento Dialogue*, 116. Although the early Quattrocento dialogues were more combative than the later ones, even the early dialogues can be distinguished from the classical *contentio*. For example, while Vegio, in Valla's *De voluptate*, compares himself to an orator in court, he contrasts himself to the Stoics, who "think it unlawful to abandon a belief once they have adopted it. . . . As for me," he writes, "if someone makes a better point than I do, I yield, and am grateful besides." Cited in Marsh, *Quattrocento Dialogue*, 66. Cf. Valla, in *De libero arbitrio*, where he denies that he fights "for the sake of victory rather than truth." Valla, *Dialogue on Free Will*, in Cassirer, Kristeller, and Randall, *Renaissance Philosophy of Man*, 166. See also Petrarch's *Secretum*, where Augustinus argues for a mean between two much and too little contention: "For if, as a learned man said, 'truth is lost by quarreling too much,' yet a moderate contention often leads to the truth." Cited in Marsh, *Quattrocento Dialogue*, 21.

173. Marsh, *Quattrocento Dialogue*, 21, 32, 50–51, 68–69. See also Struever, *Language of History*, 160–61.

174. Cicero *De officiis* 1.37.132; CWE 25:20–21, 74, 76–78. See also the Introduction note 104.

the epideictic. These three classes of letters do not closely resemble *sermo*, as described in the previous chapter. Although they are, stylistically, more personal than their public oratorical counterparts, their subject matter, like the subject matter of the three dominant genres, is directed toward specific and immediate matters—the *definite* question. And the three "oratorical" classes of letters, unlike Ciceronian *sermo*, employ appeals to the emotions, including fear, hatred, and rivalry.[175]

It is in Erasmus's discussion of the fourth class of letters, the familiar class, however, that the characteristics of classical *sermo* can be found. It is difficult to generalize about this class of letters, which Erasmus uses as a miscellaneous category for all letters that do not belong to the previous three, such as letters of information, instruction, commendation, lamentation, congratulation, and so on. Nonetheless, the different kinds of letters that make up this hodgepodge class share traits that hark back to the conception of *sermo* sketched earlier: they are friendly, rather than agonistic; and they do not appeal to negative emotions, like anger.[176] Still, because the broad class of familiar letters includes far more than learned conversations, it is distinct from Cicero's philosophical dialogues. Erasmus, however, offers an epistolary analogue to Ciceronian *sermo* when he discusses the last subdivision of the familiar class, which he terms "letters of discussion [*disputatoriae genus*]." This category, Erasmus writes, is "a class of letters quite common among scholars, in which they carry on a reciprocal scholarly exchange among themselves, when they wish to learn about some topic, or reply to an enquirer, or dispute some point on which they fail to agree."[177] Although Erasmus gives no set account of this class, "as it is so varied," he does refer to some examples. These examples permit Erasmus to imply something about the *decorum* of scholarly discussion, implications that echo the Ciceronian model of *sermo*.

Erasmus cites ten examples of letters of discussion from three authors: Cicero; Pliny the Younger (62–c. 113 C.E.), Roman writer, statesman, and orator; and Angelo Poliziano (1454–94), Tuscan humanist, writer, and lecturer.[178] Although the subject matter of the letters is diverse—for ex-

175. See, for example, CWE 25:79–83, 221–22.
176. CWE 25:71–72, 225–54.
177. CWE 25:254; ASD, vol. 1, part 2, 578.
178. Erasmus offers ten citations: two from Cicero; two from Pliny; and six from Poliziano. In fact, however, five letters are from Poliziano and one from the Renaissance philosopher Giovanni Pico della Mirandola (1463–1533), which was included in Poliziano's collected works.

ample, a legal question, Stoic linguistic usage, the best style for forensic speech, a scientific mystery, and the relationship between eloquence and philosophy—upon close examination, certain common themes emerge. The first is that of the appropriate language for scholarly discussions. For example, Cicero alludes to the *decorum* of such discussions by declaring his personal devotion to civility. Although the Stoics deny that language can be obscene or indecent, Cicero writes that "for myself, I adhere (and shall so continue, since it is my habit) to the modesty of Plato. That is why I have written to you in guarded language on a theme which the Stoics handle with complete freedom."[179] For Cicero, freedom of discussion does not extend to inappropriate language. The need for rhetorical propriety is also addressed in Poliziano's letters, where philosophical conversation is said to require a different *decorum* than that of other forms of speech. "There is no one single face of eloquence itself," Poliziano writes, and "no one has been considered eloquent by universal approval." Instead of a single standard of good speech, there are different standards for different occasions: "There is one language, as it were, in which we play and another in which we prosecute serious matters. You would not address a boy in the same manner of speaking as you would a learned person." Like Cicero, Poliziano here recognizes a separate type of speech for philosophy as well as for the educated elite that discusses such complex matters.[180]

A second theme underlying Erasmus's examples is that truth is the goal of the scholarly letter. Poliziano proclaims that truth supersedes prevailing in a scholarly argument: "I am accustomed to dispute about ambiguous matters in such a way that I truly rejoice in a discovery more than in a victory." Adhering to the dictates of classical *sermo*, the authors cited by Erasmus avoid rhetorical jousting out of their concern for truth.[181] Similarly, the authors cited by Erasmus value truth above their own prestige. Accordingly, Poliziano praises the deceased Ermolao Barbaro for the courage it took to declare publicly his change of opinions. Poliziano writes that Barbaro

179. Cicero *Ad familiares* 9:22. From *Cicero's Letters to His Friends,* trans. D. R. Schackleton Bailey (Atlanta: Scholars Press, 1978), 311–14.

180. Pico della Mirandola, in a letter included in the Poliziano collection, makes much the same point. Pico argues that the eloquence demanded in other settings is unsuited to philosophy and that if a choice must be made between wisdom and eloquence, then wisdom must be chosen. Thus, he writes, "Cicero prefers an ineloquent prudence to a stupid loquacity." Angelo Poliziano, *Opera omnia Angeli Politiani* (Venice: Aldine Press, 1498), 3.15, 5.1., 9.4.

181. For example, Pico's letter, which speaks of examining the subject in a "friendly manner" (*amice*) and without "contention" (*contentione*), can be understood in terms of the Ciceronian view that contention obstructs discovery of truth.

practiced his freedom of speech "not so much against others as against himself, and he refuted many things in later commentaries which he would have defended in prior commentaries."[182] Because truth is the ultimate value in a "letter of discussion," reason is the only legitimate proof. Thus Pliny writes that "on an important question like this [that is, the merits of brevity versus a more abundant style in forensic oratory] I would rather yield to a reasoned argument than to authority alone." Pliny refuses to change his view based only on an *ipse dixit*. He demands a rational argument.[183]

Finally, a third theme that appears in the letters cited by Erasmus is the uncertainty of the issues discussed in them. For example, Cicero underscores the uncertainty of a legal question and Pliny points up the uncertainty surrounding a question of style.[184] Similarly, the issues considered in the other "letters of discussion" cited also concern "ambiguous matters." The authors of these letters respond to the uncertainty of their subject matter by adopting the position Cicero enunciated in his philosophical dialogues: they permit freedom of judgment. As seen above, Poliziano praises Barbaro for changing his stand. When truth is at stake, people—at least scholars—must be free to choose, even if it means choosing against one's previous beliefs.[185]

The above-mentioned themes, implicit in Erasmus's examples, reflect the Ciceronian conception of *sermo*. But Erasmus was not the first to revive Ciceronian *sermo*. As seen above, the Quattrocento humanists made use of this type of rhetoric. Nevertheless, the dialogues of Erasmus's humanist predecessors did not generally concern religious doctrine and were written before the Reformation forced the question of religious toleration to the fore.[186] Confronting the disintegration of Christian unity, Erasmus was the first to see dialogue as the ideal method of handling nonessential doctrinal

---

182. Poliziano, *Opera omnia*, 1.20, 12.1.

183. Pliny the Younger *Epistles* 1.20. From *The Letters of the Younger Pliny*, trans. Betty Radice (Harmondsworth: Penguin Books, 1969), 55.

184. Cicero *Ad familiares* 7.22, in *Cicero's Letters to His Friends*, 499; Pliny the Younger *Epistles* 1.20, in *The Letters of the Younger Pliny*, 52.

185. In addition, Pliny supports freedom of judgment in a letter to Licinius Sura about a natural anomaly: a spring that "three times a day . . . fills and empties with a regular increase and decrease of water." After raising a number of possibilities to explain this strange phenomenon, Pliny closes the letter without passing judgment himself on any of the possibilities. Instead, he obliges Sura to decide for himself. "It is for *you* [emphasis added] to investigate the cause of this phenomenon," Pliny writes, "as you have the ability. I have done more than enough if I have managed to describe it clearly." Pliny the Younger *Epistles* 4.30, in *The Letters of the Younger Pliny*, 132–33.

186. Lorenzo Valla did anticipate the Erasmus-Luther debate on free will, in his dialogue *De libero arbitrio*, but he emphasized the philosophical, not the doctrinal, nature of the question.

differences. For example, in the colloquy *Inquisitio de fide*, Erasmus uses dialogue to demonstrate that Catholic and Lutheran only differ on non-essentials. Or, in the colloquy *Convivium religiosum* ("The Godly Feast"), Erasmus depicts an intellectual exchange between nine educated laymen who interpret Scripture without impinging on the fundamentals of faith. As the character Eusebius says there of his own interpretation: "Whether it's correct I don't know; I'm satisfied that the idea isn't irreverent or heretical." The interlocutors there do not claim certainty, but try to find the most probable interpretation "by comparing passages, an excellent method of biblical study."[187]

In his *Disputatiuncula* (*Little Disputation*), Erasmus uses the form of dialogue with a missing interlocutor (his friend John Colet) to investigate an adiaphoristic question: whether or not Jesus suffered in anticipation of his crucifixion. Responding to Colet, who maintains that Jesus' divinity prevented him from actually feeling pain, Erasmus takes the position that Jesus, because he also possessed a human nature, did indeed experience dread, fear, and sadness before his death. Because his debate with Colet does not concern an essential of faith, however, Erasmus concedes the possibility of error. Erasmus claims that he would even prefer being mistaken, since his mistakes offer him the opportunity to learn. Thus, implicitly contrasting his *Disputatiuncula* with the oratorical agon, he states: "In a battle of words, whoever is wise does not want to conquer so much as to be conquered; that is, he does not want so much to teach as to learn. If I lose, I go away more learned, but if I win, I leave you just as happy."[188] Like the Quattrocento humanists who

---

187. *Colloquies*, 58, 61; Boyle, *Erasmus on Language and Method*, 138. The dialogue *Convivium religiosum* is reminiscent of the Ciceronian dialogues in a number of ways: it is set in the garden of a rural villa; the size of the company is limited—Eusebius restricts the group to nine, "the number of muses"; the discussion is moderate and tranquil; it is directed, ultimately, to action, as Eusebius departs the colloquy to conduct acts of charity in other villages. See *Colloquies*, 49, 78; Lawrence V. Ryan, "Erasmis Convivia: The Banquet Colloquies of Erasmus," *Medievalia et Humanistica: Studies in Medieval and Renaissance Culture*, n.s., 8 (1977): 205; and Boyle, *Erasmus on Language and Method*, 139. In contrast to the Ciceronian dialogue, however, Erasmus sanctions such colloquies "even for sailors, . . . provided they're cautious about passing judgment." *Colloquies*, 57. Cf. Erasmus's condemnation of debates among the common people about contentious issues, such as "free will" or his novel translation of the New Testament. LB 9:121B–C (*Apologia de in principio erat sermo*, 1520); Boyle, *Erasmus on Language and Method*, 6–7.

188. LB 5:1265D–E (*Disputatiuncula de taedio, pavore, tristitia Jesu, instante supplicio crucis: deque verbis, quibus visus est mortem deprecari, 'Pater, si fieri potest, transeat a me calix iste'* [Little Disputation on the Dread, Fear, and Sadness of Jesus, when the Punishment of the Cross was pressing upon him and on the words with which he seemed to be averting death "Father if it can be done let this cup pass from me"]).

preceded him, Erasmus manifests a skeptical tolerance of divergent opinions. But Erasmus differs from earlier humanists because he specifically acknowledges the legitimacy of doctrinal diversity. The full potential of this tolerance of diversity is revealed in another dialogue with a missing interlocutor: *De libero arbitrio.*

Diatribē

Erasmus composed *De libero arbitrio* in the form of a *diatribē*, a kind of philosophical dialogue, and not a bitter, abusive denunciation, as it is defined today. In fact, Erasmus most commonly referred to his piece not as *De libero arbitrio*, but as *Diatriba.* The genre's roots are in classical antiquity, where it developed as a popularization of the philosophical dialogue, designed to investigate moral issues such as the nature of good and evil or the sufficiency of virtue for happiness. It can be distinguished, formally, from other genres of dialogue by its use of a fictional interlocutor, whose personality remains sketchy in the debate. Although Erasmus edited or translated classical *diatribai* by Galen, Plutarch, and Seneca during the years of his disputations with Luther, his most immediate classical exemplar of the genre was Cicero's *Tusculan Disputations* (books 1, 2, and 5 were written in the genre), which Erasmus edited in 1523, only a year before composing his own *Diatriba.*[189]

The most comprehensive discussion of Erasmus's use of *diatribē* in *De libero arbitrio* is M. O. Boyle's *Rhetoric and Reform: Erasmus' Civil Dispute with Luther.* Boyle acknowledges the link between *diatribē* and dialogue, but she contends that Erasmus's *Diatriba* was written in the deliberative genre.[190] Boyle supports this claim by identifying the subject matter of the *Diatriba*, that is, free will, with the Ciceronian rhetorical category "propo-

---

189. On the classical use of *diatribē*, see André Oltramare, *Les Origines de la Diatribe Romaine* (Geneva: Imprimeries Populaire, 1926), especially 9–17, 116–25; Boyle, *Rhetoric and Reform*, 6–8. Erasmus, in *Hyperaspistes* I (LB 10:1313A), finds the origin of the diatribe in the battles philosophers had among themselves, "each for his own sect." See also Augustijn's *Erasmus*, 137: "A diatribe is a treatise, known since Greek and Roman times, in dialogue form on a moral or philosophical theme." Erasmus edited or translated Galen's *Exhortatio ad bonas arteis, praesertim medicinam; de optimo docendi genere; et qualem oporteat esse medicum* (Basel: Froben, 1526); Plutarch, *Libellus* (*De non irascendo* and *De curiositate*) (Basel: Froben, 1525); *De vitiosa verecundia* (Basel: Froben, 1526); and Seneca, *Opera* (2d ed. of *Lucubrationes*, 1515) (Basel: H. Froben and J. Herwagen, 1529). Cited in Boyle, *Rhetoric and Reform*, 167–68 n. 9.

190. Following Oltramare, Boyle writes that the *diatribē* "evolved in classical antiquity as a popularization of the philosophical dialogue."

sition" (*propositum*), or *indefinite* question, which, she explains, "coincides with the genre of deliberative rhetoric, and specifically with the *diatribē*." Boyle associates the other two basic oratorical genres, epideictic and judicial, with the Ciceronian category *causa*, or *definite* question.[191] Boyle, however, is mistaken in her identification of the *propositum* with the deliberative genre. As I show in the introduction, public oratory is concerned with the *definite* question, not the *indefinite*. The *causa*, according to Cicero, encompasses all three genres of rhetoric: laudatory, judicial, *and* deliberative. Similarly, Quintilian links the *definite* question to the deliberative genre.[192] Boyle is correct in relating the *diatribē* to the *propositum*, but the *indefinite* questions of the *diatribē* (and Erasmus's *Diatriba*) belong to *sermo*, not to deliberative oratory. That Erasmus evinces his concern with the practical consequences of the debate in *Diatriba* (deploring "irreligious curiosity"), in no way brings the work's conversational status into question. As noted previously, classical *sermo* was also concerned with action.[193]

Like classical *sermo*, then, the subject matter of Erasmus's *Diatriba* is action oriented, but not toward a specific action. Its subject matter is philosophical: an investigation into the reality of free will. The nature of *Diatriba*'s topic leads Erasmus to designate his audience as the learned elite, the same class of persons that populated Cicero's philosophical dialogues. The investigation he conducts in *De libero arbitrio*, Erasmus writes, "has always been considered most proper for scholars."[194] The *Diatriba*'s limited audience contrasts with the popular audience of ancient deliberative oratory (the political assembly) and of Erasmus's own version of the deliberative genre (preaching), which was addressed to all classes of society.[195] Popular discussion of matters like free will, Erasmus maintains, is not expedient since

191. Boyle, *Rhetoric and Reform*, 10–11. Boyle also identifies the *quaestio civilis*, another name for the *propositum*, with the deliberative genre. *Rhetoric and Reform*, 15.

192. *De partitione oratoria* 20.68–70; Quintilian *Institutio oratoria* 3.5.8. Alain Michel, whom Boyle cites to support her claim that *propositum* coincides with the deliberative genre, writes: "In reality, politics are related to particular circumstances. . . . The discussions that take place in the city are *hypotheses, causae.*" *Rhetoric and Reform*, 169 n. 35. Or, referring to *De oratore*, Michel observes that all three oratorical genres concern the *definite* question; there is no analysis of the *indefinite* question. See his *Rhétorique et Philosophie*, 217–19.

193. Boyle, *Rhetoric and Reform*, 16; Introduction, 31.

194. *Luther and Erasmus*, 36.

195. Although deliberative oratory generally addresses a popular audience, there is one kind of deliberative oratory appropriate to a small audience. Cicero's association of the deliberative genre with giving advice or an opinion, *sententiae dictio*, suggests a smaller, more select audience, such as the Senate, rather than a large political audience. *De inventione* 2.4.12. In general, however, the ancient rhetoricians viewed deliberative oratory as directed to the public.

it will endanger Christian piety and harmony: "Such matters might allow-
ably have been treated in discussion by the learned world, or even in
theological schools, although I should not think even this to be expedient
save with restraint; on the other hand, to debate such fables before the gaze
of a mixed multitude seems to me to be not merely useless but even
pernicious."[196] Expediency, however, is also a characteristic of *sermo*. Thus
expediency is an accepted *telos* in such examples of *sermo* as Cicero's *De
officiis* and Valla's *De voluptate*.[197]

Erasmus's *Diatriba* seeks not only expediency but, more fundamentally,
the truth. Cicero classifies this search for truth under the rhetorical end of
honor (*honestum*), which Erasmus acknowledges in *Diatriba*. There Erasmus
states that he will "take issue solely with this one doctrine of Luther [that is,
free will], with the single aim of using various scriptural texts to illuminate
the truth, the investigation of which has always been most honorable
[*honestissima*] for scholars."[198] Erasmus's aim of discovering the truth, in
Diatriba, impels him to emulate Cicero's *sermo*, in which (destructive)

---

196. *Luther and Erasmus*, 41–42, 97. In *Hyperaspistes* I, see LB 10:1259B–C, 1260A–B,
1267B, 1276A–C, 1281D–E, and 1290B–E. Erasmus tried to restrict discussion among the
common people by composing *De libero arbitrio* in Latin. He explains: "Writing in Latin, I
disguise my thoughts from the common folk, while you [Luther] take pains to have this
disputation of yours translated into the German language so that you can make a show of
Erasmus to farmers, sailors and cobblers, people before which he is a speechless man." LB
10:1313E–F (*Hyperaspistes* I). (Erasmus similarly writes that his *Annotations*—notes on his
edition of the New Testament—"were written 'for scholars, not for the public' and that it was
wrong 'to discuss publicly among tanners, weavers, and foolish women' what was an academic
dispute." See Rummel, *Catholic Critics*, 1:124). Boyle calls attention to the expediency of
Diatriba to support her claim that *Diatriba* is composed in the deliberative genre: "Advanta-
geousness [*utilitas* or expediency] is not merely a particular argument of *Diatriba*," she writes,
but also "an essential aim of the disputation as deliberative rhetoric." *Rhetoric and Reform*,
110.

197. The fact that expediency is an end of *both* deliberative oratory and conversation should
not be surprising. Although conversation was a distinct genre, its features are influenced by the
deliberative *genus*. As J. F. Tinkler observes, "the deliberative genre was especially important for
sermocinal rhetoric, particularly the kind of philosophical literature that we find interesting in
the humanist tradition." "Renaissance Humanism," 285.

198. For Cicero, honor is "anything that is sought wholly or partly for its own sake." And
truth, as well as virtue and knowledge, is sought for its own merit. *De inventione* 2.157,
2.53.159. Erasmus links truth to honor in LB 9:1215C (*De libero arbitrio*). Boyle infers from
Erasmus's pursuit of the honorable, however, that *Diatriba* was written in the deliberative
genre, since Cicero includes honor, along with expediency, as the aim of deliberative oratory. See
Rhetoric and Reform, 15–16. But like expediency, honor is not peculiar to deliberative oratory;
sermo is also characterized by *honestum*. See Tinkler, "Renaissance Humanism," 285. Moreover, Erasmus's goal of truth is consistent with the end of classical *sermo*, as Cicero affirms in
De finibus 1.5.13: "Our object is to discover the truth."

emotional appeals are avoided and contention eschewed. Erasmus describes his disputation with Luther as "temperate . . . for the purpose of eliciting the truth." He writes that he pursues the matter without recrimination, "because in this way the truth, which is often lost amid too much wrangling may be more surely perceived." He uses gentle words in *Diatriba*, "so that truth might shine forth more unfalteringly." Erasmus denies that he is engaged in gladiatorial combat with Luther. Combat, he explains, will only obstruct the search for truth. Erasmus offers the example of "two combatants who, in the heat of a quarrel, turn whatever is at hand into a missile, whether it be a jug or a dish." He questions the reader: "What sort of sincere judgment can there be when people behave in this way? Who will learn anything fruitful from this sort of discussion—beyond the fact that each leaves the discussion bespattered with the other's filth?"[199] Like Cicero, Erasmus concludes that truth is furthered by a more harmonious relationship between interlocutors.

Because of the absence of passions and contention, the *decorum* of *Diatriba* is civil and moderate. Erasmus characterizes *Diatriba* numerous times as "civil."[200] But this is not the civility of deliberative oratory, as Boyle suggests, but of *sermo*. Contrary to Erasmus's intentions in *Diatriba*, the goal of deliberative oratory is not to moderate emotions, but to inflame them. Thus Quintilian writes: "As regards appeals to the emotions, these are especially necessary in *deliberative* oratory. Anger has frequently to be excited or assuaged and the minds of the audience have to be swayed to fear, ambition, hatred, reconciliation."[201] Quintilian singles out *ethos* as especially apposite

---

199. *Luther and Erasmus*, 36–37; LB 10:1287C (*Hyperaspistes* I). In contrast to *Diatriba*, Erasmus's stance in *Hyperaspistes*—responding to Luther's combative *De servo arbitrio*—is more contentious. See, for example, LB 10:1312A and 1364D–E. In practice, Erasmus often fell short of his ideal of civil discourse: "Invective is the dominant mode of expression [in Erasmus's apologetic writings]. Equivocation and subterfuge are weapons wielded with dexterity. Although Erasmus often adopts a superior tone, he is superior to his opponents only in learning; in pettifogging, peevishness, and intellectual pride he is their match." Rummel, *Catholic Critics*, 1:189–90. See also 2:151, 153–54.

200. See, for example, LB 10:1251B–C, LB 10:1283A–B, and LB 10:1332F (*Hyperaspistes* I). For further examples, see Boyle, *Rhetoric and Reform*, 194 n. 78, and 114–15.

201. Quintilian *Institutio oratoria* 3.8.12–13. In his exposition of the laws, however, Cicero proposes "an important and . . . excellent provision" to regulate the discussion of the Senate: "*Moderation shall be preserved in meetings of the people and the Senate.*" Cicero explains that by moderation he means "calm and quiet behavior, for the presiding officer regulates and determines not only the spirit and desires, but almost the facial expressions, of those over whom he is presiding. But though [it is hard to preserve such moderation in popular assemblies], in the Senate it is not difficult, for a senator is not the kind of person to form his opinion on the basis of another's authority; rather, he wishes to be respected for himself." *De legibus* 3.18.40.

to the deliberative genre: "But what really carries greatest weight in *deliberative* speeches is the authority of the speaker." Yet Erasmus rejects *ethos* in his debate with Luther, using Cicero's criticism of the Pythagoreans, in *De natura deorum*, against Luther's followers, who "approve with unrestrained zeal whatever you [Luther] taught: 'He, himself, has spoken it!' "[202] Although Boyle finds that Erasmus's sacred oratory and the rhetoric of *Diatriba* both possess a common deliberative character, Erasmus himself distinguishes between the two. In preaching—"exhorting or dissuading"— he writes, there is a place for emotional manipulation; such is not the case, however, "in the disputing of truth," where "it is moderation which pleases."[203] This moderation is not found in *contentio*, which is what Erasmus terms Luther's *De servo arbitrio*, but in *sermo*, which is a name he applies to his *Diatriba*.[204]

The means to arrive at the truth, in *Diatriba*, is argument *in utramque partem*. But this method, also used in the Ciceronian dialogues, can provide only probability, not certainty. Like Ciceronian *sermo*, the skepticism produced by arguing both sides of the issue in *Diatriba* is distinct from the skepticism of deliberative oratory. In political deliberations, skepticism (that is, argument *in utramque partem*) ceases with the assembly's decision. The orators in this case abide by the group's consensus. Accordingly, Boyle, who views *Diatriba* as deliberative, argues that Erasmus maintains his skepticism, vis-à-vis Luther, only until the debate is ended, at which time he "yields judgment to the consensus." And Erasmus, in fact, does conclude *Diatriba* with the words: "I have completed my discourse; now let others pass judgment."[205] The judgment Erasmus refers to here, however, is individual, at least among scholars, and does not preclude further debate. It is the judgment of *sermo*, about which Cicero writes in *Tusculan Disputations*,

---

Nevertheless, this conception of deliberative oratory is the exception in classical rhetoric— appearing here as a proposal for the ideal state.

202. LB 10:1305F (*Hyperaspistes* I). See Introduction, 34. Nevertheless, as Erika Rummel notes, Erasmus also used argumentation from authority, even quoting scholastic writers, when it served his purposes. Rummel, *Catholic Critics*, 1:186–87.

203. *Luther and Erasmus*, 96.

204. Erasmus refers to *Diatriba* as *sermo* in LB 10:1267C (*Hyperaspistes* I). He refers to Luther's argument as *contentio* in LB 10:1277B and 1290C, and to Luther as contending [*contendis*] in LB 10:1281E and 1282B. Erasmus also distinguishes between his own "well-balanced inquiries [*inquisitiones*] of learned men" and Luther's "quarrelsome disputes [*contentiones*] carried on before the populace." LB 10:1271F.

205. Boyle, *Rhetoric and Reform*, 36 and 111; *Luther and Erasmus*, 97.

"judgment is free."[206] For Erasmus, debates over doctrinal adiaphora, like Cicero's debates over philosophical questions, cannot be decided. They are questions "which do not admit of resolution." Although Erasmus believes that various degrees of consensus may form on some doctrinal adiaphora (free will, for example, the existence of which was widely accepted), he still allows the learned to debate the matter among themselves, since there is no universal consensus on the doctrine. Free will, Erasmus writes, "could have received sober treatment from learned men."[207] Erasmus recognizes the Holy Spirit's role in the evolution of dogma, effected by scholarly discussion.[208] Therefore, scholars should not be prevented from exploring, reconsidering, and possibly abandoning widely accepted doctrines, so long as they are not fundamental to the faith.

Sermo and Toleration

Traditionally, the humanists have been defined, and have defined themselves, by their opposition to the scholastics. The humanists represented the

206. See Introduction, note 144. Compare Erasmus's statement in *Diatriba*, "I play the debater, not the judge," with the conclusion to Cicero's *De natura deorum*: "My purpose was rather to discuss the doctrines I have expounded than to pronounce judgment upon them." In *De natura deorum*, the conversation ends without a consensus, each speaker holding his own view of probability. *Luther and Erasmus*, 38; *De natura deorum* 3.40.95. Like the debate over free will, Erasmus allows that the controversies raised by his edition of the New Testament can be decided individually. See Rummel, *Catholic Critics*, 1:22: "Deference is also expressed to the learned reader's opinion. ['So that no more the worse, each person may make use of his own judgment'], Erasmus wrote in the *Apologia* (166:13–14 Holborn). When he pointed out variants, it was up to the reader to decide which he would rather adopt (ibidem 170:34–5). In his preface to the *Annotations* he expressed the same attitude. He was ['leaving the final decision to the reader' (Ep 373:61 CWE 3)]. It followed that he claimed no official standing for his text." See also *Catholic Critics*, 1:89.

207. LB 10:1276A–C. Cf. *De oratore* 2.29.78. Erasmus invites Luther to participate in the reexamination of earlier conciliar decisions, but counsels him, because of expediency, to attribute any earlier errors to the needs of that time: "If I were convinced that at a certain council some wrong decision or definition had been made, I should have the right to proclaim the truth, but it would not be expedient, lest wicked men be given a handle to scorn the authority of the Fathers, even in those decisions which they have taken in a godly and devout spirit. I would rather say that they took a decision that seemed reasonable from the point of view of their own times which present needs suggest should be repealed." *Luther and Erasmus*, 41; See also Boyle, *Rhetoric and Reform*, 107–8.

208. McConica, "Grammar of Consent," 93, 96; Payne, *Erasmus: His Theology of Sacraments*, 27; Boyle, *Rhetoric and Reform*, 26, 158. Erasmus translates *logos*, in the Johannine prologue, as *sermo*. Thus, not only human truth, but also God's truth is identified with conversation. See Boyle, *Erasmus on Language and Method*, especially 3–33, and McConica, "Grammar of Consent," 90–91.

new philosophy of the Renaissance; the scholastics stood for the old philosophy of the Middle Ages. In contrast, Paul Oskar Kristeller has argued that humanism and scholasticism were not antithetical movements, but "that they coexisted and developed all the way through and beyond the Renaissance period as different branches of learning."[209] Defenders of either position can find support in Erasmus. The Dutch humanist was, as Kristeller himself concedes, a frequent critic of the scholastics.[210] But Erasmus also found the scholastic debates on nonessentials to be useful, so long as they were conducted with *decorum*. Erasmus's language here is guarded. He does not consider scholastic debates irreverent, if conducted properly; thus, he does "not disapprove of these debates on [nonessential] matters being treated in the schools, as long as this is not done wantonly but soberly." These questions are advantageous, "provided they are moderate and gone into as far as is right."[211]

The scholastics anticipate Erasmus's argument that truth emerges from the discussion of opposing views. Nevertheless, scholastic debate, by itself, cannot provide Erasmus with a model of toleration, since scholastic argument *in utramque partem* did not always betoken skepticism. The example of the scholastic *disputatio*, "a formal discussion of a subject by two or more people, who take opposite or differing sides," is instructive. Although the *disputatio* consisted of arguments *pro* and *contra*, it was usually resolved by the master's *determinatio* (determination) of the correct or approved answer. That a question can be argued on either side, therefore, does not preclude the existence of one right answer. A work like Aquinas's *Summa theologiae*, which reflects the method of *disputatio*, points up the unskeptical character of scholastic argument. The openness of the *Summa*'s discussion, where objections to the initial proposition are entertained, is only apparent. Like the *disputatio*, the *Summa* contains an authoritative *determinatio*. Counterarguments function, for Aquinas, as prompts to defend and develop his own thesis, and not as serious attempts to investigate a question. Consequently, because stating a position, in scholastic disputation, was not tantamount to believing (or even possibly believing) in that position, scholastics could even propose heretical views in order to refute them.[212]

---

209. Paul Oskar Kristeller, *Renaissance Thought and Its Sources*, ed. Michael Mooney (New York: Columbia University Press, 1979), 103.

210. Ibid., 90.

211. LB 10:1260A; LB 10:1265A–B (*Hyperaspistes* I).

212. James J. Murphy, *Rhetoric in the Middle Ages: A History of Rhetorical Theory from St. Augustine to the Renaissance* (Berkeley and Los Angeles: University of California Press, 1974),

Not all questions the scholastics debated, however, required a single, certain answer. The scholastics, like Erasmus, recognized the category of nonessential doctrines, which were genuinely open to debate, though Erasmus believed that their list of nonessentials was not long enough.[213] Even when they were skeptical, though, the scholastics were unable to anticipate Erasmus's defense of toleration because they largely overlooked the role of emotions in the search for truth.[214] Erasmus grounds *sermo*—like all rhetorical *genera*—on the principle of *decorum*, that is, the accommodation of the speaker to the emotional condition of the listener. In contrast, the scholastics simply assumed that rational debate was sufficient to reveal the truth. From Erasmus's perspective, the scholastics' neglect of *decorum* increased the likelihood of verbal intolerance, even in discussion of nonessentials. Their confidence in the sufficiency of reason, however, promoted still greater intolerance of those who denied the fundamentals of faith. Unwilling to consider the emotional causes that preclude someone from realizing the truth, the scholastics viewed heretics as either malicious or insane. Absent from the scholastics is Erasmus's rhetorical insight that heretics must be accommodated, until they are capable of seeing the truth. Accordingly, typical of the scholastics is the assumption, expressed by Aquinas, that heretics were motivated by either "pride or covetousness . . . or some illusion of the imagination." He did not consider that heretics may honestly be mistaken; to him the heretic always chose to disbelieve.[215]

The skepticism and *decorum* missing from scholastic disputation are present in Erasmian *sermo*. It is the presence of these two rhetorical qualities that accounts for the tolerance of *Diatriba* and other Erasmian dialogues. The effect of Erasmus's skepticism is to deny any person or institution the ability to justify religious persecution by claiming knowledge; the subject

---

102–4; Tinkler, "Humanism and Dialogue," 200–203; Byrne, *Probability and Opinion*, 161–62.

213. Byrne, *Probability and Opinion*, 118–19.

214. See, for example, Aquinas's view in ibid., 144, 146.

215. St. Thomas Aquinas *Summa theologiae* 2, 2, q. 11, a. 1; Byrne, *Probability and Opinion*, 118–19, 121–23, 161–62. Cf. Perelman and Olbrechts-Tyteca, *New Rhetoric*, 33: "If argumentation addressed to the universal audience and calculated to convince does not convince everybody, one can always resort to *disqualifying the recalcitrant* by classifying him as stupid or abnormal. This approach, common among thinkers in the Middle Ages, is also used by some modern writers. There can only be adherence to this idea of excluding individuals from the human community if the number and intellectual value of those banned are not so high as to make such a procedure ridiculous."

matter of *sermo* is inherently disputatious, resolved by the individual's determination of what is most probable. The effect of Erasmus's *decorum*, governed by the search for truth, is to foster controlled debate in the interest of truth. Because Erasmus sees conversation as the means to reveal greater truth, he supports discussion of nonessential doctrines. Yet he also regulates the discussion to ensure the proper rhetorical environment. For Erasmus, discussion must be free of both physical and verbal abuse, lest the discovery of truth be obstructed.

The theory of toleration implicit in Erasmian *sermo* is nothing short of an early version of the argument from truth, that is, the argument that free speech should be safeguarded because it leads to the discovery of truth.[216] Erasmus anticipates Milton and Mill's defense of free speech, as well as the particular version of the argument from truth known as "the marketplace of ideas." For Erasmus, as for his successors, truth emerges from the discussion of ideas. This type of toleration, in Erasmus, stands in contrast to the toleration derived from the model of preaching. In preaching, the speaker presumes to know the truth already. In *sermo*, however, the speakers are engaged in a joint effort to discover the truth. And though each speaker may have tentatively arrived at a point of view, the other interlocutors and their opinions must be accorded full respect. Such mutual respect signals a discussant's readiness to reconsider in light of the others' opinions.[217] Chaim Perelman and Lucie Olbrechts-Tyteca express a similar sentiment in *The New Rhetoric*: "To agree to discussion means readiness to see things from the viewpoint of the interlocutor, to restrict oneself to what he admits, and to give effect to one's own beliefs only to the extent that the person one is trying to persuade is willing to give assent to them."[218] Of course, Erasmus

216. Frederick Schauer, *Free Speech: A Philosophical Inquiry* (Cambridge: Cambridge University Press, 1982), 15.

217. Note the similarity between the *decorum* of Erasmian conversation and Amy Gutmann and Dennis Thompson's discussion of mutual respect as a virtue of political deliberation in "Moral Conflict and Political Consensus," in *Liberalism and the Good*, ed. R. Bruce Douglass, Gerald M. Mara, and Henry S. Richardson (New York: Routledge, 1990), 134–42. For example, Gutmann and Thompson argue that "in seeking for political consensus in the face of fundamental moral disagreement, we need to attend not only to the nature of the positions but also the way in which people hold or express positions. Morally respectable positions can be defended in morally disrespectful ways. It is the role of the principles of accommodation to restrain those ways. . . . The principles are best conceived as expressing a virtue that lies at the core of moral deliberation in a democracy—*mutual respect*." Like Erasmus, Gutmann and Thompson value mutual respect, primarily, for its consequences.

218. "The use of argumentation implies that one has renounced resorting to force alone, that value is attached to gaining the adherence of one's interlocutor by means of reasoned

does not apply this full toleration to all religious opinions—only the nonessentials; and he does not grant this freedom of discussion to all individuals—only the learned elite. Nevertheless, he establishes a paradigm for toleration that will be expanded beyond these limitations. It will be left to future humanists and their successors to broaden the area of debate and to expand the category of persons considered competent to engage in it.

---

persuasion, and that one is not regarding him as an object, but appealing to his free judgment. Recourse to argumentation assumes the establishment of a community of minds, which, while it lasts, excludes the use of violence." Perelman and Olbrechts-Tyteca, *New Rhetoric*, 55. See also 16.

2

Acontius and the Revision of the Humanist Defense

After Erasmus

Erasmus's Successors

Erasmus's vision of a reunited Christendom attracted other Catholic humanists, among them the bishop of Naumburg, Julius Pflug (1499–1564).[1] Pflug believed that only Erasmus could reconcile Catholic and Lutheran. Thus he wrote to Erasmus in 1531: "The eyes of all those who seek peace look towards you alone. For immortal God has given you the authority and the power so that you alone of everybody are able to cure especially these evils."[2] Erasmus, in turn, dedicated his *De sarcienda ecclesiae concordia* (*On Establishing Concord in the Church*) in 1533 to Pflug. To make Erasmus's vision of unity a reality, Pflug took part in colloquies between Catholics and Lutherans with the hope that doctrinal agreement could be reached. Pflug also composed the first draft of Emperor Charles V's *Interim* of Augsburg, a "declaration of His Imperial Majesty on the manner of behaving in religious matters until the conclusion of the ecumenical Council."[3] The *Interim*, published as a law of the empire on 30 June 1548, presented a doctrinal formula, in twenty-six articles, to be embraced by both

---

1. For a general discussion of Erasmus's humanist successors, see Lecler, *Toleration and the Reformation*, 1:224–41, 261–76.
2. Erasmus, *EE* 9:265 (Letter from Julius Pflug, 12 May 1531).
3. Lecler, *Toleration and the Reformation*, 1:234.

Catholics and Protestants until a final determination was made. Neither the colloquies nor the *Interim*, however, brought the two sides together.

Like Pflug, George Witzel (1501–73), German humanist and priest, looked to Erasmus's "middle course," for inspiration. In Witzel's words: "Luther should not be listened to, the Sophists should not be listened to, but Erasmus and those like him, that is, those who support no faction but Christianity, wholeheartedly and sincerely."[4] Witzel agreed with Erasmus that heretics should not be persecuted. He also supported Erasmus's claim that the differences between Catholics and Lutherans did not touch on essential doctrine. With no fundamental differences to justify Christian division, Witzel first sought to effect unity through an ecumenical Council. With the Council delayed, he next advocated the policy of colloquies, in which he, like Pflug, took part. Ultimately, Witzel despaired of the efficacy of colloquies. Nevertheless, he continued to maintain that Catholics and Lutherans were in substantial agreement. Thus, in his book *Via regia, sive de controversis religionis capitibus conciliandis sententia* (first published in 1600), Witzel showed that Catholic and Lutheran doctrine were consistent with each other. An Erasmian to the end, Witzel, in the same work, called upon Catholics, Lutherans, Calvinists, and Zwinglians to unite in Christ: "Is Christ divided?" he asked. "Has the Pope been crucified for us? Have we been baptized in the name of Luther, Zwingli, Rink, or Calvin?"[5]

A generation later than Pflug and Witzel was the Belgian humanist and Catholic theologian George Cassander (1513–66). Following the example of Erasmus, whom he greatly admired, Cassander also hoped to reconcile Catholics and Protestants. But he could no longer anticipate, as did Pflug and Witzel, full reconciliation. By his time, they had grown too far apart for that. Instead of complete unity, Cassander proposed in his principal work *De officio pii ac publicae tranquillitatis vere amantis viri in hoc religionis dissidio* (1561) that the Churches agree on "the elements of Apostolic doctrine."[6] Making use of Erasmus's idea of a brief list of fundamental doctrines, Cassander argued that agreement on the fundamentals of faith would allow Churches to "differ in certain opinions and rites"(19). Cassander recognized that institutional divisions created by the Reformation

---

4. Erasmus, *EE* 10:188 (Letter from George Witzel, 20 March 1533).

5. George Witzel, *Via regia, sive de controversis religionis capitibus conciliandis sententia* (Helmstedt: H. Conring, 1650), 53; cited in Lecler, *Toleration and the Reformation*, 1:270. Rink was a Hessian reformer who preached Anabaptism.

6. George Cassander, *De officio pii ac publicae tranquillitatis vere amantis viri in hoc religionis dissidio* (1562), 15.

would not disappear. But all Churches that accepted the fundamentals—and for Cassander this meant all Catholic and Protestant Churches, except the Anabaptists and anti-Trinitarians—would be counted members of the one true invisible Church: "And that Church that is based on the foundation of true and Apostolic teaching, which is contained in that very short Symbol of Faith, and does not separate itself by wicked schism from the communion of the remaining Churches, I consider a true Church and a member of the true Catholic Church, the Church of Christ. And I am thinking not only about the Western Churches, but also about the Eastern Churches"(25). As members of the comprehensive invisible Church, the various visible Churches were only obligated to treat each other with charity: "One is separated from the body, which is the Church . . . , only by the lack of charity"(19). Unable to achieve institutional unity among the Churches, Cassander would have been satisfied with mutual toleration.

Failure of Erasmus's Dream

Despite the attempts of his disciples, Erasmus's dream of Catholic-Protestant reconciliation, even along Cassander's minimal lines, was not realized. Rather than moving closer together, Roman Catholicism and Protestantism were becoming two separate religions. Protestantism itself was subdividing into a multitude of sects—Lutheran, Calvinist, Zwinglian, Anglican, and Anabaptist. By the middle of the sixteenth century, the vision of a reunited Christendom was all but abandoned, supplanted by each group's more limited goal of unity within its own ranks. For the Catholics, this unity was accomplished at the Council of Trent. Convened in 1545, the Council provided the Church with an authoritative declaration of Catholic doctrine to unite the faithful. The Protestant sects, unable to reach doctrinal concord as a single body, attained dogmatic coherence individually through a series of confessions and theological works.[7] Lutheranism's Augsburg Confession, promulgated in 1530, was the first Protestant attempt to define doctrine in a denominational book; the Calvinists relied upon Calvin's *Institutio Religionis Christianae* and Geneva Catechism, as well as a number of other national statements of doctrine; and the Anglican Church was united by the Thirty-Nine Articles, the product of the Convocation of 1563.

7. The Protestants were unable to reach doctrinal concord primarily because they disagreed on the nature of Christ's presence in the Eucharist and because they had no single ecclesiastical structure to enforce unanimity.

The consensus arrived at by each faction further nullified Erasmus's vision of toleration based on comprehension. For Erasmus, consensus served as a defense of toleration because agreement was likely on only the few fundamentals of faith. The possibility that consensus would extend beyond the fundamentals had not worried Erasmus. In the wake of the Council of Trent, which had defined the new Catholic orthodoxy, however, consensus became a tool of intolerance; Erasmus's presumption was no longer true. To distinguish orthodox dogma from Protestant heresy, the Council emphasized heretofore undetermined doctrines, most of which Erasmus would never have considered fundamental to Christianity. Thus, in response to the Lutheran heresies on grace and justification, the Council devoted sixteen dogmatic chapters and thirty-three canons![8] And so it went with the rest of the Council's declarations. It pronounced on the number and nature of the sacraments and on the divine origins of the Roman Catholic ecclesiastical organization precisely because those were the areas in which Luther and the other reformers departed from the Church. Because Luther considered transubstantiation an inadmissible speculation, the Council declared it an article of faith; to counter the Lutheran doctrine of justification by faith alone, the Council presented the belief in justification by good works; and in response to Luther's heresy that original sin remained after baptism, the bishops asserted the doctrine of the remission of original sin through baptism. Even the dead Erasmus did not escape the Church's anti-Lutheran reaction. Many of Erasmus's ideas were, falsely, branded as Lutheran, and his works were said to "have opened the door to all heresy." Consequently, in 1559, all his books were placed on the *Index*.[9] The Tridentine consensus was anything but tolerant; it declared dissent from previously debatable subtleties as heresy, punishable by burning at the stake. Similarly, the Protestant Churches expanded their fundamentals of faith to distinguish themselves from Catholics, as well as from one another. For example, Lutherans, Zwinglians, and Calvinists debated the real presence of Christ in the Eucharist, with each denomination considering its own doctrine to be a necessary belief.[10] Accordingly, Lord Acton has argued that the reformers'

---

8. Hubert Jedin, *Reformation and Counter Reformation*, vol. 5 of *History of the Church*, ed. Hubert Jedin and John Dolan (New York: Seabury Press, 1980), 470–71. For a more detailed discussion of the Council of Trent, see Hubert Jedin, *Geschichte des Konzils von Trient* (Freiberg: Herder, 1951–57).

9. Augustijn, *Erasmus*, 198–99; Menchi, *Erasmo in Italia*, 308–21.

10. Menchi, *Erasmo in Italia*, 245–49, 356–61. So great were the divisions between Protestant denominations that the Lutheran poet and theologian Paul Gerhardt (1606–76)

preoccupation with doctrine made them more intolerant than the old Church from which they split.[11]

Intellectual Changes

The Reformation

Although, as W. K. Jordan notes, "nothing was further from the minds of the reformers than the toleration of doctrines other than their own," the Reformation gave rise to an individualistic mentality, which promoted toleration despite the reformers' personal intolerance. The Reformation, Jordan states, "led men to judge what is true and good by the test of reason rather than by the tenets of tradition." And W.E.H. Lecky observes that the Reformation "issued in a diffusion of a rationalistic spirit which no Church, however retrograde or dogmatic, has been able to exclude."[12] The reformers themselves, however, were no rationalists. Faith, not reason, is the basis of Reformation theology. Reason, for the reformers, stood in opposition to faith. According to Luther, "reason rejects faith."[13] But the reformers did vest the authority of scriptural interpretation in the individual, not the Church. This theological break with Roman Catholicism, though not itself rationalist, would support the growth of rational discussion as a tool of religious toleration.

"Scripture alone," *scriptura sola*, was the slogan of the Reformation. In Luther's words, Scripture "alone is the true lord and master of all writings and doctrine on earth."[14] Scripture, Luther argues, is clear in itself, without

---

wrote: "I cannot regard the Calvinists, *quatenus tales*, as Christians." E. W. Zeeden, *Die Entstehung der Konfessionen* (Munich: Oldenbourg, 1965), 96; cited in *History of the Church*, 428–29.

11. Lord Acton argues that Protestantism is less tolerant than Catholicism because the Protestant theory of persecution is dogmatically motivated, in contrast to the Catholic theory of persecution, which is impelled by a concern with social order. John Emerich Edward Dalberg Acton, "The Protestant Theory of Persecution," in *Essays on Freedom and Power* (New York: Meridian, 1955), 113–40.

12. Jordan, *Religious Toleration in England*, 1:32; W.E.H. Lecky, *History of the Rise and Influence of the Spirit of Rationalism in Europe* (Bombay: Longmans, Green, 1913), 1:365.

13. WA 39.1:90 (*The Disputation Concerning Justification*, 1536).

14. *Luther's Works: American Edition* 32:11–12 (*Defense and Explanation of all the Articles*, 1521).

need of a church to interpret it. But while Scripture is objectively clear in itself, it is subjectively clear only to those whom the Spirit has illuminated: "For the Spirit is required for the understanding of Scripture, both as a whole and in any part of it."[15] Without the Holy Spirit, Luther explains, one "sees but does not perceive and hears but does not understand"(166). Or as Calvin writes: "To those whom He pleases not to illumine, God transmits His doctrine wrapped in enigmas in order that they may not profit by it except to be cast into greater stupidity."[16] Because the illumination of the Spirit is personal, the search for scriptural truth must be an individual one. Of course, Luther and Calvin did not, in practice, permit their followers to arrive at their own conclusions. For them, there was only one correct interpretation of the Bible, and that was the Bible according to Luther—or Calvin.[17] The ultimate effect, however, of the Protestant doctrine of *scriptura sola* and its corollary that each person must interpret the Bible for him or herself was to liberate the believer from the authority of the Church, the traditional restraint on religious inquiry.

It was Church authority, embodied by consensus, that had restricted Erasmus's field of discussion. The greater the consensus, the more restricted the discussion: doctrines with universal consensus were completely beyond question, whereas doctrines that garnered lesser degrees of consensus were to be debated only among the scholarly elite. The reformers, however, eliminated consensus as a reason to restrict religious discussion because consensus was no longer a criterion of truth. Luther himself makes this point in his debate with Erasmus on free will. The reformer concedes that the consensus of so many centuries stands against him. He even admits that in the past this fact had prevented him from opposing the Church. "I myself," Luther writes, "was so impressed by [Church authorities] for more than ten years that I think no one else has ever been so disturbed by them."[18] He eventually breaks with the Church, though, because he believes Scripture is on his side. Human consensus, that is, "the judgment of that whole choir of saints . . . or rather of the whole world," means nothing when it conflicts with God's word (152). The reformers further rejected Erasmus's distinction between the learned, who were permitted to dispute doctrines, and the public, who were to be shielded from these debates. Because it was the Holy

15. *Luther and Erasmus*, 112.
16. *Institutes* 3.24.13.
17. Jordan, *Religious Toleration in England*, 1:31.
18. *Luther and Erasmus*, 145.

Spirit, and not scholarly expertise, that enabled the believer to understand Scripture, there was no reason to limit doctrinal discussion to the learned. All Christians had an equal obligation to discover true doctrine and preach it, which is implicit in the Protestant concept of the priesthood of all believers. By allowing more people to discuss doctrine, Luther and other reformers had, unwittingly, made it possible to expand the *sermo*-based defense of toleration beyond the limits set by Erasmus.

Method

There was another intellectual influence, besides the Protestant Reformation, that had positive implications for the growth of the *sermo*-based defense of toleration. This influence was the search for "method." In the late sixteenth century, those raised in the humanist tradition attempted to reform and simplify the content of the traditional course of studies. They termed this attempt at reform "method." Girolamo Borro, professor of philosophy at Pisa, defined method as the "brief way under whose guidance we are led as quickly as possible to knowledge."[19] Although they attempted to simplify and give order to the full range of university subjects such as grammar, rhetoric, history, law, and mathematics, these education reformers focused their efforts on "finding the method" of logic, in particular.

The single individual most associated with the movement to reform traditional logic is Peter Ramus. His attacks on Aristotelian logic resulted in what he considered a more ordered and teachable conception of dialectic and rhetoric. In fact, what Ramus did, according to Walter J. Ong, was to expand dialectic at the expense of rhetoric.[20] Through his writings on dialectic and the work of his close associate Omer Talon on rhetoric, Ramus

19. Neal W. Gilbert, *Renaissance Concepts of Method* (New York: Columbia University Press, 1963), 71.

20. Thus Ramus "simplified" the five traditional stages of rhetoric by eliminating the first two stages and the fourth stage, that is, invention, which concerns itself with finding the subject matter of the speech; arrangement or disposition, which relates to the organization of the speech's arguments; and memory, which pertains to the use of mnemonic devices. These three stages, he contends, belong to dialectic. Rhetoric, according to Ramus, consists of only the third and fifth stages, that is, style, which involves the use of proper language and ornamentation, and delivery, which concerns the control of the voice and of body gestures in the speech. This new division of rhetoric was anticipated by the humanist, Rudolph Agricola. Walter J. Ong S.J., *Ramus, Method, and the Decay of Dialogue: From the Art of Discourse to the Art of Reason* (Cambridge: Harvard University Press, 1983), 270–77; Wilbur Samuel Howell, *Logic and Rhetoric in England, 1500–1700* (Princeton: Princeton University Press, 1956), 151–52; Conley, *European Tradition*, 128–33.

profoundly influenced the theories of dialectic and rhetoric during the late-sixteenth and seventeenth centuries. But I am less concerned in this discussion with the specifics of Ramus's theory or with his influence on other theories of logic than with how Ramus is representative of an attitude shared by other, lesser-known proponents of method toward reason and the passions.

Ramus defines method as the orderly arrangement of arguments in which the more conspicuous ideas precede the less conspicuous ideas.[21] Because arguments can be conspicuous in either an absolute sense or relative to the perceptions of the listener, Ramus distinguishes between two types of method: a method of teaching and a prudential method. In the more preferable method of teaching the "general and universal explanations precede"; the "special explanation by distribution of the parts" follows; and "last of all comes the definition of the singular parts and clarification by means of suitable examples."[22] In other words, the method of teaching presumes to pattern itself after a naturally logical order of ideas—from the most general statements to the less general, more concrete ones. This method of teaching, however, conflicts with the rhetorical principle of *decorum* because the order of speech is determined by logical considerations, not by whether the projected audience will understand or find this ordering persuasive. The speaker can arrange the material without any reference to the circumstances of its presentation. Through this method, Ramus excludes human needs and emotions.

The method of teaching is Ramus's primary method, but he touches on a second, less significant method, which entails accommodation not to the inherent logical disposition of ideas but to "the condition of persons, things, times, and places."[23] According to this method of prudence, arguments are to be arranged according to expediency. The "prudent" orator recognizes that many minds will not conform to the logical ordering of the first method and that the audience's emotional state must influence the speaker's arrangement. Ramus, however, is not altogether sure that the method of prudence should be considered a bona fide method, referring to it as "dissimulation" and "imperfect."[24] The use of prudential method to persuade the common

21. Howell, *Logic and Rhetoric in England*, 152–53.

22. Peter Ramus, *Dialectici comentarii tres authore Audomaro Taleo editii* (Paris, 1546), 83–84; cited in Ong, *Ramus*, 245. See also Gilbert, *Renaissance Concepts*, 142–43.

23. *Dialectici*, 87–90; cited in Ong, *Ramus*, 246. In his later writings Ramus speaks of only one method with two uses. Ong, *Ramus*, 252.

24. Ong, *Ramus*, 253.

people—that "many-headed monster"—is anathemized by Ramus as a deception perpetrated by orators and poets. He opposes the *decorum* of the prudential method because accommodation to the listener unsettles the natural order of ideas.

Despite its idiosyncracies, Ramus's exposition of method is typical of others in the late sixteenth century in that method is supposed to be logical, based on reason and not the passions.[25] Ramus's emphasis on reason manifests itself in his depreciation of the method of prudence because it deceives by pleasure. The end of this type of method is not teaching, but delighting and moving.[26] The method of prudence serves "no other purpose than that of pulling along the troublesome and mulish auditor"(254). If the auditor were not obstinate and perverse, Ramus explains, the method of teaching, organized according to natural logic, would be sufficient. As his discussion of method reveals, Ramus links rationalism to the rejection of rhetorical *decorum*. The two, however, are not necessarily linked. It is possible, as in the case of *sermo*, to have a rational rhetoric that is still sensitive to the condition of the listener. Ramus himself, in his early writings, refers to rational speech as dialectic, which he defines as "the ability to discourse" or the "power of discoursing."[27] Unlike his later conception of method, which organizes ideas in abstraction from people and in opposition to *decorum*, Ramus's early definition of dialectic suggests the Ciceronian conception of *sermo*.[28] By itself, therefore, the turn to method merely indicates a shift toward a different kind of rhetoric, that is, a rhetoric that eschews emotional appeals. The rise of method does not signal a general rejection of rhetoric. Even in his later days Ramus was never wholly opposed to rhetoric. He was motivated by a desire to make traditional logic accessible to a broader audience than was the traditional logic of the medieval scholastics. It is only his neglect of *decorum*, the human element in rational discussion, that ultimately defines his legacy as antirhetorical.

25. Gilbert, *Renaissance Concepts*, 9–10. The elevation of intellect and distrust of passions is not limited to the reformation of method, but is typical of the late Renaissance in general. See Bouwsma, "Changing Assumptions."

26. Ong, *Ramus*, 253.

27. "Dialectica virtus est disserendi." Ramus, *Dialecticae institutiones* (1543), fol. 5; cited in Ong, *Ramus*, 349 n. 23.

28. Ramus equates discoursing, which is the activity of dialectic, with "conversing" and with "using one's reason." *Dialecticae institutiones*, fol. 5; cited in Ong, *Ramus*, 349 n. 24. See also 176.

Acontius: The New Humanist

The Protestant Reformation and the reformation of method influenced the evolution of the humanist defense of religious toleration. Although Erasmus's rhetorically based arguments continued to undergird later humanist theories, the expansion of *sermo*, made possible by Protestantism and method, effected a shift in the humanist case for toleration; conversation, rather than preaching, would become the dominant model of toleration. The continuity and changes in the humanist defense of toleration are exemplified by Jacobus Acontius. Born in the early sixteenth century, in Ossani, near Trent, Acontius defended toleration in a series of books, the most noteworthy being *Satan's Stratagems*. He justified the toleration of religious dissent on rhetorical grounds, at the same time that he adapted his rhetorical arguments to fit the new theological and intellectual climate. Acontius revived the humanist plea for toleration by incorporating Protestantism's individualism and method's rationalism into his conception of rhetoric.

The evidence available on Acontius confirms his status as a humanist. Professionally, he was engaged in the respected humanist occupation of court counselor, serving in the entourage of the king of Bohemia and as secretary to Cardinal Madruzzo, governor of Milan.[29] He also associated with other humanists. Thus, following his departure from Italy in 1567, Acontius proceeded first to Switzerland, then to England, where he established his closest social and intellectual links with that group of humanists known as the Italian Academicians.[30] Acontius's writings also bear out their author's humanism. His early *Dialogue of Giacopo Riccamati*, a conversation between two men in search of religious truth, exemplifies the humanists' stylistic preference for dialogue.[31] And Acontius's magnum opus, *Satan's*

29. This king of Bohemia would later become Emperor Maximilian II. Jacobus Acontius, *Satan's Stratagems*, ed. P. Radin (San Francisco: California State Library, 1940), ii. For a complete discussion of Acontius's life, see Charles Donald O'Malley, *Jacopo Aconcio*, trans. into Italian by Delio Cantimori (Rome: Edizioni Di Storia and Letteratura, 1955), 1–51. See also Briggs, "Jacopo Aconcio." On humanists as advisers to the court, see Quentin Skinner, *The Foundations of Modern Political Thought* (Cambridge: Cambridge University Press, 1980), 2:213–21. Also see Kristeller, *Renaissance Thought*, 11.

30. This group, which included Celso, Curio, and Faustus Socinus, is characterized by Jordan as "among the finest products of humanism and free thought in Renaissance Italy." While in Basel Acontius probably also met the famed humanist and defender of toleration, Sebastian Castellio. Jordan, *Religious Toleration in England*, 1:305–10. See also Frederic C. Church, *The Italian Reformers: 1534–1564* (New York: Columbia University Press, 1932), 8.

31. Acontius's *Dialogue* was probably written somewhere between 1550 and 1555 but

Stratagems, evinces the humanists' belief that words, not force, will eventually overcome religious error.

The details of Acontius's life, however, distinguish him from earlier humanists such as Erasmus. First, Acontius abandoned the Catholic faith for Protestantism. Although the exact date and conditions of his conversion are unknown, it is clear that he openly accepted Protestantism by 1557, the year he left Italy. After that date Acontius began publishing a variety of books, including at least three on theological matters.[32] In 1558, while in Switzerland, he published the finished version of the aforementioned *Dialogue of Giacopo Riccamati* and a *Summary of the Christian Religion*, the latter being a discussion of Protestant doctrine coupled with a condemnation of Catholic dogma. In 1564 (wrongly dated 1565) Acontius published *Satan's Stratagems*, in which he argues that religious persecution is indefensible on religious grounds. In these three works Acontius manifests his Protestantism by defending the following propositions: the Bible is the sole source of religious truth;[33] the individual is responsible to find sure knowledge of the truth through Scripture without relying upon priests, popes, or councils (86–87, 93–97, 136); consensus does not determine the truth (143); the Holy Spirit empowers our understanding of the Word (41); the pope is not the vicar of Christ (177); salvation is received only through faith, not good works or the intercession of saints (80–81); and baptism and the Lord's Supper are the only sacraments with a scriptural basis.[34] Acontius's Protestant theology influenced his theory of toleration. Whereas Erasmus could accept consensus as a criterion of truth or relegate religious disputes to the scholarly, Acontius could not.

Second, Acontius was distinguished from earlier humanists through his pursuit of logical method. Method for Acontius meant, as it did for Ramus, that discourse should be logically arranged and unemotional. This conception of speech was at odds with the view of earlier humanists, such as Erasmus, who emphasized pathetic appeals. Thus, Acontius begins his *De*

---

remained unpublished until much later, because Acontius feared to publicize its anti-Catholic stance while still in Italy.

32. It seems apparent that Acontius did not publish these works while in Italy because of their anti-Catholicism. A fourth book on religious matters, *Una Essortatione al timor di Dio*, was published posthumously in 1580 by Acontius's executor, Castiglione.

33. *Satan's Stratagems*, 139.

34. Concerning the pope being the vicar of Christ, also see O'Malley, *Jacopo Aconcio*, 164–65. Erich Hassinger emphasizes the orthodoxy of Acontius's Protestantism in *Studien zu Jacobus Acontius* (Berlin: Grünewald, 1934). He does so, however, to the neglect of Acontius's humanism. O'Malley voices a similar criticism of Hassinger in *Jacopo Aconcio* 97 and 110.

Methodo, published in 1558, arguing, as did Ramus, that a proper method is necessary to reform the study of logic.[35] He defines this method as "a certain correct rationale by which one shall be able to prosecute an inquiry into the truth and knowledge of anything and be able to teach properly what has been found."[36] Like Ramus, Acontius uses method as a means of ordering his material. But because Acontius, like Ramus, appeals to reason and not the emotions, his method conflicts with the main genres of classical rhetoric, which rely on emotional persuasion.[37] This difference between method and the main oratorical genres is due to their different goals. Method is intended for students of logic; oratory is used to persuade a general audience. In the former, emotions are ignored; in the latter *pathos* often determines the outcome. Since method calls for terseness and logical lucidity, Acontius condemns the use of metaphor in defining terms, arguing that it obscures the concept at hand. Consistent with his vision of a nonemotional rhetoric, mathematics is Acontius's model for discourse.[38]

Still, logical speech by itself will not always persuade. What, according to the proponents of method, is a speaker to do when logic alone proves ineffective? Ramus's Puritan followers answered that those who rejected the logic of Scripture must be coerced. As William Perkins, Puritan writer and disciple of Ramus, states: "Now unto those that fall . . . , that doctrine which doe crosse their error, is to be demonstrated and inculcated (or beaten upon them) together with brotherly affection." The fallen, in order to ensure

35. "Since the usefulness of the arts does not derive from understanding them but from applying them, and since it is necessary—if one is to apply some art—that the teaching of that art be practicable (just as for one who desires to write or read the letters of the alphabet), it seems good that all verbosity should be earnestly avoided in transmitting the arts." Jacobus Acontius, *De Methodo e Opuscoli Religiosi e Filosofici,* ed. Giorgio Radetti (Florence: Vallecchi, 1944), 84, also 86–88; O'Malley, *Jacopo Aconcio,* 115.

36. Acontius, *De Methodo,* 86; quoted in Gilbert, *Renaissance Concepts,* 183.

37. Ramus recognized similarities and dissimilarities between his own method and Acontius's when in a letter to Acontius he wrote: "*De Methodo* is not completely different from my own *Institutes,* yet not completely the same." Peter Ramus, *Praefationes, Epistolae, Orationes* (Paris, 1577), 203–4; cited in Acontius, *De Methodo,* 410. Acontius's method is more rhetorically inclined than Ramus's. Whereas Ramus's method of teaching arranges its propositions in a supposedly objective manner, Acontius's method uses the subjective standard of personal knowledge to order its material, descending from better to lesser known. See *De Methodo,* 164. Ramus also wrote a letter approving Jacobus Acontius's defense of toleration, *Satan's Stratagems.* Ramus, *Praefationes,* 203–4, quoted in Acontius, *De Methodo,* 410, 203–4.

38. *De Methodo,* 134. See *Satan's Stratagems,* 46. "Mathematicians furnish the best established and most convincing demonstrations." Also *De Methodo,* 341, in a letter to Giovanni Wolf, Acontius writes of the clarity of exposition found in mathematics.

their return, "must be very earnestly beaten upon, and those that are unwilling must in a manner bee constrained."[39] Ramist method, which disparages *decorum*, prevented Perkins from acknowledging the emotional impediments to conversion. Acontius, however, assumed a different position toward coercion because he recognized the role of emotions in religious persuasion. He tried to unite a logician's suspicion of emotions with a humanist's appreciation of them.

Rhetoric and Toleration: Continuities and Changes

Dialogue of Giacopo Riccamati

Acontius's Protestantism led him to look for a way the average person could discover religious truth, independently of Church authority, and his commitment to logical method inclined him to search for a rational rhetoric. Acontius found both in the traditionally humanist genre of *sermo*. As noted above, Acontius himself made use of the genre in his *Dialogue of Giacopo Riccamati*. In this early work, Acontius already signals his choice of conversation as the primary model of toleration.[40]

The *Dialogue* is a conversation between two men, Riccamati and Mutio, on the well-being of the soul. It is eventually revealed that Riccamati, the dominant speaker and voice of Acontius, is Lutheran;[41] Mutio is Catholic.

39. William Perkins, *The Art of Prophecying or a Treatise Concerning The Sacred and Onely True Manner and Methode of Preaching*, trans. Thomas Tuke, in *Works* (London: John Legatt, 1631), 2:652; Perry Miller, *The New England Mind: The Seventeenth Century* (Cambridge: Harvard University Press, 1982), 338–39. See relevant sections of Miller for a discussion of Ramus's influence on the Puritans.

40. For a discussion of the *Dialogue*, see O'Malley, *Jacopo Aconcio*, 77–99. Cf. the work of Bernardino Ochino (1487–1565), a humanist contemporary of Acontius, who defended religious toleration in his twenty-eighth dialogue (1563). Like Acontius, in the *Dialogue of Giacopo Ricammati*, Ochino used the dialogue form to explore religious issues. See Ochino's *Dialogi XXX in duos libros divisi*, 2 vols. (Basel, 1563). For a discussion of Ochino's views on religious toleration, see Karl Benrath, *Bernardino Ochino of Siena: A Contribution Towards the History of the Reformation*, trans. Helen Zimmern (New York: Robert Carter & Brothers, 1877), 293–94; Jordan, *Religious Toleration in England*, 1:309–10; and Lecler, *Toleration and the Reformation*, 1:367–69.

41. Riccamati is from Acontius's own town of Ossani, and he offers Mutio "a little book,"

Although this description may call to mind another religious conversation between a Lutheran and a Catholic, Erasmus's *Inquisitio de fide*, Acontius's *Dialogue* does not emphasize the proximity between Lutheran and Catholic dogmas as did Erasmus's colloquy. Unlike the Catholic Aulus and the Lutheran Barbatius in *Inquisitio de fide*, who appear willing to accept each other's creed as orthodox, Riccamati, in the *Dialogue*, argues that the pope and the Roman Catholic Church are the Antichrist (192). Lutherans and Catholics, he explains, are unlikely ever to reconcile, since the Catholic Church will not abandon its errors (201). And while the interlocutors in *Inquisitio de fide* depart still committed to their respective faiths, Mutio leaves the *Dialogue* ready, presumably, to forsake his Catholic beliefs for Lutheranism.[42]

It is not surprising that the gulf between Catholic and Lutheran is greater in Acontius's dialogue than in Erasmus's. Relations between the two faiths had further degenerated over the intervening quarter century. But while Acontius's vilification of the Catholic Church may be viewed as less tolerant than Erasmus's moderation toward the Lutherans, the wide-ranging inquiry that Acontius encourages in the *Dialogue* surpasses anything found in Erasmus. The *Inquisitio de fide* is not an inquiry into religious doctrine itself. Rather, the colloquy is structured as a test of Barbatius's orthodoxy based on the Apostles' Creed—a test that Barbatius passes. It does not question orthodoxy. The *Dialogue*, by contrast, is an investigation in which all dogmas are open to scrutiny. Because ignorance is the cause of damnation, Riccamati contends that people must be willing to question their most sacred assumptions:

> Each religion and sect is firmly persuaded that theirs is the true religion, while it can only be true that one of these religions is true. Think of the infinite multitude of those being deceived. I would like to be assured of what certainty there is that my religion is good. I want to listen to those who condemn it. I want to understand the reasons and proofs that they allege. I want to investigate the responses that they could give to me in opposition and in diligently comparing, I want to try (if I can) to assure myself of the truth. . . . It certainly

which is Acontius's *Somma brevissima della dottrina Christiana. Dialogo di Giacopo Riccamati Ossanese*, in *De Methodo*, 208.

42. Mutio tells Riccamati, at the end of the *Dialogue*, that "you have transformed me from a beast to a man. You know what comes to my mind? I believe firmly that those who live in the deception in which I lived need to be undeceived with the same dexterity with which you undeceived me. . . . You would make a useful work if you reduced all your reasoning to written form with a false title, so as not to scare the scrupulous men." Ibid., 209.

seems to be the case that men of all these sects are committing a grave error in not employing this diligence (189).

Mutio agrees with Riccamati, observing that it is better to question true beliefs than to accept false beliefs unquestionably. The worst penalty for questioning true beliefs is excommunication. In that case, Mutio says, "I can be sure that the road I have chosen is good, and knowing this when I go to confess my sins, I should easily obtain absolution for my excommunication." But the penalty for accepting false beliefs unquestionably is damnation (199). Even if a person's unquestioned beliefs happen to be true, he or she still sins. Riccamati confirms Mutio's views. A person who walks on the right path without being certain, Riccamati argues, is doing the same thing as someone who walks on the wrong path: "For don't they do the same dishonor to God, and in his eyes aren't they both an abomination?" (204). God does not neglect the subjective element of effort in judging humankind: "If God were to have mercy on those who erred, it is more likely [that He will extend his mercy] on those who diligently searched for truth rather than on those who did not bother" (198–99).

Riccamati suggests two acceptable ways to investigate the truth. The first is to examine Scripture for oneself. The second is to seek out others' opinions, that is, to "ask everybody what the right way is," and then to judge between the different opinions. This second method of consulting with others is nothing other than *sermo*. Unlike Erasmus, however, Acontius does not limit *sermo* to doctrinal adiaphora but includes the fundamentals of faith. Neither does he restrict doctrinal conversation to the scholarly. Revealing his Protestant outlook, and his break with Erasmus, Acontius has Riccamati say that this method of comparison "is not only for priests and brothers, but for all who honor God and hope for salvation" (195). Quoting St. Jerome, Riccamati states: "'The Lord does not write in the gospels like Plato or Aristotle, that is, for the few and obscurely, but He wrote for the people, that is, clearly so that all could understand'" (196).

Why does *sermo* yield knowledge of the truth? Acontius believes that truth will emerge from conversation because truth is more powerful than error. "It seems to me," Mutio declares, "that truth compared to lies would always seem all the more clear and illustrious" (199). This assumption that truth will triumph is not new to Acontius; it dates back to antiquity.[43] But

---

43. This belief in truth's ability to triumph presupposes a rational faith. The Socratic elenchus, for example, is premised on such a faith. Similarly in the Third Book of *Esdras* 4:41

Acontius uses it to bolster the argument, already made by Erasmus, that discussion must be protected in the interest of truth. Because truth will eventually triumph, Acontius argues, conversation should be viewed as a tool of progress that will produce more truth. *Sermo*, for Acontius, is a collective effort to advance divine knowledge: "Today, we do our part; tomorrow, two or three others, and so on. All those who esteem God and their salvation will kindle the desire in others to study Scripture, to understand everybody's opinion, to compare them, and to see which opinions conform to Scripture. And above all, in trusting God, it is impossible that the truth will not come to light."[44] By explicitly introducing his claim for the superior power of truth, Acontius moves closer to the modern "marketplace of ideas" theory than Erasmus. Acontius even cites John Chrysostom's use of the marketplace metaphor in the search for religious truth: " 'Will the ignorant people be excused? No. Because if you want to buy a dress, you should go from one merchant to another until you find the best dress for the best price and buy it. Therefore, the people would do well to go seek all doctors (of religion) asking where one sells sincere truth and where one sells corrupted faith; because it is not forbidden to hear the confessions of everyone and choose the best. Try everything, and hang on to the good one' " (195).

Acontius, however, observes in the *Dialogue* that while truth is stronger than error, truth is not universally embraced. Roman Catholics, for example, reject the truth because "they want to maintain their reputations, riches, grandeurs, and comforts" (201). And the ancient pagans rejected Christianity, though "their religion was ridiculous and crazy." They still maintained their false beliefs because "the power of superstition is almost infinite. Anything, no matter how absurd or impossible can be made to seem true and even infallibly true" (188). Later, in *Satan's Stratagems*, Acontius explains more fully why truth, despite its superiority, does not prevail in all cases. There he shows that truth will triumph only in the proper rhetorical context.

A Theology of Skepticism

Erasmus envisioned preaching as the rhetorical genre of essential doctrines and conversation as the genre of doctrinal adiaphora. Acontius, however,

---

it is written that "truth is mighty and will prevail." See Schauer, *Free Speech*, 209–210 n. 9. See also Walter Bagehot, "The Metaphysical Basis of Toleration," in *Literary Studies*, ed. R. H. Hutton (London, 1884), 425.

44. *De Methodo*, 202.

did not recognize this rhetorical distinction. In *Satan's Stratagems*, Acontius presents conversation as the best genre for treating all doctrine, adiaphoral and essential. Preaching is almost never mentioned in *Satan's Stratagems*, although the work focuses on religious doctrine: how to discover true doctrine, how to communicate it, and how to confront erroneous doctrine. Acontius's choice of *sermo* as the genre of all doctrinal matters, however, blurs Erasmus's line between doctrines that are known with certainty, which are preached (but not discussed), and doctrines that are not known with certainty, which can be debated. Because all beliefs are open to question in conversation, Acontius cannot insulate some beliefs—the fundamentals— from scrutiny, as Erasmus wished. Thus, even when Acontius intends to use *sermo* as a tool of persuasion, that is, to win over the heretic, he recognizes that "orthodox" speakers are simultaneously forced to examine their own beliefs. Unlike preaching, conversation is not simply directed toward effecting a change in the listener; it is also turned inward on the speaker: "No man whatsoever, being but a man, ought to be so confident as to be persuaded that he cannot err and to imagine, when controversy arises on any matter, that it will be but lost labor for him to hear any one who speaks about it."[45] For though there are only two states in which people can find themselves, the light of truth or the darkness of error, it is a "matter of fact . . . that there is never so much light that some clouds of error do not still remain" (8). Since there is only one truth but many opinions on every matter, we can only conclude that many of these opinions are wrong. Even the ostensibly wise are not immune to error, seeing that they disagree among themselves over what the truth is (51). Acontius, therefore, calls for an initial skepticism toward all beliefs. He lays the foundation for this skepticism in orthodox Christian terms.

It was the Fall, in Acontius's view, that rendered humanity corrupt and lustful. Hence the present human condition is "very little unlike the nature of the foul demons" (7). Yet human beings are not thoroughly corrupt. Certain traces of our former nature still remain, which goad us to some understanding of God. With the help of the Spirit, Acontius believes, we may even receive eternal salvation (8). But Satan, that "wily old fox," seeks to destroy us in any way possible. When we know God's truth, Satan attempts to lead us into error. If we are already in error, Satan tries to ensure that we remain ignorant. What are Satan's means? Our passions, the fruit of the Fall. Taking advantage of human pride and hate, Satan is able to prevent us from

45. *Satan's Stratagems*, 20.

thinking rationally and, therefore, from discovering our errors. To increase the influence of the passions, Satan fosters bitter arguments in which the participants engage in verbal abuse rather than rational discussion. Our conviction, derived from pride, that we alone possess the truth is reinforced by hate for opponents who "have put all their confidence in mere violence and insolence" (14–15). The result of Satan's instigations is that we, already prone to irrationality, are deprived of any vestige of judgment. Satan has created a world populated by those who are certain they know the truth, but are actually compelled to error by their passions.

On the basis of his pessimistic view of human nature, Acontius concludes that the perceived truth must always be questioned. Because of our propensity to err, we must be willing to consider opposing viewpoints. Like Erasmus, Acontius recognizes the implications of this argument. If we cannot be sure of our own beliefs, then we cannot impose them on others. Yet, like Erasmus, he is also unwilling to reject the possibility of religious knowledge. Acontius asks, "Are we to approve of perpetual faltering in matters of faith?" "Not so," he answers (20). Acontius does not accept the conclusions of the ancient skeptics who, after presenting the probable arguments on both sides of every issue, "maintained that all things were a matter of opinion and that there was no certain knowledge of anything" (175). Acontius wants certainty, but must reconcile this certainty with his skepticism. He accomplishes this by adopting Erasmus's distinction between the fundamentals of faith and the adiaphora: "For all the articles of the true doctrine are not of one kind. There are some so necessary to be known, that they ought to be fixed and certain in the minds of all. There are others which, though matters of controversy among the churches, nevertheless do not destroy agreement in the faith" (54). But, as a Protestant, Acontius cannot simply identify the fundamentals with the universal consensus of the Church and exclude those doctrines from his skepticism. Instead, Acontius develops two forms of skepticism: one for the fundamentals of faith, the other for the nonessentials. The difference between these two skepticisms permits him to condemn the view that "there is no place for certainty in divine matters" (23), while still advising others to be skeptical of all dogmas until they have been carefully examined (19).

The skepticism Acontius extends to the fundamentals of faith acts as an impetus to the discovery of truth. People must be skeptical of what they believe are the fundamentals, according to Acontius, because without such skepticism, they will continue to cling to their errors. Not even Acontius's own Protestant beliefs escape skeptical scrutiny. "Although in our age the gospel has, as it were, come to life again, . . . [each person] must again and again see whether any blemish is still left, or whether in any part [the gospel] has not been fully restored to its original purity and original lustre" (88). We must make certain for ourselves that we know the fundamentals, and doubt is the first step to certainty. "No one," Acontius writes, "is more averse from [skepticism] than I—But on no account," he continues, "would I have a man, who has not yet arrived at any certainty and is perhaps still plunged in false beliefs, lay claim to knowledge" (23). Even when someone has received correct beliefs from others, unless he personally knows that these doctrines are true, he is in danger of lapsing into error. Imperfect persuasion, Acontius argues, is an unstable basis for faith. Once knowledge is attained, however, the believer can never be brought to error: "The man in whom sure knowledge resides, so that he has true, consistent and infallible reasons to give for the opinion he holds, cannot be brought to doubt that matter or be seduced" (20). We should understand the transient doubts accompanying the search for truth as we do the pain associated with healing: uncomfortable yet necessary.[46] Although many will not reach knowledge immediately but only after lengthy inquiry, it is more hazardous for them to accept their beliefs without such examination than to embrace them blindly.

Skepticism of the fundamentals, however, is only temporary for Acontius. Because every person, with the help of the Spirit, is capable of finding the fundamentals of faith, there is no need for "perpetual faltering in matters of faith." Scripture is never so obscure that at least those articles, "which are necessary to be known for the attainment of salvation, can[not] easily be understood" (83). Therefore, those who continue to deny the essentials of faith may be excommunicated from the Church, though Acontius believes excommunication is a last resort, reserved for malicious heretics.[47] But while skepticism of the fundamentals is temporary, it is not pathological. This attitude distinguishes Acontius from Erasmus. Although Erasmus did not demand immediate orthodoxy of all Christians, he would have preferred it. He was willing to tolerate error or uncertainty, *ad tempus*, only because it was expedient to do so. But Acontius viewed uncertainty as healthy. He encouraged it as a necessary step in the search for religious knowledge. And for Acontius, unlike Erasmus, the need to inquire applied not only to the

---

46. Pain, "although it is always regarded as bad, nevertheless if accepted for the sake of getting rid of some grave sickness, appears to assume the character of that which is good, and not only good but notably good." Ibid., 21.

47. Ibid., 34–35, 61–62; Jordan, *Religious Toleration in England*, 1:352–54.

learned but to the common man: "For a man is guilty of no sin, even if he is only a porter, because he reads Holy Writ, because he inquires into the sure foundations of salvation, because he confers with his friends or his equals or even with those more learned than himself. Nay rather, he is worthy of the highest praise on that account, and all men should be encouraged to do the same."[48]

In contrast to the temporary skepticism of the fundamentals, Acontius permits continued skeptical investigation of adiaphora. Like Erasmus, however, Acontius limits skeptical inquiry in adiaphora to "profitable" questions that do not derive from "impertinent curiosity." Echoing Cicero's principle that speech should ultimately effect action, Acontius excludes "futile and vain questions" from discussion.[49] But on profitable questions, Acontius writes, "one man may rightly hold one opinion on this point and one another" (58). To distinguish essential from nonessential doctrines, Acontius composes a "watchword of the faith," in which the few fundamentals are enumerated.[50] This minimal list, more explicit than anything Erasmus or Cassander composed, was latitudinarian in intent. Acontius hoped that the watchword would unite all who professed it "as Christians and brothers," equally deserving of "the same religious rights" (203). And for all matters not included in the confession, that is, "whatever controversies were still left," Acontius called for toleration: "Those who accept the necessary things [should] forbear one another and discuss their controversies lovingly and kindly as brothers."[51]

48. *Satan's Stratagems*, 136.

49. Ibid., 25–31, 87. Like Erasmus, Acontius accepts the idea that doctrines can be nonessential yet useful. Thus he distinguishes between "those things which are necessary" and "whatever things have any use at all." Ibid., 198.

50. The following are the beliefs that make up Acontius's confession: (1) That there is one true God and he whom he sent, Jesus Christ, and the Holy Spirit. And that it is not right to deny that the Father is one and the Son another, because Jesus Christ is truly the Son of God; (2) that man is subject to the wrath and judgment of God. And that the dead will come to life again, the just to everlasting happiness, but the wicked to everlasting torments; (3) that God sent his Son Jesus into the world, who, being made man, died for our sins and was raised from the dead for our justification; (4) that if we believe in the Son of God, we shall obtain life through his name; (5) that there is salvation in none other; not in the blessed virgin, or in Peter, or in Paul, or in any other saint, or any other name whatever. And that there is no righteousness in the law or in the commandments or inventions of men; (6) that there is one baptism in the name of the Father and of the Son and of the Holy Spirit. With the exception of article 5, which is directed against Roman Catholics, the beliefs listed above would include all Trinitarian Christians. Ibid., 201–2.

51. Ibid., 203, 199. Acontius implies that there are doctrines intermediate between the essentials that must be believed and the nonessentials that are fully left to individual judgment.

Forms of *Sermo*

The skeptical inquiry that Acontius urges is *sermo*. His version of *sermo*, like Cicero's and Erasmus's, consists of argument *in utramque partem* in which the individual can compare contrary opinion and decide truth for himself. But *sermo*, for Acontius, can assume a variety of forms. It can occur as an internal conversation, in which each person considers both sides of an issue to arrive at the truth:

> Now it would be one means of arriving at the truth, if having found an interpretation which appeared to support your opinion, you assumed the character of the objector and diligently inquired what could be said against it, and did not at once applaud your own cleverness. The result would be that those who disagree with one another would not be in perpetual disagreement, but that those who err would in the end give way to those who think aright.

Sermo can also take the traditional form of a conversation between individuals, each searching for truth. The product of such discussion, like the product of one person's inner debate, is greater truth: "He who doubts is stimulated to investigation of what is true, and when many investigate, it is strange if none finds it; moreover if, when the truth is found, liberty of discussion is granted, when a comparison is made, that which is best must needs come to light" (132). Therefore, Acontius concludes, prohibiting discussion is in Satan's interest: "It is not expedient for Satan to allow freedom of inquiring in his kingdom" (133).

Acontius's conception of *sermo* is more expansive than Cicero's intimate gathering of friends or Erasmus's small scholarly discussion. Conversation, according to Acontius, is the method that churches, though large and diverse, should use to investigate doctrinal matters. He describes the long-standing tradition of "common prophecy," in which all are given the opportunity of expressing their opinion in the church, even the most

---

These doctrines are not "chief articles of the faith," but they may still involve deadly error: "For just as one science is derived from another, so errors grow from errors." In these doctrines, one may maintain error privately and "nevertheless be of the number of the brothers." But if such a one seduces others, he or she should be excommunicated. Acontius, however, does not pursue the matter elsewhere. It would seem that Acontius justifies this seducer's excommunication, in part, on the grounds of causing disorder among the believers—"for he sorely offends the brothers." Ibid., 61.

unlearned or those suspected of heresy (89–92): "It will be time enough for a man to be condemned, when he has been fully and carefully heard, and when the weight of his reasoning has been tested to a nicety" (174). After everyone has had the opportunity to speak, debate stops and the church arrives at a collective decision: "Wherefore when each man has expressed his opinion, he must abide by the decision of others, and not persistently contend" (92). Despite this consensus, Acontius does not deny the individual's right to maintain his or her own position. Rather, Acontius only insists that the dissenter cannot continue to harangue the other members of the church. "Unless this is done, sure it is that there will be no end to contentions" (92). Acontius desires concord in the church, but makes no claims that the church's opinion is decisive. He reemphasizes the voluntary nature of consensus in his discussion of another form of *sermo*, the Church council.

Acontius explains that because he is writing to a Protestant audience, he does not have to argue at length that the decision of a Church council is not in-and-of-itself binding. "No one," Acontius asserts, "is compelled to agree with the decisions of councils" (94–95). Nevertheless, Acontius believes that "councils should indeed be convened." The purpose of councils, he explains, is to present a variety of opinions, so that each person can compare and judge for himself.

> Councils come together, that, when any controversies that disturb the church are laid before them, and each person is given the opportunity of free speech, . . . others then decide, not that on a show of hands the decision may rest with the majority, every one being under the necessity of agreeing thereto—for so the greater part of meeting would generally outvote the better part—, but that each man might weigh what has been said, so that, if it seemed to be proved by fitting testimonies of Holy Writ, he would embrace it himself and endeavor to persuade others of it, not on the authority of the council, but by those testimonies of the word of God, which he had learnt in the council. (95–96)

The importance of a council, then, does not lie in its pronouncement, but in the occasion it provides for discussion of the issues. What the council participants contribute is their viewpoint. Consequently, prestige should not influence a person's selection to a council. Unlike Erasmus, who emphasizes the elitist nature of *sermo*, Acontius writes of the council's members that "there will be no need for a man to be either a bishop or an archbishop or the pope of Rome, or one with any distinguished reputation for learning" (97). No one should be excluded that "is seen to be at all endowed with godliness and God's Spirit." And if it happens that a fool or an ungodly man is somehow admitted to a council, "since no regard is to be had to the number of votes, but only to what is said, . . . he will not be able to do much harm, if only he is looked upon as such as his own words show him to be" (97–98).

The *Decorum* of Doctrinal Conversation

Consistent with *sermo*, à la Cicero and Erasmus, Acontius's paradigm of conversation appeals to reason, not the emotions. Reason, which Acontius identifies with the spirit of God, should hold sway, and the passions— "anger, arrogance, and clamor, . . . which Satan governs"—should be banished (18). Judgment must be "free from every mental emotion," if we are to arrive at knowledge. "All mental emotion weakens and obscures the judgment."[52] Acontius rejects the emotionalism of the main genres of classical rhetoric, which rely on *pathos* and *ethos*, as well as *logos*, to persuade. For Acontius, the passions are the reason why true doctrine is perverted.[53] If passions were eliminated, then human beings would be able to arrive at the truth by themselves. Anticipating Milton's argument in the *Areopagitica* by over a hundred years, Acontius writes: "Let truth contend warily with impostures, and nevertheless it needs prove the stronger."[54] Acontius maintains here that the individual's *logos*, with the aid of the Spirit

52. Ibid., 139–40, 54. Cf. John Goodwin's preface to the English edition of *Satan's Stratagems*: "It is hard to say, whether that hand which desires to be lifted up against Error and Heresie, with success, had more need of *softness or strength*. Few mens Errors finde access to their judgments, but by way of their affections:

> He that will the Judgment win,
> With th' Affections *must begin*

"Nor will it be easie for men to come at them to dethrone them but by making their approaches the same way; I mean, by making friends of their affections, that they may not side with their Judgments against them." Jacobus Acontius, *'Darkness Discovered' or the Devils Secret Stratagems laid open whereby He labors to make havock of the People of God, by his wicked and damnable Designs for destroying the Kingdom of Christ* (London: J. Macock, 1651; rpt., Delmar, N.Y.: Scholars' Facsimiles & Reprints, 1978).
53. *Satan's Stratagems*, 9.
54. Ibid., 74. Milton's words are: "Let her [Truth] and Falsehood grapple; who ever knew Truth put to the wors, in a free and open encounter?" See John Milton, *Areopagitica*, in *Complete Prose Works of John Milton* (New Haven: Yale University Press, 1953–74), 2:561.

(the universal *logos*), will perceive the truth on its own, provided that the passions do not obscure its judgment.

Acontius's faith in the power of truth is conditional. Truth must "contend *warily* [my emphasis] with impostures" if it is to prove stronger. Acontius elucidates what it means for truth to contend warily: "If all our hope were placed in [the Lord], if we fought with his word, inspired with his Spirit (which is to be gained by unceasing prayer), carefully and discreetly avoiding those wiles of Satan, of which we have hitherto been speaking, truly there would be naught for us to fear from heretics."[55] The wiles of Satan, to which Acontius refers, are Satan's attempts to stir up the passions through persecutions and quarrels. Acontius accepts that truth is naturally stronger than error, but he is also aware that when truth is not presented properly, the emotions, not reason, will determine judgment. There is no inevitability, he argues, to the triumph of truth. Truth is never so apparent that it will be recognized under all conditions.

Like his trust in the superior power of truth, Acontius's recognition that truth does not always succeed is not peculiar to him. For example, Aristotle in the *Rhetoric* takes a similar position to Acontius. There Aristotle justifies rhetoric for its capacity to ensure that "the true and the just [which] are naturally superior to their opposites" are not defeated, the presumption being that truth will not always succeed on its own if it is delivered improperly.[56] Acontius's fellow humanists also joined him in their qualified faith in the triumph of truth. Thomas More assumes in *Utopia* that "truth by its own natural force would finally emerge sooner or later and stand forth conspicuously," yet he adds the proviso "provided the matter was handled reasonably and moderately."[57] And the Socinian humanist Johannes Crell (1590–1633) writes that "it is indeed the nature of truth, particularly celestial and salutary truth, that it penetrates more easily than lies and errors into a well-disposed mind," but only "when it is suitably expressed and set out with solid arguments."[58] Likewise, Milton's apotheosis of truth is tempered by his confession that truth, "to our eyes blear'd and dimm'd with prejudice and custom, is more unsightly and unplausible then many error."[59]

Underlying the preceding observations is the rhetorical principle of *deco-*

---

55. *Satan's Stratagems*, 74.
56. *Rhetoric* 1355a20–25.
57. *Complete Works of St. Thomas More*, 4:221.
58. Johannes Crell, *Vindiciae pro religionis libertate*, 2d ed. (Eleutheropolis, 1650), 35; cited in Lecler, *Toleration and the Reformation*, 1:419.
59. *Complete Prose Works of John Milton*, 2:565.

rum, more specifically, the *decorum* of *sermo.* Because truth is the speaker's goal, this speaker must neutralize the passions of the listeners. In line with his condemnation of the passions as destructive, Acontius describes the speaker's accommodation to listeners in terms reminiscent of homeostasis. Believers must adapt themselves to the conditions of those who err in order to rehabilitate them. Like true homeostasis, accommodation, if it is to effect equilibrium, must take into account the various unnatural situations which surround the individual.[60] Acontius argues that to restore reason to a position of dominance, one must actively nullify the influence of the passions. This holds true not only for heretics, who must be brought to the truth, but also for those who have found the truth, seeing that there is no guarantee that reason will continue to predominate in them. To negate the baneful effect of *pathos,* one must first understand its appeal. Rhetoric supplies Acontius with this understanding. By understanding how someone can be led astray by anger or pride, Acontius seeks to ensure that believers will avoid these emotions. Believers engaged in conversations with heretics will only persuade them by using that reasoning and language which would have the "power of inducing that tranquillity of mind and . . . healthiness of judgment" necessary to rational thought.[61] Because intellectual conversation requires a proper rhetorical setting, Acontius distinguishes the marketplace of ideas from the economic marketplace. The economic marketplace, Acontius implies, functions without controls on speech. In this marketplace, everyone speaks "what comes to his tongue's end."[62] In the marketplace of ideas, however, attention must be given to speech and demeanor. Anyone accorded the right of speaking in the church should "have all rashness and shamelessness kept at a distance."[63] Unless the

---

60. On homeostasis, see Walter B. Cannon, *The Wisdom of the Body* (New York: W.W. Norton, 1939).

61. *Satan's Stratagems,* 11. Acontius alludes to the *decorum* of conversation, which eschews emotional manipulation, in his citation of Ennius's contrast of the good orator with the rude soldier. See *Satan's Stratagems,* 190. Acontius's faith in rhetorical accommodation would seem to be at odds with the Protestant doctrine of predestination. If one assumes that God grants faith and that human beings cannot influence the outcome, then it is beyond our control to manipulate persuasion. This apparent conflict makes it unlikely that Acontius, who recognized the role of rhetoric in religious conversion, held to a strict predestinarian view. O'Malley, *Jacopo Aconcio,* 153, argues that the contents of *Satan's Stratagems* opposes a belief in predestination. For further discussion of Acontius and predestination see O'Malley, *Jacopo Aconcio,* 108, 110, 130, and 132.

62. Acontius, *Darkness Discovered,* 129.

63. *Satan's Stratagems,* 92–93.

marketplace of ideas is regulated to ensure tranquillity, truth is unlikely to be discovered.

Acontius's position on *ethos* illustrates his attempts to neutralize, but not ignore, the passions. Like Cicero, who rejected *ethos* in conversation, Acontius contends that authority has no bearing on the truth. Judging an opinion on the basis of who said it will only promote error. For example, if heretics' views were condemned *in toto* on the basis of their evil character, then not only their errors but also their truths would have to be rejected. Or, if we accept an individual's beliefs because that person is reputed to be good, we are quite likely accepting erroneous beliefs, given that the appearance of morality often stands in inverse proportion to its actual existence.[64] Consequently, the people must be exhorted to ignore *ethos* and pay attention instead to what is said: "For even if Satan asserts what is true, it still remains true, while on the contrary, if an angel from heaven asserts what is false, it cannot be made true on that account."[65] We should not, for example, believe that Luther's argument against justification by works is true because Luther said it, but because we see that the Bible and the Spirit testifying to our hearts confirm its truth.[66] As it is our responsibility to eliminate the effect of *ethos* on the formation of our own beliefs, so too we ought not persuade others by employing argument from character.

Nevertheless, Acontius understands that most listeners base their beliefs on their assessment of the speaker's character: "For man, as a rule, is so disposed, that he believes regard must be had not to what is said, but to who has said it" (142). Therefore, while Acontius will not use *ethos* positively to persuade, he tries to ensure that the speaker's character will not work

64. Ibid., 142, 84–86. "Simple men, enemies of guile and all other evil arts, since they suppose they should take greater pains to be good than to seem so, will very easily be outdone in acquiring a reputation for saintliness by skilful men greedy of office; for they will be less careful in hiding their blemishes. . . . He who has set his heart on office will be most careful to hide all his faults."

65. Ibid., 142. Acontius's rejection of *ethos* as a legitimate proof explains why he consciously avoided the citation of authorities, save the Bible, in *Satan's Stratagems*. This is in marked contrast to the other great sixteenth-century defender of toleration, Sebastian Castellio, who in his *De haereticis* supported his case by citing the writings of various authors.

66. Ibid., 97. Acontius's opposition to *ethos* is consistent with his argument against the authority of church councils. Although "in the councils of the apostles regard had to be paid not so much to what was decided, as to those by whom it was decided," this is not true of the councils of their successors, where "it matters not so much who they are who have issued any decree, but we have much more to consider what it is they have decreed and of what nature, what testimonies are quoted from Holy Writ, how plainly and clearly those testimonies show the proposition which is being asserted."

negatively to inflame the listener's passions and render the listener incapable of rational thought. By permitting the audience's negative impression of him to obscure the truth of his words, the speaker makes the auditors vulnerable to the *ethos* of another speaker. Therefore, "the advocates of truth" must ensure that they are not only free of crime, "but (if it may be) all suspicion of crime also."[67] Although Acontius's position here runs counter to the basic genres of classical rhetoric, it accords with Cicero's conception of *sermo*. Both Cicero and Acontius distinguish between *ethos*, which is inappropriate to *sermo*, and the credibility of the speaker, which is necessary in *sermo*, if the speaker's message is to be heard.

Toleration: Precondition to Conversation

The *decorum* of conversation is at the bottom of Acontius's theory of toleration. Like Erasmus, Acontius believes that religious persecution obstructs the search for truth. Prudence has shown that harassment only confirms the erring in their errors. Therefore, those suspected of error must be approached with patience and moderation, so that they may calmly arrive at the truth.[68] The whole of the second book of Acontius's *Satan's Stratagems* is a practical guide to rhetorical *decorum*. In it he describes how to conduct a conversation with those in error.[69] His advice to the speaker includes the following: the speakers' tone and words should be conducive to calm debate; speakers must adapt themselves to what the person, time, and place demand; they must begin with their audiences' presuppositions, not

67. Ibid., 165. "Every offence is in itself worthy of the very severest punishment, but if a man commits it, who has lent his name to the Gospel truth, and commits it in the sight of the ungodly, so that occasion is hereby given them of bringing the Gospel into ill repute, or if the minds of the weak are thereby offended, so that they think those dogmas cannot be pious and godly, when those who profess them lead such a life, then verily will God very greatly abhor it." See also 38–39, and 130–31.

68. Ibid., 17–19, 36–37. Acontius does permit the use of sharp language under rare circumstances, but essentially rules it out: "But this nevertheless I do maintain, that a great and serious and very certain cause is needed, before recourse is had to it [strong words], for instance the discovery that what you are attacking is an error, and a great one, and that the author of it is a man of perverse and obstinate disposition, who will not assent to the truth even when he learns it." Ibid., 113.

69. Cf. "A Letter of the learned and judicious Mr Dury (one of the Assembly of Ministers) to Mr Samuel Hartlib touching the Author," written about Acontius in 1648: "I make no doubt but it [that is, *Satan's Stratagems*] will be convincing sufficiently to such as are free from *hardness of heart* in the ways of factiousness; and are not blinded with *carnal ends*, in the prosecution of Religious Controversies." Acontius, *Darkness Discovered*.

their own; and they should be very careful never to misrepresent their opponents' position. Common to all these various strategies is the assumption that it is not enough for the speech's contents to be true. Speakers are also obligated to foster an environment in which their listeners are capable of understanding that truth. This means that speakers should eschew all verbal abuse. They must do so not only for the sake of their interlocutors, but also out of concern for the nonparticipating spectators, who are affected by a speaker's abusive language. As some onlookers will identify the means of debate with the argument itself, improper means will come to be equated with erroneous doctrine, even if the doctrine itself is true. Hence, some will presume a mean-spirited presentation to be prima facie evidence of error. Others will be so repulsed at the sight of these contentions that they will lose interest in religion altogether.[70] Either way, Satan will have achieved his aim of bringing greater darkness to mankind.

Acontius applies his argument against verbal abuse even more forcefully to physical compulsion, directing his words here particularly to the magistrates. Contrary to the claims of many in the clergy, Acontius states that the persecution or execution of heretics does not alleviate error. Quite the opposite, it exacerbates heresy by magnifying the role of the passions. Thus, if kept alive, heretics will hold firm to their beliefs. Anger and pride prevent them from accepting the possibility that their persecutors may be correct. And if killed, heretics are forever denied the opportunity for reform. They will only stand as martyrs to others. For persecution proves no more helpful to those who are not heretics than to the heretics themselves. The witnesses to such acts of compulsion will be moved to sympathize with the heretic, believing that it is the "lot of the godly to endure persecution, disgrace and affliction for the sake of religion" (64). The people's hatred of the pastors who support persecution, already viewed as tyrants, will also be strengthened. All too often the public's perception of the clergy as evil will prevent the minister's truth from being heard. The heretic's views, however, will find support as a result of the *ethos* that heretic acquires through being persecuted.

Because persecution is inimical to the discovery of truth, Acontius implores magistrates to refrain from using force against heretics. But Acontius also seeks a positive role for the state, based on its religious function to facilitate its citizens' knowledge of the divine law. The state can increase the amount of truth found in its jurisdiction, according to Acontius, by guaran-

---

70. *Satan's Stratagems*, 15–16.

teeing religious toleration and the free flow of ideas: "But the magistrate's authority is chiefly necessary herein, that he suffer not lack of self-restraint and lust of evil-speaking in any man, whosoever he be. . . . If there are controversies about religion, let the contest be carried on by testimonies and arguments on either side, but as to anything that tends to mutual exasperation, let the magistrates take diligent care that they abstain therefrom in fear of the penalty enacted for so doing" (78–79). In contrast to the modern theory of the state, which guarantees religious liberty out of an obligation to protect its citizens' individual rights, Acontius viewed the state as a rhetorical arbiter, which interceded to moderate speech for the communal interest in religious truth. He hoped that by curbing passionate and unrestrained disputation, the magistrate would encourage reasoned discussion, which would yield greater knowledge.

Acontius envisioned his minimal creed as another institutional restraint on heated and excessive debate. As seen earlier, he identified this "watchword" with the limits of uncertainty. But Acontius, more explicitly than any of his contemporaries, also pointed up the rhetorical advantages of compiling a confession. Although Acontius agreed with Erasmus that the fewer the essentials of faith, the more room there was for tolerance, he went on to suggest that a confession would lead to toleration by regulating the acrimony of religious discussion. To Acontius treating something as essential, when it was not, hindered rational discourse. For example, if those unsure of a doctrine's necessity are persuaded that it is in fact necessary, their judgment will be determined by their emotions, not their reason; since the threat of eternal damnation is so awesome, it is nearly impossible for anyone to consider rationally the doctrine in question.[71] "And in the case of those in whom the error has already taken root, what is so great an obstacle to the possibility of their being weaned from error as the idea that they cannot surrender their opinion without forfeiting their salvation?" (55). When every person presents personal beliefs as articles of faith, which all must accept, discussion degenerates into "discords, dissensions, and brawlings," further strengthening the rule of the passions (189). Acontius's solution is to propose a confession in which only those doctrines necessary to salvation are included. This, he hoped, might mitigate the intensity of the disputants' emotions, thereby reducing the number of quarrels and persecutions (198, 203).

71. Ibid., 54. "So far is this alarm from helping the judgment in any way to judge aright, that it actually hinders it in a very great measure. For all mental emotion weakens and obscures the judgment."

Acontius and Mill: A Comparison

About two hundred years after Acontius composed *Satan's Stratagems*, John Stuart Mill wrote in *On Liberty*: "The dictum that truth always triumphs over persecution, is one of those pleasant falsehoods which men repeat after one another till they pass into commonplaces, but which all experience refutes. . . . It is a piece of idle sentimentality that truth, merely as truth, has any inherent power denied to error, prevailing against the dungeon and the stake."[72] Mill's argument here is that persecution, in the past, and social convention, in the present, were and are able to stifle truth. He concludes in favor of liberty of discussion. Contrary to common opinion, however, Mill's argument and conclusion are not novel; Acontius anticipates both.[73]

Like Mill, Acontius understands that truth can be hindered through physical and nonphysical restraints on free discussion. Concerning physical coercion, Acontius believes that Satan tries to limit the spread of religious knowledge by "restraining and removing" the right to free discussion.[74] To counter Satan, Acontius advocates liberty of discussion; by allowing true and false opinions to be compared, truth will be advanced (132). Again like Mill, he recognizes that formal liberty of discussion does not guarantee that the discussion will be genuinely free.[75] But whereas Mill focuses on social convention as the prime threat to open discussion, Acontius concentrates on

72. John Stuart Mill, *On Liberty*, in *Collected Works of John Stuart Mill*, ed. J. M. Robson, vol. 18 (Toronto: University of Toronto Press, 1977), 238.

73. See Schauer, *Free Speech*, 22, who maintains that prior to Mill, "truth was considered self-evident, needing only to be expressed to be recognized."

74. *Satan's Stratagems*, 132.

75. Acontius anticipates another of Mill's arguments for free discussion. Mill writes that unless the received opinion is "vigorously and earnestly contested . . . the meaning of the doctrine itself will be in danger of being lost, or enfeebled, and deprived of its vital effect on the character and conduct: the dogma becoming a mere formal profession, inefficacious for good, but cumbering the ground, and preventing the growth of any real and heartfelt conviction, from reason or personal experience." *On Liberty*, 258. Acontius similarly describes a society in which heresy and disagreement have been silenced by the sword and finds that true religion does not benefit. Without the freedom to discuss religious issues publicly, the people forget religious doctrine: "Discipline is gradually relaxed, godliness grows cold and a strange forgetfulness of God and his law creeps over [this society]." This allows for seducers to change the original doctrine subtly, over a long period of time, without the knowledge of the people. The churchmen, at the same time, are unaware of any such changes in doctrine, for the dissemination of error must be spread behind their backs to avoid punishment. Furthermore, since the pastors place all their hopes for preserving doctrine and resisting heresy in the use of the magistrate's sword, they do not realize that they must defend the doctrine with the word of God. Their learning weakens and they become lazy, allowing for ignorance to settle in. These pastors become incapable of defending true doctrine against heresy, "so that afterwards Satan can

improper rhetoric. The easiest way to stop free discussion, according to Acontius, is to prevent the listener from believing the speaker. This may be effected through attacking the speaker's *ethos*: "Now the calumniator's art is this, that when he falsely accuses any man, he may so engage either ear of him, before whom he accuses, that the accused cannot get a hearing; but that he may be condemned without ever being given an opportunity of speaking in the presence of an impartial judge, as if the accusation were absolutely certain and absolutely just" (154). Liberty of opinion does not exist under such conditions. Nor is it correct to call a quarrel, though formally unrestrained, a free discussion, for the passions are then in control. Free discussion, requisite for the truth to triumph, can only be achieved through the use of proper rhetoric. Since bad rhetoric obstructs the quest for truth, Acontius's solution is to employ good rhetoric—*sermo*—through which the passions may be neutralized.

Taken by itself, belief in the power of truth does not lead to toleration. In fact, historically it has often meant quite the opposite. If truth is presumed inevitably to win, if it is seen as self-evident, then in a uniform society the dominant opinions will be accepted as true. The few who disagree will be viewed as obstinate and evil; the possibility that they may be good, rational men who want to know the truth but are unable to find it is not considered. Nor does the assumption that truth will always reveal itself justify tolerating those you deem to be in error. The argument that the heretic is needed because he shows others what to avoid is met with the counterclaim that since truth will inevitably be revealed, the heretic is therefore expendable. For example, although St. Thomas Aquinas allowed that heresy played a positive role in the search for truth since it provided the faithful with an opportunity to contrast truth with error, his willingness to apply the death penalty to heretics implied that their error was not essential to the discovery of truth.[76] It is Acontius's rhetorical concern, a concern with the effects of

---

without any difficulty thrust upon men every kind of superstition and error." *Satan's Stratagems*, 63–64.

76. St. Thomas Aquinas *Summa theologiae* 2, 2, q. 11, art. 3. St. Thomas quotes St. Augustine's statement (*De Gen. cont. Manich.* i. I) that because of heresy " 'we may shake off our sluggishness and long to know the divine Scriptures.' " See *On Genesis: Two Books on Genesis Against the Manichees* and *On the Literal Interpretation of Genesis: An Unfinished Book*, trans. Roland J. Teske, S. J. (Washington, D.C.: Catholic University of America Press, 1991), 48. Nevertheless, St. Thomas writes that "we should consider what they directly intend, and expel them" and that "if heretics be altogether uprooted by death, this is not contrary to Our Lord's command."

words and actions on the listener, that transforms the rationalist faith in the supremacy of truth into an argument for toleration.

Acontius and the Practice of Toleration

The practical implications of Acontius's theory of toleration can be analyzed on two levels: secular and spiritual.[77] First, in the secular realm, toleration is delimited by two conflicting duties: the duty to tolerate heretics and the duty to protect and foster true religion. Like Erasmus, Acontius finds scriptural support for the state's toleration of heretics in the parable of the tares (Matthew 13). Temporal rulers, according to Acontius, must not kill heretics: the tares (the heretics) cannot be uprooted (killed) before the harvest (the last judgment), lest some of the wheat (the godly) also be removed with them.[78] Moreover, heretics should not even be persecuted because persecution is both rhetorically ineffective and presumes an unwarranted infallibility on the part of the persecutor. Nevertheless, Acontius writes:

> There are other things that [the magistrate] can and ought to do, such as to punish irreverent words against God, to chastise those who have ventured to abandon the whole Christian religion and who have ventured to induce any one else to abandon it. If any strange forms of worship have been set on foot or any images put up, he should remove them; he should shield the necks of the godly from the violence and injury of the ungodly, keep the public peace, and other things of that kind.[79]

---

77. Acontius recognizes the Gelasian division between secular and spiritual swords, as did Erasmus.

78. Both Erasmus and Acontius use the parable of the tares to support toleration, but whereas Erasmus prohibits the killing of heretics in the hope that the heretics may repent, Acontius interprets the parable as a safeguard in the interest of the godly, lest they be mistaken for heretics and executed. Acontius does not believe that the possibility of a heretic's reform is sufficient reason to spare his life. *Satan's Stratagems*, 71–72.

79. Ibid., 73. I have previously mentioned the magistrate's duty to ensure that discussions are kept within proper bounds.

Acontius argues here that the magistrate has another religious duty, in addition to the protection of heretics: he must further the faith. This duty, however, limits Acontius's toleration. It permits the magistrate to punish apostates in the interest of true religion. Thus, we can say that it runs counter to the more pervasive demands for toleration advanced in *Satan's Stratagems*. Yet the persecution of apostates makes sense within the context of his Christian humanist argument, which distinguishes Acontius from later proponents of religious liberty. As a humanist, Acontius accepts the utility of the Word in bringing people to the truth. He understands that attention must be paid to the rhetorical packaging of the message. Therefore, physical and verbal coercion are to be eschewed. But if someone renounces Christianity— the Word in its totality—then that person stands outside the bounds of reasoned discussion. Unlike the heretic, the apostate cannot be persuaded of the truth, but ought to be punished to serve as an example to deter others "from any thought of altogether abandoning [God's] worship and depriving his word of all credit": "For an apostate not only abandons the true worship of God, but also deprives the word of God of all credit; with the heretic its authority still remains intact. And so you have other arms besides stones and the sword, wherewith to destroy the heretic and resist him, to wit the word of God, whereas in the case of the apostate you have not."[80] Acontius, the Christian humanist, stops short of full religious toleration. He neither questions the religious basis and character of the civil magistrate's office nor the certainty and singularity of Christianity's truth. On the contrary, he uses rhetoric and toleration to promote the true faith. Full religious liberty could only be promoted either after the state was secularized or Christianity's truth itself was questioned.

Second, regarding the spiritual realm, Acontius maintains that the most extreme punishment available to the Church is excommunication, which can be administered to those who continue to deny the fundamentals of faith.[81] It is unclear whether Acontius believes that Roman Catholics adhere to the fundamentals. Although at one point he recognizes the right of Roman Catholics, "except some few," to belong to the *communio sanctorum*, implying that most Catholics do accept the fundamentals, his articles of faith

---

80. Ibid., 69. Although Acontius does not speak directly of non-Christians, it would seem likely that those who have never accepted Christianity are not liable to punishment. Church tradition, theoretically accepted even by the proponents of persecution, opposed the coercion of non-Christians. See O'Malley, *Jacopo Aconcio*, 163.

81. *Satan's Stratagems*, 54.

would seem to exclude most of them.[82] Thus, in his confession he renounces justification by works and requires belief in salvation solely through Christ, not Mary, Peter, Paul, or any other saints.[83] Acontius's articles of faith, however, are broad enough to comprehend all the Protestant sects. He, unlike almost all other Protestants, would have even accepted the Anabaptists, given that he was excommunicated for defending a minister charged with leniency toward that group.[84]

As excommunication would excite the passions of the excommunicant and those around him, it was to be applied sparingly and cautiously. Only those who persisted obstinately in their heresy were to be cast out. Further, if anyone was to be excommunicated, it was to be done in a manner that was rhetorically correct, since someone who was not only excommunicated but also berated would be disposed to attack the Church and turn others away from it. Acontius draws the parallel between the excommunicant and the private individual trying to persuade another of the truth. In both instances, "more disadvantage than advantage may result from bitterness of language." Therefore, the heretic should be condemned "without any abuse or reproach . . . with signs of sorrow rather than of any anger or hatred."[85] The heretic must be treated, like anyone else, with kindness and moderation. For while toleration in Acontius's view involved legal questions, it demanded much more. It required treating others, including heretics, in a manner conducive to reasoned discourse. In the final analysis Acontius implies that rhetoric, not law, will effect such a climate.

82. O'Malley, *Jacopo Aconcio*, 164.

83. "There is salvation in none other [than Christ]; not in the blessed virgin, or in Peter, or in Paul, or in any other saint, or any other name whatever. And that there is no righteousness in the law or in the commandments or inventions of men." *Satan's Stratagems*, 202.

84. Archbishop Grindal appears to have excommunicated Acontius in 1562 for defending Adrian Haemstade, the minister of the Dutch Church in London. Haemstade was accused of accepting Anabaptists into his congregation, and Acontius wrote a letter in his defense. See O'Malley, *Jacopo Aconcio*, 35–39; Briggs, "Jacopo Aconcio," 484–86; and Jordan, *Religious Toleration in England*, 1:316. Acontius's toleration would have probably extended to the Socinians too; at least the Socinians themselves viewed Acontius as sympathetic. See O'Malley, *Jacopo Aconcio*, 165.

85. *Satan's Stratagems*, 62.

3

Chillingworth: Humanism in the Seventeenth Century

Hooker

Following in the tradition of Erasmus, Acontius, and other Northern humanists was the English theologian Richard Hooker (1554–1600). In his multivolume work *Of the Laws of Ecclesiastical Polity*, Hooker defended the Anglican religious and political order against the Puritans, who denied a scriptural basis to Anglican customs.[1] According to Hooker, the Anglican Church did not need an express scriptural source for its practices since, to him, they were adiaphoral. In such nonessentials, he argued, the Church is permitted to establish its own laws on the basis of rational principles.[2] Like previous humanist defenders of toleration, Hooker viewed the Church as an inclusive institution. For Hooker, the Church could comprehend both Anglican and Puritan beliefs. He went so far as to concede that even the Roman Catholic Church, though a Church of "little power" (Revelation 3:8) and a "crazed Church,"[3] was nevertheless a Church, in communion with other Churches: "Notwithstanding so far as lawfullie we may, we have held, and doe hold fellowship with them [Roman Catholics]. . . . [W]ith Rome we

---

1. The Preface and first four volumes were published in 1593; volume 5 in 1597. The last three volumes, which were partial or unfinished drafts, were published after his death: volumes 6 and 8 in 1648, volume 7 in 1661.

2. Richard Hooker, *Of the Laws of Ecclesiastical Polity* 3.9.1, 3.3.3–4. All citations from Hooker, unless otherwise indicated, are from *The Folger Library Edition of the Works of Richard Hooker*, ed. W. Speed Hill (Cambridge: Harvard University Press, 1977). See also Lecler, *Toleration and the Reformation*, 2:401–2, and Jordan, *Religious Toleration in England*, 1:226–28.

3. Cited in Lecler, *Toleration and the Reformation*, 2:402.

dare not communicate concerning sundrie hir grosse and greevous abomi-
nations, yet touching those maine partes of Christian truth wherein they
constantlie still persist, we gladly acknowledge them to be of the familie of
Jesus Christ."[4] Although a virtuous life and "inward beleefe of hart" are
ultimately necessary for salvation, everyone who claims to be a Christian
should be considered a member of the visible Church: "If by externall
profession they be Christians, then are they of the visible Church of
Christ . . . , although they be impious idolators, wicked heretiques, persons excommunicable, yea, and cast out for notorious improbitie" (3.1.7).

Like Acontius, Hooker believed that all religious beliefs, including the
fundamentals of faith, should be investigated rationally. "Exclude the use of
naturall reasoning about the sense of holy scripture concerning the articles
of faith," he asks, "and then that the scripture doth concerne the articles of
faith who can assure us?" Hooker commends, as did his predecessors,
argument *in utramque partem*. He writes: "Our Lord and Saviour him selfe
did hope by disputation to doe some good, yea by disputation not onely of
but against the truth, albeit with purpose for the truth" (3.8.16–17). Such
disputation should take place in a tranquil environment. Thus, addressing
the Puritans in his Preface to *Ecclesiastical Polity*, Hooker requests that any
debate between them and his own Anglicans should be by "solemne conference in orderlie and quiet sort" (Preface 5.3).

Reminiscent of his intellectual forbears, Hooker observes that much of
what is discussed cannot be determined with certainty, only probability. In
these cases, people cannot be forced to subscribe to what are, at best, only
probable beliefs: "Now it is not required or can be exacted at our hands, that
we should yeeld unto any thing other assent, then such as doth answere the
evidence which is to be had of that we assent unto." Therefore, it is
permissible, "even in matters divine," to "doubt and suspend our judgement" about some doctrinal issues, "inclyning neyther to one side nor other,
as namely touching the time of the fall both of man and Angels." About
other doctrines, Hooker continues, "we may very well retaine an opinion
that they are probable and not unlikely to be true, as when we hold that men
have their soules rather by creation then propagation or that the mother of
our Lorde lived alwaies in the state of virginitie as well after his birth as
before" (2.7.5).

Although Hooker supports conversation as a means of investigating truth,
he is wary of the strife and confusion that ensue from discussion without any

4. *Of the Laws of Ecclesiastical Polity* 3.1.10.

authoritative arbiter. Therefore, contrary to Ciceronian *sermo*, in which there is no final judgment, Hooker's "conference or disputation" needs a conclusion: "Of this we are sure, that nature, scripture, and experience it selfe, have all taught the world to seeke for the ending of contentions by submitting it selfe unto some judicial and definitive sentence, whereunto neither part that contendeth may under any pretense or coulour refuse to stand."[5] Hooker's form of conversation resembles more the public oratory of the deliberative or judicial genres than *sermo*. Accordingly, Hooker compares a possible religious debate between Puritans and Anglicans to the debates before "Parliament where the place of enacting is" (Preface 6.5). Similarly, he likens the determination of religious controversy to a "judiciall decision" (Preface 6.2). And in contrast to Cicero's injunction against using personal authority in *sermo*, Hooker finds *ethos* an acceptable proof in religious controversy.[6] Hooker admits that argument from authority is not demonstrative, that is, cannot provide certainty, but he contends that "in defect of proofe infallible," the opinion of the learned elite is proof of probability: "Although it did not appeare what reason or what scripture led them to be of that judgement, yet to their very bare judgement somewhat a reasonable man would attribute, notwithstanding the common imbecilities which are incident into our nature" (2.7.5).

Like the public decision of the political assembly or the court, Hooker believes that the Church's decision of a religious controversy is binding. The individual must submit to the Church's judgment, Hooker maintains, because the issues under contention cannot be known with certainty, only probability, and while no one can be forced to *believe* that one opinion is more probable than another, a person can be compelled to *act* according to the Church's determination, which is the most probable: "For the publike approbation given by the body of this whole Church unto those things which are established, doth make it but probable that they are good."[7] The Jews

5. Ibid., Preface 6.1. See also 2.7.6, 1.16.7, and 5.10.1.

6. "For if the naturall strength of mans wit may by experience and studie attaine unto such ripenes in the knowledge of thinges humaine, that men in this respect may presume to build somewhat upon their judgement; what reason have we to thinke but that even in matters divine the like wits, furnisht with necessarie helpes, exercised in scripture with like diligence, and assisted with the grace of almightie God may growe unto so much perfection of knowledge, that men shall have just cause, when any thing pertinent to fayth and religion is doubted, the more willingly to incline their mindes towards that which the sentence of so grave, wise, and learned in that faculty shall judge sound." Ibid. 2.7.4.

7. Ibid., Preface 6.6. Cf. ibid., 1.8.3: "The most certaine token of evident goodnes is, if the generall perswasion of all men do so account it. . . . The generall and perpetuall voyce of men

during biblical times, for example, followed the determination of the Council of Jerusalem: "Things were disputed before they came to be determined; men afterwards were not to dispute any longer, but to obey. The sentence of judgement finished their strife, which their disputes before judgement could not doe. This was ground sufficient for any reasonable mans conscience to build the dutie of obedience upon, whatsoever his owne opinion were as touching the matter before in question" (Preface 6.3). Hooker thinks that Christians, similarly, "are all bound for the time to suspend" their personal beliefs and to observe the Church's laws. Truth and tranquillity require obedience to the Church's consensus. The Church's decision represents both "the probable voice of everie intier societie" and the side of "peace and quietnes." "God being author of peace and not of confusion in the Church," Hooker explains, "must needs be author of those mens peaceable resolutions"(Preface 6.6).

Hooker, intellectual scion of Erasmus, points up a dilemma within the humanist argument for toleration. The concept of adiaphora is a double-edged sword. It permits the humanist to argue for a more comprehensive Church on the ground that differences between denominations are not essential to faith. (Thus Hooker accepted Puritans and even Catholics as bona fide Christians.) But the concept of adiaphora can also be used to argue for greater state intervention in religious matters. By characterizing a practice as nonessential, it becomes possible to limit that practice while still claiming that no one's religious freedom has been infringed. Hooker himself wielded this argument against the Puritans, who believed that they were being denied the opportunity for true worship. Although granting Puritans the right to their opinions,[8] he demanded outward conformity from them in

---

is as the sentence of God him selfe. For that which all men have at all times learned, nature her selfe must needes have taught; and God being author of nature, her voyce is but his instrument. By her from him we receive whatsoever in such sort we learn." Hooker's statement here is similar to Erasmus's conception of consensus.

8. At one point, Hooker states that the Puritans have never been denied the opportunity of discussing their views: "Wherein if the things ye crave be no more than onely leave to dispute openly about those matters that are in question, the schooles in Universities (for any thing I know) are open unto you: they have their yerely Acts and Commencements, besides other disputations both ordinary and upon occasion, wherein the severall parts of our owne Ecclesiasticall discipline are oftentimes offered unto that kind of examination; the learnedest of you have beene of late yeares noted seeldome or never absent from thence at the time of those greater assemblies; and the favour of proposing there in convenient sort whatsoever ye can object (which thing my selfe have knowen them to graunt of Scholasticall courtesie unto straungers) neither hath (as I thinke) nor ever will (I presume) be denied you." Ibid., Preface 5.1.

what he believed were indifferent matters, that is, in those matters in which they departed from the Anglican Church.[9]

The humanists' expansion of the adiaphora enabled the state to limit religious liberty on the grounds that its restrictions affected only the nonessentials of faith. Two responses to this intolerant consequence developed. First, the Church was depicted more as a forum for the exchange of ideas than as an authoritative decision maker (the Church's rhetoric was characterized as sermocinal, not deliberative or judicial), making it less likely that the Church, via the state, would impose a determination upon its members. Second, the subjective nature of religious obligation was underscored, in other words, the belief that a person's inner sense of what religion requires should be protected regardless of whether or not this opinion is objectively true. This is the argument from conscience. Both these responses, in varying degrees, were found in Hooker's successor, William Chillingworth. Although Chillingworth defended primarily freedom of discussion and not freedom of practice, the logic of his arguments opposed restriction of religious belief and action.

Chillingworth: Heir to a Tradition

Early Years

Although humanism achieved its fullest expression in the Renaissance, the humanists' emphasis on classical studies and their propagation of the rhetorical tradition did not cease with the close of the sixteenth century. Virtually all the great writers of the seventeenth century were schooled in the *studia humanitatis*, with many of the period's seminal works still composed

---

9. The distinction between religious belief, which is protected, and religious action, which is not, has also appeared in the decisions of the U.S. Supreme Court. In *Reynolds v. U.S.*, 98 U.S. 145 (1878), a case involving Mormon claims to polygamy as a religious duty, the Court wrote that "Congress was deprived of all legislative power over mere opinion, but was left free to reach actions which were in violation of social duties or subversive of good order." The Court found that "to permit [polygamy] would be to make the professed doctrines of religious beliefs superior to the law of the land, and in effect to permit every citizen to become a law unto himself."

in Latin.[10] Because of humanism's influence, rhetoric pervaded the life of the student and scholar in the seventeenth century.[11] And, most important for the present discussion, the rationalist tendency within rhetoric, exhibited earlier by Ramus, Acontius, and Hooker, prevailed.[12]

One of the most influential humanists in the first part of the seventeenth century was the Englishman William Chillingworth. The biographical details of his life attest to the persistence of the humanist tradition, particularly in its emphasis on conversation and toleration. Chillingworth was born in 1602, son of the mayor of Oxford and godson to William Laud, then fellow of St. John's College and later archbishop of Canterbury. He began his education, in humanistic fashion, studying under Edward Sylvest, "a noted Latinist and Greecian," and proceeded, at the age of sixteen, to Trinity College, Oxford, where after passing "with ease" through his courses in logic and philosophy, he devoted himself to the study of divinity and mathematics.[13] While at Oxford, Chillingworth showed his predilection to conversation, albeit with youthful vigor. Anthony a'Wood, in his *History of Oxford Writers*, described Chillingworth's manner at Oxford in the following passage: "He would often walk in the College Grove and contemplate,

10. John Milton, for example, knew Latin, Greek, and even Hebrew, composed many of his works in Latin, and was thoroughly imbued with the classical tradition.

11. Harris Francis Fletcher, *The Intellectual Development of John Milton* (Urbana: University of Illinois Press, 1956–61), 2:201–70. Classical rhetorical theory was maintained in the seventeenth century by rhetoricians who sought to reconcile Ramism with the traditional five-part division of rhetoric. Howell, *Logic and Rhetoric in England*, 318–41. The humanists' practice of eloquence continued in Jacobean and Caroline England among the Anglican preachers. See W. Fraser Mitchell, *English Pulpit Oratory from Andrewes to Tillotson* (London: Society for Promoting Christian Knowledge, 1932), 140. The style of these preachers, generally termed "witty" or "metaphysical" is most often contrasted with the plain style of the Puritans.

12. The century's denigration of passionate discourse is most commonly associated with the new science's apotheosis of reason: the objective reconstruction of knowledge based on fact and experience. Natural scientists rejected the emotionalism of traditional rhetoric and sought, instead, a plain style. Thomas Sprat (1635–1713), propagandist of the new science, described the linguistic style of the Royal Society, center of scientific activity in England, in the following terms: "They have exacted from all their members, a close, naked, natural way of speaking; positive expressions; clear senses; a native easiness: bringing all things as near the Mathematical plainness, as they can: and preferring the language of Artizans, Countrymen, and Merchants, before that of Wits, or Scholars." Thomas Sprat, *History of the Royal Society*, ed. J. I. Cope and H. W. Jones (St. Louis: Washington University Studies, 1959), 113. See also Shapiro, *Probability and Certainty*, 232–46. The desire to build a rhetoric free of passions, however, was not limited to the scientific community. Humanists also used rational rhetoric, as they had earlier, to explore religious doctrines.

13. P. des Maizeaux, *An Historical and Critical Account of the Life of William Chillingworth* (London, 1725), 2.

but when he met with any Scholar there, he would enter into discourse, and dispute with him, purposely to facilitate and make the way of wrangling common with him; which was a fashion used in those days, especially among the disputing Theologists, or among those that set themselves apart purposely for divinity."[14] Likewise, John Aubrey, in his *Brief Lives*, writes that Chillingworth "was the readiest and nimblest Disputant of his time in the University, perhaps none haz equalled him since."[15]

Chillingworth's studies at the university ended, somewhere near the close of 1628. At that time John Fisher, one of several Jesuit missionaries present in England, persuaded him to convert from Anglicanism to Roman Catholicism, after which Chillingworth departed the country for the Catholic seminary at Douai, in northwest France.[16] Chillingworth turned to the Catholic Church with the hope that this institution, with its claims to universalism, would accommodate itself to a broad spectrum of beliefs and practices.[17] He soon understood, however, that the post-Tridentine Church was unwilling to tolerate religious diversity. Disillusioned with Catholicism, Chillingworth returned to England, initially uncommitted to any church but eventually reconciling himself to Protestantism, probably by the end of 1634. According to his biographer des Maizeaux, he decided to come back after searching the subject through the method of conversation. He "took all opportunities of arguing with learned Men of both persuasions, in order to find what they could say for themselves, or object against their adversaries. At last, the Protestant Principles appearing to him the most agreeable, both to the Holy Scripture and right Reason, he declared for them."[18] But he did

14. Anthony a' Wood, *Athenae Oxoniensis* (London: R. Knaplock, D. Midwinter, and J. Tonson, 1721), 2:40.

15. John Aubrey, *Brief Lives*, ed. Oliver Lawson Dick (London: Secker & Warburg, 1949), 64. See also a' Wood, *Athenae Oxoniensis*, 2:42: "He was a subtle and quick Disputant, and would several times put the King's Professor to a push. Hobbes of Malmsbury would often say, that he was like a lusty fighting Fellow, that did drive his Enemies before him, but would often give his own Party smart backblows."

16. Des Maizeaux contends that John Fisher was the alias of John Perse or Percey. *Chillingworth*, 5. There is disagreement among Chillingworth's contemporaries about which seminary Chillingworth attended. Some think that he attended the College of English Jesuits at St. Omer, not Douai. See Robert R. Orr, *Reason and Authority: The Thought of William Chillingworth* (Oxford: Clarendon Press, 1967), 26–27, for a more complete discussion of the matter.

17. Chillingworth initially believed that the Catholic Church had adapted the language of the Gospel to non-Christian traditions and that, in the Council of Florence, it had diligently tried to accommodate the Greek Church in the interest of unity. Orr, *Reason and Authority*, 11–19.

18. Des Maizeaux, *Chillingworth*, 15–16.

not commit himself to Anglicanism at this point. Repelled by the doctrinal rigidity of the Thirty-Nine Articles, Chillingworth did not subscribe to them until 1637, when he decided that he could accept them as principles of unity without acknowledging their dogmatic infallibility.[19]

Great Tew

Following his rejection of Catholicism, Chillingworth continued his inquiries into religion at Great Tew, the Oxfordshire house of his friend, Lucius Cary, second viscount Falkland. Great Tew was the intellectual meeting place, before the Civil War, of England's new generation of humanists. Besides Falkland and Chillingworth, the Great Tew circle included a future archbishop of Canterbury, Gilbert Sheldon; a future lord chancellor and historian, Edward Hyde, earl of Clarendon; the father of English biblical criticism, Henry Hammond; the political philosopher Thomas Hobbes; and the scholar John Hales.[20] The circle included others too: "all Men of eminent Parts and Faculties in Oxford, besides those who resorted thither from London."[21] The ideas that most influenced the men of Great Tew, as can be seen in their writings, were those of their Northern humanist forbears: Erasmus, Castellio, Acontius, Ochino, Cassander, Socinus, Hooker, and, most immediately, the Dutch jurist and statesman, Hugo Grotius (1583–1645).[22] Like these earlier humanists, most participants at Great Tew believed in a tolerant and comprehensive Church. So long as a person accepted the fundamentals of faith, they thought, he should be free to disagree on the rest. Clarendon observed this attitude in Falkland, leader of the circle. In controversial points, Clarendon writes, "He had so dispassioned a Consideration, such a Candour in his Nature, and so profound a Charity in his Conscience, that in those Points, in which He was in his own Judgment most clear, He never thought the worse, or in any Degree declined the Familiarity of those who were of another Mind; which, without Ques-

19. Ibid., 33–34, 42; Henry G. Van Leeuwen, *The Problem of Certainty in English Thought, 1630–1690* (The Hague: Martinus Nijhoff, 1963), 16.
20. Trevor-Roper, *Catholics, Anglicans and Puritans,* 166–67, 175.
21. Edward Hyde, earl of Clarendon, *The Life of Edward Earl of Clarendon* (Oxford: Clarendon Press, 1759), 42–43.
22. Grotius has been described as "the Erasmus of the seventeenth century." Trevor-Roper, *Catholics, Anglicans, and Puritans,* 189–92.

tion, is an excellent Temper for the Propagation, and Advancement of Christianity."[23]

Another sign of the humanist influence on Falkland's group was that the meetings at Great Tew were patterned after Cicero's and Erasmus's models of *sermo*. Like Cicero's philosophical dialogues, the discussions at Great Tew took place in a country home. Both Cicero's interlocutors and the guests at Great Tew were educated men of leisure, who engaged in amicable conversation. And like the characters in some of Erasmus's colloquies, the Great Tew circle gathered around the dinner table to engage in conversation. Alluding to this similarity between the two, Clarendon refers to Falkland's conversation as "a *Convivium Philosophicum*, or *Convivium Theologicum*," a philosophical or theological feast—a description resembling Erasmus's colloquy *Convivium religiosum*, "the Godly Feast."[24] In addition, as was the case with Cicero's and Erasmus's interlocutors, the participants at Great Tew were free to come to their own conclusions about the issues under debate. Clarendon makes this point about Chillingworth, who composed his chief work, *The Religion of Protestants: A Safe Way to Salvation*, while at Great Tew. He wrote his work, Clarendon observes, "after frequent Debates upon the most important Particulars; in many of which, He suffered himself to be over-ruled by the Judgment of his Friends, though in others He still adhered to his own Fancy, which was sceptical enough, even in the highest points" (ibid.).

The Religion of Protestants

Chillingworth wrote *The Religion of Protestants*, published in 1637, as a rejoinder to *Mercy and Truth, or Charity Maintained by Catholics*, written by Edward Knott, pen name of the Jesuit Matthew Wilson. In his work, Knott maintained that unrepented Protestantism destroys the hope of salvation.[25] Chillingworth denies Knott's claims, defending the essence and

---

23. *Clarendon*, 43–44; Orr, *Reason and Authority*, 37. Jordan notes that the Great Tew group and their sympathizers "sprang from the humanistic tradition, which in the previous century had contributed notably to the development of the theory of toleration." *Religious Toleration in England*, 2:350. See also Trevor-Roper, *Catholics, Anglicans, and Puritans*, 166–230. For further discussion of Falkland's toleration and humanism, see Jordan, *Religious Toleration in England*, 2:371–77; and Tulloch, *Rational Theology*, 1:76–169. On John Hales, see Jordan, *Religious Toleration in England*, 2:400–412, and Tulloch, *Rational Theology*, 1:170–260.

24. *Clarendon*, 42–43.

25. *Mercy and Truth, or Charity Maintained by Catholiques* (St. Omer, 1634). *The Religion*

virtues of Protestantism. *The Religion of Protestants* contributes to the cause of toleration because Chillingworth, as part of his defense, contrasts the authoritarianism of the Roman Catholic Church with what he perceives as the tolerant attitude of the Protestant religion.

In *The Religion of Protestants*, Chillingworth accepts Cicero's injunction that *sermo* should be a rational rhetoric. Undergirding the entire work is the assumption that we must seek divine truth through reason, which manifests itself rhetorically in discourse. Chillingworth defines discourse as "right Reason, grounded on Divine Revelation and common notions, written by God in the Hearts of all Men; and deducing according to the never failing Rules of Logick, consequent Deductions from them." He continues: "And though by Passion, or Precipitation, or Prejudice, by want of Reason, or not using what they have, Men may be, and are oftentimes, led into Errour and Mischief: Yet that they cannot be mis-guided by *Discourse*, truly so called."[26] Thus, for Chillingworth, the rule of reason entails the pacification of the passions. Prudence, the orator's watchword, "requires not only a good discerning judgement and apprehension, but a Serenity and Calmness in the Passions." Those who possess "piercing, discerning Judgement in speculative Sciences, as the Mathematicks, Metaphysicks, and the like," but are still ruled by their passions and affections, "are notwithstanding utterly invincibly imprudent."[27] Stated in the language of rhetorical theory, Chillingworth negates *ethos* and *pathos* in favor of logical explanation. Against his Catholic adversaries who reject what he says because of his character, Chillingworth writes that persuasion should not be based on character, but on reason: "The Christian Reader, knowing that his Salvation or Damnation depends upon his impartial and sincere Judgement . . . will . . . regard

---

of Protestants was only the latest polemical piece written in the war of letters between Jesuits and Protestants. In 1630, Knott published *Charity mistaken, with the want thereof Catholics are unjustly charged, for affirming, as they do with Grief, that Protestancy unrepented destroys salvation.* In 1633 Christopher Potter, provost of Queen's College, Oxford, replied with the *Want of Charitie, iustly charged, on all such Romanists, as dare (without truth or modesty) affirme, that Protestancie destroyeth Salvation. In answer to a late Popish Pamphlet intituled 'Charity Mistaken.'* Potter was answered in the following year by Knott, who wrote *Mercy and Truth, or Charity Maintained by Catholiques* and who, after being apprised of Chillingworth's upcoming *The Religion of Protestants*, also published a pamphlet condemning Chillingworth's views prior to the publication of *The Religion of Protestants.* See des Maizeaux, *Chillingworth*, 43–45, and Van Leeuwen, *Problem of Charity*, 17–18.

26. William Chillingworth, *The Religion of Protestants*, in *The Works of William Chillingworth*, . . . 9th ed. (London: B. Motte, 1727), Preface, 12 (citations to *The Religion of Protestants* are by chapter and section). See also ibid., Preface, 3; Answer to Preface, 13; and 2.110.

27. *Sermons*, in *The Works of William Chillingworth*, 18.

not the Person, but the Cause and the Reasons of it; not who speaks, but what is spoken."[28] Like Acontius, Chillingworth opposes the Roman Catholic Church's pretensions to being the sole judge of truth. He argues that reason cannot be submitted to an external authority, "for he that doth it to Authority, must of Necessity think himself to have greater Reason to believe that Authority."[29]

After the publication of his magnum opus, Chillingworth grew despondent over England's descent into Civil War. Evincing the humanist trust in rhetoric, he sought to counter the rebellion against the king and to effect a moral reformation of the English people through preaching. Chillingworth directed his oratory primarily to the reason of the listener, although he preached a sermon before the king, in Oxford, that was described as "not only remarkable for that strength of reason, which seems to have been [his] peculiar talent: but also for the eloquent addresses, pathetick and affectionate exhortations, whereby he endeavors to enforce the practice of Virtue and Piety."[30] Chillingworth's enemies also noted his eloquence. Thus, the Puritan Francis Cheynell observes of him: "Never did I observe more acuteness and eloquence so exactly tempered in the same person: *Diabolus ab illo ornari cupiebat* [the Devil desired to be praised by him]; for he had eloquence enough to set a faire varnish upon the foulest designe."[31] Apparently, Chillingworth believed that emotional appeals are inappropriate to

---

28. *The Religion of Protestants*, Preface, 29. Chillingworth opposes not only Catholic rejection of rational argument, but also Protestant. To those Protestants who see the Holy Spirit, not human reason, as the ultimate source of faith, Chillingworth argues that since reason is a faculty common to all, rational propositions can be verified by others; personal truths cannot. Therefore, a personal revelation by the Holy Spirit is not a legitimate criterion of truth: "For is there not a manifest Difference between saying, *The Spirit of God tells me that this is the Meaning of such a Text* (which no Man can possibly know to be true, it being a secret Thing) and between saying, *These and these Reasons I have to shew, that this or that is true Doctrine, or that this or that is the Meaning of such a Scripture?* Reason being a public and certain Thing, and exposed to all Men's Trial and Examination." *The Religion of Protestants*, 2.110; 3.27. The Puritan Cheynell, recognizing Chillingworth's attack on the doctrine of illumination, writes of Chillingworth: "He . . . raised a battery against the Popes chaire, that he might *place Reason in the chaire in stead of Antichrist.*" Francis Cheynell, "A Speech made at the Funerall of Mr Chillingworths mortall Booke," *Chillingworthi Novissima: Or the Sicknesse, Heresy, Death, and Buriall of William Chillingworth* (London, 1644), part D.

29. *The Religion of Protestants*, 2.114. Besides reflecting the rational character of *sermo*, *The Religion of Protestants* also eschews contentiousness, in line with the genre's *decorum*. Chillingworth tells Knott that he undertook writing *The Religion of Protestants* "with a full Resolution to be an Adversary to your Errors, but a Friend and Servant to your Person." Ibid., Preface, 3. Like Erasmus in the *Diatribe*, Chillingworth debates civilly with his opponent.

30. Mitchell, *English Pulpit Oratory*, 282–83; des Maizeaux, *Chillingworth*, 284.

31. Cheynell, "Speech."

doctrinal conversation, but legitimate in persuading an audience to act virtuously. Chillingworth's eloquence, however, did not bring about a victory for the Royalist cause—nor did his military skills. Having joined the Royalist armies in August 1643, Chillingworth was taken prisoner by the Parliamentary forces in January 1644, dying shortly thereafter.[32]

Chillingworth's legacy to the humanist defense of toleration was to recognize the logical implications of the humanists' rhetorical principles, which induced him to adopt positions more radical than his predecessors'. His analysis of two principles in particular, probability and accommodation, led him to conclude that all religious knowledge is intrinsically probable and that doctrinal requirements of faith must be adapted to the individual. Chillingworth developed these views, to which neither Erasmus nor Acontius would have assented, in *The Religion of Protestants*.[33]

Rhetoric and Probability

All Religion Is Only Probable

Despite their propensity to probabilistic reasoning, the humanists did not apply argument from probability to the fundamentals of faith before the seventeenth century. Thus while Erasmus used "consensus" to determine the fundamentals of faith, he did not accept that consensus, in this case, demonstrated probability. He was unwilling to apply probability, despite its legitimacy in rhetoric, to essential doctrine. Similarly, Acontius demanded certainty of the believer, despite conceding that no individual could be sure he knew the truth. To Acontius, requiring anything less than certainty in the

---

32. Des Maizeaux, *Chillingworth*, 313–46. Ironically, it was the Puritan enemy of Chillingworth, Cheynell, who attempted to nurse Chillingworth to health. Cheynell, in his *Chillingworthi Novissima*, describes his unsuccessful attempts to cure Chillingworth of both his physical and spiritual ills.

33. I choose to discuss Chillingworth's arguments from probability and accommodation for their novelty and for being exemplary of the further extension of humanist-rhetorical principles. Chillingworth, however, advances other significant humanistic grounds for toleration that I will not examine here. For example, Chillingworth takes up the Erasmian position that Christianity, more than a series of doctrines, is a religion of ethical practices: "A worthy Doctor of our Church did well define Faith to be a *spiritual Prudence*, that is, a Knowledge sought out only for Practice." Chillingworth, *Sermons*, 20. Chillingworth's argument promotes toleration insofar as sin is defined more in terms of living an unethical life than in committing doctrinal error.

essentials of religion was tantamount to full-blown skepticism. The fundamentals, according to these humanists, were to be immune from the calculus of rhetorical probability. This immunity, however, was withdrawn during the seventeenth century. Relying on the classical rhetorical principle that probability was an adequate proof, Chillingworth contended that, in religion, high probability was the best one could attain.

Chillingworth develops his argument that religion is probable, not absolutely certain, by distinguishing between two different kinds of knowledge. The first concerns matters perceived through sense experience, mathematical demonstration, or direct divine revelation, which are therefore known with metaphysical or absolute certainty.[34] The second, and for Chillingworth more significant, concerns all other matters, which are known with only probable or moral certainty. Knowledge of the existence of Rome and Constantinople acquired through actually seeing them, for example, belongs to the first category, since such knowledge is based on sense experience. But belief in their existence that is not based on personal experience can only be held with moral, not metaphysical, certainty. In practice, Chillingworth notes, "my certainty that there are such cities in the world, would not be one scruple augmented" by physically seeing them.[35] Theoretically, however, metaphysically certain knowledge is beyond question, whereas knowledge that is probable can be questioned.

Although those who require sure knowledge of dogma assert that Christian truths can be known with absolute certainty, Chillingworth argues that religious knowledge can only be had with moral certainty. Insofar as people—save prophets—are denied divine revelation, the evidence that Christianity is true, like the evidence that Rome and Constantinople exist, is only probable.[36] Christians rely on the Bible as their source of truth, but the

---

34. William Chillingworth, Wharton MSS 943, f. 871, Lambeth Palace Library, London; quoted in Orr, *Reason and Authority*, 51–52. Chillingworth is not systematic in his discussions of knowledge and certainty. Thus, at one point he refers to an absolutely infallible certainty. This reference leads Van Leeuwen to conclude that Chillingworth has three categories of knowledge, the highest being "not attainable by mortal man." *Problem of Certainty*, 22. Since Chillingworth concedes (*The Religion of Protestants*, 2.152) that what one claims with absolute certainty may, in fact, only be a dream, one can never truly reach absolute certainty. Still, Chillingworth does refer to the highest level of certainty attainable by mortals as "absolute" or "metaphysical" certainty.

35. On the contrary, actually viewing the cities would only increase the possibility of being fooled, seeing that "it would be far easier, for a company conspiring together by some art, to persuade me, that I see not what I see, but am deluded by my imagination." Ibid.

36. Chillingworth effectively excluded the possibility of prophecy: "To place a belief on this level of direct revelation we need to be 'certain of our certainty', and this, as Chillingworth

Bible is a secondhand account of events that we ourselves did not witness. As is the case with our knowledge of Rome and Constantinople, our assurance of the Bible's truth does not come from direct sense experience but from "the *Speech* of People," and though this "speech" is probable—even highly probable—it is not absolutely certain.[37] The speech of a people or, as Chillingworth more frequently terms it, "tradition," consists here of the "Testimony of the Primitive Christians" and of all later churches that the Bible is the true word of God.[38] Chillingworth's argument that we know Christianity's truth through tradition restates Erasmus's argument from consensus in Protestant terms—the difference being that Chillingworth wants the individual to interpret "consensus," whereas Erasmus vests the power of interpretation with the Church.[39] Tradition is the agreement of the

---

explained, leads to an infinite regress—you then need to be 'certain' of your second order 'certainty', and so on." Wharton MSS 943, f. 876; quoted in Orr, *Reason and Authority*, 53.

Chillingworth's argument that religion is only probable is anticipated by the sixteenth-century humanist Sebastien Castellio (1515–63), in *De arte dubitandi et confidendi, ignorandi et sciendi*. In this work Castellio, like Chillingworth, distinguishes between different levels of certainty in religion: doubt, belief, ignorance, and knowledge. Again like Chillingworth, Castellio argues that religious knowledge must be evaluated by the same criteria used to evaluate secular knowledge. For Castellio, the criteria are sense and reason. See Sebastian Castellio, *De arte dubitandi et confidendi ignorandi et sciendi* (Leiden: E. J. Brill, 1981); Van Leeuwen, *Problem of Certainty*, 27–28 n. 34; Popkin, *History of Scepticism*, 10–14; and Shapiro, *Probability and Certainty*, 76–77. A more direct influence on Chillingworth's epistemology is Hugo Grotius's *Truth of the Christian Religion* (Paris, 1624). Grotius argues that there are different kinds of proof, with their own levels of certainty, for different subject matters. Proofs, and thus the certainty, in matters of faith, he points out, are not as strong as mathematical demonstrations. In fact Chillingworth quotes Grotius's discussion of the different types of proof available: "Thus is there one way in Mathematicks, another in Physicks, a third in Ethicks, and lastly, another kind when a Matter of Fact is in question. . . . Now it is the pleasure of Almighty God that those Things which he would have us to believe (so that the very Belief thereof may be imputed to us for Obedience) should not so evidently appear, as those Things which are apprehended by Sense and plain Demonstration, but only be so far forth revealed as may beget Faith, and a Perswasion thereof in the Hearts and Minds of such as are not obstinate." Grotius, *Truth of the Christian Religion*, 2.19; quoted in *The Religion of Protestants*, 6.51. See Orr, *Reason and Authority*, 106–7, and Van Leeuwen, *Problem of Certainty*, 21–22.

37. *The Religion of Protestants*, 4.53.

38. Ibid., Preface, 13. "Such a Tradition . . . involves an Evidence of Fact, and from Hand to Hand, from Age to Age, bringing us up to the Times and Persons of the Apostles, and our Saviour himself, cometh to be confirmed by all these Miracles and other Arguments, whereby they convinced their Doctrine to be true." Ibid., 2.53.

39. Chillingworth is willing to show greater respect than Acontius for the pronouncements of Church councils. See Ibid., 4.18: "I willingly confess the Judgement of a Council, though not infallible, is yet so far directive and obliging, that without apparent Reason to the contrary, it may be Sin to reject it, at least not to afford it an outward Submission for publick peace sake."

faithful, the standard of truth, for both humanists. But unlike Erasmus, Chillingworth remains loyal to the rhetorical origins of "consensus," explicitly stating that consensus is only probable.[40] Tradition furnishes moral assurance, not "physical" or "moral" certainty, that *Scripture hath been preserved from any material Alteration.*[41] Although he cannot know with absolute certainty that every element of the Holy Scripture is infallibly true, as does his adversary Knott, Chillingworth contends that we must certainly believe in the truth of the Religion of Christ.[42] Since it is reasonable for us to accept probability in religion as the criterion of truth, and because Christianity, on the evidence of tradition, is more probable than any other religion or than the possibility of no religion at all, then, Chillingworth concludes, "it is infallibly certain that we are to firmly believe the Truth of the Christian Religion."[43]

Restatement of a Classical Idea

Chillingworth's support for argument from probability harks back to the classical rhetoricians in two ways: first, he accords probable knowledge epistemological legitimacy; second, he points up the persuasive power of arguments from probability. In arguing that probability is a valid form of knowledge, Chillingworth places himself in the rhetorical tradition. His argument that probability is the proper standard for religion parallels Aristotle's affirmation of the rhetorical syllogism and induction. Both consider it impossible to impose a standard of certainty on material that does not permit it. Aristotle rejects Plato's condemnation of rhetoric as based on opinion, not knowledge, because the orator addresses issues in which true knowledge, necessary and certain, cannot be attained.[44] Similarly, Chillingworth counters Knott's call for certainty based on an infallible Church with the argument that no one can claim or demand certainty in matters that can only be known with probability.[45] Those who condemn probability as a

40. Although Cicero conceded that when "all men throughout the world agree" on some belief, then "we too are bound to hold the same opinion," he was speaking then as a Stoic. Paradoxically, he asserted his Skeptical freedom to depart from skepticism.

41. *The Religion of Protestants,* 2.24.

42. E. Knott, *Mercy and Truth,* chapter 2; quoted in Orr, *Reason and Authority,* 84; Chillingworth, *The Religion of Protestants,* 6.8.

43. *The Religion of Protestants,* 6.8.

44. See the Introduction, page 24.

45. "Now nothing is more repugnant, than that a Man should be required to give most certain Credit unto that which cannot be made appear most certainly credible; and if it appear

legitimate criterion of the truth, Chillingworth maintains, view all knowledge that is less-than-certain as identical. Like Cicero, who uses *verisimile* (like truth) to denote probability in contrast to plausibility, Chillingworth argues that high probability should not be viewed as tantamount to mere possibility, for on a continuum, beginning with possibility and ending with absolute certainty, high probability is closest to absolute certainty.[46] It is thus erroneous to consider "whatsoever is but probable, though in the highest Degree of Probability, [as if it] were as likely to be false as true! Or because it was but morally, not mathematically certain, that there was such a Woman as Queen Elizabeth, such a Man as Henry VIII, that is in the highest Degree probable, therefore it were an even Wager there were none such!"[47] We must make the same calculus of probability in religion as the gambler does in betting. Like the gambler, we need to distinguish between an overwhelming favorite and an even bet; the former, though not absolutely certain, is very probable, whereas the latter is not.

Chillingworth also understands the practical motivation behind the orator's use of probability: that probable arguments are an effective means of persuasion. The classical rhetorician's justification of probability as theoretically legitimate is matched by his recognition that arguments from probability lead listeners to action, both in the courts and in the political assemblies. As was true of most rhetorical principles, the practice of argument from probability preceded the theoretical explication. Ancient orators used such arguments, first and foremost, because they worked. In like manner, Chillingworth states that probability is as likely to persuade a person to act as is absolute certainty. If great numbers of people endure extreme hardships in the present out of "a probable hope of some future gain and commodity, and that not infinite and eternal, but finite and temporal," then how much more reasonable is it to assume that a highly probable hope of eternal salvation awaiting those that obey Jesus Christ "may be able to sway our will to Obedience?" (6.5). Probability, Chillingworth argues, is sufficiently powerful to lead men to serve God. In line with his rejection of *ethos* and *pathos*,

---

to him to be so, then is it not obscure that it is so. . . . For you to require a strength of Credit, beyond the Appearance of the Objects Credibility, is all one as if you should require me to go ten Mile an Hour upon an Horse, that will go but five." *The Religion of Protestants*, 6.7. Cf. Hooker's similar statement earlier in *Ecclesiastical Polity*, 2.7.5.

46. Cicero *Academica* 2.32; Lisa Jardine, "Lorenzo Valla: Academic Skepticism and the New Humanist Dialectic," in *The Skeptical Tradition*, ed. Myles Burnyeat (Berkeley and Los Angeles: University of California Press, 1983), 263.

47. *The Religion of Protestants*, 4.57.

Chillingworth argues that probability's persuasiveness is not based on its emotional appeal but on its reasonableness.[48] The most probable religion, Christianity, is the rational choice.

Chillingworth's position that all religious knowledge is only probable bolsters religious toleration. By requiring certainty in the fundamentals of faith, Erasmus and Acontius deny the possibility of continual discussion on the fundamentals of faith. Anything known with absolute certainty is, in the final result, precluded from debate. Chillingworth, however, cannot as easily foreclose discussion of any religious doctrine, seeing that nothing in religion is known with absolute certainty. While he asserts above that "we must certainly believe in the truth of the Religion of Christ," he blurs the line between what can be perpetually questioned and what must ultimately be protected from scrutiny. Echoing Cicero's skepticism, Chillingworth does not commit himself to any permanent position, only to a "Constancy in following the Way to Heaven which for the present seems to me the most probable."[49]

Accommodation, Fundamentals, and the Variable Standard

Traditional Distinction

While, as Chillingworth asserts, we can know that the Bible as a whole is true with the highest degree of probability, we should not conclude that all our interpretations of the Bible carry with them that same degree of moral certainty. Chillingworth acknowledges that the meaning of the Bible is not always clear. But he opposes Knott's conclusion that because it is sometimes obscure, the Bible needs a judge, the Roman Catholic Church, to interpret it. Chillingworth writes: "God hath appointed no . . . Judge of Controversies, . . . though it seems to us convenient there should be one, yet it is not so: . . . it hath pleased God (for Reasons best known to himself) not to

---

48. As Kennedy observes, the rhetorical origins of argumentation from probability are tied to the ancient Greeks' increased interest in rational argument. Seeing that witnesses could be bought, but that probabilities could not be bribed, the ancient Greeks realized that probabilities were a more reliable means to determine truth. *Art of Persuasion*, 89–90.

49. *The Religion of Protestants*, Preface, 5.

allow us this convenience."[50] True, the meaning of some parts of the Bible is not always apparent. For example, Chillingworth grants that the Bible offers no certain answers to questions about predestination, the Immaculate Conception, or the pope's indirect power in temporalities. Still, the individual is capable of distinguishing, by dint of his own reason, between what does and does not need to be known, between the fundamentals and adiaphora: "Christians . . . have and shall have *Means sufficient* (though not always effectual) *to determine*, not all *Controversies*, but all *necessary to be determined*."[51] Chillingworth assumes that people can reach a consensus on the essentials by looking to the Bible alone for truth: "For if Men did really and sincerely submit their Judgements to Scripture, and that only, and would require no more of any Man but to do so, it were impossible but that all Controversies touching Things necessary and very profitable should be ended; and if others were continued or increased, it were no Matter" (2.4).

Chillingworth's discussion of the fundamentals of faith is influenced by the rhetorical principle of accommodation. As adapted to Christianity by Erasmus, accommodation signifies both God's accommodation to humanity—best exemplified by God's incarnation in Christ—and, emulating God, human beings' accommodation of themselves, their words and actions, to the circumstances of their fellows.[52] Chillingworth applies Erasmus's sense of divine accommodation to the fundamentals of faith, arguing that because God accommodates Himself to humanity, He only requires us to believe those parts of Scripture which we can clearly understand:[53] "God," Chillingworth writes, "will require no impossibilities of us" (2.152). Accordingly, the "plain places" of the Bible, those places where "we are sufficiently certain of the Meaning," contain all things necessary for belief.[54] We, in turn, cannot require "harder or heavier conditions . . . than God requires" (3.64). Heretics are not those who deny any part of the Bible, but only those

---

50. *Mercy and Truth*, chapter 2; *The Religion of Protestants*, 2.85. See also 3.7.

51. *The Religion of Protestants*, 1.7.

52. Christianity, Erasmus argues, must consider "the ignorant multitude for whom Christ died." *EE* 4:345.40–46 (Letter to Paul Volz, August 1518). Christianity speaks to all: "The sun itself is not as common and accessible to all as is Christ's teaching. It keeps no one at a distance, unless a person begrudging himself, keeps away. . . . The mysteries of kings, perhaps, are better concealed, but Christ wishes his mysteries published as openly as possible." *Paracelsis*, trans. in Olin, *Christian Humanism*, 96–97.

53. *The Religion of Protestants*, 2.84.

54. Ibid., 2.84. See 2.127, where Chillingworth writes: "How can it consist with his [that is, God's] Justice to require of Men to know certainly the Meaning of those Words, which he himself hath not revealed?" See also Orr, *Reason and Authority*, 61–63.

who "obstinately contradict the Truth of any Thing plainly delivered in Scripture."[55] They spurn God's accommodation, His plain and clear message, choosing for themselves the path to eternal damnation.

The result of Chillingworth's argument from accommodation is a call to limit the fundamentals of faith to a minimum, similar to the earlier suggestions of Erasmus and Acontius. Chillingworth himself was aware that his support for a minimum number of essentials, "a Common Profession of those Articles of Faith, wherein all consent," derives from his humanist predecessors (4.40). He cites Erasmus to substantiate his view that the Roman Church expanded doctrine beyond the necessary articles of faith. Erasmus, Chillingworth notes, recognized that Luther's doctrinal departures could not have justified his excommunication (5.91). Although at the time of his conversion to Catholicism Chillingworth believed the Roman Church was inclusive, he came to understand that it had reacted to the Reformation with dogmatic inflexibility. Erasmus, he argued, implied as much by criticizing the Protestants for leaving the Church and thus causing Rome to tighten its reins on doctrinal dissent. The post-Tridentine Church, according to Chillingworth, was no longer comprehensive in the way that the medieval Church was; it was no longer a catholic church.[56] The Roman Catholic Church excluded from its communion those believers who disagreed with it on nonessentials. Chillingworth uses Acontius to make the same point about the Protestant sects. We Protestants, Chillingworth writes, are guilty of "restraining . . . the World of God from that latitude and generality, and the Understandings of Men from that liberty, wherein Christ and the Apostles left them."[57] That Christian, in particular Protestant, intolerance has been the "common Incendiary of Christendom," Chillingworth observes, "is no singularity of mine, but the Doctrine which I have learned from Divines of great learning and judgement. Let the reader," Chillingworth continues, "be pleased to peruse the seventh book of Acontius's *de Strat. Satanae* . . . and he shall confess as much" (4.16n). In proposing that the true articles of faith are far fewer than those propounded by most Catholics

55. Ibid., 2.127. Chillingworth further limits heresy when he writes that the doctrine denied must also be revealed with a "Command that all should believe it." Ibid., 6.12.

56. "I should have represented . . . Erasmus's Complaint against Protestants, whose departing from the Roman Church occasioned the determining and exacting the Belief of many Points as necessary, wherein, before Luther, Men enjoyed the Liberties of their Judgements, and Tongues, and Pens." Chillingworth, *Additional Discourses*, in *The Works of William Chillingworth*, 42.

57. *The Religion of Protestants*, 4.16.

and Protestants, Chillingworth consciously attaches himself to the tradition of the Renaissance humanists.[58]

Like preceding humanists, Chillingworth extends full toleration on the nonessentials. All Christians who agree on the "high Points of Faith" are "in one Communion" with one another. They may jointly worship God, "after such a Way as all esteem lawful," and they must mutually perform "all those Works of Charity, which Christians owe to another."[59] But no unity is demanded on nonessentials, "the obscure and controverted Questions of Religion." In these arguments "as may with probability be disputed on both Sides (and such are the Disputes of Protestants;) good Men and Lovers of Truth on all Sides may be saved."[60] Such controversies, Chillingworth explains, differ from civil controversies, in which "either the Plaintiff must injure the Defendant by disquieting his Possession, or the Defendant wrong the Plaintiff by keeping his Right from him." When debating adiaphora, every person can maintain his own opinion without harming another: "I may hold my Opinion, and do you no wrong, and you yours and do me none. Nay, we may both of us hold our Opinion, and yet do our selves no Harm; provided, the Difference be not touching any Thing necessary to Salvation."[61] Similarly, Chillingworth writes, "in such points which may be held diversly of divers men *Salva Fidei compage* [excluding the structure of faith], I would not take any Man's liberty from him, and humbly beseech all Men, that they would not take mine from me."[62]

Chillingworth describes the debates over nonessentials in terms that are reminiscent of earlier accounts of *sermo*. Argument *in utramque partem* is undertaken with the aim of discovering the most probable truth. Chillingworth even compares adiaphoral debates among Protestants to the exchange of opinions in Cicero's *Tusculan Disputations* (7.34). But Chillingworth does not discuss debates over essential beliefs. His intention is to emphasize the unity of all Christians on fundamentals, not their differences. He simply posits that because Christians believe in the Bible, they also agree on the essentials: "Now that Christians do generally agree in all those Points of

58. In addition to Erasmus and Acontius, Chillingworth recognizes that the humanists George Cassander and Hugo Grotius influence his support for a comprehensive Church based on limited fundamentals. Chillingworth's links to Grotius are especially strong. Orr, *Reason and Authority*, 106–7, 122–24.

59. *The Religion of Protestants*, 4.40.

60. Ibid., Preface, 31. See also Answer to Preface, 26, and 1.13.

61. *The Religion of Protestants*, 2.20.

62. Ibid., Preface, 28. See also 2.85, 3.46, 4.13, 4.16, and 6.56.

Doctrine, which are necessary to Salvation, it is apparent, because they agree with one accord in believing all those Books of the Old and New Testament, which in the Church were never doubted of to be the undoubted Word of God" (4.40). The problem, however, is that agreement on the authority of the Bible says nothing about the content of the Bible. Thus, the Socinians accept the Bible, yet Chillingworth implies at one point that they are not orthodox on the fundamentals of faith.[63] Defining the fundamentals in terms of "the BIBLE only," as he sometimes does, evades the question of what dogmas are essential to salvation.[64]

Defining the Fundamentals

What, then, are the fundamentals of faith? Although unequivocal in his stand that they are fewer than the doctrines demanded by most sects, Chillingworth is more ambiguous about their actual composition. He writes, for example, that the Apostles' Creed contains all the beliefs necessary for salvation, thereby suggesting, in contrast to Acontius, that Catholics are true believers.[65] Elsewhere, he maintains that the Thirty-Nine Articles, "in themselves," are true.[66] Neither confession, however, is equivalent to the fundamentals of faith. In fact, Chillingworth never explicitly states what the essentials of faith are.[67]

---

63. "Yet this much I can say (which I hope will satisfie any Man of reason), that whatsoever hath been held necessary to Salvation, either by the Catholic Church or all Ages, or by Consent of Fathers, measured by Vincentius Lyrinensis his Rule, or is held necessary, either by the Catholic Church of this Age, or by the Consent of Protestants, or even by the Church of England, that against the Socinians, and all others whatsoever, I do verily believe and embrace." Ibid., Preface, 28.

64. "The BIBLE, I say, the BIBLE only, is the Religion of Protestants! Whatsoever else they believe besides it, and the plain, irrefragable, indubitable Consequences of it, well may they hold it as a Matter of Opinion: But as matter of Faith and Religion, neither can they with coherence to their own Grounds believe it themselves, nor require the Belief of it of others, without most high and most schismatical presumption." Ibid., 6.56.

65. *The Religion of Protestants*, 4.22.

66. Orr, *Reason and Authority*, 88.

67. At one point he includes among the plainly stated truths of Christianity the following: a belief in a God who is "Omnipotent, Omniscient, Good, Just, True, Merciful, a Rewarder of them that seek him, a Punisher of them that obstinately offend him; that Jesus Christ is the Son of God, and the Saviour of the World, that it is He, by Obedience to whom Men must look to be saved . . . [we must further believe in] his Birth, or Passion, or Resurrection, or Ascension, or Sitting at the right Hand of God: His having all Power given him in Heaven and Earth: That it is he whom God hath appointed to be Judge of the Quick and Dead; that all Men shall rise again at the last Day; that they which believe and repent shall be Saved; that they which do not believe and repent shall be damned." In addition, Chillingworth enumerates here the need to

His equivocation over what is fundamental to the faith appears in his discussion of the Trinity. In *The Religion of Protestants* Chillingworth implies that belief in the Trinity is essential to salvation, describing those who deny the Trinity "as being but a Handful of Men, in respect of all, nay, in respect of any of these Professions which maintain it" (4.45). In an earlier letter to an unknown correspondent named Harry, however, Chillingworth views Arian doctrines as consistent with the fundamentals of Christianity.[68] Further, Cheynell, in his account of Chillingworth's last days, quotes Chillingworth as saying that he "did not absolve . . . and would not condemne" Turk, Papist, or Socinian, leaving open the question of whether belief in the Trinity or even in Christianity is necessary for salvation.[69] In the end, Chillingworth skirts the question of what particular doctrines are essential to Christianity by asserting that since the Bible contains all necessary dogmas, then a general belief in the Bible—as opposed to its specifics— protects the believer from heresy.[70] Chillingworth thought that Christianity's disparate sects could unite on the lowest common denominator of their faith: belief in the Bible.

Chillingworth's unwillingness to define the fundamentals of faith is not, in and of itself, unusual. Erasmus and Acontius, as well, were willing to suggest but not to declare authoritatively what is essential to salvation. This reluctance on the part of these three to define the fundamentals stems, in part, from their fear that a specific formula, instead of acting to unite Christians, would only engender greater divisiveness.[71] Nevertheless, Chillingworth's refusal to commit himself to any particular formula cannot be explained solely on the grounds of such fear. More than evading the issue of necessary dogma, Chillingworth assumes a relativistic position in much of *The Religion of Protestants* that is theoretically inconsistent with the very enterprise of defining the minimum articles of faith. Chillingworth, responding to Knott's criticism that he would not "give in a particular Catalogue what

---

deny that either the Mosaic Law or good works are necessary to salvation. *The Religion of Protestants*, 2.127. But even this long list is not intended as a precise tally of the fundamentals of faith; rather it is only Chillingworth's surmise of the unambiguous doctrines found in Scripture.

68. Orr, *Reason and Authority*, 98–99.

69. Cheynell, *Chillingworthi Novissima*, C4.

70. *The Religion of Protestants*, 6.56–57. See also 3.50 and 6.48.

71. Thus Acontius proposes a confession for consideration but states that it should not be seen as the final word. See *Satan's Stratagems*, 203. The problem Acontius and other humanists faced in forwarding their creeds is that while they wanted to include as many Christians as possible, a creed, by its nature, is exclusive.

Points be fundamental," argues that he gives no such catalogue because human variability makes compilation of such a list impossible:

> God himself hath told us, "That where much is given, much shall be required; where little is given, little shall be required" [Luke 12:48]. To Infants, Deaf-men, Mad-men, nothing, for ought we know, is given; and if it be so, of them *nothing* shall be required. Others perhaps may have Means only given them to believe, "That God is, and that he is a Rewarder of them that seek him" [Hebrews 11:6]; and to whom thus much only is given, to them it shall not be damnable, that they believe but only thus much.[72]

The fundamentals of faith, according to this explanation, depend on the individual's level of understanding. To those who have no understanding, no knowledge is demanded. For those endowed with reason, "the *minimum quod sic*, the lowest Degree of Faith," required is a belief that God is a rewarder of those who seek him, which can be fulfilled by non-Christians as well.

Chillingworth endorses the same variable standard of faith when he considers the case of the Catholics. The relevant factor in determining whether a Catholic—or Protestant for that matter—is to be saved is the individual's level of knowledge. Those Catholics who "want Means to find the Truth, and so die in Errour; or use the best Means they can with Industry, and without Partiality to find the Truth, and yet die in Errour, these Men, thus qualified, notwithstanding these Errours, may be saved."[73] But if a Roman Catholic goes against his conscience and knowingly professes erroneous beliefs, even if his errors do not concern any of the articles of faith (and Chillingworth is willing to concede that Roman Catholicism may be consistent with the fundamentals of faith), then he will most certainly be damned.[74]

The difficulty with Chillingworth's argument for a variable standard of faith, however, is that it vitiates his earlier quest for the essentials of faith. Once the points necessary for salvation are tailored to everyone's needs, the whole notion of a single set of fundamentals becomes indefensible. Different sets of fundamentals must be designed for the slightly weak of mind, for

72. *The Religion of Protestants*, 3.13.
73. Ibid, 3.12. See also 1.4, where Chillingworth tells Knott: "I know no Protestants that hath any other Hope of your Salvation, but upon these Grounds, that unaffected ignorance may excuse you, or true Repentance obtain Pardon for you."
74. Ibid., 3.56 and Answer to the Preface, 29.

average intellects, and for those with superior intelligence or for those unfamiliar with Christian beliefs, those only slightly familiar, those well-versed, and so on. Some may be excused for knowing less than even the most basic principles of Christianity, whereas others must know more.[75]

How is this contradiction between Chillingworth's desire to define the fundamentals and his relativization of faith to be explained? The answer lies in his criterion for determining the fundamentals of faith: accommodation. Since God accommodates Himself to us, Chillingworth argues, He will not require more than is humanly possible. So too, we cannot require of our fellows a knowledge of doctrine that is beyond their capabilities. Initially Chillingworth defines our capacity for knowledge in terms of an objective standard—the fundamentals of faith—even if Chillingworth does not state what these fundamentals are. Until this point, Chillingworth's conception of the fundamentals is in accordance with the earlier humanists'. Although they do not frame their arguments for fundamentals in precisely the same fashion as Chillingworth, arguing (unlike Chillingworth) that the fundamentals can be known with absolute certainty, they (like Chillingworth) desire a single minimal standard by which believers can be distinguished from heretics. Chillingworth recognizes, however, that the logical implications of "accommodation" demand more than a compilation of the articles of faith. Accommodation, understood rhetorically, means accommodation to a particular set of circumstances. "To consider Men of different Religions . . . in their own nature and *without circumstance*," Chillingworth writes, "must be to consider them, neither as ignorant, nor as knowing; neither as having, nor as wanting means of Instruction; neither as with Capacity, nor without it; neither with erroneous, nor yet with unerring Conscience." Abstracting persons in this manner tells us nothing about the persons themselves. "What Judgement can you pronounce on them," Chillingworth asks, "all the Goodness and Badness of an Action depending on the Circumstances? Ought not a Judge being to give sentence of an Action, to consider all the Circumstances of it?"[76] Certainly any creed cannot accommodate the feeble-minded. But what of those whose environment prevents them from hearing

75. "I add now, that what may be enough to Men in Ignorance, may be to knowing Men not enough; according to that of the Gospel, *to whom much is given, of him much shall be required*: That the same Errour may not be capital to those who want Means of finding the Truth, and capital to others who have Means, and neglect to use them: that to continue in the Profession of Errour, discovered to be so, may be damnable, though the Errour be not so." Ibid., 5.66. See also 5.88 and 4.14.

76. Ibid., Answer to the Preface, 29.

the truth? Would not any list of fundamentals demand more from them than they were capable of? Or what of those who know more than the minimum number of fundamentals, yet profess other than they know? Does not any shortened list of fundamentals demand too little of them? Chillingworth seems to be saying here that "accommodation" obviates the need for a single set of fundamentals because no catalogue of essentials can truly accommodate all.

Herein lies Chillingworth's great innovation. Neither Erasmus nor Acontius took "accommodation" to its limits. They would not question the assumption that at least some beliefs were necessary for all Christians; to them the idea was too extreme. Chillingworth, however, does. As his Puritan opponents suspected, the logic of Chillingworth's argument would not only extend salvation to Catholics, provided they sought the truth, but also to non-Christians who were genuine in their beliefs.[77] Chillingworth's standard is subjective, based on the individual's conscience. It implies that fidelity to one's convictions is more important than adherence to objective truth. Regardless of what the oracle is, Chillingworth states, whether it is believable or not,

> though it were, if it were possible, the Barking of a Dog, or the Chirping of a Bird, or were it the Discourse of the Devil himself, yet if I be, I will not say convinced but, persuaded, though falsely, that it is a divine Revelation, and shall deny to believe it, I shall be a formal though not a material Heretick. For he that believes, though falsely, any Thing to be divine Revelation, and yet will not believe it to be true, must of Necessity believe God to be false, which . . . is the Formality of an Heretick.[78]

Although Chillingworth applies this subjective standard to the realm of beliefs and not action, the logic of Chillingworth's argument runs counter to Hooker's claim that nonessential ceremonies can be restricted by the state because they are not objectively required. Implicit in Chillingworth's approach is the attitude that a ceremony's religious importance cannot be divorced from the individual's perception of its religious importance.[79]

---

77. See Cheynell, *Chillingworthi Novissima*, C3; Orr, *Reason and Authority*, 81–82; and Jordan, *Religious Toleration in England*, 3:394–95.

78. *The Religion of Protestants*, 2.121.

79. Chillingworth quotes Hooker's argument without comment, neither approving nor rejecting it. Ibid., 5.110. Elsewhere, however, Chillingworth shows his willingness to depart

Nevertheless, Chillingworth does not abandon his belief in the existence of the fundamentals of faith; rather, this belief coexists with his radical sense that doctrine must be accommodated to the individual. While he acknowledges that doctrinal requirements must be adapted to circumstance, he asserts that the fundamentals are apparent to any rational person who hears them clearly expounded.[80] The tension within Chillingworth's argument is between his more traditional view that accommodation can be objectively ascertained and his revolutionary view that accommodation is wholly subjective. According to the former, we are justified in deciding upon a minimum number of beliefs that all rational Christians should be expected to agree upon. Beyond that, the demands of accommodation are left to God. If someone knows a nonfundamental truth and denies this truth, then God may deny him salvation, but the visible Church cannot exclude him. In the latter, more radical, opinion, *all* is left to God, since there is no way to discover the capacities of each individual. There is no such thing as one catalogue of fundamentals suitable to all—even to all Christians. This latter view, however, would have eliminated the grounds for a comprehensive Church, the common dream of the humanists. Without any fundamentals to bind them, Christians would become discrete individuals, with their own needs, capacities, circumstances and without a creed to distinguish them from the rest. This Chillingworth could not accept. His solution, though unsatisfactory, is to ignore the tension between the two views and to assume that the objective and subjective aspects of accommodation coincide: all rational Christians will certainly agree upon the fundamentals. Although Chillingworth reached the limits of humanism, he would not go beyond them.

Religion versus Politics

Chillingworth's two arguments, that all religious knowledge is probabilistic and that the essentials of salvation must be accommodated to the individual, represent a continuation as well as a further development of the humanists' rhetorical defense of religious toleration. Nevertheless, Chillingworth also

---

from Hooker. He writes that "Mr. Hooker, though an excellent man, was but a man." Ibid., 5.109.

80. Orr, *Reason and Authority*, 81.

points the way to the decline of the humanist defense of toleration. One aspect of this decline, which has already been mentioned, is the growing amorphousness of the humanist concept of fundamentals, expressed in Chillingworth's own vacillation between leaving the fundamentals undefined, defining them broadly, or interpreting them subjectively. The result of such doctrinal vagueness is that the fundamentals no longer function as the humanists (including Chillingworth) intended, that is, as the charter for an inclusive church. Instead, they reflect the popular sentiment that all Christians, or at least Protestants, agree on the basics, though what these basics are is not specified.

There is another reason, besides a weaker conception of fundamentals, why Chillingworth's arguments signal the decline of humanist toleration: because he accepted the humanists' political assumptions, he was unable to come to terms with the turmoil of the period. The humanist defense of toleration required a balance between individual freedom and political obedience. On the one hand, the *decorum* of *sermo* presupposed free discussion. Therefore, the humanists condemned religious coercion. On the other hand, the search for truth demanded a tranquil environment. Hence, the humanists emphasized the necessity of political and social order. But the English Civil War proved that the humanists' political balance was no longer viable. Although Chillingworth tried to maintain the humanist equilibrium between liberty and order, he was, in the end, unsuccessful; he could not escape the limitations of the humanist framework.

Both Erasmus and Acontius deny the sovereign's right to coerce his subjects' beliefs: the people engaged in a search for truth must be permitted to discuss their religious differences. Acontius even argues that the magistrate must not only himself eschew religiously based persecution, but must also ensure that his people refrain from verbal abuse and unrestrained speech in religious matters. In doing so, Acontius contends, the magistrate will encourage reasoned discussion and thus, ultimately, the truth.

The ruler's duty to tolerate religious diversity, however, does not imply, to the humanists, that a subject can use religion to escape his political obligations. Rather, these humanists emphasize the religious need, grounded in rhetorical *decorum*, for political obedience. Without political obedience, they argue, there can be no tranquillity, and without tranquillity, the search for religious truth is hobbled. The motivation behind humanist toleration and the humanist call for political obedience is the same: the desire for a proper rhetorical setting. Erasmus and Acontius understood that neither the climate of fear and anger brought on by religious persecution nor the state of anarchy caused by political rebellion were proper rhetorical settings. Despite his tolerance in religion, Erasmus excoriated those who threatened public peace and obedience to authority: "Who would prevent the princes from putting to death those heretics who upset the public peace, since pagan princes have the same right, and our sovereigns themselves may use it against Catholics?"[81] Erasmus maintained that Anabaptists should not be tolerated, because they disturb the peace, and Lutherans should be condemned, since they upset the tranquillity of Christendom. He opposed Luther's invective because he believed it would repel people from the truth. The speaker, if he is to persuade, must foster a climate of moderation; Luther, he believed, was doing just the opposite. Acontius evinced the same obedience to political authority. He took pains to deny the "calumny" that Lutherans "are a seditious people and hostile to princes and all good practices."[82] "Where the Gospel has been received, the same rulers are on the throne, as were on it before, and no change has been made or attempted through our agency, or even dreamed of" (4.13). Neither Erasmus nor Luther suggested that rebellion was an option when confronting an intolerant ruler.

Chillingworth accepted the humanist balance between the individual's freedom in religion and political obedience. He trusted reason's capacity to find the truth and was concerned that the rhetorical prerequisites of this search be fulfilled. Truth will triumph over error so long as they are on an equal footing: "Falsehood and Errour could not long stand against the Power of Truth, were they not supported by Tyranny and worldly Advantage."[83] Those who are coerced, however, will be tempted to lie: "Worldly Terrour may prevail so far as to make Men profess a Religion they believe not" (2.18). Terror must therefore be eliminated from religious discussion.[84] Chillingworth's justification of political obedience is also the same as the earlier humanists. Rhetoric needs a stable political authority.[85] But what if

81. Erasmus, LB 9:581 (*Suppatio errorum in Censuris Beddae*); cited in Lecler, *Toleration and the Reformation*, 1:123–24.

82. Acontius, *Satan's Stratagems*, 156.

83. *The Religion of Protestants*, 4.13.

84. A subtle difference between Acontius and Chillingworth seems to be that whereas Acontius believed that coercion, because of its ability to excite the passions, could affect perception of the truth, Chillingworth was less wary of coercion's perversion of the senses than its propensity to make people profess that which they did not believe. In any event, Chillingworth was aware that the propagation of truth depended on the proper external circumstances.

85. Therefore, whereas there is no judge to determine religious disputes, there must be one to decide in matters of sedition: "For though we deny the Pope or Church of Rome to be an infallible Judge, yet we do not deny, but that there are Judges which may proceed with Certainty

the legitimate secular power is removed? Chillingworth argued that with the removal of the king, social and political order cease to exist. Oaths, having been broken once (that is, by the rebels), can be broken again. Without a lawful king there is no security against life and property.[86] The prerequisites for religious and all other types of discussion have been removed.[87]

Conditions, however, pushed Chillingworth to weight the balance, especially in his later years, in the direction of political obedience. Although faithful to the humanist ideal of toleration, his emphasis on order progressively overshadowed his concern for toleration. Writing on the eve of the English Civil War, Chillingworth was more acutely aware than either Erasmus or Acontius of religion's role in subverting the power of the Crown. He acknowledged, for example, that his hostility to the Roman Church resulted, in part, from its attempts to undermine the English monarchy.[88] In *The Religion of Protestants* he condemned the Catholic doctrine that any monarch whom the pope declares heretical should not be obeyed: "Whereas if I follow the Scripture, I may, nay I must obey my Sovereign in lawful Things, though an Heretick, though a Tyrant."[89] Nor are the Protestants permitted to use force against the king. Violence against anyone's conscience is impermissible, but violence against the monarch is especially sinful:

> Therefore if Protestants did offer Violence to other Mens Consciences, and compel them to embrace their Reformation, I excuse them not; much less if they did so to the sacred Persons of Kings, and those that were in Authority over them, who ought to be so secured from Violence, that even their unjust and tyrannous Violence, though it may be avoided (according to that of our Saviour, *When they persecute you in one City flee unto another,*) yet may it not be resisted by opposing Violence against it. Protestants therefore that were guilty of this Crime are not to be excused; and blessed had they been had

---

enough against all seditious Persons, such as draw Men to Disobedience against Church or State, as well as against Rebels, and Traitors, and Thieves and Murderers." Ibid., 2.122.

86. Wharton MSS 943, ff. 889 and 893; cited by Orr, *Reason and Authority*, 192.

87. Orr offers a similar explanation of Chillingworth's political conservatism, writing that toward the end of his life Chillingworth became more preoccupied "with what he had always regarded as the social preconditions for intellectual freedom, namely an ordered political structure and a single Church." *Reason and Authority*, 185–86. I differ with Orr in my emphasis on the rhetorical aspect of Chillingworth's theory.

88. Tanner MSS 278, f. 126, Bodleian Library, Oxford; cited by Orr, *Reason and Authority*, 187.

89. *The Religion of Protestants*, 6.65.

> they chosen rather to be Martyrs than Murderers, and to die for their
> Religion rather than to fight for it. (5.96)

When facing a tyrant, the faithful have one of two options: submit to persecution or leave. They can do no more.

With the onset of hostilities, Chillingworth devoted himself wholeheartedly to the Royalist cause. In a sermon preached before the Court in 1643, Chillingworth upheld the rightness of the king's position, notwithstanding the personal immorality of the king's soldiers ("Publicans and sinners"), and he condemns the Puritan cause as wrong and sinful, though the actors themselves are personally moral:

> They that made no Scruple at all of fighting with his Sacred Majesty, and shooting Muskets and Ord'nance at him (which sure have not the Skill to chuse a Subject from a King) to extreme Hazard of his Sacred Person, whom by all possible Obligations they are bound to defend; do they know, think you, the general Rule without exception or limitation left by the Holy Ghost for our Direction in all such Cases, *Who can lift up his Hand against the Lord's Annointed, and be innocent?*[90]

In the "Unlawfulness of Resisting the Lawful Prince," Chillingworth echoed the same sentiments expressed in his sermon: violent resistance to the king is never permitted. Christianity, he writes here, " 'commands to pay all manner of subjection and obedience, not only to lawful princes, but to the most impious infidel and idolatrous princes, such as Nero . . . and Diocletian.' "[91] Not content to support the Royalist cause with words, Chillingworth translated his theoretical pronouncements into action by designing some siege engines used at Gloucester.[92] He even took up arms fighting for the king, dying in the custody of the Puritan forces.

Chillingworth differed from his humanist predecessors in the emphasis he placed on political obedience. In the balance between liberty and order,

90. Chillingworth, *Sermons*, 6–7.
91. Wharton MSS 943, f. 895; quoted in Orr, *Reason and Authority*, 194. In addition to his *Sermons* and his "Unlawfulness of Resisting the Lawful Prince," Chillingworth also decries the rebellion in two complementary essays, "Passages Extracted out of the Declaration of the Scots" and "Some Observations on the Scottish Declaration." See Orr, *Reason and Authority*, 190–93.
92. Orr, *Reason and Authority*, 188.

Erasmus and Acontius stressed liberty, Chillingworth, during his later years, order: Erasmus and Acontius spent more of their time seeking to gain, from those in authority, greater religious freedom for the people; Chillingworth, toward the end of his life, expended more effort on persuading the people that obedience is paramount. Yet ultimately all three humanists called for both obedience *and* toleration. Thus, while Chillingworth's emphasis on political obligation did, in a sense, pave the way for those like Thomas Hobbes who would totally subordinate toleration to the primacy of the state, he never himself abandoned the cause of toleration. He only displayed more clearly the political conservatism implicit in the other Northern humanists—a conservatism whose rhetorical motivation also underlay the humanist defense of religious toleration.[93]

---

93. See Trevor-Roper, *Catholics, Anglicans, and Puritans*, 193.

4

Hobbes: Humanism Turned Against Itself

Hobbes's Humanism

Humanism's Internal Tensions

Humanism was a balancing act: humanists had balanced rhetoric's skepticism against religion's demands for certainty, the need for religious discussion against the requirements for tranquillity. This balance, however, was difficult to maintain. Hooker, for example, believed in a comprehensive, dogmatically tolerant Church, but did not tolerate Puritans. Chillingworth alternated between the competing claims of religious liberty and political order. Despite humanism's inherent tensions, however, Hooker and Chillingworth accepted its assumptions. Thomas Hobbes, however, abandoned humanism's shaky equilibrium for the firmer foundations of science. As Hobbes saw it, scientific knowledge, unlike humanism, was univocal, and when applied to politics and religion, taught that a single sovereign should rule and define the religious truth for his subjects.

Because he empowered the sovereign to control all public aspects of religion, Hobbes also negated any guarantees of toleration. Superficially, he retained certain humanist shibboleths, such as the distinction between fundamentals and adiaphora and the conviction that religion is a matter of persuasion. However, he reinterpreted these humanist principles to his own ends. He used humanism to undermine the humanist defense of religious toleration. But while he rejected the humanists' arguments for toleration, he did not dismiss the possibility of toleration. Hobbesian political theory, I argue, is, in principle, neutral on the question of toleration since there is nothing in Hobbes's argument that actually precludes it.

Humanist Beginnings

Hobbes's education bore the stamp of humanism: a firm grounding in the classics and rhetoric. At the age of eight, Hobbes was tutored in Greek and Latin, and by the age of fourteen his facility was so great that he translated Euripides' *Medea* from Greek into Latin iambics for his tutor.[1] At fifteen, Hobbes entered Magdalen Hall, Oxford. His studies there were primarily scholastic in nature, with an emphasis on logic and Aristotelianism, but the humanist influence on Hobbes and his fellow students was apparent in the requirement of four terms of rhetoric.

After receiving his bachelor of arts from Oxford, Hobbes found employment as tutor to William, son of William Cavendish, baron of Hardwick and later first earl of Devonshire. As a tutor in the Cavendish household, Hobbes was hard-pressed to continue his personal studies.[2] But Hobbes remained in the Cavendish household long after his tutoring duties had ended, and he was able to pursue his humanistic interests in the family's ample library at Chatsworth. The crowning glory of his humanistic endeavors is his English translation of Thucydides' *History of the Peloponnesian War*, completed in 1628, just after his departure from the Cavendish family.[3] As a translation, Hobbes's Thucydides is noteworthy for being far superior to its predecessor, by Thomas Nichol.[4] The significance of this translation for present purposes, however, is not its quality but the insight it provides into the character of Hobbes's humanism. Both his decision to translate Thucydides and the ideas he presented in his introduction to the *History* place Hobbes in the same late-humanist tradition as Chillingworth: Hobbes appreciated the power of eloquence; he adopted rhetoric's standard of probability; he opposed a

1. Aubrey, *Brief Lives*, 148. My discussion of Hobbes's early life relies heavily on chapter 1 of Miriam Reik, *The Golden Lands of Thomas Hobbes* (Detroit: Wayne State University Press, 1977).

2. Hobbes was even reported to have carried books with him (particularly Caesar's *Commentaries*) so that he might read them in lobbies and antechambers, "whilest his Lord was making his Visits." Aubrey, *Brief Lives*, 149.

3. Hobbes's departure followed the death of his former pupil, William—by then, second earl of Devonshire.

4. Nichol's version, published in 1550, was based on the French of Claude de Seyssel, which was based, in turn, on the Latin of Lorenzo Valla. Hobbes translated directly from the Greek edition of Aemilius Porta. Reik, *Golden Lands*, 36.

rhetoric based on appeal to the passions; he supported monarchy; and, in an indirect manner, he even sided with those who championed greater religious latitude. If Hobbes had produced no other work, he would undoubtedly have been considered a typical, albeit minor, humanist.

Hobbes begins his translation with an "Epistle Dedicatory" to his former pupil, William of Cavendish, in which he recommends the writings of Thucydides "as having in them profitable instruction for noblemen, and such as may come to have the management of great and weighty actions."[5] The profitable instruction, Hobbes proceeds to tell us, consists of the examples and precepts of heroic virtue, "actions of *honour* and *dishonour*," held up before the reader in plain view (8:vi). Thus, like Erasmus and Thomas Elyot, humanists who composed handbooks on the education of the young nobleman, Hobbes translated the *History* for its edifying examples of the virtuous life.[6] But while Hobbes valued Thucydides' matter, he was equally concerned with Thucydides' method.

It was Hobbes's realization that both content *and* form are required in teaching that drew him to history, in general, and to Thucydides' *History*, in particular. Content and form, or what Hobbes termed "truth" and "elocution," complement each other, and good history contains both. "For in *truth*," Hobbes writes, "consisteth the *soul*, and in *elocution* the *body* of history. The latter without the former, is but a picture of history; and the former without the latter, unapt to instruct."[7] For truth unadorned is philosophy, and philosophy, which conveys knowledge through precepts, is an inferior means of instruction.[8] Philosophy can teach a student the truth, but it may not move him to apply it. History, by contrast, will move the student to act. History presents its message in a rhetorically suitable form, teaching through examples, which are far more likely to inspire the listener than are dry precepts.[9] This link between history and rhetoric was not lost

---

5. Thomas Hobbes, *The English Works of Thomas Hobbes of Malmesbury* (hereafter referred to as *EW*), ed. Sir William Molesworth, vol. 8, *The History of the Grecian War Written by Thucydides* (London: Bohn, 1843), v.

6. Erasmus's and Elyot's works are, respectively, the *Education of a Christian Prince* and the book of the *Governour*. Other similar examples are Guillaume Budé's *Education of the Prince* and Antonio de Guevara's *Dial of Princes*.

7. *EW* 8:xx.

8. Ibid., xxii; David Johnston, *The Rhetoric of Leviathan: Thomas Hobbes and the Politics of Cultural Transformation* (Princeton: Princeton University Press, 1986), 20–21.

9. By making the reader feel as if he were actually witnessing the events himself, history firmly impresses the mind and soul of the student. This technique of presenting a "speaking picture" is a traditional element of classical rhetoric. Quintilian speaks of it (*Institutio oratoria*

on classical rhetoricians like Cicero and Quintilian, who placed history in the orator's domain.[10] In turn, their observations did not elude Hobbes, who cited the rhetoricians Cicero and Lucian as his authorities for his views on history.[11] Hobbes praised history for its rhetorical effectiveness and chose to translate Thucydides because Thucydides is the most rhetorical of historians.[12] Thus Hobbes quoted Plutarch as saying: Thucydides "maketh his auditor a spectator," casting his reader into "the same passions they were in that were beholders."[13]

By turning to history as his source of knowledge, Hobbes implicitly accepted rhetoric's epistemological standard of probability. Although he does not expressly say so in Thucydides, as he did in his later political works, all historical knowledge is of necessity probable.[14] First, facts, the building blocks of history, are open to error. For if an eyewitness can err through misperception or, more likely, the dimming of memory, then the odds are much greater that someone far removed from the original event, subject to

---

6.2.29–32) in the following words: "There are certain experiences which the Greeks call *fantasia*, and the Romans *visions*, whereby things absent are presented to our imagination with such extreme vividness that they seem actually to be before our very eyes. It is the man who is really sensitive to such impressions who will have the greatest power over the emotions. . . . From such impressions arises that *energaia* which Cicero calls *illumination* and *actuality*, which makes us seem not so much to narrate as to exhibit the actual scene, while our emotions will be no less actively stirred than if we were present at the actual occurrence."

10. Cicero writes: "And as History, which bears witness to the passing of the ages, sheds light upon reality, gives life to recollection and guidance to human existence, and brings tidings of ancient days, whose voice, but the orator's, can entrust her to immortality?" *De oratore* 2.9.36. Quintilian comments similarly on the orator's need to move beyond the study of "the precepts of philosophy alone" to include the more important study of "all the noblest deeds that have been handed down to us from the ancient times. . . . For if the Greeks bear away the palm for moral precepts, Rome can produce more striking examples of moral performance, which is a far greater thing." *Institutio oratoria* 12.2.29–30.

11. *EW* 8:xxxi, xiii; Leo Strauss, *The Political Philosophy of Hobbes: Its Basis and Its Genesis*, trans. Elsa M. Sinclair (Chicago: University of Chicago Press, 1952), 82.

12. For a discussion of Hobbes's understanding of the link between history and rhetoric, see Strauss, *Political Philosophy,* 79–86. Hobbes's interest in history, as Strauss points out, was typical of the humanists in general. Ibid., 82. Italian humanists such as Machiavelli and Guicciardini, for example, composed histories, and even Acontius wrote a work on historical methodology.

13. *EW* 8:viii, xxii.

14. Hobbes implies that he does not view history as possessing the certainty of the apodictic sciences—mathematics or logic—when he approves Thucydides' use of fictive speeches like Pericles' Funeral Oration, that is, what Hobbes and the rhetoricians called "deliberative orations," in historical narrative. Ibid., xxi. In fact, Hobbes's contemporaries saw a connection between fictive speeches and probability: "Such speeches were often considered allowable only if they were 'probable.'" Reik, *Golden Lands,* 47–49.

the distortions of many generations, will be mistaken about some of the facts. Thus, facts cannot be known with certainty, only with probability. Second, since induction can never yield certainty, the conclusions derived from historical facts are themselves probable at best. Causal statements about history, though they may be generally true, are not infallible. There are no sure predictors for wars or seditions. Historians, Hobbes among them, have had to content themselves with Chillingworth's standard of moral certainty, not the absolute certainty of the logician.

Hobbes, however, was by no means uncritical of rhetoric in his introduction to Thucydides. Rhetoric is already associated here with public disorder, a constant theme in his later writings. Hobbes writes that, in the Athenian political assemblies, the unsound advice of rhetorical demagogues was preferred over the "temperate and discreet advice" of men like Thucydides.[15] In public deliberations before many people, "fear (which for the most part adviseth well, though it execute not so) seldom or never sheweth itself or is admitted" (ibid.). Rather than taking counsel from realistic fear, as one would do in more private discussions, the assemblies of the multitude are ruled by negative passions, particularly the demagogue's pursuit of glory.

Hobbes does not condemn rhetoric, per se, but only a rhetoric that permits the passions to obscure the truth. Like *sermo*, Hobbes's rhetoric of history is not directed to emotional manipulation. Hobbes believed that eloquence in history is ideally intended to confirm in the reader what reason already has shown to be the case. Although some rhetoricians subordinate truth to rhetorical ornamentation and affect, Hobbes argues that this need not be the case.[16] Thus Thucydides, who refused to sway the assemblies to reckless action, demonstrates the possibility of good oratory. Unfortunately, his

15. "It need not be doubted, but from such a master Thucydides was sufficiently qualified to become a great demagogue, and of great authority with the people. But it seemeth he had not desire at all to meddle in the government: because in those days it was impossible for any man to give good and profitable counsel for the commonwealth, and not incur the displeasure of the people. For their opinion was such of their own power, and of the facility of achieving whatsoever action they undertook, that such men only swayed the assemblies, and were esteemed wise and good commonwealth's men, as did put them upon the most dangerous and desperate enterprizes. Whereas he that gave them temperate and discreet advice, was thought a coward, or not to understand, or else to malign their power." *EW* 8:xvi.

16. Ibid., xxvi. Hobbes singles out the rhetorician Dionysius of Halicarnassus, a vociferous critic of Thucydides, as exemplary of the orator who lets "affection to his country" and desire to please the hearer predominate. "Yet," Hobbes continues, "Lucian, a rhetorician also, in a treatise entitled, *How a history ought to be written*, saith thus: 'that a writer of history ought, in his writings, to be a foreigner, without country, living under his own law only, subject to no king, nor caring what any man will like or dislike, but laying out the matter as it is.' "

example also proved to Hobbes that bad rhetoric will often triumph over good: the warmongering orators prevailed, while Thucydides withdrew from public life, "that he might not be either of them that committed or of them that suffered the evil" (ibid., xvi).

Hobbes contrasts the rational character of historical oratory, as evidenced by Thucydides, with the unreflective nature of public oratory. Thucydides' eloquence, Hobbes writes, is "rather to be read than heard. For words that pass away (as in public orations they must) without pause, ought to be understood with ease, and are lost else: though words that remain in writing for the reader to meditate on, ought rather to be pithy and full." Hobbes distinguishes Thucydides' oratory, specifically, from the rhetoric of the courtroom. Thucydides' style, Hobbes writes, "was not at all fit for the bar." Hobbes's source for the distinction is Cicero, who observes that while Thucydides' goal is "to hold an auditor while telling a story," the judicial orator intends "to arouse him." In addition, Cicero notes, Thucydides' rhetoric, as opposed to the courtroom orator's, is not designed "to clinch a case against an opponent, or to refute a charge." Like *sermo*, the ancient historian's rhetoric is neither passionate nor agonistic.[17]

Hobbes's politics in Thucydides are, like other humanists', traditionally promonarchical. Hobbes writes approvingly of Thucydides' preference for monarchy over democracy. His conception of monarchy (or of state power in general) is traditional, that is, neither rigid nor absolute: governments can be mixed between the few and the many, and states may be "democratical in name but in effect monarchical."[18] More specifically, Hobbes's politics are like Chillingworth's, overtly concerned with the problem of order. Chillingworth and Hobbes, writing in anticipation of the English Civil War, both responded to the prospects of social disorder by emphasizing the connection between monarchy and stability. Chillingworth did so in his exhortations to obey the king. Without such obedience, Chillingworth argued, social and political order disappear. Hobbes made the same connection between monarchy and order by citing Thucydides' rationale for the superiority of monarchy. Because the public assemblies were controlled by the rhetoric of demagogues, Hobbes argued in the name of Thucydides that democratic governments are more prone to sedition and dissolution than monarchies: "So it seemeth," Hobbes continues, "that . . . [Thucydides] approved of

17. Ibid., xxxi; Cicero *De optimo genere oratorum* 5.15–16.
18. *EW* 8:xvii.

the regal government" (ibid.). Already in Hobbes's introduction to Thucydides, the exigencies of order outweigh the claims of liberty.

How did Hobbes's concern for order affect his views on toleration? Although Hobbes does not directly address the issue of toleration in his introduction, the sympathy he shows for those ancient Greeks—Anaxagoras, Socrates, and Thucydides—who questioned religious convention implies a sensitivity toward the plight of the heterodox in his own day. All three, because they questioned the accepted religion, were considered atheists by their countrymen. This charge, Hobbes asserts, was false. They were criticized not for their atheism, but only for their courage in rejecting the superstitions of those around them.[19] Hobbes's comments are more than historical musings about ancient thinkers; they allude to the religious struggles of his own seventeenth-century England. As Hobbes's praise of Thucydides' monarchism reflects his support of the English monarch, his sympathy for the religious nonconformists of ancient Greece signals his affinity for contemporary religious dissenters.[20] While the practical implications of this affinity cannot be known with certainty, it seems likely that Hobbes's stand on toleration at this point approximated Chillingworth's. Because Hobbes was not yet committed to the centralization of all power and decision-making in the person of a single sovereign—witness his recognition of mixed government in Athens—the existence of independent religious institutions does not threaten the safety of the Commonwealth, as it will in his mature theory.

In 1628, then, Hobbes, by virtue of education, interests, and opinions, was a humanist, much along the lines of Chillingworth. Consistent with his humanism, Hobbes found in Thucydides' *History* a proper model of rhetoric, a probable standard of knowledge, and a justification for monarchy. Hobbes, however, moved away from these humanist elements. His anxiety about the degeneration of the polity impelled him to nonhumanist solutions. Nonetheless, he retained an interest in Thucydides to the very end: he made sure that his translation was reprinted three times, the last being in 1676,

19. Ibid., xiv–xv. Hobbes even makes Thucydides into something of a pagan humanist, who opposed the overpunctual observation of religion, but approved the "worshipping of the gods."

20. That Hobbes himself was accused by his contemporaries of atheism, does not detract from my argument. For even if Hobbes's sympathy for the ancient Greek thinkers derived from his personal identification with their plight, he does not deny here, as he does in his later political thought, the right of nonconformists to make their views known. For a discussion of contemporary views of Hobbes as an atheist, see Samuel I. Mintz, *The Hunting of Leviathan* (Cambridge: Cambridge University Press, 1962), especially chapter 3.

three years before his death; and in his verse biography, written at the age of 84, Hobbes still considered Thucydides to be his favorite classical writer.[21] Thucydides remained significant to Hobbes because the Greek historian provided him with a conception of science and a distinction between nature and convention crucial to his later thought.[22] Hobbes received from Thucydides, first, a scientific method that supplied natural explanations for all social phenomena. Thucydides excludes, for example, the religious and metaphysical interpretations that are sometimes found in Herodotus, and he generalizes from individual cases to society at large, based on the assumption of a common human nature.[23] This notion that knowledge must be scientific will feature prominently in Hobbes. Second, Hobbes received from Thucydides a framework in which *nomos* and *physis*, convention and nature, are opposed. This antithesis, which Thucydides shares with the Sophists, contrasts human law and morality, derived from convention, with nature or reality. For the Sophists, justice and injustice, right and wrong were not part of the immutable order of things, but artificial.[24] Thucydides uses this distinction to argue that although human beings sometimes appeal to the conventional principles of justice and law, they are in reality motivated by self-interest, that is, nature.[25] Later Hobbes applied the *nomos-physis* antithesis to his theories of knowledge and politics in order to argue that univocality in both is a product of convention.

21. *Hobbes's Thucydides*, ed. Richard Schlatter (New Brunswick: Rutgers University Press, 1975), xx.

22. The importance of Thucydides' ideas to Hobbes's mature political theory was suggested to me by Amos Funkenstein.

23. On Thucydides as scientist, see Charles Norris Cochrane, *Thucydides and the Science of History* (New York: Russell & Russell, 1965); and Gigliola Rossini, "The Criticism of Rhetorical Historiography and the Ideal of Scientific Method: History, Nature and Science in the Political Language of Thomas Hobbes," in *The Languages of Political Theory in Early-Modern Europe*, ed. Anthony Pagden (Cambridge: Cambridge University Press, 1987), 305–10.

24. W.K.C. Guthrie, *The Sophists* (Cambridge: Cambridge University Press, 1971), 21–24, 55–60.

25. Thucydides finds confirmation for this opinion from the Athenians, who not only acted on the basis of self-interest but openly conceded that interest, not justice, was the sole determinant of human action. Guthrie, *Sophists*, 84–88; John H. Finley, *Thucydides* (Cambridge: Harvard University Press, 1942), 54–60.

Hobbes the Scientist

The "Break" Debate

Sometime around 1630, soon after publishing his English translation of Thucydides' *History of the Peloponnesian War*, Hobbes chanced upon a copy of Euclid's *Elements*. The epiphanic character of this incident is described by Hobbes's first biographer, John Aubrey:

> He was 40 years old before he looked on Geometry; which happened accidentally. Being in a Gentleman's Library, Euclid's Elements lay open, and 'twas the 47 *El. libri* I. He read the Proposition. *By G——*, sayd he (he would now and then sweare an emphaticall Oath by way of emphasis) *this is impossible*! So he reads the Demonstration of it, which referred him back to such a Proposition; which proposition he read. That referred him back to another, which he also read. *Et sic deinceps* [and so on] that at last he was demonstratively convinced of the trueth. This made him in love with Geometry.[26]

Euclid's geometry sparked in Hobbes a passion for science that dominated his writings from 1630 until his death.[27]

What Hobbes's newfound scientific interest signifies for the chronology of his intellectual development, however, is the subject of much debate. On the one hand, there are those like Leo Strauss who distinguish between a humanistic period (1608–ca. 1630) and a scientific period (1630–79) in Hobbes.[28] They contend that there is an apparent disjunction between the

---

26. Aubrey, *Brief Lives*, 150.

27. Hobbes's pursuit of science is first seen in the *Short Tract on First Principles* (unpublished during his lifetime but written possibly as early as 1630), in which Hobbes argues for a mechanistic scientific position; it continues in his subsequent studies of optics, geometry, motion, and mechanics in such works as *De Corpore* of 1655, the *Problemata physica* of 1662, and the *Decameron physilogicum* of 1678. His science of politics is enunciated in three works: *The Elements of Law*, written in 1640 and published in 1650 as two treatises, *Human Nature* and *De Corpore Politico*; *De Cive*, written after the *Elements*, but published in 1642; and, last, *Leviathan*, published in 1651. See Frithiof Brandt, *Thomas Hobbes' Mechanical Conception of Nature* (Copenhagen: Levin & Munksgaard, 1928), 55; and J.W.N. Watkins, *Hobbes's System of Ideas: A Study in the Political Significance of Philosophical Theories* (London: Hutchinson University Library, 1973), 13–14.

28. Strauss's conception of Hobbes's break with humanism is complex. For while Strauss states that Hobbes broke with his humanist past before he wrote any of his major works on

years leading up to Hobbes's exposure to geometry, which are identifiably humanistic, and the years following his Euclidean revelation: in the former, exemplified by Hobbes's translation of Thucydides, history is the source of knowledge, and in the latter, it is science, particularly geometry. On the other hand, recent scholars like Miriam Reik and David Johnston seek to minimize, if not dismiss altogether, the presumed discontinuity between Hobbes's humanist and scientific periods.[29] Hobbes's humanistic concerns, they point out, did not disappear: his devotion to literature persisted, witness his translations of Homer's *Iliad* and *Odyssey* into English late in life; he was still preoccupied with the influence of speech and eloquence on human actions, as he was earlier in his translation of Thucydides; despite his criticisms of rhetoric, he made use of rhetoric himself, especially in *Leviathan*; and he even published *A Briefe of the Art of Rhetorique* in 1637, an English translation and adaptation of Aristotle's *Rhetoric*. These facts, they contend, along with the implausibility of a forty-one-year-old philosopher totally breaking with his previously held ideas—ideas held for over twenty years—argue against the idea of two completely disconnected periods in Hobbes's career.

Neither the proponents nor the critics of the "break hypothesis," however, can maintain their position absolutely, since Hobbes's "discovery" of science involved both his abandonment of some previously held ideas and his retention of others.[30] The question, then, is not "did he or did he not reject humanism in toto," but "what did Hobbes reject, and what did he retain, and why." I contend that from the standpoint of the humanist defense of toleration Hobbes rejected far more than he preserved. The reason for his rejection of humanist toleration was the English Civil War. Hobbes's experience with civil war led him to conclude that, if chaos was to be avoided, the humanists' epistemological, political, and religious assumptions, which suggested ambiguity, had to be abandoned. And because the humanists based

political theory, Strauss also argues that the essence of Hobbes's political theory derives from his humanist period. The essence, according to Strauss, is Hobbes's "moral attitude," which posits an "antithesis of fundamentally unjust vanity and fundamentally just fear of violent death." See *Political Philosophy*, 27–29.

29. Reik, *Golden Lands*, chapter 2; Johnston, *Rhetoric of Leviathan*, chapter 1.

30. And so Strauss speaks of a humanist essence that remains throughout Hobbes's later political theory, whereas Reik and Johnston find new emphases and interests—though Reik deems "the path that led from . . . humanistic studies to political and scientific concerns . . . a natural one for the seventeenth-century mind, just as it was natural then for a poet like Milton to write a textbook in logic as well as his poems." *Reik, Golden Lands*, 51.

their defense of toleration on these assumptions, Hobbes concomitantly abandoned humanist toleration.[31]

The Failure of Rhetoric

Hobbes's rejection of humanism is epitomized by his attack on the hallmark of humanism: rhetoric.[32] As both sides of the "break hypothesis" acknowledge, humanism was tied to the study of rhetoric.[33] Throughout his mature political writings, Hobbes consistently links civil war and sedition to rhetoric, particularly religious rhetoric. In *The Elements of Law* (completed in 1640), he asserts again, as he did in his introduction to Thucydides, that the rhetoric of the public assemblies is apt to bring about civil war and that, therefore, monarchy is preferable to democracy.[34] Aware of, even obsessed with, the role of Presbyterian preachers in causing the Civil War, rhetoric becomes, for Hobbes, a tool employed by those outside the government to overthrow the duly constituted authorities. There are men, Hobbes warns in *De Cive* (published in 1642), who preach a doctrine of the private knowledge of good and evil. This opinion, Hobbes continues, "sprang from sick-brained men, who having gotten good store of holy words by frequent reading of the Scriptures, made such a connexion of them usually in their preaching, that their sermons, signifying just nothing, yet to unlearned men

31. See Richard Ashcraft, "Ideology and Class in Hobbes' Political Theory," *Political Theory* 6 (1978): 27–62. Ashcraft argues here that not only is the Civil War to be understood as the background to Hobbes's political views, but that it shapes the substance of his political theory.

32. For a discussion of Hobbes's assault on rhetoric, see Frederick G. Whelan, "Language and Its Abuses in Hobbes's Political Philosophy," *American Political Science Review* 75 (1981): 61–67, especially 62–63.

33. Strauss finds Hobbes's humanism linked to his interest in history, which is, in turn, connected to the rhetorical tradition. For a discussion of Hobbes's understanding of the connection between history and rhetoric, see Strauss, *Political Philosophy*, 79–86. Hobbes's interest in history, as Strauss points out, was typical of the humanists in general. Ibid., 82. As for Johnston and Reik, their rejection of the "break hypothesis" is based on Hobbes's continuing interest in the rhetorical tradition, which they perceive to be characteristic of humanism. While the two sides of the "break hypothesis" debate whether Hobbes abandoned his rhetorical stance after his translation of Thucydides or always maintained it, a third position is taken by Gigliola Rossini, who argues that Hobbes was consistently antirhetorical, even in Thucydides. "Criticism," 303–18.

34. Thomas Hobbes, *The Elements of Law*, ed. Ferdinand Tönnies (Cambridge: Cambridge University Press, 1928), 2.5.8, pp. 112–13.

seemed most divine."[35] By persuading the people to act out of their own judgment, not the sovereign's, Hobbes concludes that these preachers cause "the ruin of all governments." In his history of the English Civil War, *Behemoth* (finished in 1668), Hobbes is still more explicit: "The mischief [the Civil War] proceeded wholly from the Presbyterian preachers, who, by a long practised histrionic faculty, preached up the rebellion powerfully."[36] These Presbyterian ministers were so artful in their rhetoric that they seduced the people to disobedience unawares. Rhetoric allowed them to conceal "the ambitious plot in them to raise sedition against the state," making them appear to be motivated solely by true religious zeal (193–94).

It would seem that Hobbes's chief criticism of rhetoric was that, by manipulating the listener's passions, rhetoric masks the truth. In *The Elements of Law*, for example, Hobbes writes that eloquence values winning above the truth and that its practitioners "make good and bad, right and wrong, appear great or less, according as it shall serve their turns."[37] Similarly, in *De Cive* Hobbes writes that it is "the nature of eloquence" to make all things—"good and evil, profitable and unprofitable, honest and dishonest"—appear other than they are in reality, "according as it shall best suit with his end that speaketh. . . . Nor is this fault in the man, but in the nature itself of eloquence, whose end (as all masters of rhetoric teach us) is not truth (except by chance) but victory, and whose property is not to reform, but to allure."[38] Rhetoric is almost always divorced from wisdom, making "things to them who are ill-affected seem worse, [and] to them that are well-affected seem evil"; instead of explaining things as they really are, it presents the preconceived notions of the orator as reality (2.12.2, pp. 138–39). Hobbes persists in this sentiment through *Leviathan* (published in 1651), where he describes eloquence as "seeming prudence" and "seeming wisedome," which deceives not only the listener but the speaker too.[39] Seen from this perspective, Hobbes most resembles that ancient critic of rhetoric,

35. Thomas Hobbes, *De Cive or The Citizen*, ed. Sterling P. Lamprecht (Westport, Conn.: Greenwood Press, 1982), 2.12.6, pp. 133–34.

36. *EW* 6:363 (*Behemoth*).

37. *Elements of Law*, 2.8.14, pp. 140–41.

38. *De Cive*, 2.10.11, p. 123.

39. Thomas Hobbes, *Leviathan*, ed. C. B. Macpherson (New York: Penguin Books, 1968), 151 and 164, where Hobbes writes: "Eloquence seemeth wisedome, both to themselves and others." Hobbes also argues that the rhetoricians "could not poison the people with those absurd opinions contrary to peace and civil society, unless they held them themselves, which sure is an ignorance greater than can well befall any wise man." *De Cive*, 2.12.12, pp. 138–39.

Plato.[40] Like Plato in the *Gorgias*, Hobbes may also be said to uphold genuine truth against rhetoric's apparent truth, the only difference being that for Plato the villains are the Sophists, and for Hobbes they are the Puritan preachers.

If Hobbes's criticisms were grounded simply on this traditional argument, his position could be interpreted not as a rejection of rhetoric, per se, but only of bad rhetoric, thus supporting the position that Hobbes did not abandon the rhetorical tradition and humanism. Later humanists, including Acontius and Chillingworth, would have especially agreed with Hobbes's rejection of a rhetoric that appeals to the passions.[41] Hobbes's language in *De Cive* condemning rhetoric for not being based on right reason but on "a certain violence of the mind" seems reminiscent of Acontius's *Satan's Stratagems*.[42] His willingness at the end of *Leviathan* to entertain a positive sort of rhetoric that is allied, not opposed, to reason further seems to testify to the compatibility of Hobbes's and the humanists' views on rhetoric.[43] And, in fact, those who argue against the "break hypothesis" maintain that Hobbes does distinguish between a good and a bad rhetoric—just as he did in his humanist days.[44] Hobbes's critique of rhetoric, however, is not based primarily on the power of eloquence to distort the facts. The main fault of rhetoric, for Hobbes, and the reason for his break with humanism, is that rhetoric is equivocal.

40. Terrence Ball makes this comparison of Hobbes to Plato: "Hobbes' defense of linguistic austerity must be viewed against the background of an older rhetorical tradition in which the aim of political speech is to kindle the passions and direct the interests of the audience. Hobbes is as critical as Plato of appeals to passions and mere 'opinions' of the masses." Terrence Ball, "Hobbes' Linguistic Turn," *Polity* 17 (1985): 755–56. Strauss also compares Hobbes with Plato on rhetoric in *Political Philosophy*, 148–49 n. 5.

41. Cf. Bouwsma, "Changing Assumptions in Later Renaissance Culture." Hobbes's rejection of passionate appeals is consistent with the *decorum* of *sermo*.

42. *De Cive*, 2.10.11, p. 123.

43. "So also Reason, and Eloquence, (though not perhaps in the Naturall Sciences, yet in the Morall) may stand very well together. For wheresoever there is place for adorning and preferring of Errour, there is much more place for adorning and preferring of Truth, if they have it to adorn." *Leviathan*, 718.

44. See, for example, Johnston, *Rhetoric of Leviathan*, 59–60, or Reik, *Golden Lands*, 52: "Even after Hobbes made politics a subject for science, there was no 'break' in its relation to rhetoric as he saw it in his early years. When he raged against rhetoric and said that impudence was the 'goddess of rhetoric,' as he did in *Behemoth*, he was speaking of the confusion wrought by oratory in 'democratical assemblies'—a position he already took in the Thucydides essay. . . . But side by side with passages where he is critical of those who abuse rhetoric, one finds others where he reiterates his early conviction that rhetoric, properly employed, has its place in the moral sciences." See also Reik, *Golden Lands*, 149–50 and 220 n. 39.

Rhetoric is unacceptable to Hobbes because it promotes ambiguity, and it is ambiguity, not falsehood, that Hobbes fears most. It is in the nature of rhetoric to adapt itself to the individual's passions.[45] But when words "have a signification . . . of the nature, disposition, and interest of the speaker"— which is rhetoric's aim—they "can never be true grounds of any ratiocination." Especially when we come to moral words, people's diverse prejudices lead them to different conceptions of the same term: "For one man calleth Wisdome, what another calleth feare; and one cruelty, what another justice; one prodigality, what another magnanimity."[46] As Quentin Skinner shows, such rhetorical redescription was a time-honored classical rhetorical technique known as *paradiastole*, defined by Quintilian as the means "by which we distinguish between similar things, as 'When you call yourself wise instead of astute, brave instead of rash, economical instead of mean.'"[47] Hobbes, however, condemns paradiastole because it makes moral agreement impossible. Hobbes disapproves of the use of metaphors and tropes in reasoning on similar grounds: "All metaphors," he writes in *The Elements of Law*, "are (by profession) equivocal. And there is scarce any word that is not made equivocal by divers contextures of speech, or by diversity of pronunciation and gesture."[48] Hobbes, unlike Plato, does not condemn literary "adornments" because they are mere appearances, imitations of reality.[49] Rhetorical devices are unsuitable, to Hobbes, because they foster conceptual diversity and, ultimately, civil war: "Metaphors, and senslesse and ambigu-

45. Conal Condren contends that Hobbes himself adopted rhetoric's equivocal style, offering varied and inconsistent arguments depending on circumstance. Condren links this Hobbesian characteristic specifically to the rhetoric of Lorenzo Valla. Because Hobbes uses a humanist's rhetorical techniques, Condren maintains that "too simple an opposition [is] being posited by modern scholars between Hobbes and 'humanism.'" "On the Rhetorical Foundations of *Leviathan*," *History of Political Thought* 11 (1990): 715.

46. *Leviathan*, 109–10.

47. Quintilian, *Institutio oratoria* 9.3.65. Expanding upon Quintilian's understanding of the concept, the Tudor rhetorician George Puttenham writes in *The Arte of English Poesie* (1589) that we make use of the figure of paradiastole when we "call an unthrift, a liberall Gentleman: the foolish-hardy, valiant or couragious: the niggard, thriftie: a great riot, or outrage, an youthfull pranke, and such like termes: moderating and abating the force of the matter by craft and for a pleasing purpose." George Puttenham, *The Arte of English Poesie*, ed. Gladys Doidge Willcock and Alice Walker (Cambridge: Cambridge University Press, 1936), 184–85. For a historical account of paradiastole, particularly as it relates to Hobbes, see Quentin Skinner, "Thomas Hobbes: Rhetoric and the Construction of Morality," *Proceedings of the British Academy* 76 (1990): 1–61. See also Quentin Skinner, "Moral Ambiguity and the Renaissance Art of Eloquence," *Essays in Criticism* 46 (1994): 267–92.

48. *Elements of Law*, 1.5.7, p. 16; *Leviathan*, 102, 109, 114–15.

49. Plato *Republic* 601A–C.

ous words, are like *ignes fatui*; and reasoning upon them, is wandering amongst innumerable absurdities; and their end, contention, and sedition, or contempt."[50] So too rhetoric's reliance on arguments from authority. By turning to "opinions already received, what nature soever they are," the rhetoricians breed controversy.[51] Each side cites its own authorities, persuasive to its own group, but in doing so they abandon any common ground with those outside: "PERSUASION . . . begetteth no more in the hearer, than what is in the speaker, bare opinion." But the aftermath of persuasion is only "two opinions contradictory one to another, namely affirmation and negation of the same thing."[52] Presbyterians, Independents, Anglicans, and Roman Catholics may construct internally persuasive arguments—for Hobbes their arguments had been all too effective—nevertheless, Hobbes asserts, their use of rhetoric will produce civil war, not a broader consensus.

The humanists would have agreed with Hobbes that rhetoric could foster contention. Much of the contemporary religious controversy and intolerance, in their view, resulted from the malevolent use of persuasion. They discerned, however, a solution to Hobbes's dilemma. The humanists argued that Christians possessed sufficient certainty of the fundamentals of faith and of ethical precepts to achieve unity.[53] Even Chillingworth, who conceded that all religious knowledge was at best only probable, maintained that the fundamentals were so highly probable that they could be accepted by everyone. The essentials of faith, the humanists claimed, were apparent, and therefore, almost all Christians agreed on them. The consensus that was visible in doctrine, according to the humanists, was even broader in ethical matters, where non-Christians also accept the fundamentals of moral living. The universal agreement on moral truths is noted by the sixteenth-century humanist Sebastian Castellio:

> But to judge of doctrine is not so simple as to judge of conduct. In the
> matter of conduct, if you ask a Jew, Turk, Christian, or anyone else,

50. *Leviathan*, 116–17. Hobbes himself, ironically, used rhetoric to make his case against rhetoric. Thus, Hobbes's condemnation of metaphor as *ignes fatui* is itself metaphoric. See Kahn, *Rhetoric, Prudence, and Skepticism*, chapter 6, and Whelan, "Language and Its Abuses," 71.

51. *De Cive*, 1.12.6, pp. 133–34.

52. *Elements of Law*, 1.13.2, p. 50.

53. Although Erasmus is the best known advocate of the importance of ethics to Christianity, this principle is common to all the Christian humanists. See, for example, Chillingworth, *Sermons*, 77, and Orr, *Reason and Authority*, 158–59.

what he thinks of a brigand or a traitor, all will reply with one accord that brigands and traitors are evil and should be put to death. Why do all agree in this? Because the matter is obvious. For that reason no controversies are raised and no books are written to prove that brigands, etc., should be put to death. This knowledge is engraved and written in the hearts of all men from the foundation of the world.[54]

For humanists like Erasmus and Chillingworth, the consensus on doctrine and ethics also had veridical implications. Like the classical rhetoricians, they saw consensus as a criterion of the truth.

Hobbes, however, rejects the humanists' conception of consensus on the grounds that it, like the practice of rhetoric, is ambiguous. Like Chillingworth, he argues that consensus can only determine probability. But, for Hobbes, probability is an insufficient standard of knowledge. His rejection of probability as a criterion of knowledge emerges out of his discussion of prudence.[55] In Hobbes's terminology, prudence is knowledge of the future based on past experience.[56] Thus history, which Hobbes relied upon in his translation of Thucydides, is a kind of prudence, since it seeks to apply past lessons toward the future. In *The Elements of Law* and later in *Leviathan*, Hobbes makes clear that such prudence is insufficient because it is probable, not certain.[57] Signs from the past, he states:

are but conjectural; and according as they have often or seldom failed, so their assurance is more or less; but never full and evident;

54. Bainton, *Concerning Heretics*, 131.

55. Although in his translation of Thucydides Hobbes relies on probability, qua history, as the basis of knowledge, he no longer does so in his mature political writings. The first evidence of Hobbes's ambivalence toward probability is in his *Briefe of the Art of Rhetorique*, the first English translation of Aristotle's *Rhetoric* (published in 1637). Hobbes departs here from Aristotle's original by obscuring probability's role in rhetoric. Whereas Aristotle based the rhetorical syllogism, the enthymeme, on probability, Hobbes defines it instead as a short syllogism, leaving out any mention of probability. See John T. Harwood, ed., *The Rhetorics of Thomas Hobbes and Bernard Lamy* (Carbondale: Southern Illinois University Press, 1986), 1–2, 14, 40, and Walter J. Ong, S.J., "Hobbes and Talon's Ramist Rhetoric in England," *Transactions of the Cambridge [England] Bibliography Society* 1 (1951): 261–62, 267–68.

56. Human beings gain prudence, according to Hobbes, by observing the relationship between "signs" — "the Event Antecedent of the Consequent" — and what follows them. For a discussion of the differences between prudence in *Elements of Law* and *Leviathan*, see Marshall Missner, "Skepticism and Hobbes's Political Philosophy," *Journal of the History of Ideas* 44 (1983): 418–19.

57. *Leviathan*, 97–98. On Hobbes's movement from history to science, see Strauss, *Political Philosophy*, chapters 7–8; Rossini, "Criticism," 318–24.

for though a man hath always seen the day and night to follow one another hitherto; yet can he not thence conclude they shall do so, or that they have done so eternally. Experience concludeth nothing universally. If the sign hit twenty times for once missing, a man may lay a wager of twenty to one of the event; but may not conclude it for a truth.[58]

In a reversal of Chillingworth, whose metaphor of the gambler was designed to show the absurdity of equating high probability with mere possibility, Hobbes highlights the inadequacy of probability when compared with certainty.[59] While prudence, according to Hobbes, is useful and necessary for daily life, it is never certain. Prudence will not guarantee us that because one event followed another in the past, it will do so again. In addition, prudence can never take into account all the circumstances that may affect an outcome.[60] Moreover, since there is no direct correspondence between external objects and our impressions of them (Hobbes assumes that sense impressions are caused by the motion of matter impinging first on the sense organs and then, eventually, on the brain and heart), we can never be positive that our sense impressions, upon which prudence is based, are not the products of dreams or our eyes having been rubbed.[61] Therefore, Hobbes writes in *Leviathan*, the conclusions derived from experience—no matter how probable—are "not with certainty enough."[62] At this point, one might pause to ask, "certain enough for what?" "Certain enough," Hobbes might reply, "to avoid any disagreement." Hobbes's problem with prudence, and therefore with probability, is that because it "concludeth nothing universally," it permits of various opinions. On everyday concerns such as weather—do the clouds signify rain?—there is no harm in uncertainty and diversity. But in religion and morals, Hobbes believes, epistemological

58. *Elements of Law*, 1.4.10, pp. 12–13. Hobbes anticipates Hume's point that it is not valid to infer from "every observed A has been B" to "every A is B." Watkins, *Hobbes's System*, 20.

59. Chillingworth, *The Religion of Protestants*, 4.57.

60. "*Prudence* . . . , through the difficulty of observing all circumstances, be very fallacious." *Leviathan*, 97. "Signes of prudence are all uncertain; because to observe by experience, and remember all circumstances that may alter the sucesse, is impossible." Ibid., 117. Prudence, Hobbes writes, is "found as well in Brute Beasts, as in Man; and is but a Memory of successions of events in times past, wherein the omission of every little circumstance altering the effect, frustrateth the expectation of the most prudent." Ibid., 682.

61. Steven Shapin and Simon Schaffer, *Leviathan and the Air-Pump* (Princeton: Princeton University Press, 1985), 101–2. See also *Leviathan*, 85–86.

62. *Leviathan*, 97.

uncertainty spells social ruin. In these areas, it is necessary to have knowledge that can compel assent.[63]

Though religious doctrine, according to Hobbes, requires an unequivocal basis, rhetoric's "consensus" does not provide such a standard. For even if the consensus over Christian doctrine made it probable, as Chillingworth contends, there would still be some doubt, and, therefore, the possibility of debate. Hobbes implies, however, that our knowledge of Christian doctrine is not even probable. The religious consensus of the Christian Church, for Hobbes, has no greater validity than the beliefs of the pagans. All men, in Hobbes's opinion, are naturally drawn to religion out of fear of the unknown, and they select their particular form of religion by their feelings toward the religion's living representatives. The early Christians accepted their religion, in large part, because of "the contempt, into which the Priests of the Gentiles of that time, had brought themselves, by their uncleannesse, avarice, and juggling between Princes." And the Anglican Church owes its acceptance to the people's dissatisfaction with the Catholic priests' "fayling of Virtue" and the "contradictions and absurdities" of scholasticism.[64] The consensus of the Christian faithful, therefore, is no more a sign of Christianity's truth than the fact of consensus among other religions demonstrates the truth of their faiths.

But more unsettling for Hobbes than the objective meaninglessness of consensus is its transience. Without the fear of the civil sword, the multitude's faith in any specific religion will inevitably cease over time (179). Christianity, left to itself, is as ephemeral as any other religion.

To the humanists' argument that Christians can find agreement on the essentials of an ethical life, Hobbes replies that since moral concepts have no objective foundation, no consensus on morality is possible. For while all language for Hobbes is, in a superficial sense, artificial and arbitrary, moral language is artificial and arbitrary in a very profound sense. Descriptive terms like apple and tomato, in Hobbes's linguistic theory are artificial and arbitrary because (1) there is no necessary connection between the names used and the object to which the name refers, that is, we could have easily called an apple a tomato as vice versa, and (2) because the names "apple" and "tomato" cannot capture all the specific attributes of these fruits (color,

---

63. "For Hobbes there was no philosophical space within which dissent was safe or permissible. . . . The aim of philosophy was the highest degree of certainty that could be obtained. . . . The production of certainty would terminate disputes and secure total assent." Shapin and Schaffer, *Leviathan and the Air-Pump*, 107–8.

64. *Leviathan*, 181–82.

size, location, and so on). Nevertheless, Hobbes is not a true nominalist regarding such descriptive words, since he argues that there exists some objective characteristic or characteristics to distinguish apples from tomatoes: we can impose a "universal" name like apple or tomato on many different apples or tomatoes "for their similitude in some quality, or other accident."[65] When treating of moral epithets, however, Hobbes is a complete nominalist. Such terms, he contends, have no objective qualities. In *Leviathan* Hobbes writes:

> But whatsoever is the object of any mans Appetite or Desire; that is it, which he for his part called *Good*: And the object of his Hate, and Aversion, *Evill*; And of his Contempt, *Vile*, and *Inconsiderable*. For these words of Good, Evill, and Contemptible, are ever used with relation to the person that useth them: There being nothing simply or absolutely so; nor any common Rule of Good and Evill, to be taken from the nature of the objects themselves; but from the Person of the man (where there is no Common-wealth;) or, (in a Common-wealth,) from the Person that representeth it.[66]

In the absence of an objective basis for moral epithets, human beings—given the freedom—will define their terms subjectively, according to their passions. Subjective definition of moral terms, however, will necessarily preclude consensus. Seeing that such terms only denote likes and dislikes, the diversity of our emotions will cause each of us to define our terms differently.[67] Moreover, even on those terms of moral opprobrium that are universally condemned, like theft and adultery, agreement is only apparent,

65. Ibid., 103. See Watkins, *Hobbes's System*, chapter 8, for an excellent discussion of Hobbes's theory of language.

66. *Leviathan*, 120.

67. "For though the nature of that we conceive be the same; yet the diversity of our reception of it, in respect of different constitutions of body, and prejudices of opinion, gives everything a tincture of our different passions. . . . For one man calleth *Wisedome*, what another calleth *feare*; and one *cruelty*, what another *justice*; one prodigality, what another *magnanimity*; and one *gravity*, what another *stupidity*, &c." Ibid., 109–10. Likewise, Hobbes states: "Every man, for his own part, calleth that which pleaseth and is delightful to himself, GOOD; and that EVIL which displeaseth him: insomuch that while every man differeth from other in constitution, they differ also one from another concerning the common distinction of good and evil." *Elements of Law*, 1.7.3, p. 29. See also *De Cive*, 2.14.17, p. 166.

not real: "We demand not whether theft be a sin, but what is to be termed theft, and so concerning other, in like manner."[68]

As in his discussion of doctrine, Hobbes fears most the social effects of ambiguity. The consequences of equivocal words like "good" and "evil," he predicts, are "Disputes, Controversies, and at last War."[69] Hobbes identifies this condition of verbal discord as the natural state, in which life, in the now famous words, is "solitary, poore, nasty, brutish, and short."[70] Consensus on moral terms is an artifact. In nature there can be no right and wrong, just and unjust. "Force and Fraud" are the "two Cardinall vertues" (188).

The Promise of Science

In place of the humanists' rhetorical epistemology, exemplary of equivocation, Hobbes offers what he believes is an unequivocal theory of knowledge. What makes knowledge unequivocal, he argues, is human imposition; we can know something with certainty only when we make it ourselves.[71] In developing this argument, Hobbes harks back to the Sophists' *nomos-physis*, convention-nature, antithesis. Hobbes creates an epistemology and a political theory that, despite having their source in nature, achieve their legitimacy through convention, that is, through human construction.[72] Applying the convention-nature distinction to knowledge, Hobbes finds that "there is no conception in a mans mind, which hath not at first, totally, or by parts, been begotten upon the organs of Sense."[73] Accordingly, we cannot conceive of anything that is imperceptible, like God, because its existence lies outside the natural world.[74] Notwithstanding the fact that all thinking must begin in nature, Hobbes asserts that nature alone cannot produce certain knowledge. Prudence, for example, is based on the senses, yet is uncertain. Univocal knowledge can only be gained through convention. Such knowl-

68. *De Cive*, 2.14.17, pp. 166–67.

69. *Leviathan*, 216. Also *De Cive*, 1.3.31, p. 57.

70. *Leviathan*, 186.

71. Hobbes's theory of knowledge fits more broadly in the *verum factum* tradition, which conceives of knowing as a kind of making or as a capacity to make. For further discussion of this tradition, see Antonio Pérez-Ramos, *Francis Bacon's Idea of Science and the Maker's Knowledge Tradition* (Oxford: Clarendon Press, 1988), particularly 186–89 on Hobbes.

72. Hobbes's use of the convention-nature distinction is discussed in Amos Funkenstein, *Theology and the Scientific Imagination from the Middle Ages to the Seventeenth Century* (Princeton: Princeton University Press, 1986), 331–38.

73. *Leviathan*, 85.

74. *EW*, vol. 1, *Elements of Philosophy* (1655), 1.1.8, p. 10; Watkins, *Hobbes's System*, 45.

edge, according to Hobbes, is the product of science. In contrast to memory, which is innate, or prudence, which is gotten by experience, science is "attayned by Industry."[75] Human beings, not external facts, create science. They do so, "first in apt imposing of Names," second, by forming these "names" into assertions, and, then, by connecting one assertion to another to form syllogisms, "till we come to a knowledge of all the Consequences of names appertaining to the subject in hand" (115). Scientific truth, for Hobbes, consists in the logical ordering of words, "the right ordering of names in our affirmations" (105). But the meanings of words, as seen in the previous discussion of moral epithets, are not preexistent. Meaning is derived from our own arbitrary impositions: "The first truths were arbitrarily made by those that first of all imposed names upon things."[76] Thus, Hobbes explains, while it is true that "man is a living creature," it is only true by virtue of our having imposed the name "living creature" on a certain class of things.

This arbitrariness of science makes geometry, not experimentation and empirical observation, the model of science. "Geometry," Hobbes writes in *Leviathan*, "is the onely Science that it hath pleased God hitherto to bestow on mankind."[77] For Hobbes, science at its best is artificially constructed, like the definitions and figures of geometry; it is not the passive replication of objective phenomena.[78] By beginning with settled definitions that are humanly devised, geometry ends with indisputable conclusions.[79] This absence of controversy, characteristic of geometry, becomes, for Hobbes, an inherent quality of truth. Hobbes writes as if truth and agreement were indistinguishable: "Doctrine repugnant to Peace, can no more be True, than Peace and Concord can be against the Law of Nature."[80] As Hobbes earlier identified rhetoric with contention, he now equates truth with unanimity. Science and rhetoric, in Hobbes's framework, stand in antithesis to each

75. *Leviathan*, 115.

76. *EW*, vol. 1, *Elements of Philosophy*, 1.3.8, p. 36; Sheldon S. Wolin, *Politics and Vision: Continuity and Innovation in Western Political Thought* (Boston: Little, Brown, 1960), 246.

77. *Leviathan*, 105.

78. Although, as Funkenstein points out, Hobbes sometimes emphasizes the thetic-arbitrary beginnings of science (from definitions) and, at other times, its hypothetical-experimental beginnings, nevertheless, his science is arbitrary throughout. Even in experimental science, there is never a one-to-one relation between phantasms—our perceptions of external reality—and things; "The congruence is guaranteed by the strict material causation in the universe." Funkenstein, *Theology and the Scientific Imagination*, 333–34 n. 20.

79. *Elements of Law*, 1.13.3, p. 50; *Leviathan*, 114, 117.

80. *Leviathan*, 233.

other: "the signs of this being controversy; the sign of the former, no controversy."[81]

As should be apparent from his conception of science as the absence of controversy, Hobbes's rejection of the humanists' rhetorical epistemology does not involve a repudiation of consensus per se. Hobbes is never willing to divorce knowledge from consensus. On the contrary, his problem with a rhetorical epistemology is that it, being based on probability, cannot provide as firm a consensus as science's artificially produced certainty can. By Hobbes's own definition, however, science, since it is grounded in sense experience, cannot address religion or morals and, therefore, cannot create a consensus in these areas. Yet, from Hobbes's perspective, it is religious and moral agreement that is most crucial for social order. Hobbes solves this quandary by arguing that while science cannot compel assent in doctrine or morals, it can spell out the conditions under which a doctrinal and moral consensus can be reached. True science, as Hobbes writes in *Leviathan*, is conditional, composed of "if-then" clauses: "As when we know, that, *If the figure showne be a circle, then any straight line through the Center shall divide it into two equall parts.*"[82] Since, according to Hobbes, we cannot arrive at any agreement on doctrine or morality on our own, that is, in the state of nature, we must create a decisive authority that will do so. A conditional statement that reflects Hobbes's views can be formed as follows: if moral and doctrinal consensus is to be reached, then it can only be the result of a common power, appointed by us, that will impose such a consensus. To explain the artificial creation of this common power, the sovereign, Hobbes once again turns to nature and convention.

Nature, Hobbes argues, drives pre-political humanity to confer its rights on a sovereign (184). Because we are both equal by nature (and, therefore, equally vulnerable) as well as naturally fearful of violent death, we are impelled to escape the state of nature (188). These natural facts alone, however, cannot make allegiance to the sovereign absolutely binding.[83] Nature, as the Commonwealth's sole justification, is an unstable foundation for political obligation. Since the passions that drive us sometimes change, some who now wish to obey the sovereign, may wish to disobey later. To ensure univocality, Hobbes grounds the creation of the sovereign in convention. His means for producing this convention is a covenant in which the

---

81. *Elements of Law*, 1.13.3, p. 51
82. *Leviathan*, 147.
83. Funkenstein, *Theology and the Scientific Imagination*, 335.

covenanting parties agree among themselves to give up their rights to self-government and authorize a single will—whether an individual or an assembly—as the absolute sovereign.[84] In return, the subjects of the Commonwealth are shielded from the conditions of the state of nature. The covenant to form the Commonwealth, like knowledge, receives its univocality from an arbitrary act of the covenanting individuals. It is an artificial construction.[85] Thus Hobbes describes the Commonwealth as an "Artificiall Man" and civil laws as "Artificiall Chains," which we "[ourselves,] by mutuall covenants, have fastened at one end, to the lips of that Man, or Assembly, to whom they have given the Soveraigne Power; and at the other end to [our] own Ears."[86] The paradigm for Hobbes's political science, as with his scientific knowledge in general, is geometry. As geometry is demonstrable because it is artificial—"for the lines and figures from which we reason are drawn and described by ourselves"—so civil philosophy, Hobbes's science of politics, "is demonstrable because we make the commonwealth ourselves."[87]

Hobbes's ruler can, and must, determine religious doctrine and practice. Hobbes dismisses any epistemological basis for opposing such authority with the presumption that nothing can be known of God and His precepts, except His existence.[88] Satisfied that he has also demonstrated the destructive potential of religious ideas, Hobbes proclaims the sovereign's right to judge opinions and doctrines to be absolute.[89] Without a personal revelation concerning God's will, a subject has to obey the command of the Commonwealth. The alternative, where all are free "to take for Gods Commandments, their own dreams, and fancies, or the dreams and fancies of private men" would end in a religious anarchy, where subjects would find commonality only in their mutual hatred of the Commonwealth's laws.[90]

The sovereign exercises the same prerogative, according to Hobbes, in the moral sphere. Seeing that moral epithets are defined solely by the individual's passions, these terms can have no social meaning independent of the

---

84. *Leviathan*, 227.
85. *Elements of Law*, 1.19.5, p. 80; *Leviathan*, 226.
86. *Leviathan*, 263–64.
87. *EW*, vol. 7, "Epistle Dedicatory" to *Six Lessons to the Professors of Mathematics*, 184.
88. Watkins, *Hobbes's System*, 45.
89. *Leviathan*, 233. In *The Elements of Law* and *De Cive*, by contrast, Hobbes saw the Apostolic Church, not the sovereign, as authorized to interpret Scripture. See Richard Tuck, "Hobbes and Locke on Toleration," in *Thomas Hobbes and Political Theory*, ed. Mary G. Dietz (Lawrence: University of Kansas Press, 1990), 162–63.
90. Funkenstein, *Theology and the Scientific Imagination*, 333–34.

Commonwealth. In the natural state, "notions of Right and Wrong, Justice and Injustice have there no place."[91] As with doctrine, the absence of a moral arbiter leads inevitably to civil war, in which moral disputes are settled by violence.

Hobbes's sovereign, then, has the power to create a religious and moral consensus where none previously existed. To the extent that it was the covenanting individuals who created the sovereign, this consensus can be said to derive its validity from those individuals. But insofar as they have no right after the covenant to question the sovereign's moral and religious pronouncements, Hobbes's consensus is only formally linked to the public. Unlike the humanists, who believed that the whole body of the faithful, that is, the Church, continued to express the *consensus fidelium*, Hobbes allows those who are to form the Commonwealth just a single opportunity to agree that they are incapable of doctrinal and moral consensus and thus require an external consensus-maker. After the covenant, their personal moral and religious opinions cease to matter.

Toleration: Hobbes versus the Humanists

Neutralizing Humanist Toleration

Paradoxically, while Hobbes rejects the humanists' epistemological assumptions, on which the fundamentals of faith are based, he formally retains their conception of the fundamentals of faith. Like the humanists, Hobbes maintains that the fundamentals are the only legitimate measure by which to judge the orthodoxy of other Christians. Only those "propositions and articles . . . the belief whereof our Saviour or his apostles have declared to be such, as without believing them a man cannot be saved" are essential. All other beliefs that may distinguish "Papists, Lutherans, Calvinists, Arminians, &c" that are not requisite for salvation are "superstruction," external to Christianity.[92] Hobbes writes, in typical humanist fashion, that the fundamentals are determined by finding those necessary doctrines that are

91. *Leviathan*, 188.
92. *Elements of Law*, 2.6.5, p. 116.

"without obscurity."[93] This task, he cautions, is not as easy as the Puritans would have it. Besides avoiding "obscure, or controverted Interpretation," Scripture must be interpreted rhetorically. To understand what the Bible signifies, he explains, the words of the Bible must be understood in their proper rhetorical context: "For it is not the bare Words, but the Scope of the writer that giveth the true light, by which any writer is to be interpreted."[94] Thus, literal adherence to Scripture is not always called for. Such passages that are rhetorically obscure must be excluded from the necessary dogma. The fundamentals are limited to those precepts "so easy, as not to need interpretation."[95] Given these restrictions, the fundamentals are inescapably minimal.[96]

In addition to "the fundamentals," Hobbes retains the humanists' conception of persuasion. Following in the tradition of Erasmus, Hobbes has Christ deliver his message through persuasion, not compulsion: "It was not congruent to the style of the King of Heaven to constrain men to submit their actions to him, but to advise them only."[97] Further, he commands his apostles and disciples to do the same. According to Christ's commission, they were to proclaim his Word wherever it would be received. But where it was not received, they were "to shake off the dust of their feet against them; but not to call for fire from heaven to destroy them, nor to compel them to obedience by the Sword. In all which there is nothing of Power, but Perswasion."[98] Accordingly, when his apostles proclaimed Christ to the world, they eschewed all coercion. Hobbes recounts in Erasmian imagery how Paul accommodated his speech to his different audiences. To the Jews of Thessalonica he either performed miracles, "as Moses did to the Israelites in Egypt," or adduced "already received Scripture." But to the Gentiles, "there was no use of alledging the Scriptures, which they beleeved not." The Apostles, therefore, turned to reason to refute the Gentiles' idolatry and then "to perswade them to the faith of Christ, by their testimony of his Life, and Resurrection" (542–43). Hobbes, however, does not restrict his discussion to the ancient Church. Not only the early apostles, but present-day

---

93. *Leviathan*, 615.
94. Ibid., 626. See also Johnston, *Rhetoric of Leviathan*, 141, who writes that Hobbes's minimum theology "can be traced back to the immensely popular writings of Erasmus."
95. *Behemoth*, 232–33.
96. "I confess I know very few controversies amongst Christians, of points necessary to salvation." *Behemoth*, 243.
97. *Elements of Law*, 2.7.9, p. 130.
98. *Leviathan*, 551. Also 525–26.

ministers, in their capacity as ministers, must avoid all religious violence. Because it is impossible to force someone to believe, Hobbes argues in *Leviathan*, coercion of religious beliefs is useless and, therefore, senseless: "Faith hath no relation to, nor dependence at all upon Compulsion, or Commandment, but onely upon certainty, or probability of Arguments drawn from Reason, or from something men beleeve already. Therefore the Ministers of Christ in this world, have no Power by that title, to Punish any man for not Beleeving, or for Contradicting what they say."[99] Hence, all of Christ's ministers, past and present, are empowered to teach and no more.

Taken on their own, the above statements are a forceful reiteration of the humanist defense of religious toleration. But with his unwillingness to accept the humanist principles of probable knowledge and religious consensus as well as his delegating of all religious decisions to the sovereign, the obvious question becomes "why does Hobbes hold on to these humanist principles?" The answer, in short, is because Hobbes redefines these concepts in such a way that rather than threaten his theory of undivided and absolute sovereignty, they actually justify total political obedience. Hobbes exploits the humanist defense of toleration for his own purposes, beginning with his argument that the fundamentals are not contradictory to sovereign power. The Puritans had justified their right to rebel by arguing that the king was infringing on his subjects' right to practice true religion.[100] Hobbes counters this claim with the humanists' fundamentals pared down to the minimum. If the essentials of religion are so few that the king's laws are considered true to the faith, then the Puritans' religious grounds for overthrowing the monarch are neutralized.

Always implicit in the humanists' attempts to simplify dogma was the possibility that the "fundamentals" might become so reduced that they would eventually be drained of all meaning.[101] This possibility was partially realized in Hobbes, when accepting the humanist dicta that the scriptural source of the fundamentals must be unambiguous and that the essential doctrines must be comprehensible to all, he concludes that belief in Jesus as

99. Ibid., 526. As Hobbes has explicitly eliminated certainty from faith, his statement here that faith may be derived from certainty is inconsequential.

100. *The New Cambridge Modern History*, vol. 4, ed. J. P. Cooper (Cambridge: Cambridge University Press, 1970), 127. See also J. W. Allen, *English Political Thought, 1603–1660* (London: Methuen, 1928), 1:404–5.

101. Lecler, for example, believes that secularism was the unintended result of humanism. *Toleration and the Reformation*, 1:132, 380.

Christ is the only belief necessary for salvation.[102] All other doctrines, excluding those deducible from belief in Christ—such as the existence of God the Father and the Resurrection—are not fundamental; for Hobbes, questions about the Trinity, Eucharist, predestination, and free will are inessential.[103] Like Hooker, Hobbes uses doctrinal minimalism to undermine the Puritan case against the sovereign. Hobbes surpasses Hooker, however, in abridging the fundamentals of faith. With faith in Christ the sole demand, no one can accuse a king, so long as he is Christian, of denying the essential belief: "Under the sovereign power of a Christian commonwealth," Hobbes states confidently, "there is no danger of damnation from simple obedience to human laws."[104] Since a Christian sovereign will most certainly permit belief in Christ, we can all be good Christians. As for other laws, even on ostensibly religious matters, they do not contradict the fundamental points. They are adiaphora, legislated by the sovereign and dictated by prudential considerations.

Hobbes's radical reduction of fundamental doctrine also refutes the Roman Catholics' claim that subjects need not keep faith with heretical kings. Because all Christian sovereigns, regardless of sect or denomination, will agree that Jesus is the Messiah, there is no basis for labeling them heretics. Hobbes further rebuts the Catholics' charge with an etymological discourse on the meaning of the term "heresy." In his essay *Concerning Heresy and the Punishment Thereof* (probably composed in 1666), Hobbes explains: "The word *heresy*, is Greek, and signifies a taking of any thing, and particularly the taking of an opinion."[105] Originally it had no pejorative sense but only referred to the various schools of Greek philosophy, such as the Pythagoreans, Academics, Platonists, and so on. Sometime after the advent of Christianity, however, "heretic" took on a negative connotation and came to mean someone who adhered to an opinion in opposition to the whole Church. Still, Hobbes argues, "*catholic* and *heretic* were terms

102. "[T]aken from places expresse, and such as receive no controversie of Interpretation . . . this Article beleeved, *Jesus is the Christ*, is sufficient . . . to our Reception into the Kingdome of God, and by consequence, onely Necessary." *Leviathan*, 617–19. For Hobbes's argument that the fundamentals must be comprehensible to all, see *Elements of Law*, 2.6.8, pp. 119–20; *De Cive*, 3.18.10, pp. 203–4; and *Leviathan*, 617.

103. *Elements of Law*, 2.6.9, pp. 120–22. Hobbes also excludes the traditional belief in the Trinity when he identifies the triad with Moses, Jesus, and the Apostles. *Leviathan*, 522–24; Mintz, *Hunting of Leviathan*, 45.

104. *Elements of Law*, 2.6.11, p. 124.

105. *EW*, vol. 4, *Concerning Heresy, and the Punishment Thereof*, 387. Hobbes composed this work to defend himself against charges that *Leviathan* was heretical.

relative" (390). Heresy is no different than other moral epithets. Without a sovereign definer it only reflects the subjective tastes of the individual: when someone approves of a private opinion, they call it "opinion"; when they do not, they call it "heresy."[106] Like "justice" and "injustice," "heresy" receives a univocal meaning in the Commonwealth. Since there is no standard by which to designate heresy except the sovereign, it is logically absurd to condemn a sovereign as heretical.[107]

Not content with merely neutralizing the threat from "fundamentals," Hobbes also sought to incorporate into his conception of fundamentals a positive duty to obey the sovereign. He does so by differentiating between two types of essentials, the first relating to doctrine, the second to actions: "*Faith in Christ*, and *Obedience to Laws*."[108] To achieve salvation, Hobbes contends, faith alone is not sufficient. One must endeavor to obey God's commandments—a requirement variously known in the Bible as charity, love, righteousness, and repentance (611). This insistence upon action as a prerequisite to salvation is by no means novel. The idea that a Christian life is as necessary for salvation as Christian doctrine is a mainstay of Christian humanism.[109] What is distinctive about Hobbes, however, is that he equates obedience to God with obedience to the ruler. Our obligation to God, he writes in *Leviathan*, is to obey the law of nature, the Laws of Moses being no longer in force. Since the chief precept of the law of nature is to keep faith with our covenants and inasmuch as we have constituted the civil sovereign over us "by mutuall pact one with another," it follows that our obligation to God is to obey the sovereign.[110] Thus having demonstrated the necessity of political obedience, Hobbes's revision of the fundamentals is complete. Retaining the form of the humanists' conception, he nevertheless ensures that the content of the essentials will bolster his theory of political absolutism.

---

106. *Leviathan*, 165.

107. "Nor is there any Judge of Haeresie amongst Subjects, but their owne Civill Soveraign: For *Haeresie is nothing else, but a private opinion, obstinately maintained, contrary to the opinion which the Publique Person* (that is to say, the Representant of the Commonwealth) *hath commanded to be taught.* By which it is manifest, that an opinion publiquely appointed to bee taught, cannot be Haeresie; nor the Soveraign Princes that authorize them, Haeretiques. For Haeretiques are none but private men, that stubbornly defend some Doctrine, prohibited by their lawfull Soveraigns." Ibid., 604–5. Also *Behemoth*, 173–76.

108. *Leviathan*, 610.

109. *The Complete Works of St. Thomas More*, ed. Edward Surtz, S. J. and J. H. Hexter (New Haven: Yale University Press, 1965), 4:lxx–lxxvi.

110. *Leviathan*, 612.

So long as Hobbes defines the fundamentals of faith strictly in terms of their content, however, he leaves himself open to the criticism that he is mistaken about their composition: it can be suggested that Scripture, for example, demands more from the believer than faith in Christ alone. To defend himself against this objection, Hobbes goes on to argue that since the belief necessary for salvation is internal, it follows that even if the sovereign, or Hobbes, is wrong about what articles of faith are required, the believer can still fulfill his obligation to God. Regardless of the sovereign's heterodox laws, which are limited to control over the individual's actions, a subject may still be orthodox in his own personal beliefs.[111] In *The Elements of Law* and in *De Cive*, Hobbes does not draw out the full implications of his position. In these two works, martyrdom to an infidel king is still a rightful choice. Though we may not resist princes under any circumstance, we must be willing to "go to Christ by martyrdom; which if it seem to any man to be a hard saying, most certain it is that he believes not that Jesus is the Christ."[112] By the time he wrote *Leviathan*, however, Hobbes no longer viewed martyrdom as a legitimate option. Here he maintains that, with the exception of those who have an express calling to convert the infidels, there is no need to die for Christ and that if someone is foolish enough to give up his life in such a way, he does not merit the label "martyr."[113] Since faith is divorced from action, Christian subjects should avoid persecution by doing what the sovereign commands. Even if the sovereign commands one to deny Christ, one must do so, since "Profession with the tongue is but an externall thing, and no more then any other gesture whereby we signifie our obedience" (527–28).

Nonetheless, while Hobbes argues that subjects must obey any sovereign, including an infidel, Hobbes is most concerned with their obligations to the Christian ruler. Such a sovereign, according to Hobbes, is the legitimate judge of public doctrine because he alone has the power to dictate religious consensus, and we are bidden by the biblical precept of obedience to adhere to his pronouncements in all public expressions of religion.[114] Moreover,

---

111. In other words, Hobbes is advising dissenters to be what Calvin denounced as Nicodemites.

112. *De Cive*, 3.18.13, p. 208. In *De Cive*, 3.15.13, p. 192, Hobbes writes: "Those Attributes therefore, whereby we signify ourselves to be of an opinion, that there is any man endued with sovereignty independent of God, or that he is immortal, or of infinite power, and the like, though commanded by princes, yet must they be abstained from." See also Strauss, *Political Philosophy*, 72; and Hobbes, *Elements of Law*, 2.6.14, p. 125.

113. *Leviathan*, 530–31.

114. *De Cive*, 3.18.6, pp. 200–201, especially the footnote.

because the forms of worshiping and honoring God are mainly arbitrary—with the exception of universal signs of scorn like the "body's uncleanness"—a single person is necessary to decide what the Commonwealth's signs of divine honor and worship will be.[115] True, Hobbes concedes, a Christian sovereign may sometimes command public adherence to nonessentials or even absurdities—"that is, make some superstructure out of Hay, or Stubble, and command the teaching of the same"—yet we must still follow the ruler's commandments, though erroneous, because the sovereign is the sole divinely instituted authority to decide religious questions.[116]

Hobbes's separation of belief from action does safeguard an internal region, what Alan Ryan calls an "inner life," from the state.[117] On this ground, Hobbes condemns the Roman Catholic Church's extension of its legal powers beyond "the Rule of Actions onely, to the very Thoughts and Consciences of men, by Examination, and *Inquisition* of what they Hold, notwithstanding the Conformity of their Speech and Actions."[118] But as Ryan and J.W.N. Watkins recognize, Hobbes's objection to inquisitions is an epistemological, not a moral statement.[119] Beliefs are neither visible to "humane Governours" ("for God onely knoweth the heart"), nor voluntary.[120] An inquisitor, according to Hobbes, is unable to know whether or not he is truly successful, and, more important, even if the heretic wants to change his thoughts he cannot.[121] Therefore, Hobbes concludes, thought control is futile. For Hobbes, the inner region is like a hermetically sealed box, whose contents cannot be affected or exposed by force. What this means for the ruler, as just seen, is that he cannot compel the private world of thought. Because he is the public authority, however, he can still control all external behavior, including the practice of religion.

The clergy, in Hobbes's view, are the representatives of the inner conscience. They are entrusted with the duty of persuasion, which affects only the inner life. But they have no right to move from the realm of belief into the sphere of action. Contrary to the claims of both Presbyterian ministers and

---

115. Ibid., 3.15.16, p. 188; 3.15.18, pp. 190–93.

116. *Leviathan*, 624–25.

117. Alan Ryan, "Hobbes, Toleration, and the Inner Life," in *The Nature of Political Theory*, ed. David Miller and Larry Siedentop (Oxford: Clarendon Press, 1983), 197–218.

118. *Leviathan*, 700.

119. Watkins, *Hobbes's System*, 70; Ryan, "Hobbes, Toleration, and the Inner Life," 217.

120. *Leviathan*, 500–501.

121. One can only speculate whether Hobbes would have permitted inquisitions, had he been aware of the effectiveness of "brainwashing."

the pope that the sovereign is, ultimately, beholden to them, Hobbes replies that the clergy is powerless to implement its beliefs through force.[122] It is in this context of protecting the king from ecclesiastical threats that Hobbes's identification of religion with persuasion must be understood. By reaffirming this humanist principle, Hobbes emasculated the independent religious institutions in their struggles against the king. Citing the classic humanist text on toleration, the parable of the tares, to make his point, Hobbes argues, as did the humanists, that the tares must be tolerated until the Second Coming. But rather than use this passage to defend a general policy of toleration, Hobbes directed his comments to papal pronouncements against the king: as "our Saviour refused to take upon him that Power [of separating the bad from the good] in this world himself, but advised to let the Corn and Tares grow up together till the day of Judgment," so too the pope can have no power over princes, even over "those [princes] that are to bee esteemed as Heathen" (607–8).

Prudential Argument for Toleration

Having concluded that the divine status of the Bible is not knowable and that even when Scripture is accepted as true, its necessary doctrine is almost nonexistent, Hobbes grants the sovereign the same power over religion that he concedes him in the secular areas of life.[123] That Hobbes gives the ruler a carte blanche in legislating religion, however, is not tantamount to saying that he requires the sovereign to be intolerant. As in other areas of public policy, the king's actions in this sphere must be dictated by the good of the Commonwealth. Although immune from his subject's scrutiny, the sovereign is presumed by Hobbes to do only that which is necessary for the security of

122. *Leviathan*, 592.

123. Hobbes's rejection of religion's epistemological claims not only safeguards the sovereign from theological attack, but also undercuts the orthodox justification of religious coercion. Traditionally, the use of compulsion against heretics was justified on the grounds that heretics obstinately turn away from the truth. See, for example, Aquinas *Summa Theologiae* 2, q. 11, a.3. By denying objective epistemological status to dogmatic truth, though, Hobbes invalidates orthodoxy's claims that heretics pertinaciously repudiate obvious truths; it does not make sense to accuse someone of obstinately denying a truth that is, by its nature, unknowable. As seen earlier, Hobbes considered the term *heresy* to have only subjective meaning. Alan Ryan maintains that Hobbes's orthodox contemporaries recognized that he undermined their defense of persecution. See "A More Tolerant Hobbes?" in *Justifying Toleration: Conceptual and Historical Perspectives*, ed. Susan Mendus (Cambridge: Cambridge University Press, 1988), 37–59.

the state, and no more.[124] Hobbes's sovereign, therefore, ought to be as tolerant as possible, in accordance with the interests of the state.

Since the sovereign will be guided by prudential, not scientific, considerations in fixing the level of toleration, Hobbes does not, and cannot, prescribe an unconditional course of action for the ruler; toleration will depend on circumstance. Nevertheless, Hobbes, in various places, hints at the kind of religious restrictions and liberties he believes consistent with political exigency. Hobbes distinguishes between public and private manifestations of religion. He asserts that all public worship should be controlled by the state, but assumes that the Commonwealth may be tolerant of private acts of worship. Hobbes will not consider the possibility of free public worship because he cannot conceive of a state without an official religion. Once his assumption of the necessity of a civil religion is granted, his conclusions follow: there can be no public religion without public worship and no public worship without uniformity. As Hobbes states in *Leviathan*:

> But seeing a Common-wealth is but one Person, it ought also to exhibite to God but one Worship; which then it doth, when it commandeth it to be exhibited by Private men, Publiquely. And this is Publique Worship; the property whereof, is to be *Uniforme*: For those actions that are done differently, by different men, cannot be said to be a Publique Worship. And therefore, where many sorts of Worship be allowed, proceeding from the different Religions of Private men, it cannot be said there is any Publique Worship, nor that the Commonwealth is of any Religion at all.[125]

Hobbes's intolerance of diverse public worship, however, is tempered by a tolerance of private worship: "Private worship may be voluntary, if it be done secretly; for what is done openly is restrained, either by laws or through modesty, which is contrary to the nature of a voluntary action."[126] Hobbes's concern throughout his political theory, and the standard by which he judges religion, is the good of the state.[127] Private worship, which is unseen, cannot harm the state. Therefore, Hobbes is willing to permit it.

---

124. *Leviathan*, 228–39. It is because the sovereign does not have the right to impose doctrines on his citizens unless he sincerely believes that doing so would preserve them that, according to Tuck, "*Leviathan* is a defense of toleration." "Hobbes and Locke on Toleration," 165.

125. *Leviathan*, 405. Also *De Cive*, 3.15.15, p. 187; and 3.15.17, pp. 189–90.

126. *De Cive*, 3.15.12, p. 182.

127. See Strauss, *Political Philosophy*, 74.

Although he subordinates religion to *raison d'etat*, Hobbes is sympathetic to the idea of toleration. He writes approvingly of the ancient Romans who, having "conquered the greatest part of the then known World, made no scruple of tollerating any Religion whatsoever in the City of Rome it selfe; unlesse it had something in it, that could not consist with their Civill Religion"—the Jews being the sole exception because of their belief that they owed no obedience to any mortal state.[128] Similarly, Hobbes though placing the lion's share of blame for the Civil War on the rebels, does acknowledge in *Behemoth* the imprudence of the king's religious legislation. The opposition to the king, Hobbes surmises, "would never have ventured into the field, but for that unlucky business of imposing upon the Scots, who were all Presbyterians, our book of Common-prayer."[129] Finally, in his most explicit statement on behalf of toleration, Hobbes depicts England's current state of religious anarchy in positive terms. Summarizing the history of Christianity leading up to his time, Hobbes distinguishes between two periods: the first characterized by the loss of freedom, the second by its restoration. In the first period, religious liberty was lost initially to the presbyters, next to the bishops, and then to the bishop of Rome—with greater privations at each progressive level. In the second period, freedom of religion was recovered beginning with Queen Elizabeth's renunciation of papal power, and following that with the Presbyterians' "putting down of Episcopacy" and the almost concurrent removal of Presbyterian power: "And so," Hobbes continues, "we are reduced to the Independency of the Primitive Christians to follow Paul, or Cephas, or Appolos, every man as he liketh best." Rather than lamenting this situation, Hobbes seems to prefer it. If only this condition of freedom could "be without contention, and without measuring the Doctrine of Christ, by our affection to the Person of his Minister," it would be "perhaps the best." There should be no power over others' consciences, Hobbes declares, but the Word itself. Further, he notes, it is unreasonable to require one to follow the opinion of another on such a crucial matter as salvation.[130]

For Hobbes, toleration is the ideal, but contemporary English society, in his view, was too contentious and factious to permit trafficking in ideals. While leaving the hope of toleration open to future generations, he could not champion its cause in his own day.

---

128. *Leviathan*, 178.
129. *Behemoth*, 198.
130. *Leviathan*, 710–11.

5

Bodin: A Different Kind of Humanist Toleration

Between Hobbes and Humanism

Hobbes feared the disruptive power of religious rhetoric. Thus he blamed the English Civil War on the oratory of Presbyterian preachers, "who, by a long practised histrionic faculty, preached up the rebellion powerfully." Like Hobbes, such humanists as Erasmus, Acontius, and Chillingworth had also perceived the dangers of demagogic, religious oratory, but they had assumed that the destructive effects of religious rhetoric would be checked by the unity attained on the fundamentals of faith. According to these humanists, once the broad consensus on fundamentals was recognized, once rhetorical or actual warfare between Christians could no longer be justified, then Christians, of whatever stripe, would learn to tolerate one another. Hobbes, by contrast, denied the stabilizing effect of consensus. Left to themselves, he explained, people would not agree on a core of doctrinal and ethical truths. Such truths, Hobbes maintained, could not be known, only believed. And beliefs—derived from the passions, not reason—are fleeting. Religious unity could be effected and maintained, Hobbes said, only through the force of a common sovereign: the sole legitimate judge of religious dogma, practice, and morals within each commonwealth.

In spite of their differences, however, both the Erasmian humanists and Hobbes assumed that the state must have only one religion. These humanists sought uniformity of religion because they still clung to the ideal of a single, albeit latitudinarian, *respublica Christiana*. Hobbes, too, never seriously considered a multireligious state, though he was motivated by reason of state, not by any sentimental attachment to the seamless robe of Christendom. Accordingly, neither these humanists nor Hobbes enunciated a theory of toleration that would include non-Christians. To the Erasmian humanists, non-Christians stood beyond the pale of reasonable discourse, given that they denied the fundamentals of faith. To Hobbes, non-Christians were aliens in a commonwealth in which religion and politics were inextricable. There was, however, a rare humanist in the period under study that was willing to consider non-Christians as full members of the community: Jean Bodin. He did so in the *Colloquium heptaplomeres de rerum sublimium arcanis abditis* (*Colloquium of the Seven about Secrets of the Sublime*).

Bodin completed the *Colloquium* in 1588; however, the first complete printed edition was not published until 1857.[1] Thus, he wrote the *Colloquium* well before Chillingworth and Hobbes had composed their works. Nevertheless, I have chosen to discuss Bodin *after* these writers because Bodin anticipated some of the problems with the "humanist defense of religious toleration" that Hobbes would later elaborate, such as its trust in rational discussion to arrive at religious truth; its optimistic assumption that religious discussion and religious oratory are consistent with the state's well-being; and its belief that Christianity, as the sole true religion, could be distinguished from all other religions. It is because Bodin, like Hobbes, viewed these widely held humanist assumptions as problematic, that I consider him, for purposes of this book, outside the "mainstream" of humanism. (The breadth of toleration permitted in the *Colloquium*— greater than in later humanists like Chillingworth, or even than in the liberal Locke—also distinguishes Bodin from other humanists, and further justifies discussing him out of strict chronological sequence.)[2] But Bodin, unlike Hobbes, retains essential elements of the humanist defense of religious toleration: while treating religious matters, Bodin selects the humanist genre of *sermo* and observes its rules of *decorum*; like the aforementioned humanists, he accepts the objective existence of religious truth; and like them, he extends toleration to those who, in his mind, possess religious truth. Therefore, I do not think it improper to label the theory he develops in

---

1. Marion Leathers Daniels Kuntz, *Colloquium of the Seven about Secrets of the Sublime* (Princeton: Princeton University Press, 1975), xxxvii.

2. It is often noted that Bodin and his *Colloquium* were ill-suited for their time. See, for example, *New Cambridge Modern History*, 3:486–87: "So little did [the *Heptaplomeres*] represent any phase of sixteenth-century thinking that Bodin dared not publish it." See also Donald R. Kelley, "The Development and Context of Bodin's Method," in *Jean Bodin: Verhandlungen der internationalen Bodin Tagung in München* (Munich: C. H. Beck, 1973), 124; and *New Cambridge Modern History*, 3:486–87.

the *Colloquium* a *humanist* response to the Hobbesian critique, even if it argues for a different kind of humanist toleration.

Bodin before the *Colloquium*

The Making of a Humanist

Like Erasmus, Bodin's earliest education was more religious than classical. Bodin was schooled by the Carmelite order, first in his native Angers, and then in the Carmelite house in Paris, where he lived as a brother in the monastery from 1545 to 1547. His goal at the time was to become a priest. Bodin's stay in Paris brought him into contact with leading humanist scholars, whose lectures he attended at the trilingual Collège Royal—the future Collège de France. While pursuing his studies in Paris, Bodin became fluent in Greek and gained a working knowledge of Hebrew. He also broadened his knowledge of the classics. Thus, by the time he left Paris, around 1550, he "had acquired a truly formidable humanist education."[3] As a result of this phase of his education, Bodin published, in 1555, an edition of Oppian's *Cynegetica*, a didactic poem on hunting. Bodin displayed much humanist scholarship in this work, translating the Greek text into Latin verse and adding a commentary that referred to more than two hundred different authors and sources—an accomplishment that has been somewhat diminished by still unproven charges of plagiarism.[4] This period in Paris marked not only Bodin's introduction to humanism, but also his departure from the Carmelites. Deciding that he no longer wanted to be a priest, he obtained release from his vows in 1549 on the grounds that he had been too young at the time that he professed them.

In the 1550s, Bodin studied civil law at the University of Toulouse, the center of legal studies in France. At Toulouse, Bodin's studies and writings continued to reflect his attachment to humanism, but he now applied his

---

3. Jean Bodin, *On Sovereignty: Four Chapters from the Six Books of the Commonwealth*, ed. and trans. Julian H. Franklin (Cambridge: Cambridge University Press, 1992), ix; Jean Bodin, *The Six Bookes of a Commonweale*, trans. Richard Knolles, ed. Kenneth Douglas McRae (Cambridge: Harvard University Press, 1962), A3–A4.

4. Bodin was accused of plagiarizing some of his textual emendations from Adrian Turnebus, professor of Greek at the Collège Royal. McRae's introduction to *Six Bookes*, A4.

humanist approach to the study of legal, not literary, texts.[5] Although Toulouse was not particularly receptive to "legal humanism," it was there that he became a devotee of the new school of humanist jurisprudence known as the *mos gallicus*, which interpreted texts contextually by using the new philological techniques developed by the humanists.[6]

Near the end of his stay in Toulouse (1559), Bodin wrote the *Oratio de instituenda in republica in juventute ad Senatum Populumque Tolosatem* (*Address to the Senate and People of Toulouse on Education of Youth in the Commonwealth*), which has been described as "an advertisement" for the "new learning" of the Renaissance.[7] In the *Oratio*, Bodin called for the creation of a publicly supported college of liberal arts in Toulouse that would be based on the humanists' educational reforms, similar to the Collège de France. Like other humanists, Bodin emphasized the special role of rhetoric in the curriculum. His statements on rhetoric are reminiscent of those made by humanists in earlier chapters. To achieve eloquence, Bodin recommends that students practice, à la Cicero, argument *in utramque partem*: "But of how great value is the following, that the boys, as they have begun to speak clearly, be exercised in speaking on all matters on each side, first in Greek, then Latin, then French."[8] Again, as with the other humanists studied, Bodin wanted argumentation to be limited by the rules of *decorum*, so that reason may prevail. The "litigious manner of some of publicly vociferating," Bodin explains, disturbs "the quiet and moderate minds by nature . . . not only from tranquillity and clear-headedness, but also renders them unrestrained beyond nature." Therefore, the students' discus-

---

5. Pierre Mesnard, "Jean Bodin à Toulouse," *Bibliothèque d'Humanisme et Renaissance* 12 (1950): 54.

6. This school stood in opposition to the more traditional *mos italicus*, which worked with a system of principles derived from Justinian's *Corpus Juris* and applied the techniques of scholasticism. As with other elements of his humanism, Bodin's adherence to the *mos gallicus* was not doctrinaire, and he eventually developed a respect for the *mos italicus*, which he tried to reconcile with the humanist approach. See Richard J. Schoeck, "Humanism and Jurisprudence," in *Renaissance Humanism: Foundations, Forms, and Legacies*, ed. Albert Rabil Jr. (Philadelphia: University of Pennsylvania Press, 1988), 3:312–14; Kelley, "Bodin's Method," 126–27.

7. Kelley, "Bodin's Method," 125–26. Kelley also points out that the studies Bodin celebrated "were exclusively neither ancient nor Italian," but included the entire cultural past of Europe. "Being heir to such eclecticism," Kelley concludes, "Bodin could hardly help breaking out of the humanist mold."

8. Jean Bodin, *Address to the Senate and People of Toulouse on Education of Youth in the Commonwealth*, trans. George Albert Moore (Chevy Chase, Md.: The Country Dollar Press, 1965), 39.

sions should "be controlled by the great prudence of somebody . . . ; so that they consider that sometimes it is safer to leave an opinion than life, sometimes more glorious to be conquered than to conquer."[9] The students, Bodin suggests here, must be taught the difference between *sermo*, where truth is the ultimate goal, and *agon*, where victory is all that matters.

The *République*

After he was unable to secure a professorship at the law school, Bodin left Toulouse for Paris, around 1560, where he practiced law for a number of years. But Bodin aspired to a political life, and by the late 1560s, he had begun a public career. At first he assumed only minor posts, though in a short time Bodin had come to the attention of important members of the court, and in 1571 he was appointed master of requests and counselor to Francis, duke of Alençon, the youngest brother of King Charles IX and next in line to the throne after Henry III. In 1576 Bodin was chosen as a deputy for the Third Estate of Vermandois to the Estates General at Blois.

It is often thought that Bodin's movement from academic to political life also indicates a parallel intellectual shift from humanism to conservative, pragmatic legalism. But, as Julian Franklin argues convincingly, there was no such shift. Bodin remained a consistent defender of humanism. In his writings of the period, he still contrasts the humanist enlightenment with medieval ignorance, adopting a stance almost indistinguishable from the one he adopted in the *Oratio*. If Bodin was critical of some humanists, it was because they avoided all practical experience. In contrast to these "extremist" humanists, who used classical philological methods to study the law but never entered a courtroom, Bodin considered himself a "moderate" humanist, who favored a combination of the academic and the practical.[10]

Humanism's enduring influence on Bodin is seen in the universal, comparative approach he adopted in his legal and political classic, the *Six livres de la république* (1576). Bodin arrived at this approach through the analyses of French legal humanists studying the Roman law. Bodin came to understand from these legal humanists that the problem with applying Roman law was not simply that it was corrupted by medieval jurists, but that the original

9. Ibid., 37. Cf. Erasmus, LB 5:1265D–E: "In a battle of words, whoever is wise does not want to conquer so much as to be conquered."

10. Julian H. Franklin, *Jean Bodin and the Sixteenth-Century Revolution in the Methodology of Law and History* (New York: Columbia University Press, 1963), 59–67.

system of Roman law itself was inapplicable to contemporary France.[11] Bodin concluded, therefore, that he must widen his search beyond ancient Rome to include a comparative historical study of the most famous legal systems as the basis of a universal legal science. This was his approach in the *République*, a systematic treatise on French and universal public law, derived from a comparison and synthesis of all juridical experience.

Although the *République* grew out of the tradition of legal humanism, it also expressed some of the same nonhumanist concerns that would come to underpin Hobbes's critique of the humanist defense of religious toleration. Like Hobbes, Bodin saw the pernicious effects of religious conflict. Both men composed their great works during religious civil wars: Hobbes wrote the *Leviathan* during the English Civil War; and Bodin wrote the *République* during the French Wars of Religion, a series of wars between the majority Roman Catholics and the minority Calvinists known as Huguenots, which lasted over twenty years (1562–93). Because of their experiences with civil wars of religion, both Hobbes and Bodin feared that religious disputation would lead to political upheaval. For Bodin, religion was a bulwark of the state, and he maintained, in the *République*, that whatever damaged that bulwark—such as religious disputation—must be prohibited. "Even the very Atheists themselves," he states, in the *République*, "are of accord, That there is nothing which doth more uphold and maintaine the estates and Commonweals than religion: and that it is the principall foundation of the power and strength of monarchies and Seignories."[12] For this reason, "every man ought to be most certainly resolved and assured" of religious truth. But Bodin concedes, as Hobbes would later, that religious truth cannot be known with certainty. Religion rests "not so much upon demonstration or reason, as uppon the assurance of fayth and beleefe onely" (535C–D). Therefore, to avoid weakening the subjects' faith in religion, Bodin opposes any religious disputation: "Disputation was invented but for things probable and doubtfull; and not for things religious and necessarie, and such as every man is bound to beleeve: which by disputations are alwaies made doubtfull. Wherefore seeing that disputations of religion bring not only the doubt and overthrow of religions, but even the ruine and destruction of Common-weales also; it behooveth them to be by most strait lawes forbidden" (536H–I). A ban on religious disputation is especially necessary in states where the

---

11. Julian H. Franklin, *Jean Bodin and the Rise of Absolutist Theory* (Cambridge: Cambridge University Press, 1973), 25–26.

12. *Six Bookes*, 536I–K.

people commonly agree on a single religion, so that "all the wayes and entrances unto sedition and faction may be stopped, and the assurances of unity and peace strengthened" (535C). But Bodin believes that disputation should be outlawed even in multireligious states. For example, Bodin notes that in Germany, where Roman Catholicism and Lutheranism are both legal, the law still states that "no man should upon paine of death dispute of the religions." And as a consequence of carrying out the law in some cases, he observes, "all Germany was afterwards at good quiet and rest: no man daring more to dispute of matters of religion" (536I).

Bodin finds that religious oratory, like religious disputation, also threatens political stability. He anticipates Hobbes's emphasis on the negative political effects of oratory, particularly as practiced by preachers. Of oratory, in general, Bodin writes that it "is oftner emploied to evill, than to good.

> For seeing that this is nothing else but a disguising of the truth, and an art to make that seeme good, which is indeed naught, & that right which is wrong, and to make a great matter of nothing, as of an Emot an Elephant (that is to say, an art to lie cunnungly) wee need not doubt, but that for one which useth this art well, fiftie use the same evill, & that amongst 50 Orators it is hard to find an honest man. For that to seeke after the plaine and bare truth, were a thing altogether contrarie unto their profession.

The evil of these orators, according to Bodin, has political ramifications. Thus he goes on to explain that if we were to look more closely at all those reputed to have been "the most noble and famous Orators, we shall find them to have beene still the stirrers up of the people to sedition, to have oftentimes changed the laws, the customs, the religions, and Commonweals, yea & some others of them to have utterly ruinated the same" (543D–E). In his own time, Bodin singles out religious orators as especially menacing to the state. These preachers "have troubled all the empires both of Affrike & of the West: yea and many of them so wrested the scepters even out of the kings hands." As examples, Bodin cites the preacher-led uprisings in Morocco and Persia, and, closer to home, John Beukels of Leyden's revolt in Münster and Girolamo Savonarola's republican reforms in Florence (543E–544G).

Although both Bodin and Hobbes criticize rhetoric for threatening the Commonwealth, Bodin takes a somewhat more sympathetic approach to rhetoric than Hobbes. After enumerating the various civil ills brought on by rhetoric, Bodin also acknowledges, in classical rhetorical fashion, its civilizing power. "For them which well use it," Bodin writes, rhetoric is a means "to reduce the people from barbarisme to humanitie, to reforme disordered maners, to correct the lawes, to chastise tyrants, to cast out vices, to maintaine vertue." And while oratory is most commonly the cause of political unrest, he states: "Neither is there any other greater or better means for the appeasing of seditions & tumults, and to keepe the subjects in the obedience of their princes, than to have a wise and vertuous preacher, by whom they may bend and bow the hearts of the most stubborne rebels, especially in a Popular estate, wherein the ignorant people beareth the sway, and cannot possibly bee kept in order but by the eloquent Orators." Because of the preachers' ability to cure civil disorder, Bodin implies that sometimes even the sovereign himself must rely on their power to achieve what he himself cannot—a proposition that would have been anathema to Hobbes. Recognizing reality, Bodin writes that orators have "always holden the chiefe degree of honour and power in [the] Popular estates, causing the honourable commissions, gifts and rewards, to be still given to whom they saw good." Therefore, "both peace and war, arms and laws, wholy depended on the pleasure of the Orators" (544H–K). Under these conditions, the ruler could not possibly act on his own, but would have to work together with the orators.

Just as Bodin's attitudes toward religious disputation and religious oratory were determined by the good of the Commonwealth, so too was his stand on religious toleration. He shared this prudential approach to toleration with Hobbes. Hobbes, however, believed that prudence required unity of religion within the state and tolerated religious differences solely when they were practiced privately and secretly. Bodin, by contrast, was more tolerant of religious diversity than Hobbes, recommending that religious unity be preserved through force only when unity already existed. Here, the king may exercise his absolute sovereignty, legalizing only one religion to preserve religious uniformity.[13] For Bodin, a single established religion is to be preferred since religious uniformity strengthens the state.[14] But when a new

13. The French Wars of Religion persuaded Bodin, as the English Civil War persuaded Hobbes, that sovereign power must be absolute. Although the political theories of Bodin's *Rèpublique* and Hobbes's *Leviathan* are very different from each other, they both develop theories of absolute sovereignty in response to religious threats against the monarchy: in Bodin's case, the Huguenot arguments for a right of resistance; and in Hobbes's case, the Puritan claims to prefer their own scriptural interpretations above the sovereign's.

14. "But religion by common consent once received and setled, is not againe to be called into

religion is established and cannot be easily dislodged, Bodin counsels toleration.[15] In adopting this position, Bodin reflects the viewpoint of that group known as "the *Politiques*," who believed that the question of religious toleration should be determined by what best furthered political stability. Like them, he argues that in states, such as France, where a religious minority has grown too large to be easily suppressed, toleration should be granted. In just over ten years, though, Bodin moved beyond the limited toleration of the *Politiques* to support full toleration for almost all religious convictions.

The *Colloquium*

The Purpose of Dialogue: Bodin's Alternative

In the *République*, Bodin's views on religious toleration had more in common with Hobbes's than with those of the humanists previously discussed. He condemned religious discussion for spreading religious skepticism, though he himself believed that religious truths could not be demonstrated. Moreover, he condemned religious debate for bringing "the ruine and destruction of Commonweales," arguing that, as a political threat, religious disputation should be prohibited. In the *République*, political stability is the primary good, and, accordingly, the question of toleration is decided by *raison d'etat*.

In the *Colloquium*, however, Bodin rejects his earlier nonhumanist, proto-Hobbesian position on religious toleration. Although he retains the same

---

question and dispute, that so all the wayes and entrances unto sedition and faction may be stopped." Ibid., 535C. Bodin also argues that where a religion is generally received, the people themselves "cannot but most hardly endure any rights and ceremonies" differing from their own religion. Ibid., 381B–C.

15. "But it may be, that the consent and agreement of the nobilitie and people in a new religion or sect, may be so puissant & strong, as that to represse or alter the same, should be a thing impossible, or at leastwise marvelous difficult, without the extreame perill and daunger of the whole estate." In such a case, Bodin argues, the best advised rulers imitate prudent navigators, who when unable to reach their desired port, sail to whichever port they are able, changing their course often, yielding to storms and tempests, knowing that if they persist in their original plans, they will suffer shipwreck. "Wherefore," Bodin concludes, "that religion or sect is to be suffered, which without the hazard and destruction of the state cannot be taken away: The health and the welfare of the Commonweale being the chiefe thing the law respecteth." Ibid., 382F–G. See also 537A–B and 382H–I.

concerns as in the *République*, he addresses them from within a humanist framework—a framework that he, admittedly, alters. Thus, in the *Colloquium*, Bodin uses humanist *sermo* to discuss religious differences, but he transforms *sermo* so that it will neither promote skepticism nor endanger the state. Similarly, like the other humanists examined here, Bodin in the *Colloquium* links *sermo*-based toleration to the expansion of truth. But Bodin moves beyond a Christian, monistic conception of religious truth to a pluralistic conception of truth, in which various religions represent different aspects of a complex, contradictory whole. The result of Bodin's transformation of humanist concepts is a theory of religious toleration that is as inclusive as possible, while remaining humanist in the broad sense.

The *Colloquium heptaplomeres* is a series of conversations, divided into six books, between men of seven different religions: Paulus Coronaeus, a Catholic; Fridericus Podamicus, a Lutheran; Antonius Curtius, a Calvinist; Salomon Barcassius, a Jew; Octavius Fagnola, a Moslem; Diegus Toralba, a proponent of natural religion; and Hieronymus Senamus, a skeptic. Unlike the participants in earlier interreligious dialogues, the participants in the *Colloquium* are presented as equals, without an acknowledged arbiter to judge between them.[16] They discuss a wide variety of topics, including the nature of God, how He expresses himself through nature and the spirit world, our role in the universe, the natures of interpretation, music and musical harmony, and good and evil. The *Colloquium*'s central discussion, which takes place mostly in Book 4, concerns the question of the true religion.

Consistent with the humanist conception of *sermo*, Bodin creates a dialogue in which the interlocutors observe the rules of *decorum*. Their conversation is courteous, even affectionate at times. They were united by "innocence and integrity." And "they were not motivated by wrangling or jealousy but by a desire to learn; consequently they were displaying all their reflections and endeavors in true dignity." Again, like the previously dis-

---

16. Georg Roellenbleck, "Der Schluss des <<Heptaplomeres>> und die Begründung der Toleranz bei Bodin," in *Jean Bodin: Proceedings of the International Conference on Bodin in Munich* (Munich: C. H. Beck, 1973), 57. In one medieval interreligious dialogue, Peter Abelard's *Dialogue of a Philosopher with a Jew, and a Christian* (c. 1136), the judge is Peter Abelard, a Christian. In the *Kuzari* (1140), a similar dialogue between a philosopher, a Christian, a Moslem, and a Jew, written by the Jewish philosopher Rabbi Yehuda Halevi, the judge is the king of the Khazars, who is persuaded by the Jewish speaker. Peter Abelard, *Dialogue of a Philosopher with a Jew, and a Christian*, trans. Pierre J. Payer (Toronto: Pontifical Institute of Mediaeval Studies, 1979); Yehuda Halevi, *The Kosari of R. Yehuda Haleví*, trans. and ed. Yehuda Even Shmuel (Tel-Aviv: Dvir Publishing, 1972).

cussed humanists, who maintained that philosophical and theological conversation should be limited to a small educated elite, Bodin portrays the seven interlocutors in the *Colloquium* as "exceptionally well trained in the disciplines of the liberal arts," with "each seem[ing] to surpass the others in his unique knowledge."[17] The dialogue's setting was designed to foster moderate, learned discussion. The group meets in the Venetian home of Coronaeus. Venice, as is noted in the *Colloquium*, offers its people "the greatest freedom and tranquillity of spirit," and Coronaeus's home itself "was considered a shrine of the Muses and virtues" (3). To encourage scholarly conversation, Coronaeus had filled his home "not only with an infinite variety and supply of books and old records, but also instruments either for music or for all sorts of mathematical arts." Among these artifacts was the *pantotheca*, an unusual armoire built of olive wood, which housed in its 1296 small boxes "the universe, its goods, and materials." In this collection, were "likenesses of sixty fixed stars," "replicas of planets, comets and similar phenomena, elements, bodies, stones, metals, fossils, plants, living things of every sort," and so on. These assorted objects could be viewed and studied to sharpen the minds of the interlocutors (4–5). And to calm the spirits of the interlocutors, Coronaeus arranged for choirboys to sing divine praises at the end of each day's discussion.[18]

Although the discussion in the *Colloquium* adheres to the *decorum* of *sermo*, when judged by the goals of humanist *sermo*, it is a failure. It is this traditional conception of *sermo* that most scholars implicitly accept when they brand the *Colloquium* a failed dialogue. In Georg Roellenbleck's words, "the *Heptaplomeres* is the protocol of a failure, a failure of dialogue, a failure of rational discussion of religious material."[19] For the humanists, as for Socrates and Cicero before them, the participants in a conversation work together to discover the truth.[20] And the closer the participants approach the

---

17. Kuntz, *Colloquium*, 4.

18. Ibid., 15. Sometimes the interlocutors would also entertain themselves "by singing a hymn to the accompaniment of lyres and flutes." Ibid., 89. See also Marion Leathers Kuntz, "The Home of Coronaeus in Jean Bodin's *Colloquium Heptaplomeres*: An Example of a Venetian Academy," in *Acta Conventus Neo-Latini Bononiensis*, Proceedings of the Fourth International Congress of Neo-Latin Studies, ed. R. J. Schoeck (Bologna, 26 August to 1 September 1979), 278–79.

19. Georg Roellenbleck, "Les Poèmes Intercalés Dans L'Heptaplomeres," in *Jean Bodin: Actes du Colloque Interdisciplinaire d'Angers, 24 au 27 mai 1984* (Angers: Presses de l'Université D'Angers, 1985), 2:448.

20. On the Socratic dialogue as a "common search" for the truth, see W.K.C. Guthrie, *Socrates* (Cambridge: Cambridge University Press, 1971), 129.

truth, the more they will agree. But the interlocutors in Bodin's *Colloquium* do not agree. In fact, the dialogue's characters are never able to move any of their fellow speakers from their original beliefs. As Quentin Skinner explains, the participants recognize in their inability to persuade the futility of religious discussion. It is because religious discussion is useless, Skinner argues, that we are told in the dialogue's conclusion that "afterwards they held no other conversation about religions."[21] Similarly, Joseph Lecler writes that the speakers' lack of consensus signals Bodin's belief that "the old policy of colloquies, which had once been advocated by the Christian humanists, had been finally condemned by experience."[22] Notwithstanding these opinions, however, I do not believe that Bodin's *Colloquium* is a failed dialogue. Rather, I agree with Marion Leathers Kuntz that the interlocutors in the *Colloquium* have achieved a successful dialogue.[23]

The *Colloquium* is only a failure if we accept the traditional conception of *sermo*. Roellenbleck declares the *Colloquium* a failure because he presupposes this conception, even though he concedes that the participants in the dialogue have "learned alot."[24] This benefit does not count, for Roellenbleck, because "in the end, nothing has changed. . . . Nobody has been convinced or has modified his position." But what if, *pace* Roellenbleck et al., "learning alot" does matter, learning both about others' beliefs and, through them, about your own? Then the lack of unity would not, by itself, indicate a failed dialogue.

The inability of Bodin's interlocutors to agree on religion stems from their differing assumptions. Unlike the other humanists' conversations on doctrinal adiaphora, the discussions in Bodin's *Colloquium* revolve around the fundamentals of faith, and there is no consensus among the interlocutors about the fundamentals. The Jew, the Moslem, and the follower of natural religion reject Christ as Lord. The Christians' proofs derived from New Testament citations are meaningless to them. Yet for Christians, as Coro-

21. Kuntz, *Colloquium*, 471; Skinner, *Foundations of Modern Political Thought*; 2:249. George Sabine notes similarly that the *Heptaplomeres* "reinforces the futility of religious disputation, for again and again each speaker is driven back to the position which he has already stated, and the dispute begins anew." See George H. Sabine, "The *Colloquium Heptaplomeres* of Jean Bodin," in *Persecution and Liberty: Essays in Honor of George Lincoln Burr* (New York: Century, 1931), 290, 307.

22. Lecler, *Toleration and the Reformation*, 2:180.

23. Professor Kuntz graciously shared with me her views on the *Colloquium* as anything but a failed dialogue. She expresses some of these ideas in her essay "Structure, Form and Meaning in the *Colloquium Heptaplomeres* of Jean Bodin."

24. Roellenbleck, "Les Poèmes Intercalés Dans L'Heptaplomeres," 448.

naeus explains, "If you reject the evangelical testimonies, it is as if you denied the principles of the sciences, without which not even the geometricians will have any proof."[25] Unable to agree on the basic proofs of argument, the interlocutors lack the tools of persuasion. Accordingly, Senamus states: "I think those discussions about religion will come to nothing" (170).

Paradoxically, although Bodin's characters discuss religion, they criticize discourse between religions because it may lead to skepticism. In line with the humanists, they believe that questioning the fundamentals of faith imperils one's soul. And reflecting Bodin's concerns about the good of the Commonwealth, the characters in the *Colloquium* fear the effects of religious skepticism on the state's stability.[26] In Book 4 of the Colloquium, Fridericus raises the question of religious discussions between members of different faiths, while attempting to lure Salomon into debate. Fridericus maintains that though "it is both dangerous and destructive for the masses to engage in discussions about the accepted and approved religion unless one can control the resisting common people . . . , private discussion about divine matters among educated men" is most fruitful.[27] The other speakers respond in turn that debates about religious fundamentals should be avoided. Thus, Toralba observes that people should keep away from religious discussion lest it cause a believer "to abandon the religion of his ancestor" (165), tearing him away from the faith "which God has bestowed from his bountiful goodness" (169). Salomon declares that "according to our laws and customs we are prohibited from discussing religion . . . lest divine laws seemed to be called into doubt"—doubt that "produces the opinion of impiety" (166). Senamus, citing Siena's ban on "discussions about divine matters and the decrees of the popes," links the prohibition on religious disputes to civil peace (167). Similarly, Octavius proclaims the danger of religious debate—"dangerous enough in private but even more so in public." According to Octavius, "if it is not permissible to argue about human laws [in the Florentine republic and in ancient Sparta] so that there

---

25. Kuntz, *Colloquium*, 292.

26. "But religion by common consent once received and setled, is not againe to be called into question and dispute, that so all the wayes and entrances unto sedition and faction may be stopped, and the assurances of unity and peace strengthened." *Six Books*, 535. See also 536: "Wherefore seeing that disputations of religion bring not only the doubt and overthrow of religions, but even the ruine and destruction of Commonweales also; it behooveth them to be by most strait lawes forbidden."

27. Kuntz, *Colloquium*, 165.

will be no approach for breaking the laws through disputation, how much less should this be done about divine laws."[28] And Curtius states that the ancient prophets thought it laudable to abstain from discussions about one's own religion with outsiders. Therefore, Curtius continues in a relativist fashion, "Christians should not cast doubt on the articles of their own faith, nor should Jews among each other or Mohammedans among each other" (170).

Even Coronaeus, who favors religious dialogue and who, along with Fridericus, implores Salomon to enter the discussion about religion, concedes that he is unwilling to question his own religious doctrines. Religious discussion, for him, is a means "to lead into the proper pathway of salvation the converts, catechumens, the demoniacs, the Ismaelites, Jews, Pagans, and Epicureans who have wandered from the straight path." But Coronaeus opposes Christians discussing the tenets of their faith among themselves, for fear that they become "hopelessly entangled by doubtful considerations and involved in various errors" (170). Coronaeus wants non-Catholics to question their religions, but as for himself, he states: "I shall not allow myself to be carried away by the arguments of any one or to be separated from the accepted religion of the Roman pontiffs" (205). Only the dogmatic Fridericus, so confident that his faith cannot be shaken, unequivocally supports religious dialogue.[29] The rest assert that it is wrong to engage in any activity that casts doubt on their own dogmas.

The speakers find support for their fears in the fact that religion is inherently uncertain. "Religion," Toralba explains, "will be grounded either in knowledge or opinion or faith." Knowledge cannot be the sole basis of religion, since true knowledge requires "proof based upon the surest prin-

28. Ibid., 169–70. Octavius further observes: "The edicts of the Persians and the Turks also warned that no discussions about religion may be carried on. Also the kings of the Muscovites and the princes of the Germans at a great assembly at Augsburg, after destructive and lengthy wars, proclaimed that there would be no more discussion about religion among Catholics and priests of the Augsburg confession. When one man rashly violated this edict, he was put to death, and the uprisings in that city were quelled to the present"(167).

29. Tellingly, Bodin casts Fridericus as the speaker fooled by artificial apples that Coronaeus had mingled with their real counterparts: "When Fridericus, good man that he was, bit into an artificial apple, being deceived by its appearance, he said: 'I do not see how any one of you could have not been deceived.' After the others looked more closely at the apples which were so cleverly fashioned that they seemed freshly plucked, Coronaeus said: 'If the eyes which are the keenest of the senses are so irrationally deceived in insignificant matters, how can it happen that the mind, which gathers everything from the senses, attains certain knowledge in difficult and sublime matters?'" Bodin thus uses Fridericus to make the skeptical point that reality and appearance are often indistinguishable. Ibid., 233.

ciples and fortified by necessary conclusions," and the different religions have not provided such proof. We are left, therefore, with opinion and faith, neither of which is certain. "If religion depends on opinion, that ambiguous opinion wavers between truth and falsehood and totters during hostile discussion." And faith, which is "pure assent without proof," can be lost. For if we receive our faith from our trust in another person's word, when "we reject this opinion of his uprightness or erudition, we lose faith."[30] And if faith is granted by divine infusion, it can, by definition, be lost: any belief that is "inevitable and fixed so that it cannot be lost . . . is force, not faith."[31]

Despite agreeing that religious dialogue is dangerous, the characters of the *Colloquium* still go on to discuss religion; they reject the traditional model of *sermo* in which everyone's beliefs are open to scrutiny, but are still willing to present their religious views. The *Colloquium*'s speakers reconcile their criticism of religious discussion with their participation in it by creating a kind of conversation that does not bring about the skepticism they dread. In contrast to the traditional dialogue, their conversations reinforce their original beliefs. The final words of the *Colloquium* confirm this deepening of opinions. The speakers, the text states, spoke no more about religions, "although each one defended his own religion with the supreme sanctity of his life."[32]

How can a dialogue across religious lines strengthen the believer's faith? Toralba provides the answer. Anticipating an argument made centuries later by John Stuart Mill, he argues that we understand ourselves only by way of contrast with others. Justice, integrity, or virtue would not be perceived "unless wicked men mingled with the good, sane with the mad, brave with the cowardly, rich with the poor, low with the noble. . . . Indeed, these discussions which Coronaeus began would offer no purpose or pleasure unless they took lustre from opposing arguments and reasons."[33] The exercise of defending his religious beliefs against those of the others clarifies each speaker's views to himself. What is initially held as an unreflected prejudice

---

30. Cf. Hobbes, *Leviathan*, 132–34; 179–83.

31. Kuntz, *Colloquium*, 169. Cf. Bodin, *Six Bookes*, 535.

32. Kuntz, *Colloquium*, 471.

33. Kuntz, *Colloquium*, 148. Cf. John Stuart Mill, *On Liberty*: "But on every subject on which difference of opinion is possible, the truth depends on a balance to be struck between two sets of conflicting reasons . . . and it has to be shown why that other theory cannot be the true one; and until this is shown, and until we know how it is shown, we do not understand the grounds of our opinion."

is retained, after discussion, as an intellectually defensible—if not fully demonstrable—opinion.

In addition to reinforcing their beliefs through argumentation, the *Colloquium*'s speakers also intensify their religious resolve through poetry. There are eleven poems exalting God that the interlocutors recite in the *Colloquium*; six are recited after the discussion of religious differences begins.[34] And of these six poems, at least five either single out the speaker's own religion for praise or condemn the theology of a competing religion. For example, in his poetry, Salomon praises the unique nature of the Hebrews: their covenant with God on Sinai, where they were given the divine laws; and the special protection God grants them.[35] And in his poem, Coronaeus celebrates Christ, the redeemer of humankind, as the source of earthly kings (390–91). Finally, Octavius directs his poem against the Christian doctrine of original sin (406–7).

Like the speakers' arguments in the *Colloquium*, this tendentious poetry does not persuade anyone to change religions. Such poetry is never intended to persuade nonbelievers. Rather, the speakers recite poetry to arouse their own faiths. By turning to poetry, the participants indicate that when dealing with religion, rational argument is not enough. It is not sufficient for the participants to intellectualize about their specific doctrines. They must also feel their religion. And poetry is the means by which the characters impress their religion upon their souls.

Although Bodin values the utility of defining one's own religion vis-à-vis another's, whether through conversation or poetry, this benefit alone is insufficient to justify toleration. St. Thomas Aquinas, for example, allowed that heresy played a positive role in the search for truth since it permitted the faithful to contrast truth with error. Nevertheless, he supported the death penalty for heretics. To Aquinas, their error was not essential to the discovery of truth.[36] Why, then, does Bodin grant his characters the opportunity to defend and praise their religions, when none of his contemporaries

34. Each of the Christians recites one poem. Toralba and Octavius each recite two, and Salomon recites four. Only Senamus, the skeptic, avoids poetry. See Kuntz, "Structure, Form and Meaning in the *Colloquium Heptaplomeres*," 24–25. See also Roellenbleck, "Les Poèmes Intercalés Dans L'Heptaplomeres," 445–47.

35. Kuntz, *Colloquium*, 191–92, 261–62, 411–12.

36. St. Thomas Aquinas *Summa theologiae* 2, 2, q. 11, a. 3. St. Thomas quotes St. Augustine's statement (*De Gen. cont. Manich.* i. I) that the profit derived from heresy is that "'it makes us shake off our sluggishness, and search the Scriptures more carefully.'" Nevertheless, St. Thomas writes that "we should consider what they directly intend, and expel them" and that "if heretics be altogether uprooted by death, this is not contrary to Our Lord's command."

do so? Humanists that supported limited toleration do not grant equal status to heretics and non-Christians because these humanists believe the heretics' errors to be damnable. The key to Bodin's exceptionalism is his conception of religious truth.

The Nature of Truth

Bodin sees religious truth as a complex whole—what Marion Daniels Kuntz refers to as "a unity based on multiplicity (*concordia discors*)"[37]—with each religion forming a part of the greater whole. Bodin, however, does not view these elements as thoroughly consistent with one another, but as subsisting in a state of tension. Taken together, the different religions express the unity of truth, yet each particular religion conflicts with the others. Bodin relies on a musical metaphor to convey his idea. In a conversation about harmonic theory that he initiates, Coronaeus opines that the sweetest harmony is achieved "with the full system of the highest tone blended with the lowest, with the fourth and fifth interspersed." In contrast, "harmonies in unison, in which no tone is opposite, are not pleasing to the trained ear."[38] This idea that harmony or truth inheres in different opposing elements is voiced by other speakers. Toralba observes that what is most pleasing to the senses is "a harmony which depends on the blended union of opposites."[39] And Curtius recites a poem praising God for His universe based on opposites: "This greatest harmony of the universe though discordant contains our safety" (147).

Nature's blending of opposites does not destroy the individual components. The elements retain their separate identities. The opposing elements of nature, Toralba explains, are forms, like the contrary forms of fire and water. And "things which are contrary to each other in nature herself cannot be mingled by design, but only blended, joined, or united so that they seem to be one" (146). Like nature, religious truth is also composed of distinct elements whose differences cannot be ignored. Although tolerant of different religions, Octavius still declares: "Truly we ought to despise the blending of sacred rites" (157). We cannot treat opposing religions as if they were the same. Similarly, Salomon rebukes Senamus, who adopts the practices of all

---

37. Marion Daniels Kuntz, "Harmony and the Heptaplomeres of Jean Bodin," *Journal of the History of Philosophy* 12 (1974): 35–36.

38. Kuntz, *Colloquium*, 144. See also Kuntz, "Harmony and the Heptaplomeres of Jean Bodin," 35–36; and "Home of Coronaeus," 279–80.

39. Kuntz, *Colloquium*, 145.

religions: "I would prefer that you were hot or cold rather than lukewarm in religion, Senamus. And yet, how is it possible to defend the religions of all at the same time, that is, to confess or believe that Christ is God and to deny that He is God, that He has been overcome by death and snatched from torment, that bread becomes God, and does not become God, which things cannot happen at the same time through nature" (465). Salomon's fellow participants follow his advice, remaining steadfast in their convictions. Each person believes that by doing so he protects the purity of his faith, which alone reveals the full truth. Bodin, however, does not identify with any single religion.[40] He recognizes the divine descent of all religious beliefs.[41] Thus for him, religious differences should not be retained for the sake of any single religion, but because they, collectively in their opposition to one another, contain the whole truth. The variety of religions mirrors the contrariety of the universe. In Curtius's words, it is "the variant natures of individual things [that] combine for the harmony of one universe."[42]

Bodin emphasizes that the opposition of individual elements must be kept within limits, that the contrariety of extremes must be curbed. The participants in the *Colloquium* point to intervening elements as a moderating force. In music, "extreme opposites are brought together by intermingling of the middle tones (Fridericus)." In nature, opposites are "united by the interpolation of certain middle links." These links "present a remarkable harmony of the whole which would otherwise perish completely if this whole world were fire or moisture (Toralba)." In planetary movements, "the contrary force of Mars and Saturn is restrained by the intermediate light of Jupiter

40. Bodin's own religious allegiances are unclear. He was born a Roman Catholic, supported the Catholic League against the then Protestant Henry of Navarre (King Henry IV), and was buried a Catholic in the Church of the Franciscans at Laon, at his request. Nevertheless, throughout his life Bodin was dogged by the widespread suspicion that he was a Protestant heretic. He was probably charged with heresy as a youth in 1547; he was arrested and imprisoned for a year and a half, from 1569 to 1570, for being a Protestant; and because of continuing fears that he was a heretic, he was questioned (but cleared) by the lieutenant-general of Laon in 1587. Bodin was also, from very early on, suspected of being a closet Jew or at least a Judaizer. See Paul Lawrence Rose, *Bodin and the Great God of Nature: The Moral and Religious Universe of a Judaiser* (Geneva: Librairie Droz, 1980). For a summary of Bodin's religious life and views, see Kuntz, *Colloquium*, xv–xlvi.

41. Kuntz, *Colloquium*, xli–xlii.

42. Ibid., 149. Like Machiavelli in the *Discourses*, Curtius saw the opposition between parts of the whole as a source of liberty: "The Roman state flourished when the patricians blocked the plebs and the tribunician power thwarted the consular greed." See Niccolò Machiavelli, *The Discourses of Niccolò Machiavelli*, trans. Leslie J. Walker (London: Routledge and Kegan Paul, 1950), 1.4, vol. 1, 218–19.

(Fridericus)." And among philosophic schools, "the opposite camps of Epicureans and Stoics were joined, as if by certain bonds, midway by the Academicans and Peripatetics (Toralba)." Such intermediate schools were necessary, for "if one opposite were joined to another opposite with no middle ground between, there would necessarily be continual battle." It is also safer when a political office is divided between three persons instead of two. "For a third party forces two opposing factions toward harmony, when the others have allied themselves (Coronaeus)." Finally, a state split into two factions, divided about laws, honors, or religion, is bound to destroy itself. "If, however, there are many factions, there is no danger of civil war, since the groups, each acting as a check on the other, protect the stability and harmony of the state (Curtius)" (146–51).

To moderate conflict, Bodin does not construct the *Colloquium* as a bipolar dialogue between extremes. Instead, he includes in the *Colloquium* a spectrum of religious opinions. The opposition between the three Christians, who believe in divine revelation and in Christ as the son of God, and the natural philosopher and skeptic, who deny or question these beliefs, is mediated by the Jew and the Moslem, who believe in divine revelation, but deny Christ's divinity. Bodin also curbs the opposition between speakers by following the rhetorical rules of *decorum*. As noted earlier, the *decorum* of the *Colloquium* resembles the *decorum* of humanist *sermo*. Unlike the humanists of previous chapters, however, Bodin does not follow these rules for the purpose of finding the one truth. For Bodin, the rules of *decorum* represent the unity of the parts within the whole. Like the opposing elements of nature, the interlocutors in the *Colloquium* are part of a common universe and conflicts between them must be restrained. Despite their differences, they are described at the end of the dialogue as brothers living in unity.[43]

The passage in which Bodin points up the fraternity of the interlocutors also alludes to the higher level of understanding reached on account of their diversity. The passage, which is based on Psalm 133, is sung by Coronaeus as follows: "Lo, how good and pleasing it is for brothers to live in unity, arranged not in common diatonics or chromatics, but in enharmonics with a certain more divine modulation." Marion Kuntz suggests that this use of musical terminology means that during the course of the dialogue, the speakers traverse the range of musical genera, from the diatonic, which allows only seven tones, to the chromatic, which allows twelve, to the more complex enharmonic *genus*. The numerous intervals in the enharmonic

---

43. "Lo, how good and pleasing it is for brothers to live in unity." Ibid., 471.

genus, like the varied divisions between the seven speakers, reveal the greater truth. As the advancement of musical *genera* in Coronaeus's song corresponds to the multiplication of tones in each succeeding *genus*, the participants in the *Colloquium* may, similarly, be said to have reached the highest level—the enharmonic *genus*—when they have expressed the fullness of their divisions at the end of the dialogue.[44] It may also be argued that because enharmonics is the more refined and arcane *genus*, it represents, for Bodin, greater understanding. As Nicolo Vicentino argues in his *L'antica musica ridotta alla moderna prattica* (1555), enharmonics is reserved "for the few—for people with cultivated taste, not for the common folk."[45] And Bodin, influenced by "the Hermetic belief that the deepest truths cannot be revealed to the multitude," equates the esoteric with the deeper truth.[46] Coronaeus's paraphrase of Psalm 133 implies, then, that the speakers in the *Colloquium* hold no further conversations about religion, not, as most commentators contend, because they have given up on religious discourse, but because they have reached a higher level.[47] They have achieved their goal.

Consistent with the view that each religion possesses some aspect of truth, all the participants call for toleration. Coronaeus assures his guests "the greatest freedom in speaking about religion" (165–66). For Toralba, "the law of nature and natural religion which has been implanted in men's souls is sufficient for attaining salvation" (186). Presumably, therefore, all religions that adhere to the natural law should be tolerated. Curtius, as already seen, argues that many sects can live together more peacefully than two. He also cites the Church Fathers and the Church Councils as supporting the principle of toleration: " 'It is not for religion to compel, which ought to be undertaken of one's own accord, not by force.' "[48] Senamus holds up the example of Jerusalem, where eight Christian sects, Jews, and Moslems coexisted, each group tolerating the rest (465–66). Octavius applauds the

---

44. Ibid., 471; Kuntz, "Structure, Form and Meaning in the *Colloquium Heptaplomeres*," 26–28.

45. Edward E. Lowinsky, *Secret Chromatic Art in the Netherlands Motet*, trans. Carl Buchman (New York: Russell & Russell, 1946), 90.

46. Frances E. Yates, "The Hermetic Tradition in Renaissance Science," in *Art, Science, and History in the Renaissance*, ed. Charles S. Singleton (Baltimore: Johns Hopkins University Press, 1967), 264. On Bodin's ties to Hermeticism and other mystical traditions, see Kuntz, *Colloquium*, liv–lvi.

47. "The beauty of the enharmonic mode and the awe which it had inspired leave the seven speakers with no need to discuss religion again." Kuntz, "Structure, Form and Meaning in the *Colloquium Heptaplomeres*," 28.

48. Ibid., 468. See also ibid., 469–71.

tolerance of the kings of the Turks and Persians and the religious freedom of Venice.[49] And Salomon affirms that no "more serious insult against God can be conceived than to wish to force anyone to obey Him" (468–69). Because religion should not be coerced, he explains, Jews do not force their religion on gentiles—although Salomon is unwilling to tolerate Jewish apostates.[50] By the conclusion, even Fridericus, the most dogmatic of the interlocutors, agrees that faith cannot be compelled. The Emperor Theodoric's opinion, he states, "is worthy to be inscribed in golden letters on the door posts of princes . . . , that we are unable to command religion because no one can be forced to believe against his will" (471).

The Argument from Conscience

I have until now discussed what I see as Bodin's primary argument for religious toleration: that each religion represented in the *Colloquium* can claim for itself a right to be tolerated because it is a part of the truth. Bodin, however, offers another, seemingly more modern justification for toleration that does not depend on a religion's veracity: the argument from conscience. Bodin's use of the argument from conscience in the *Colloquium* is another example of how his approach to toleration is humanist, yet different from the mainstream humanist defense of toleration. In line with other humanist defenders of toleration, Bodin does not rely on the right to conscience as his principal justification for toleration. Yet he differs from them insofar as he develops the argument from conscience further than most other humanists, thus anticipating the liberal argument from conscience.

Many of the humanist defenders of religious toleration, particularly Protestant humanists, call attention to the argument from conscience in their writings on toleration. Sebastian Castellio noted the hypocrisy of forcing someone to recant his beliefs against his conscience. "To force conscience," he wrote, "is worse than cruelly to kill a man."[51] Similarly, Acontius wrote that no one should be compelled to confess his opinions as error, when he

---

49. Ibid., 151, 467. Octavius, however, also praises the Persians and Turks for forbidding discussions about religion because they lead to civil unrest (167). The key for Octavius is that religious discussion must not degenerate into violence. Peace is maintained, in part, by the rules of *decorum*.

50. "If anyone of our nation seeks a foreign god and foreign sacred rites, after he has deserted the worship of God, he is ordered to be stoned, and the city to be destroyed. The same punishment follows those who have not acquiesced to the high priest's dictum." Ibid., 468–69.

51. Sebastian Castellio, *Conseil à la France désolée* (October 1562), 15; quoted in Bainton, *Concerning Heretics*, 259. See also Bainton, *Studies*, 174.

does not yet understand that he is wrong, "since, if I comply, I shall do so against my conscience, and therefore shall sin against God."[52] And Chillingworth used the argument from conscience to justify his variable standard of fundamentals. Nevertheless, despite these references to conscience, the humanists did not produce a theory of individual rights, which denied them a principled basis to protect persons outside the Church. This fact distinguishes the humanists from the liberals, who, as shall be seen later, did construct a theory of religious liberty that focused on the individual's right to conscience. Like the other humanists mentioned, Bodin did not construct a theory of religious liberty grounded on the right to conscience: his appeal to truth was still more important than his appeal to conscience; he does not present conscience as a prepolitical right, as Locke does; and he never fully spells out the implications of conscience for toleration. Nevertheless, Bodin skirts the outer limits of humanism by respecting the consciences of all sincere believers, no matter their religion.

According to the argument from conscience, as developed in the *Colloquium*, any person that is genuine in his beliefs, even if wrong, will be saved. Octavius, the most consistent defender of conscience in the *Colloquium*, includes sincere idolaters and polytheists among the saved, despite his strict monotheism, because "with pure heart and soul and an upright conscience, they were thus instructed and trained by the priests and thus worship the divinity that was known to them and related to them."[53] Octavius finds support from the other non-Christian interlocutors. Salomon, who like Octavius is repelled by the Christian doctrine of the Incarnation, concedes that "even worship which is offered in good faith to a clay god is not unpleasing to eternal God."[54] And Toralba and Senamus, agree that "a just error is erased by a just excuse" (243) and that all religions practiced "not with faked pretense but a pure mind" are "not unpleasing to eternal God" (251). The Christian interlocutors, particularly the Protestants, however, have less regard for the sincere conscience. Whereas Octavius cites both St. Thomas Aquinas and St. Augustine as respecting the erroneous conscience,[55] the Protestant participants—like the Catholic Aquinas—do not

52. *Satan's Stratagems*, 93.
53. Kuntz, *Colloquium*, 241.
54. Ibid. See also 243.
55. Octavius states: "Thomas Aquinas said: 'When errant reason has established something as a precept of God, then it is the same thing to scorn the dictate of reason and the commands of God.' Divine Augustine had confirmed this before." Kuntz, *Colloquium*, 157–58.

however, Senamus supposes that all atheists have bad intentions. And therefore, these persons who act out of bad conscience cannot assert a liberty based on a right to conscience.

A Humanist Response to Hobbes

Is the *Colloquium* a plausible humanist response to Hobbes's critique of the humanist defense of religious toleration? First, does it respond adequately to Hobbes's concerns? Hobbes's main problem with the humanist defense was his fear that it endangered the Commonwealth. It permitted religious debates that could lead to civil war. And while the humanists claimed that only nonessential beliefs could be debated, but that Christians would unite around the fundamentals of faith, Hobbes denied that there was a core of Christian truths to which all believers would agree. To Hobbes, Christianity could not be proven objectively truer than other religions. Thus Hobbes believed that rational theological discussions were useless, or rather they were worse than useless. Unable to demonstrate anything, debates between Christians about the truths of their religion would inevitably degenerate into passion-driven conflicts that would rend the body politic. In place of theological conversation, Hobbes sought to establish the sovereign as the sole arbiter of religious doctrines. And Hobbes would have left it to the sovereign to determine, on prudential grounds, the scope of toleration.

In the *Colloquium*, Bodin was similarly troubled by the political instability that religious discussions might produce. And he also implied that Christianity could not demonstrate its own truthfulness any better than the other faiths could. But Bodin neutralizes the dangers of religious discussion by changing its purpose. The purpose of religious conversation, in the *Colloquium*, is no longer for the interlocutors, collectively, to discover the truth, but for the participants to confirm themselves further in the truth of their own beliefs. Bodin, therefore, escapes the dangers of a theological debate in which each interlocutor tries to persuade the others of their errors. For in such a debate, once the participants cease to agree that they are only debating nonessentials, as Hobbes believed they inevitably would, the discussion is likely to turn violent. Jean-Jacques Rousseau's warning, that it is impossible to live at peace with people you believe are damned, is relevant here. Rousseau explains that regarding such people, "it is absolutely necessary to reclaim them or to punish them."[63] Bodin does not violate Rousseau's admonition because in a state based on the model of the *Colloquium*, Christians, as well as adherents of other faiths, will be satisfied to believe in the truth of their particular faith, without trying to dominate those who believe otherwise. They must accept that there is salvation outside the confines of their own church because their own religion is only part of a greater truth. Having accepted the legitimacy of other faiths, the subjects of Bodin's state would not require a Hobbesian judge of religious dogmas.

The second question is whether the *Colloquium* is a *humanist* response to Hobbes's concerns? I have emphasized in this chapter how the *Colloquium* departed from the humanist defense of religious toleration, which was begun by Erasmus and developed by Acontius, Chillingworth, and others. But Bodin's theory of religious toleration, implicit in the *Colloquium*, salvages key elements of the humanist defense. *Pace* most contemporary writers on the *Colloquium*, Bodin does not reject the humanist ideal of religious conversation; rather, he makes use of *sermo*. The interlocutors discuss their religious differences and learn from them. Bodin, like the humanists previously discussed, allows the participants to arrive at their own conclusions. And the interlocutors in the *Colloquium*, like those described by the other humanists, must follow the rules of *decorum*. Thus, they must not only refrain from physically persecuting but also from verbally abusing one another. In the *Colloquium*, as in other humanist accounts, the participants in *sermo* show one another mutual respect.

Where Bodin differs most from the other humanists is in his conception of religious truth. Erasmus et al. hold a monistic conception of religious truth. They presume that if "doctrine x" is true, then a competing "doctrine y" must be false. Therefore, for them, *sermo* and toleration only extend to areas that are not yet known, that is, to the adiaphora. Bodin, on the other hand, holds a pluralistic conception of religious truth, where simply because "doctrine x" is true does not mean that competing "doctrine y" cannot also be true. Accordingly, for Bodin, *sermo* can tolerate contradictory opinions, even when opposing sides are convinced that they know the truth. But even here, in their differing conceptions of religious truth, Bodin and the other humanists discussed reflect an attitude to religious truth that is characteris-

63. Jean-Jacques Rousseau, *The Social Contract and Discourse on the Origin of Inequality*, ed. Lester G. Crocker (New York: Washington Square Press, 1976), 146.

tically humanist: the balancing of skepticism and certainty.[64] Both he and the others believe in the existence of religious truth. They even maintain that we must believe wholeheartedly in our religion's core doctrines. Yet they recognize, simultaneously, that dogmas cannot be demonstrated with certainty. Their joint response is that we cannot freely question our fundamental doctrines. Although for Erasmus et al., this means that we cannot discuss these doctrines in the manner we debate nonessentials, for Bodin this only means that the speaker must use *sermo* differently, to strengthen belief in our fundamental doctrines.

One last sign of the humanist character of the *Colloquium*'s theory of religious toleration is that it links toleration to possession of the truth. The humanists discussed previously limited toleration to Christians adhering to the fundamentals of faith because they accepted the fundamental truths of Christianity, which for those humanists was the only true religion. Similarly, Bodin accepts their principle, that toleration should be granted to those possessing the truth, but because he believes that non-Christian religions are legitimate parts of a complex truth, he extends the same protection to non-Christians that the other humanists would limit to Christians. But whereas the Erasmian humanists would have viewed the *Colloquium*'s toleration as an unwarranted extension of their principle, Bodin did have humanist precedents for considering moral non-Christians capable of achieving salvation. Among humanists treated in this book, Erasmus, for example, considered it likely that ethical pagans, notwithstanding their ignorance of Christ, would be saved. Although Erasmus conceded that these pagans had little knowledge of true doctrine, their godly lives could not be overlooked.[65] Moreover, other humanists, like Guillaume Postel, did much to show the truths present in non-Christian religions.[66] Thus while Bodin followed down the road of other humanists, who minimized the differences between Christianity and other faiths, only Bodin, in the *Colloquium*, denied Christianity any special status. He took humanist concepts and altered them to give them new meaning. It could be argued that Hobbes, in a sense, did the

64. This balancing of skepticism and certainty distinguishes the humanists from dogmatists, like Luther, who condemn skepticism, and from skeptics, like Bayle, who maintain that nothing can be known about religion.

65. See Erasmus's preface to his edition of Cicero's *Tusculan Disputations* (Paris, 1549).

66. See Kuntz, *Colloquium*, xlvii–lxvi; Marion Leathers Kuntz, "Jean Bodin's *Colloquium Heptaplomeres* and Guillaume Postel: A Consideration of Influence," in *Jean Bodin: Actes du Colloque Interdisciplinaire d'Angers, 24 au 27 Mai 1984* (Angers: Presses de l'Universite D'Angers, 1985), 2:435–44; and Sabine, "The *Colloquium Heptaplomeres* of Jean Bodin," 275–89.

same. Hobbes also retained humanist concepts, like the "fundamentals of faith," and vested them with new meaning. But whereas Hobbes transformed these concepts so that he might neutralize humanist toleration, Bodin did the opposite. He took humanist ideas and adapted them so that he might expand humanist toleration. The changes he effected distinguish him from the rest of the humanists examined here, but his theory of toleration must, nevertheless, be considered a humanist theory of toleration.

6

Conclusion: The Aftermath of Humanism

Liberalism and Religious Liberty

Locke: Union of Liberalism and Humanism

By the late seventeenth century, the humanist formula of a tolerant, comprehensive Church, separate from but coextensive with the state, was no longer viable. Comprehension alone was unacceptable to the Dissenters, who demanded religious rights for those Christians excluded by or unwilling to join the established Church.[1] Nevertheless, the humanists' arguments about religious conversation, accommodation, probability, and the fundamentals of faith did not immediately disappear. Rather, they were incorporated by early liberals like John Locke into a theory of religious liberty that emphasized the individual's right to conscience.[2]

---

1. This is not to imply that the battle for comprehension was abandoned. First, many of those who supported toleration of those outside the dominant Church were concerned, at the same time, that the dominant Church itself be broad-based. Second, the latter half of the seventeenth century also found proponents of comprehension, as opposed to toleration, among such Latitudinarians as John Wilkins, John Tillotson, Sir Matthew Hale, Edward Stillingfleet, and Thomas Tenison. The Toleration Act of 1689, however, settled the debate of comprehension versus toleration in favor of toleration, although it still excluded Dissenters from public office and retained all the penal laws against Catholics and Unitarians. On Latitudinarians and comprehension, see John Marshall, "The Ecclesiology of the Latitude-Men, 1660–1689: Stillingfleet, Tillotson and 'Hobbism,'" *The Journal of Ecclesiastical History* 36 (1985): 407–27, and Shapiro, *Probability and Certainty*, 110–11.

2. Although I shall not make the case here, humanist influences are apparent in the writings

The right to conscience figures prominently in the theories of such eighteenth-century liberals as Thomas Jefferson and James Madison, as well as the contemporary liberal John Rawls, but it receives its classic exposition in Locke's *Letter Concerning Toleration*, published in 1689.[3] Here Locke provides later liberals with a rationale for safeguarding the individual's religious freedom against the coercive powers of political authority. For Locke, as for his liberal heirs, the right to conscience preceded and was independent of all political institutions; it was never abandoned by the people in their social contract. Therefore, Locke writes, the civil magistrate's power "is bounded and confined to . . . [civil] things; and that it neither can nor ought in any manner to be extended to the salvation of souls."[4] Everyone is left to the care of his or her own eternal happiness, "the attainment whereof can neither be facilitated by another man's industry, nor can the loss of it turn to another man's prejudice, nor the hope of it be forced from him by any external violence."[5]

The liberal's rights-orientation can be interpreted as indifferent, even antithetical, to the humanist defense of religious toleration. Whereas the humanist's language—discussion, consensus, and comprehensive Church—presupposes a religious community, the liberal's emphasis on rights may be said to abstract the believer from this community. Locke himself appears to support this view of liberalism. At times he implies that religion is a purely private activity, with no effect on the outside world. Every man, as Locke puts it, is allowed to decide how to spend his money, sow his land, marry off

---

of post-Restoration Dissenters such as Robert Ferguson and John Owen, who as Richard Ashcraft points out, developed the "core ingredients of liberalism." Richard Ashcraft, "John Locke, Religious Dissent, and the Origins of Liberalism" (paper presented at the Folger Institute Center for the History of British Political Thought, March 1986).

3. Jefferson writes: "But our rulers can have authority over such natural rights only as we have submitted to them. The rights of conscience we never submitted, we could not submit." Thomas Jefferson, *Notes on the State of Virginia*, ed. William Peden (Chapel Hill: University of North Carolina Press, 1955), 159. Similarly, Madison describes the right to conscience, in his *Memorial and Remonstrance Against Religious Assessment*, as "in its nature an unalienable right." Marvin Meyers, ed., *The Mind of the Founder: Sources of the Political Thought of James Madison*, rev. ed. (Hanover: University Press of New England, 1981), 5–13. For the paradigm of the right to conscience among contemporary liberals, see John Rawls, *A Theory of Justice* (Cambridge: Harvard University Press, 1971), chap. 4.

4. Montuori, *John Locke on Toleration and Unity of God*, 17.

5. Ibid., 83; John Locke, *A Second Letter Concerning Toleration*, in *The Works of John Locke in Ten Volumes*, 11th ed. (London: T. Davison, 1812), 6:119; Richard Ashcraft, *Revolutionary Politics and Locke's Two Treatises of Government* (Princeton: Princeton University Press, 1986), 493.

his daughter. "But," he observes critically, "if any man do not frequent the church, if he do not there conform his behaviour exactly to the accustomed ceremonies, or if he brings not his children to be initiated in the sacred mysteries of this or the other congregation, this immediately causes an uproar."[6] To persecute a man on religious grounds, Locke notes, is no different from discriminating against someone for the color of his hair or eyes.[7] What a Roman Catholic believes about the nature of the Eucharist, or a Jew about the New Testament, can do no injury to his neighbor. (79). The humanist's rhetorically grounded understanding that religion takes place within a social context is absent from these statements. Locke's Christian believer would seem to live in a solipsistic world, influenced by no one, and, like the spendthrift who consumes "his substance in the taverns," affecting no one except, perhaps, his immediate family (43).

Viewed within the broader context of the *Letter*, however, Locke's conception of the right to conscience does not exclude the religious community. To Locke, the individual exercises this right to conscience in consultation with other members of the community. Locke's right to conscience is not a license for religious anarchy, circumscribed only by the limits of civil law. Rather, it is a way for individuals to fulfill a religious obligation to care for their own salvation—an obligation that is carried out in the company of others.[8] The communal setting for the fulfillment of religious duties, Locke argues, is the Church. It is within the Church that people can pursue doctrinal truth.[9] Echoing the humanists' sermocinal ideal, Locke believes that discussion within the Church should be moderate and rational. Truth, he writes, "has no such way of prevailing as when strong arguments

6. Montuori, *John Locke on Toleration and the Unity of God*, 43. Jefferson's and Madison's descriptions of the independence of the right to conscience from political authority are nearly identical to Locke's. See Jefferson, *Notes on the State of Virginia*, 157–61, and Meyers, *The Mind of the Founder*, 5–13. In Rawl's version of the social contract, persons in the original position, ignorant of their own place in society, would not "take chances with their liberty by permitting the dominant religious or moral doctrine to persecute or to suppress others if it wishes." *Theory of Justice*, 207.

7. Montuori, *John Locke on Toleration and the Unity of God*, 97–99.

8. Ashcraft, *Revolutionary Politics*, 494. Ashcraft speaks of the Dissenter's emphasis on discussion as a way of choosing the right path to salvation in "John Locke, Religious Dissent, and the Origins of Liberalism."

9. We enter into religious societies, for "mutual edification," for public worship, and to draw others to true religion, "and perform such other things in religion as cannot be done by each private man apart." Montuori, *John Locke on Toleration and the Unity of God*, 57. Unlike later liberal political theorists, whose scope is limited to the state, Locke presents a dual theory of Church and state. Ibid., 15, 23.

and good reason are joined with the softness of civility and good usage."[10]

In defining the truth necessary for salvation, Locke adopts the key humanist concepts of probability, consensus, and fundamentals.[11] Like the humanists, specifically Chillingworth, Locke contends that most things can only be known with probability. "Most of the Propositions we think, reason, discourse, nay act upon are such, as we cannot have undoubted knowledge of their Truth."[12] Even religion cannot be demonstrated with certainty: "This is the highest the nature of the thing will permit us to go in matters of revealed religion, which are therefore called matters of faith: a persuasion of our minds, short of knowledge, is the last result that determines us in such truths. It is all God requires us in the gospel for men to be saved."[13] Probability for Locke, as for Chillingworth, extends not only to the adiaphora, but also to the articles of faith. God neither requires "nor has given us faculties capable of knowing in this world several of those truths, which are to be believed to salvation" (424).

How do we determine what is most probable? Locke responds in

10. Ibid., 37–39. Cf. Locke's argument in *The Reasonableness of Christianity* that because of "railing from the pulpit, ill and unfriendly treatment out of it, and other neglects and miscarriages," people who otherwise could have been brought to the Church "by friendly and christian debates . . . and by the gentle methods of the gospel made use of in private conversation" are driven from it. John Locke, *The Reasonableness of Christianity*, ed. I. T. Ramsey (London: Adam and Charles Black, 1958), 32. See also Locke's call for moderate discussion of probable matters, in *An Essay Concerning Human Understanding*: "We should do well to commiserate our mutual Ignorance, and endeavour to remove it in all the gentle and fair ways of Information; and not instantly treat others ill, as obstinate and perverse, because they will not renounce their own, and receive our Opinions, or at least those we would force upon them, when 'tis more probable, that we are no less obstinate in not embracing some of theirs. But where is the Man, that has uncontestable Evidence of the Truth of all that he holds, or of the Falshood of all he condemns; or can say, that he has examined, to the bottom, all his own, or other Men's Opinions?" John Locke, *An Essay Concerning Human Understanding*, ed. Peter H. Nidditch (Oxford: Clarendon Press, 1975), 4:16, 4.

11. Locke's intellectual debt to the humanists is more than hypothetical. Erasmus, Castellio, Acontius, Faustus Socinus, and Chillingworth were all represented in his library. Locke recommended the constant reading of Chillingworth, "who by his example, will teach both perspicuity, and the way of right reasoning, better than any book I know . . . not to say anything of his argument." James L. Axtell, *The Educational Writings of John Locke* (Cambridge: Cambridge University Press, 1968), 399.

12. Like Chillingworth, Locke observes that some propositions "border so near upon Certainty, that we make no doubt at all about them; but *assent* to them as firmly and act, according to that Assent, as resolutely, as if they were infallibly demonstrated, and that our Knowledge of them was perfect and certain." *An Essay Concerning Human Understanding*, 4:15, 2. See also John Locke, *An Early Draft of Locke's Essay*, ed. R. I. Aaron and Joceylin Gibb (Oxford: Clarendon Press, 1936), 55–56.

13. *A Third Letter for Toleration*, in *The Works of John Locke in Ten Volumes*, 6:144.

Erasmian fashion that the greater the consensus, the higher the degree of probability.[14] Accordingly, the high probability of the fundamentals of faith is confirmed by the widespread consensus of them. Locke consistently assumes that Christian brethren "are all agreed in the substantial and truly fundamental part of religion."[15] Most religious disagreements, according to Locke, concern nonessentials, matters that may "either be observed or omitted." Christians disagree among themselves about the best form of church organization and the proper form of worship, but they agree on the religious essentials.[16] Hence Locke, siding with the Dissenters against the established Church, argues that the Anglican Church, although it teaches the true faith, is not tantamount to the true faith; by demanding belief in nonessentials, it also contains elements extraneous to the true faith. What distinguishes most dissenting Protestants from Anglicans, Locke states, are discipline and ceremonies, not doctrine.[17] While not identifying what the essentials are in the *Letter*, Locke limits necessary belief—as did Hobbes—to the single conviction that Jesus was the Messiah.[18] God would not have required more, Locke assumes, because "the greatest part of mankind have not leisure for learning and logic, and superfine distinctions of the school."[19] Like the humanists, Locke believes that God accommodated Himself to us and, therefore, would not demand doctrinal knowledge beyond the capacities of most people.

But Locke goes further than the humanists in his defense of toleration because he, unlike the humanists, unambiguously affirms that conscience cannot be violated.[20] To Locke, not only is it impossible to force someone to

14. *An Essay Concerning Human Understanding*, 4:16, 6–8. Locke is speaking here of the probability of particular matters of fact. See also *An Early Draft of Locke's Essay*, 57–59. Locke's general rule for determining the level of probability is reminiscent of the Academic exercise of argument *in utramque partem*. A rational mind will reject or receive a probable proposition, Locke writes, "with a more or less firm assent, proportionably to the preponderancy of the greater grounds of Probability on one side or the other." Ibid., 4:15, 5.

15. Montuori, *John Locke on Toleration and the Unity of God*, 47.

16. Ibid., 25–27, 63–55; Locke, *A Third Letter for Toleration*, 154–58.

17. "A great, if not the greatest, part of dissenters in England own and profess the doctrine of the church of England." Locke, *A Third Letter for Toleration*, 322.

18. Locke, *The Reasonableness of Christianity*, 32. While Locke's single belief that Jesus was Messiah would include all Christians, Locke still condemns the Roman Catholics on doctrinal grounds. Thus in his *Third Letter for Toleration*, he writes that the "Romish religion" is not a true religion (422–23). Nonetheless, Locke's major disagreement with the Catholics and the reason he offers for denying them toleration is that their views pose a threat to civil society.

19. Locke, *The Reasonableness of Christianity*, 75–76.

20. "And such is the nature of understanding, that it cannot be compelled to the belief of anything by outward force." Montuori, *John Locke on Toleration and the Unity of God*, 19.

believe against his or her will, it is also an affront to God. Religious coercion conflicts with God's decision to vest each person with the responsibility for his or her own salvation. This responsibility cannot be assumed by another or abdicated: "No man can so far abandon the care of his own salvation as blindly to leave to the choice of another . . . to prescribe what faith or worship he shall embrace" (17). The consequence of the right to conscience, for Locke, is that Church and state are "absolutely separate and distinct" from each other (55, 77–79). The individual, internal nature of the right to conscience places it beyond the state's reach. Locke extends the right to conscience even to non-Christians: "The sum of all we drive at is that every man may enjoy the same rights that are granted to others . . . , neither Pagan nor Mahometan, nor Jew, ought to be excluded from the civil rights of the commonwealth because of his religion" (101–3).

Locke, however, does not support full religious liberty. Religion, he states, may be restricted when it endangers civil society. Such is the case, he implies, with Roman Catholics and, he states explicitly, with atheists. Catholics, because they believe that their religion permits them to break faith with non-Catholics and to deny allegiance to non-Catholic kings, must be deemed "dangerous to the commonwealth" (89). Atheists are not to be tolerated, since "promises, covenants, and oaths, which are the bonds of human society," can have no hold over them (93). And while Locke argues that Church and state are separate, he seems to believe that all groups will exercise their freedom within the context of a Protestant society.[21] He envisions a society that is permeated by Protestant values. Locke speaks, for example, of a "Christian commonwealth";[22] he still excludes Catholics and atheists, albeit on political grounds; and he never questions the legitimacy of a national Church, so long as "other separated congregations" are also granted their religious liberties (107).

---

21. Ibid., 39. In the Fundamental Constitutions of Carolina of 1669, which Locke drafted, the local parliament was responsible for "the building of churches, and the public maintenance of divines, to be employed in the exercise of religion, according to the Church of England; which being the only true and orthodox, and the national religion of all the King's dominions, is so also of Carolina." Despite the establishment of the Anglican Church, the religious rights of "Jews, heathens, and other dissenters from the purity of Christian religion" were to be upheld. See Bernard Schwartz, *The Bill of Rights: A Documentary History* (New York: Chelsea House Publishers, 1971), 1:121–23.

22. Montuori, *John Locke on Toleration and the Unity of God*, 105.

Bayle and the Demise of the Humanist Argument

With the development of liberalism came the gradual disappearance of the humanist belief in consensus. Thus, while Locke thought that his compatriots agreed on the fundamentals of Christianity, less than a hundred years later, Jefferson and Madison could no longer make the same claim. In turn, though Jefferson and Madison believed that free discussion would reveal religious truth, thereby at least implying the possibility of religious agreement, liberals today reject any vision of religious consensus.[23] For contemporary liberals like Rawls, religious truth lies outside the realm of common sense—those "generally shared ways of reasoning and plain facts accessible to all."[24]

The loss of religious consensus can be explained empirically by the persistence—even growth—of religious diversity, recognized and partly sanctioned in England by the 1689 Act of Toleration and fully protected in the United States since 1791 by the First Amendment.[25] The disappearance of consensus can also be accounted for, on the level of ideas, by the rise of a

---

23. Both Jefferson and Madison point out that Christian truths would have remained hidden, if not for free enquiry. "Had not the Roman government permitted free enquiry," Jefferson observes, "Christianity could never have been introduced. Had not free enquiry been indulged, at the aera of the reformation, the corruptions of Christianity could not have been purged away." See Jefferson, *Notes on the State of Virginia*, 159. Cf. Madison's *Memorial and Remonstrance*, in Meyers, *Mind of the Founder*, 11–12.

24. Rawls, *Theory of Justice*, 213. See also Bruce A. Ackerman, *Social Justice in the Liberal State* (New Haven: Yale University Press, 1980).

25. I am not suggesting that the belief in religious consensus disappeared in the United States, immediately, with the adoption of the First Amendment. First, the Bill of Rights applied only to the federal government and not the states. Second, as is clear from a variety of court decisions, freedom of religion was perceived as compatible with a view of the United States as a Christian country. In *People v. Ruggles*, 8 Johns. 290 (N.Y. 1811), the New York Supreme Court upheld the conviction of a man charged with blasphemy for having stated that "*Jesus Christ* was a bastard, and his mother must be a whore." Chief Justice Kent, writing for the Court, argued: "The free, equal, and undisturbed, enjoyment of religious opinion, whatever it may be, and free and decent discussions on any religious subject, is granted and secured; but to revile, with malicious and blasphemous contempt, the religion professed by almost the whole community, is an abuse of that right. Nor are we bound, by any expressions in the constitution, as some have strangely supposed, either not to punish at all, or to punish indiscriminately the like attacks upon the religion of *Mahomet* or that of the grand *Lama*; and for this plain reason, that the case assumes that we are a christian people, and the morality of the country is deeply ingrafted upon christianity, and not upon the doctrines or worship of those imposters." For similar statements, see Joseph Story, *Commentaries on the Constitution of the United States*, 3 vols. (Boston, 1833; rpt., New York: Da Capo Press, 1970), 3:722–28, and Thomas McIntyre Cooley, *A Treatise on the Constitutional Limitations which Rest Upon the Legislative Power of the States of the American Union* (Boston, 1868; rpt., New York: Da Capo Press, 1972), 422.

more thoroughgoing skepticism: if religious truth cannot be known, then there can be no broad agreement on religion. This religious skepticism is exemplified by Pierre Bayle, a contemporary of Locke, in his plea for religious freedom, *A Philosophical Commentary*, published in 1686. In this work Bayle undermines the humanists' (and Locke's) epistemological assumptions about religious knowledge.[26] Like Hobbes, Bayle subverts their faith in probability, the fundamentals of faith, and ultimately consensus. He differs from Hobbes, however, in his conclusion. Whereas skepticism drives Hobbes to depend on an authoritarian sovereign, it impels Bayle to rely on individual conscience.

As a practical matter, Bayle observes, people do not act as if religious truth can be known. Empirically, people's religious beliefs vary with the time and place in which they live. Education and upbringing, more than any other factors, determine a person's religion. If we had been born in China, Bayle notes, "we shou'd have bin all of the Chinese Religion; and if the Chinese were born in England, they'd have bin all Christians."[27] The educational factor is so strong that it outweighs any material advantage to be gained by conversion. Bayle notes that the Jews have historically been the most reviled of nations, "the very Scum and Off-scouring of the World, without an abiding City or Country in any part of the Earth, without Places or Preferments, frequently banish'd and persecuted from City to City."[28] Do they not realize, he asks, that they would be better off as either (contingent on location) Christian or Moslem? "Yet," Bayle continues, "nothing is more rare than the Conversion of a Jew." The cause of their stubborn convictions, in Bayle's opinion, is education: "For the same Jew, who is so obstinate now in his Errors, wou'd have bin a Christian to Fire and Faggot, if taken from his Father at two years old, and educated among conscientious and zealous Christians."

The power of education in forming opinions, Bayle explains, should come as no surprise. Human beings begin their lives as creatures devoid of reason or "Facultys for discerning Truth from Falshood," oblivious to the possibil-

26. Bayle's skepticism was not limited to religious matters. See *The Encyclopedia of Philosophy*, 1967 ed., s.v. "Bayle, Pierre."

27. Pierre Bayle, *A Philosophical Commentary on These Words of the Gospel, Luke XIV. 23. "Compel them to come in, that my House may be full"* (London: J. Darby, 1708), 1:346–47. The only other English translation is the recent *Pierre Bayle's Philosophical Commentary: A Modern Translation and Critical Interpretation*, trans. Amie Godman Tannenbaum (New York: Peter Lang, 1987). Tannenbaum appends an interpretive essay on Bayle and toleration at the end of her translation.

28. Bayle, *Philosophical Commentary*, 2:626–27.

ity that their teachers could teach them anything false (1:331–33). As a result, children accept whatever is told them no matter how absurd or incomprehensible. Then, upon maturity, people, being overcome with "a thousand unavoidably worldly Cares," do not have the opportunity to question their childhood beliefs: "The Passions and Habits of Childhood, the Prejudices of Education, take possession of us before we are aware what it is we admit to our Minds." The influence of unconscious youthful habits is so great—shrinking our souls to nothing—that it is impossible to overcome, "how great soever his Desire may afterwards be" (2:577–78).

Bayle does not base his religious skepticism solely on the influence of education. He explains that religious knowledge is also unattainable because the religious truths we seek to find cannot be distinguished from religious errors: "God has not printed any Characters or Signs on the Truths which he has reveal'd . . . they don't excite any Passions which Errors do not excite. In a word, we distinguish nothing in the Objects which appear to us true, and are so in reality, beyond what we find in Objects which appear true, and yet are otherwise" (1:331–33). The impediments to religious knowledge, in other words, are objective as well as subjective.

Bayle's doctrinal skepticism is total.[29] Like Chillingworth, Bayle denies the possibility of certain knowledge. Unlike Chillingworth, however, he also rejects mitigated skepticism, arguing that in the absence of certainty, we are condemned to total skepticism. Bayle's means of undermining probability is to erase the mitigated skeptic's distinctions between levels of probability. To Chillingworth's claim that strong probability should not be confused with mere possibility, Bayle counters that all probabilities, even those that seem close to certainty, are fallible. Whereas Chillingworth emphasized the moral certainty of high probability, Bayle focuses on its fallibility: "We may have a moral Certainty . . . founded on very high Probabilitys; but after all, this kind of Certainty may subsist in the Soul of one who is actually deceiv'd" (1:337–38). Bayle denies the objective basis of probability, equating probability with opinion (ibid). He points out, as did Hobbes, that probability does not produce unanimity. Each side in a dispute will support its case with arguments from probability, and these arguments may be equally persuasive and reasonable, the only difference being "that one sort wou'd have the misfortune of taking that for true which was not so, and the other the good

29. Bayle distinguishes between our inability to know anything about doctrine and our ability to know morality. In the latter case, Bayle feels that Scripture and our inner conscience dictate proper actions. See, for example, ibid., 1:50–52, and 310–11.

fortune of taking that for true which was really so."[30] Because there is no way to determine which claim of probability is correct, Bayle dismisses the value of probability as a criterion of religious truth. So unreliable is probability, Bayle suggests, that sometimes it even stands in inverse order to factual truth: "[Facts] in reality false, are altogether as possible, or perhaps more so than the true."[31]

Armed with his skepticism, Bayle proceeds to demolish the humanist conception of the fundamentals of faith. He does so with the humanists' own idea of accommodation. The humanists had maintained that because God accommodates Himself to us (therefore, not demanding the impossible from us), He would not have required belief in more than the few fundamentals, those comprehensible to all rational Christians. But as Chillingworth implied in *The Religion of Protestants*, true "accommodation" supports a variable standard of fundamentals adapted to the individual, not the humanists' static conception of fundamentals. Developing this point further, Bayle concludes that because we cannot know any of God's doctrinal truths, He would not have required belief in even the few fundamentals of faith. Had God "rigorously exacted the Knowledge of absolute Truth at our hands," he would not have accommodated Himself "to the State we are reduc'd to. . . . He has therefore impos'd no such Laws on us, nor Duty, but such as is proportion'd to our Facultys, to wit, that of searching for the Truth, and of laying hold on that, which upon a sincere and faithful Inquiry, shall appear such to us, and of loving this apparent Truth, and of governing our selves by his Precepts how difficult soever they may seem" (1:334–37). From Bayle's perspective, it makes no difference whether someone finds the truth or not, so long as his intentions are good and he loves the truth (1:350–51, 2:642–43).

Bayle's standard for judging a person's religious convictions is wholly subjective: fidelity to one's conscience. For him the fundamentals of faith as objective criteria are meaningless; it is the believer's perceptions of what is fundamental that counts. Those who believe they are violating the fundamentals of faith are heretics because they sin against their consciences.[32] But

---

30. Ibid., 2:694. Related to Bayle's stand that every position can be argued persuasively is his systematization of all points of view. Bayle's method in the *Dictionary*, which is to present even seemingly irrational beliefs as "systems," has the effect of making all beliefs appear reasonable and thus, by implication, worthy of toleration. This observation was made to me by Amos Funkenstein.

31. Ibid., 2:699–700. See also 1:85–86 and 2:715–19.

32. The heretic is someone who "sows Discord in the Church, and rends its Unity; his

those who maintain their beliefs with sincerity, in accordance with their consciences, are blameless. The objective significance of the beliefs are irrelevant. The subjective element is so decisive that, Bayle contends, even pagans must obey their consciences and honor their false gods, "on pain, if he reviles 'em, if he robs their Temples, &c. of incurring the Guilt of Blasphemy and Sacrilege, as much as a Christian who curs'd God, and rob'd his Churches" (1:301). Hence, Bayle writes, any pagan who blasphemes his divinities or overthrows their statues, "without a design of abjuring his Religion," should be punished by the civil magistrates. In practice Bayle acknowledges that we cannot judge the genuineness of conscience and must give individuals the benefit of the doubt and assume that their beliefs are motivated by conscience. Only atheists are excluded from toleration because denying the existence of God, the source of conscience, they cannot lay claim to the protection of conscience.[33]

Although Bayle and Locke rely on conscience as the basis for their theories of toleration, Bayle rejects the humanist principles to which Locke still subscribed. The two contemporaries agree that toleration should not be limited, as the humanists themselves envisioned, to those who adopted the minimum fundamentals.[34] But Bayle, unlike Locke, refuses to use the humanists' conception of fundamentals as an auxiliary argument for toleration. Further, Bayle rejects the very cornerstone of the humanist defense of toleration, the belief that persuasion can lead to Christian unity. Whereas Locke had accepted the humanists' vision of a comprehensive church, Bayle emphasizes the considerable differences between Christian denominations.[35] Bayle goes so far as to argue that the humanists' goal of unity is not

---

Conscience at the same time telling him, that the Doctrines he opposes are good, at least very tolerable." Ibid., 2:668–69.

33. Bayle denies toleration only to atheists who have publicly declared their atheism, even after being warned. Ibid., 1:307–8. Further, Bayle's recognition of moral atheists serves to undermine the position, accepted by Locke, that atheists should be denied toleration as threats to society. See Richards, *Toleration and the Constitution*, 96–97. Bayle also alludes to the political dangers posed by Roman Catholics. "Yet," he writes, "I can't think, unless there be other particular Reasons, that they ought to be banish'd out of Places where they behave themselves quietly." *Philosophical Commentary*, 2:771–73.

34. Bayle, for example, criticizes the position of "our Men of Half-Toleration [who] say . . . That we ought to tolerate Sects which destroy not the Fundamentals of Christianity, but not those which do." Ibid., 1:269–71.

35. According to Bayle the differences between Protestants on the nature of the Eucharist and on original sin objectively touch the fundamentals of faith (although he acknowledges that errors on such fundamentals become innocent when "they are entertain'd from a sincere Persuasion of the Truth of 'em"). Ibid., 2:524–26.

only presently unattainable in fact, but that, because of our inability to know the truth, absolutely unattainable in principle. The lack of any criterion of truth ensures doctrinal disagreement: " 'Twere to be wish'd that all Men were of one Religion; but since this is never like to happen, the next best thing they can do is tolerating each other" (1:255–56). Believing our religion to be correct, we must try to "undeceive" another of error "and reason him to the best of his Skill." But when all is said and done, and our arguments do not persuade, we "shou'd give him over, or only pray to God for him." Persuasion, Bayle implies, may work in individual cases, but ultimately there can be no religious consensus in civil society—not even a consensus on "Protestant" or "Christian" truths, as Locke still seems to have believed. Rather, Bayle maintains, we must accept that society will be multireligious, composed of various Christian sects as well as a host of non-Christian religions.

What, then, does a Bayle-like religious skepticism mean for the humanist defense of religious toleration? If we, like Bayle, have abandoned the hope of religious consensus in society, does that render the humanist defense irrelevant? Because a general agreement about religion is impossible, if not also undesirable, the humanist defense is an unsatisfactory theory of religious toleration for civil society. Nevertheless, the humanists' arguments need not be restricted to their origins in religious disputes. I argue in the next section that the late humanists and their successors expanded the humanists' religiously based arguments to secular matters and extended the humanist defense of toleration to include, first, political speech and, then, speech in general. This movement from religious toleration to freedom of speech corresponds to the growing secularization of Western society. Whereas in the sixteenth century, the goal of discovering "truth" (as a justification of freedom of debate) focused primarily on religious truth, by the mid- and late-seventeenth century, the search for truth included, but was no longer limited to, religion. Eventually, with the further passage of time, religion was no longer even viewed as something that could be discovered. Divine matters were now seen as matters of opinion, personal and idiosyncratic, not amenable to collective discussion. Thus the right to freedom of religion— notwithstanding its origins—became dissociated from the search for truth, whereas the right to freedom of speech was, in turn, defended as a means of uncovering secular truths.

In discussing the humanist legacy to freedom of speech, I identify two characteristics that distinguish humanist toleration from more radical theories of free speech: (1) the belief that some matters, because they are known with high probability (if not certainty), are excluded from discussion; and (2) a sensitivity to rhetorical *decorum*. Although these "humanist" characteristics are found in Milton's and Locke's pleas for toleration and free speech, they are less clearly visible in a twentieth-century justification of freedom of speech that resembles the humanist defense of toleration: the U.S. Supreme Court's concept of the "marketplace of ideas."

The Right to Freedom of Speech

From Religious Toleration to Freedom of Speech

John Milton (1608–74), who was "firmly in the tradition of Christian humanism," loosed the humanist defense of toleration from its exclusively religious moorings.[36] He did so in the *Areopagitica* (1644), which he composed to condemn the restrictive English Licensing Order of 1643. According to Milton, the effect of Parliament's regulation of the press would be "the stop of Truth . . . by hindring and cropping the discovery that might bee yet further made both in religious and civil Wisdome."[37] As seen in this passage, Milton linked the fates of religious and civil, that is, political, knowledge. The Licensing Order, he argued, would conceal both kinds of wisdom. Like previous humanists, Milton saw truth as progressively revealed through rational discussion: "The light which we have gain'd, was giv'n us, not to be ever staring on, but by it to discover onward things more remote from our knowledge." Those who seek to suppress discussion, therefore, hinder the discovery of truth:

> There be who perpetually complain of schisms and sects, and make it such a calamity that any man dissents from their maxims. 'Tis their own pride and ignorance which causes the disturbing, who neither will hear with meekness, nor can convince, yet all must be supprest which is not found in their *Syntagma*. They are the troublers, they are the dividers of unity, who neglect and permit not others to unite those

36. Albert R. Cirillo, "Humanism, Milton and Christian," in *A Milton Encyclopedia*, ed. William B. Hunter (Lewisburg: Bucknell University Press, 1978), 4:41. For the most complete discussion of Milton's humanism, see Fletcher, *The Intellectual Development of John Milton*.
37. *Areopagitica*, in *Complete Prose Works of John Milton*, 2:491–92.

dissever'd peeces which are yet wanting to the body of Truth.
(2:550–51)

But in contrast to earlier humanists, Milton does not limit his argument to
the search for religious truth. Not only matters of the Church, he writes, but
things "in the rule of life both economicall and politicall" must be looked
into and reformed (2:550). Thus, Milton's argument from truth justifies
greater toleration of political discussion as well as the more traditional
questioning of religious issues.

What does the discovery of political truth mean for Milton? First, by
speaking of "civil Wisdome," Milton implied that it means a better understanding of political principles. Milton believed that more freedom of
political speech would yield greater knowledge of the rules of politics. This
same assumption underlay the Putney Debates, in which the General Council of the English Army gathered, in 1647, to debate proposals for an English
constitution. Participating in these debates, then Lieutenant-General Oliver
Cromwell maintained that a consensus on a better constitution depended on
free discussion: "Truly if there be never so much desire of carrying on these
things [together], never so much desire of conjunction, yet if there be not
liberty of speech to come to a right understanding of things, I think it shall
be all one as if there were no desire at all to meet."[38] Second, Milton suggests
that discovering political truth also means being informed of the government's actions so that it may be corrected: "This I know, that errors in a good
government and in a bad are equally almost incident; for what Magistrate
may not be mis-inform'd, and much the sooner, if liberty of Printing be
reduc't into the power of a few?"[39] This second aspect of political truth is
also highlighted in a variety of Leveller tracts, during the English Civil War.[40]
For example, in the Leveller manifesto "Englands New Chains Discovered"

38. A.S.P. Woodhouse, ed., *Puritanism and Liberty: Being the Army Debates (1647–49)*
from the Clarke Manuscripts (London: Dent, 1986), 84.
39. *Areopagitica*, 570.
40. The Levellers also fell under the humanists' influence. Thus, the Leveller leader William
Walwyn is said to have "absorbed the tolerant skepticism of Renaissance humanism toward
religious dogma." See William Haller, ed., *Tracts on Liberty in the Puritan Revolution* (New
York: Columbia University Press, 1934), 2:40. Cf. humanist arguments from truth, including
Milton's, with Walwyn's declaration in *The Compassionate Samaratine* (1644): "Truth was not
used to feare, or to seeke shifts or stratagems for its advancement! I should rather thinke that
they who are assured of her should desire that all mens mouthes should be open, that so errour
may discover its foulnes, and trueth become more glorious by a victorious conquest after a fight
in open field; they shun the battell that doubt their strength." Ibid., 3:94.

(1648), Parliament is asked to "open the Press, whereby all trecherous and tyranical designes may be the easier discovered, and so prevented, which is a liberty of greatest concernment to the Commonwealth, and which such only as intend a tyrannie are engaged to prohibit: The mouths of Adversaries being best stopped, by the sensible good which the people receive from the actions of such as are in Authority."[41] About seventy-five years after the *Areopagitica* appeared, John Trenchard and Thomas Gordon defended the public's right to keep an eye on the government, in *Cato's Letters* (1720–1722): "As it is the Part and Business of the People, for whose Sake alone all publick Matters are, or ought to be, transacted, to see whether they be well or ill transacted; so it is the Interest, and ought to be the Ambition, of all honest Magistrates, to have their Deeds openly examined, and publicly scanned."[42] The examination of politicians described here, as well as the pursuit of more general political knowledge, represents the application of the humanists' arguments to political matters. The humanists' arguments, however, were progressively applied not only to the search for political truth, but also to the search for other secular truths.

Exemplary of how the humanist defense of toleration was applied to nonpolitical discussion in the First Continental Congress's statement (1774) to the inhabitants of Quebec that "the advancement of truth, science, morality, and arts in general" is an objective of the right to freedom of the press.[43] The expansion of the humanist argument is still more explicit in John Stuart Mill's classic plea for freedom of opinion, *On Liberty* (1859). Mill, though a founder of modern liberalism, was schooled humanistically. Thus, he recounts in his *Autobiography* how classical rhetoric was central to

41. William Haller and Godfrey Davies, eds., *The Leveller Tracts, 1647–1653* (Gloucester, Mass.: Peter Smith, 1964), 167. In another Leveller manifesto, "To the Right Honourable, The Supreme Authority of this Nation, The Commons of England in Parliament assembled" (1649), the authors write: "For what-ever specious pretences of good to the Common-wealth have bin devised to over-aw the Press, yet all times fore-gone will manifest, it hath ever ushered in a tyrannie; mens mouth being to be kept from making noise, whilst they are robd of their liberties; So was it in the late Prerogative times before this Parliament, whilst upon pretence of care of the publike, Licensers were set over the Press, Truth was suppressed, the people thereby kept ignorant, and fitted only to serve the unjust ends of Tyrants and Oppressors, whereby the Nation was enslaved." Don M. Wolfe, ed., *Leveller Manifestoes of the Puritan Revolution* (New York: Thomas Nelson & Sons, 1944), 327.

42. David L. Jacobson, ed., *The English Libertarian Heritage: From the Writings of John Trenchard and Thomas Gordon in The Independent Whig and Cato's Letters* (Indianapolis: Bobbs-Merrill, 1965), 39. See, in particular, numbers 15 and 38 of *Cato's Letters*.

43. The full address to the inhabitants of Quebec can be found in Schwartz, *The Bill of Rights: A Documentary History*, 1:221–27.

his education. His father, he relates, exposed him to the principle of rhetorical *decorum*, pointing out to the young Mill "the skill and art of the orator—how everything important to his purpose was said at the exact moment when he had brought the minds of his audience into the state most fitted to receive it."[44] Mill also notes in his *Autobiography* his esteem for Quintilian.[45] Like the humanists, Mill advances an argument for free speech based on the practice of argument *in utramque partem*. Only by debating both sides, Mill contends, can one arrive at the truth: "So essential is this discipline to a real understanding of moral and human subjects, that if opponents of all important truths do not exist, it is indispensable to imagine them, and supply them with the strongest arguments which the most skilful devil's advocate can conjure up." Mill cites Cicero to confirm this point. Cicero, Mill writes, "has left it on record that he always studied his adversary's case with as great, if not with still greater, intensity than even his own. What Cicero practised as the means of a forensic success, requires to be imitated by all who study any subject to arrive at the truth."[46] Like Cicero and his humanist followers, Mill defends rational conversation as the path to truth. But Mill surpassed his Renaissance forebears by calling not only for the protection of religious or even political speech, but also for the right to express opinions on "social relations" and "the business of life" (244, 245). By the time the humanist argument appears in Mill, truth no longer connotes religious doctrines but "knowledge of life" in all its complexities (250).

Milton and Mill both illustrate the humanist assumption that greater freedom of debate promotes discovery of truth. But the humanist defense of toleration consisted of more than just this assumption. The humanists were unwilling to protect speech that they knew—or at least believed—was false. Thus, they permitted debate on adiaphora, but not on the fundamentals of faith. In addition, the humanists were concerned that discussion take place in a rhetorically appropriate environment. Irrational debates, they maintained, were no more likely to foster truth than was censorship. The humanists' exclusion of "false" beliefs from protection is exemplified by Milton, the oft-presumed herald of contemporary freedom of speech and press,[47] who would have banned Catholicism because it conflicted with

44. John Stuart Mill, *Autobiography*, in *Collected Works of John Stuart Mill*, ed. John M. Robson and Jack Stillinger, vol. 1 (Toronto: University of Toronto Press, 1981), 23.

45. "I have retained through life many valuable ideas which I can distinctly trace to my reading of him [Quintilian], even at that early age." Ibid.

46. *On Liberty*, 245.

47. Francis Canavan offers a number of examples of writers who portray Milton as the

"known" truths.[48] As long as truth is in doubt, according to Milton, debate must be permitted: "To be still searching what we know not, by what we know, still closing up truth to truth as we find it . . . this is the golden rule in *Theology*."[49] But, Milton reasons, we *can* know that Scripture is absolutely and solely authoritative, and because Roman Catholicism denies this proposition, it should be proscribed. Even the early liberal Locke, who exceeds Milton in arguing for the toleration of non-Christian religions, excludes atheists from toleration; atheism lies outside the moral consensus of all religions.

Milton also reflects the humanist concern with *decorum*. He believed that only rational discussion—*sermo*—promoted the discovery of truth. The kind of writing Milton wanted to protect was the scholarly work of intellectuals. He describes the prospective writer endangered by the Licensing Order in the following passage: "When a man writes to the world, he summons up all his reason and deliberation to assist him; he searches, meditats, is industrious, and likely consults and conferrs with his judicious friends; after all which done he takes himself to be inform'd in what he writes, as well as any that writ before him."[50] Milton does not envision debate as a free-for-all, but as the "generall and brotherly search after

---

father of modern free speech in *Freedom of Expression: Purpose as Limit* (Durham, N.C.: Carolina Academic Press, 1984), 159 n. 11.

48. See *Areopagitica*, in *Complete Prose Works of John Milton*, 2:565: "Yet if all cannot be of one mind, as who looks they should be? this doubtles is more wholsome, more prudent, and more Christian: that many be tolerated rather than all compell'd. I mean not tolerated Popery and open superstition, which as it extirpats all religions and civill supremacies, so it self should be extirpat, provided first that all charitable and compassionate means be us'd to win and regain the weak and misled." Milton repeats his call to ban Catholicism elsewhere. See *A Treatise of Civil Power in Ecclesiastical Causes* (1659), where Protestants are permitted the right of "a free and lawful debate," but the "papist," whom Milton describes as the "only heretic," is barred from participation. Milton is even more vehement in *Of True Religion, Heresie, Schism, and Toleration*, where he states that Catholics should not be tolerated publicly or privately: "The exercise of their Religion, as far as it is Idolatrous, can be tolerated neither way . . . without great offence to God." Cited in Leonard Levy, *Emergence of a Free Press* (New York: Oxford University Press, 1985), 95–96.

49. *Complete Prose Works of John Milton*, 2:551.

50. *Areopagitica*, in *Complete Prose Works of John Milton*, 2:532. See also Canavan, *Freedom of Expression*, 46. Leonard Levy believes that "in all likelihood Milton never intended that anything but the serious works of intellectuals, chiefly scholars and Protestant divines, should be really free." As proof, Levy cites an essay in which Milton suggests using Latin, "which the common people understand not," when the discussion might "unsettle the weaker sort." *Emergence of a Free Press*, 95. Because Milton is concerned with rational discussion among intellectuals, *sermo* is his rhetorical paradigm, not the deliberative genre, even though the subject matter of debate includes politics.

Truth." Disputants, he writes, should exercise "a little generous prudence, a little forbearance of one another, and som grain of charity" in their communications.[51]

To foster the discovery of truth, the early defenders of free speech proposed rules to restrict irrational expression. For example, after affirming the people's liberty "to speak, write, print," the Independent Henry Burton points out the need for "wholesome and pertinent laws being made, upon penalties, to restrain all kinds of vice or violence, all kinds of reproach, slander, or injury either by word or deed."[52] Locke also couples his defense of the right to conscience with rules governing rhetorical presentation. Thus, in his Fundamental Constitution of Carolina of 1669, he states: "No man shall use any reproachful, reviling, or abusive language against any religion of any church or profession; that being the certain way . . . of hindering the conversion of any to the truth, by engaging them in quarrels and animosities, to the hatred of the professors and that profession which otherwise they might be brought to assent to."[53] For the humanists and those influenced by them, protecting a form of expression that precludes rational thought undermines the purpose of free speech.[54]

The Marketplace of Ideas

Although the First Amendment's proclamation of a right to freedom of speech is unaccompanied by any explanation of its purpose, it can be

51. *Areopagitica*, in *Complete Prose Works of John Milton*, 2:554.

52. Burton wrote this in his introduction to the 1646 edition of Leonard Busher's *Religious Peace: or a Plea for Liberty of Conscience*, a Baptist defense of religious liberty first published in 1614. Burton's introduction and Busher's pamphlet appear in Edward Bean Underhill, *Tracts of Liberty of Conscience and Persecution, 1614–1661* (London: The Hanserd Knollys Society, 1646; rpt., New York: Burt Franklin, 1966), 10. For a brief discussion of Henry Burton's views on toleration, see Jordan, *Religious Toleration in England*, 3:358–61.

53. Schwartz, *The Bill of Rights: A Documentary History*, 1:123.

54. John Stuart Mill agrees that intemperate discussion hinders the discovery of truth, especially when directed against the representatives of the minority opinion: "In general, opinions contrary to those commonly received can only obtain a hearing by studied moderation of language and the most cautious avoidance of unnecessary offense, from which they hardly ever deviate even in a slight degree without losing ground: while unmeasured vituperation employed on the side of the prevailing opinion, really does deter people from professing contrary opinions, and from listening to those who profess them. For the interest, therefore, of truth and justice, it is far more important to restrain this employment of vituperative language than the other." But, Mill concludes, "law and authority have no business in restraining either." It should be left to the individual to condemn for himself breaches of civility. *On Liberty*, 258–59.

reasonably assumed that it was intended, in part, to aid in the advancement of truth.[55] An official justification of the right to free speech, however, did not come for almost one hundred thirty years after the First Amendment's passage in 1791. In fact, the U.S. Supreme Court—with few exceptions—did not concern itself with free speech issues until after World War I.[56] It was Justice Holmes (joined by Justice Brandeis), in his famous dissent in *Abrams v. United States,*[57] who introduced the Court's first principled justification of free speech: the argument from truth—the argument that was the mainstay of the humanist defense of religious toleration.[58] The particular version of the argument from truth that he presented in his *Abrams* dissent was the marketplace of ideas.[59] For Holmes, "the best test of truth is the power of thought to get itself accepted in the competition of the market."[60] As developed by Holmes and his successors on the Court, the "marketplace" theory assumes that free speech should be protected because truth will emerge from the free interchange of ideas. State restraints on the intellectual marketplace, according to this theory, hinder the search for the truth and are, therefore, not in society's interest.[61]

Since Holmes, the marketplace of ideas theory has been the Supreme

55. See, for example, the statement of the First Continental Congress, in 1774, that one of the objectives of the right to freedom of the press was "the advancement of truth." (Cited at note 43.)

56. Harry Kalven Jr., *A Worthy Tradition: Freedom of Speech in America,* ed. Jamie Kalven (New York: Harper & Row, 1988), 130. On the U.S. Supreme Court's discussions of free speech before World War I, see Michael T. Gibson, "The Supreme Court and Freedom of Expression from 1791 to 1917," *Fordham Law Review* 45 (1986): 263–333; Howard Owen Hunter, "Problems in Search of Principles: The First Amendment in the Supreme Court from 1791–1930," *Emory Law Journal* 35 (1986): 59–137; David M. Rabban, "The First Amendment in Its Forgotten Years," *The Yale Law Journal* 90 (1981): 524–25.

57. *Abrams v. United States,* 250 U.S. 616 (1919).

58. Hunter, "Problems in Search of Principles," 108.

59. Lee C. Bollinger Jr., *The Tolerant Society: Freedom of Speech and Extremist Speech in America* (New York: Oxford University Press, 1986), 43–75; C. Edwin Baker, *Human Liberty and Freedom of Speech* (New York: Oxford University Press, 1989), 6–24; Stanley Ingber, "The Marketplace of Ideas: A Legitimizing Myth," *Duke Law Journal,* 1984: 2–3; Schauer, *Free Speech,* 15–34.

60. Although Holmes introduces the marketplace metaphor, in his *Abrams* dissent, writing there of "free trade in ideas" and "the competition of the market," it was Justice Brennan who first used the specific term "marketplace of ideas," in his concurring opinion in *Lamont v. Postmaster General,* 381 U.S. 301, 308 (1965). David Cole, "Agon at Agora: Creative Misreadings in the First Amendment Tradition," *Yale Law Journal* 95 (1986): 886, 894.

61. Using the marketplace metaphor in *Miller v. California,* 413 U.S. 15 (1973), the Court distinguished "commerce in ideas, protected by the First Amendment, from commercial exploitation of obscene material," which does not contribute to the marketplace of ideas and is, therefore, unprotected.

Court's main rationale for protecting the right to free speech. Following Holmes's *Abrams* dissent, Justice Brandeis (joined by Holmes), in his concurring opinion in *Whitney v. California* (1927), stated: "Freedom to think as you will and to speak as you think are means indispensable to the discovery and spread of political truth."[62] Another classic statement of the marketplace theory is found in Judge Learned Hand's opinion in *International Brotherhood of Electrical Workers v. Labor Board.* Underlying the First Amendment, he writes, is the assumption "that truth will be most likely to emerge, if no limitations are imposed upon utterances that can with any plausibility be regarded as efforts to present grounds for accepting or rejecting propositions whose truth the utterer asserts, or denies."[63]

Although the Court no longer relies on it exclusively, the marketplace standard has continued to dominate its analysis of First Amendment issues. In *Red Lion Broadcasting Co. v. FCC,* for example, the Court maintains that "it is the purpose of the First Amendment to preserve an uninhibited marketplace of ideas in which truth will ultimately prevail."[64] Similarly, in a dissenting opinion in *Columbia Broadcasting Co. v. Democratic Committee,* Justice Brennan writes that "our legal system reflects a belief that truth is best illuminated by a collision of genuine advocates."[65] And in *Gertz v. Robert Welch, Inc.,* Justice Powell notes that we depend "on the competition of other ideas" for the correction of pernicious opinions.[66]

The conceptual roots of the marketplace theory are humanist. It is a commonplace that the late humanist Milton and the "post-humanist" Mill

---

62. *Whitney v. California,* 274 U.S. 357 (1927). For the argument that Brandeis, in *Whitney,* did not defend the marketplace theory but an ideal of civic courage, see Vincent Blasi, "The First Amendment and the Ideal of Civic Courage: The Brandeis Opinion in *Whitney v. California," William and Mary Law Review* 29 (1988): 653–97, particularly 673–74. That individuals are given the freedom to decide political truth for themselves, even after legislative decisions have been made, is more consistent with the type of speech permitted in *sermo* than in deliberative oratory.

63. *International Brotherhood of Electrical Workers v. Labor Board,* 181 F. 2d 34, 40 (2d Cir 1950). See also Judge Hand's earlier statement in *United States v. Associated Press,* 52 F. Supp. 362, 372 (1943 District Court, S.D. New York): "[The First Amendment] presupposes that right conclusions are more likely to be gathered out of a multitude of tongues, than through any kind of authoritative selection. To many this is, and always will be folly; but we have staked our all on it."

64. *Red Lion Broadcasting Co. v. FCC,* 395 U.S. 367, 390 (1969).

65. Dissenting, *Columbia Broadcasting Co. v. Democratic Committee,* 412 U.S. 94, 189 (1973).

66. *Gertz v. Robert Welch, Inc.,* 418 U.S. 323 (1974).

were the intellectual progenitors of the marketplace of ideas.[67] Even the Court itself, which usually avoids philosophical citations, explicitly links Milton and Mill to the marketplace approach.[68] Like Milton, the Court has emphasized the protection of political speech: the primacy of political speech in "the hierarchy of First Amendment values."[69] And like Mill, the Court has not limited the First Amendment to plainly political speech. Thus, the Court has also been willing to protect, at the very least, any speech having

67. Schauer, *Free Speech*, 15; Ingber, "Marketplace of Ideas," 2–3; Baker, *Human Liberty and Freedom of Speech*, 6.

68. *New York Times Co. v. Sullivan*, 376 U.S. 254, 279, n. 19 (1964); *Red Lion Broadcasting Co. v. FCC*, 395 U.S. 367, 392, n. 18 (1969); Rehnquist, J., dissenting, *Central Hudson Gas & Electric Corp. v. Public Service Commission of New York*, 447 U.S. 557, 592 (1980).

69. *NAACP v. Claiborne Hardware Co.*, 458 U.S. 886, 913 (1982). In *New York Times v. Sullivan*, Justice Brennan writing for the Court argued that the ability of the people to rule themselves was "the central meaning of the First Amendment." *New York Times Co. v. Sullivan*, 376 U.S. 254, 273 (1964). See also *Richmond Newspapers v. Virginia*, 448 U.S. 555, 575 (1980): "The First Amendment, in conjunction with the Fourteenth prohibits governments from 'abridging the freedom of speech.' . . . These expressly guaranteed freedoms share a common core purpose of assuring freedom of communication on matters relating to the functioning of government." *Garrison v. Louisiana* 379 U.S. 64 (1964): "Speech concerning public affairs is more than self-expression; it is the essence of self-government." For a more complete list of Supreme Court cases that proclaim the primacy of political speech, see Alon Harel, "Bigotry, Pornography, and the First Amendment: A Theory of Unprotected Speech," *Southern California Law Review* 65 (1992): 1892–93 n. 9.

Many constitutional theorists have also recognized the special First Amendment status of political speech. In recent constitutional theory, Alexander Meiklejohn has argued that the First Amendment right to freedom of speech, while absolute, applies only to speech relevant to self-government. "The principle of the freedom of speech," he writes, "springs from the necessities of the program of self-government." Alexander Meiklejohn, *Free Speech and Its Relation to Self-Government* (Port Washington, N.Y.: Kennikat Press, 1972), 26. Meiklejohn, however, has justified protection of nonpolitical forms of thought and expression because they are important to democratic decision-making. Like Meiklejohn, Robert Bork also argues that the First Amendment was intended to protect political speech, though Bork goes further in this direction than Meiklejohn, protecting nothing but explicitly political speech and excluding art, literature, or science from First Amendment purview. Robert Bork, "Neutral Principles and Some First Amendment Problems," *Indiana Law Journal* 47 (1971): 1, 26–28. Bork has since abandoned his narrow definition of political speech, but continues to believe that the core of the First Amendment is political. See Robert Bork, "Judge Bork Replies," *American Bar Association Journal* 70 (1984): 132; Steven H. Shiffrin, *The First Amendment, Democracy, and Romance* (Cambridge: Harvard University Press, 1990), 210 n. 177. Also see Lillian R. BeVier, "The First Amendment and Political Speech: An Inquiry into the Substance and Limits of Principle," *Stanford Law Review* 30 (1978): 299–358; Justice William J. Brennan Jr., "The Supreme Court and the Meiklejohn Interpretation of the First Amendment," *Harvard Law Review* 79 (1965): 1; Harry Kalven Jr., "The New York Times Case: A Note on the 'Central Meaning of the First Amendment,'" *Supreme Court Review*, 1964: 191–221; and T. M. Scanlon Jr., "Freedom of Expression and Categories of Expression," *University of Pittsburgh Law Review* 40 (1979): 538.

serious literary, artistic, or scientific value.[70] But while the Supreme Court has embraced the humanist idea, via Milton and Mill, that free speech should be safeguarded in the interest of truth, it has been less faithful to two essential elements of the humanist argument. First, the Court has openly rejected the humanist distinction between matters that are known, which cannot be disputed, and uncertain opinions, which can still be debated. The Court has argued that the state must remain neutral toward the content of speech. Second, the Court has not consistently upheld the humanist principle of *decorum*. Increasingly, the Court has refused to discriminate between rational and irrational speech.

The Court has abandoned the humanist stance that known truths cannot be debated, maintaining instead that the state must remain neutral toward the content of speech and, therefore, that the state cannot decide which ideas are true and which are false.[71] The Court's position on content neutrality can be seen in *Chicago Police Department v. Mosley*, a case in which labor picketing was exempted from a general ban on picketing adjacent to a school. In his opinion for the Court, Justice Marshall wrote: "But above all else, the First Amendment means that government has no power to restrict expression because of its message, its ideas, its subject matter, or its content."[72] The government, the Court maintained, "may not grant the use of a forum to people whose views it finds acceptable, but deny use to those

---

70. In *Roth v. United States*, the Court extended constitutional protection to any speech containing "ideas having even the slightest redeeming social importance," exposing to regulation only those forms of expression, like obscenity, which are "utterly without redeeming social importance." *Roth v. United States*, 354 U.S. 476 (1957). Although the Court in *Miller v. California* (1973) eventually abandoned "the utterly without redeeming social value" test, it made clear that in addition to political speech, any speech having serious literary, artistic, or scientific value should be protected.

71. The rule against content regulation "now stands as the cornerstone of the Free Speech Tradition." Owen M. Fiss, "Free Speech and Social Structure," *Iowa Law Review* 71 (1986): 1408–9.

72. *Chicago Police Department v. Mosley*, 408 U.S. 92 (1972). See also *Erznoznick v. City of Jacksonville*, 422 U.S. 205, 209 (1975): "When the government acting as a censor undertakes selectively to shield the public from some kinds of speech on the grounds that they are more offensive than others, the First Amendment strictly limits its powers." The scholarly writings on content neutrality include Susan Williams, "Content Discrimination and the First Amendment," *University of Pennsylvania Law Review* 139 (1991): 615–730; Geoffrey R. Stone, "Content Regulation and the First Amendment," *William and Mary Law Review* 25 (1983): 189–252; Paul B. Stephan III, "The First Amendment and Content Discrimination," *Virginia Law Review* 68 (1982): 203–51; Martin H. Redish, "The Content Distinction in First Amendment Analysis," *Stanford Law Review* 34 (1981): 113–51; and Daniel A. Farber, "Content Regulation and the First Amendment: A Revisionist View," *Georgetown Law Journal* 68 (1980): 727–63.

wishing to express less favored or more controversial views." Content-based distinctions of this sort are a kind of forbidden censorship that undercuts the " 'profound national commitment to the principle that debate on public issues should be uninhibited, robust, and wide-open.' "[73]

More recently, in *Texas v. Johnson*, the Supreme Court found a Texas statute forbidding flag burning—desecration of a venerated object—to be unconstitutional on the grounds that the Texas law was not content neutral. Justice Brennan, who delivered the opinion of the Court, explained that the statute was designed to favor the government's interpretation of what the flag symbolized over the flag burner's. But, Brennan pointed out, it is unconstitutional for the state to foster its own view of the flag by restricting the flag burner's expressive conduct: "If there is a bedrock principle underlying the First Amendment, it is that the government may not prohibit the expression of an idea simply because society finds the idea itself offensive or disagreeable."[74]

The Court's advocacy of content neutrality reveals its deep skepticism, its unwillingness to commit itself to any conception of the truth. In contrast to the humanists, the Court is arguing that it is never legitimate for the state to distinguish between competing claims of truth. The First Amendment "presupposes that there are no orthodoxies—religious, political, economic, or scientific—which are immune from debate and dispute."[75] As Justice Holmes writes in his *Abrams* dissent: "Time has upset many fighting faiths." The Court's legal stand prohibiting content-based censorship finds its political analogue in the contemporary liberal "principle of neutrality," the belief that "government must be neutral on what might be called the question of the good life."[76] This principle is closely associated with such noted liberal theorists as Bruce Ackerman, Ronald Dworkin, and John Rawls.[77] It is impermissible, these theorists argue, for the state to favor "any particular conceptions of the good life or of what gives value to life."[78] A state that

73. Marshall, in *Mosley*, quoting from *New York Times Co. v. Sullivan*, 376 U.S. 254 (1964).

74. *Texas v. Johnson*, 109 Sup. Ct. 2533 (1989).

75. See Judge Hand's opinion in *International Brotherhood of Electrical Workers v. Labor Board* (1950).

76. Ronald Dworkin, *A Matter of Principle* (Cambridge: Harvard University Press, 1985), 191.

77. See Ackerman, *Social Justice in the Liberal State*; Ronald Dworkin, "Liberalism," in *Public and Private Morality*, ed., Stuart Hampshire (Cambridge: Cambridge University Press, 1978), 113–43, reprinted in Dworkin, *Matter of Principle*, 181–204; and Rawls, *Theory of Justice*.

78. Dworkin, *Matter of Principle*, 191.

favors one conception over another, they contend, does not treat its citizens as equals.

But neutrality, with its deep skepticism, and the marketplace of ideas, with its collective search for truth, make strange bedfellows. What progress toward truth can there be if it is impossible to pronounce on the truth? The Court's response is to equate survival in the intellectual marketplace with the truth, thereby treating the marketplace of ideas not as metaphor, but as reality. The value of an idea, like any other commodity, is defined by its performance in the marketplace; that idea which survives the competition is, ipso facto, the truth. Popular acceptance or, as Justice Holmes states in his *Abrams* dissent, "the power of thought to get itself accepted in the competition of the market" becomes the test for truth.[79]

Such a marketplace metaphor definition of truth, however, is not without its difficulties. To begin with, it does not make sense when applied to empirical and scientific knowledge; there are many beliefs, such as astrology, that are scientifically false, yet popular. And when applied to ethics or politics, where the truth that emerges can be identified with the best answer for society at that point in time, the extreme relativism of a marketplace-defined truth is unlikely to be acceptable. Was Nazism correct, that is, best for Germany of the 1930s, simply because it survived?[80] And if we demand that a belief triumph in the marketplace for a longer period, are we to assume that because men have dominated women since the dawn of recorded history, that such an arrangement is necessarily somehow "true"?[81]

While the Court's radical skepticism openly conflicts with the humanists' mitigated skepticism, its position on *decorum* vis-à-vis the humanists' is less straightforward. Many of the Court's early statements on freedom of speech suggest that the marketplace of ideas presupposes rational discussion.[82]

79. Cole, "Agon at Agora," 886.
80. Schauer, *Free Speech*, 21. See David Kretzmer, "Freedom of Speech and Racism," *Cardozo Law Review* 8 (1987): 469–70: "Racist views seem especially susceptible to wide-scale adoption, often at times of social or economic dislocation, even in societies in which they have had to compete with conflicting views."
81. On the historical development of male domination, see Gerda Lerner, *The Creation of Patriarchy* (New York: Oxford University Press, 1986); Riane Tennenhaus Eisler, *The Chalice and the Blade: Our History, Our Future* (Cambridge, Mass.: Harper & Row, 1987); Marija Alseikaite Gimbutas, *The Gods and Goddesses of Old Europe: 7000 to 3500 B.C. Myths, Legends and Cult Images* (Berkeley and Los Angeles: University of California Press, 1974).
82. "The classic marketplace of ideas theory assumed rationality as well as truth. It relied on reason in two ways. First, the theory assumed that people's reason enables them to comprehend a set reality and test assertions or propositions against that reality. . . . Second, the classic theory assumed that people use reason to avoid or unmask distortions in perceptions of reality

Thus, after declaring free speech indispensable to the discovery of political truth, Justice Brandeis speaks of the founders' belief in "the power of reason as applied through public discussion."[83] And Justice Frankfurter, writing for the Court in *Drivers Union v. Meadowmoor*, links freedom of speech to rational communication: "Back of the guarantee of free speech lay faith in the power of an appeal to reason by all the peaceful means of gaining access to the mind."[84] And, most prominently, in *Chaplinsky v. New Hampshire*, the Court excluded irrational speech—insulting or "fighting words," for example—from First Amendment protection.[85] The Court justified this exclusion by adopting the humanists' position that irrational speech does not promote the discovery of truth and, therefore, does not merit protection.[86] Such speech, the Court states, is "of slight social value as a step to truth." (In fact, irrational speech more likely hinders than helps the search for truth.) The Court's paradigm of the marketplace of ideas in *Chaplinsky* resembles the humanists' model of *sermo*: "a debating society, a sedate assembly of speakers who calmly discussed the issues of the day and became ultimately persuaded by the logic of one of the competing positions."[87]

The Supreme Court departed far from its position in *Chaplinsky*, as well as from the humanist view, in *Cohen v. California*, a case involving a Vietnam War protestor convicted of disturbing the peace for wearing a

---

that imbalances in message presentations might otherwise cause. In other words, reason enables people to find the truth that the theory assumes to exist." Baker, *Human Liberty and Freedom of Speech*, 14.

83. Justice Brandeis, concurring, *Whitney v. California*, 375.

84. *Drivers Union v. Meadowmoor Co.*, 312 U.S. 287, 293 (1941).

85. *Chaplinsky v. New Hampshire*, 315 U.S. 568 (1942). The Court anticipated its decision in *Chaplinsky* two years earlier in *Cantwell v. Connecticut* (1940), where it stated that the "resort to epithets or personal abuse is not in any proper sense communication of information or opinion safeguarded by the Constitution." *Cantwell v. Connecticut*, 310 U.S. 296 (1940). Cf. Justice Frankfurter's statement in *Niemotko v. Maryland*: "A man who is calling names or using the kind of language which would reasonably stir another to violence does not have the same claim to protection as one whose speech is an appeal to reason." 340 U.S. 268, 282 (1951) (Frankfurter, J. concurring).

86. This argument is almost always coupled with the argument that irrational speech endangers civil peace. In *Chaplinsky*, for example, the Court finds that " 'fighting' words . . . tend to incite an immediate breach of peace." See also *Feiner v. New York*, 340 U.S. 315, 321 (1951): "It is one thing to say that the police cannot be used as an instrument for the suppression of unpopular views, and another to say that, when as here the speaker passes the bounds of argument or persuasion and undertakes incitement to riot, they are powerless to prevent a breach of peace."

87. Mark C. Rutzick, "Offensive Language and the Evolution of First Amendment Protection," *Harvard Civil Rights–Civil Liberties Law Review* 9 (1974): 18.

jacket bearing the words "F——k the Draft" in a courthouse. Writing for the Court, Justice Harlan argued that the state must not be allowed to distinguish between appropriate and offensive speech, permitting the former and censoring the latter: "For, while the particular four-letter word being litigated here is perhaps more distasteful than most others of its genre, it is nevertheless often true that one man's vulgarity is another's lyric."[88] The form of expression is a matter of taste and style, which the Constitution leaves largely to the individual. In addition, Harlan maintained that it is impossible to sever the form from the purpose of expression since "much linguistic expression serves a dual communicative function: it conveys not only ideas capable of relatively precise, detached explication, but otherwise inexpressible emotions as well. In fact words are often chosen as much for their emotive as their cognitive force." Thus, the protestor's choice of an offensive word was essential to expressing his rage; a milder word would not have had the same effect. The Court was arguing that the protestor's medium, including his rhetorical style, was part of his message.[89] The Court in *Cohen* gave no priority to rational speech. In contrast to the humanists and its own previous position, the Court did not care whether or not the language used was conducive to rational discourse; it refused to differentiate between rational speech and emotive expression.[90]

Since *Cohen*, most of the Court has been reluctant to assume the role of rhetorical arbiter.[91] But while the Court majority has generally attempted

88. *Cohen v. California*, 403 U.S. 15 (1971). Justice Brennan makes a similar point in *Texas v. Johnson* when he argues that the right to free speech "is not dependent on the particular mode in which one chooses to express an idea."

89. Dworkin, *Matter of Principle*, 63; John Hart Ely, *Democracy and Distrust: A Theory of Judicial Review* (Cambridge: Harvard University Press, 1980), 114.

90. In addition to *Cohen*, the Court's opinion in *Terminiello v. Chicago*, 337 U.S. 1 (1949), rejects the primacy of rational speech: "A function of free speech under our system of government is to invite dispute. It may indeed best serve its high purpose when it induces a condition of unrest, creates dissatisfaction with conditions as they are, or even stirs people to anger." The Court's neutrality toward the speech medium stands in marked contrast to the procedures that regulate jury trials, which are designed to ensure that both sides are represented without inflammatory speech or prejudicial evidence. The sensitivity, implicit in these rules, to how the form of speech influences the jurors' search for truth is absent from society's search for truth embodied in the First Amendment. See Bollinger, *Tolerant Society*, 56.

91. See Robert C. Post, "Cultural Heterogeneity and Law: Pornography, Blasphemy, and the First Amendment," *California Law Review* 76 (1988): 297–335; Robert C. Post, "The Constitutional Concept of Public Discourse: Outrageous Opinion, Democratic Deliberation, and *Hustler Magazine v. Falwell*," *Harvard Law Review* 103 (1990): 601–86. Even when the Court has permitted restrictions on offensive speech, it has emphasized the exceptional nature of these limitations. In *FCC v. Pacifica Foundation*, 438 U.S. 726 (1978), for example, the

to remain neutral toward the form of speech, a minority on the Court has continued to scrutinize the speaker's medium or style. For example, in his *Cohen* dissent, Justice Blackmun found the case "to be well within the sphere of *Chaplinsky v. New Hampshire.*" Likewise, Chief Justice Rehnquist's dissent in *Texas v. Johnson* (joined by two other justices) cites *Chaplinsky* approvingly. According to Rehnquist, "the burning of the American flag," like *Chaplinsky*'s "fighting words," "was no essential part of any exposition of ideas." It was not the flag burner's message that was banned: "[The flag burner] was free to make any verbal denunciation of the flag that he wished. . . . [He] conveyed nothing that could not have been conveyed and was not conveyed just as forcefully in a dozen different ways." The medium the flag burner chose was designed to provoke. Reflecting the humanists' sense of *decorum*, Rehnquist states that "flag burning is the equivalent of an inarticulate grunt or roar that, it seems fair to say, is most likely to be indulged in not to express any particular idea, but to antagonize others." Implicit in Rehnquist's dissent is the assumption, basic to the marketplace of ideas, that freedom of speech is supposed to serve the audience's interest in discovering truth. Because people are often resistant to new ideas, this interest is even served by exposing people to ideas that they oppose. Flag burning, however, is unlike the expression of an unpopular idea because it does not inform; rather, it blocks the transfer of information. The ideas connoted by flag burning are lost on the audience because flag burning is tantamount to an assault, more likely to elicit an irrational response from the audience than a rational reconsideration of its previous beliefs.

In addition to the above-cited majority and dissenting opinions, it is worthwhile to note one other Court opinion that harks back to the humanists' efforts to oversee the tone of public discussion: *Bethel School District No. 403 v. Fraser*. This opinion, unlike the previous ones, does not deal directly with the full right of freedom of speech, enjoyed by adults, but concerns the limited First Amendment rights of adolescents. In *Bethel*, the Court holds that a high school student's offensive speech was not protected by the First Amendment.[92] The case involved the disciplining of a high

---

Court majority justified restrictions on the broadcast of indecent and profane language by noting the distinctiveness of broadcasting — its "uniquely pervasive presence in the lives of all Americans." Unregulated broadcasting, the Court argued, forces indecent materials on us and on our children in the privacy of our own homes.

92. *Bethel School District No. 403 et al. v. Fraser, a minor, et al.*, 478 U.S. 675 (1986).

school student, whose speech nominating a fellow student for a student elective office included the use of sexual innuendo. The Court justified the school's action against the offending student by pointing to the role and purpose of the American public school system in preparing future citizens. The goal of public education, the Court states, is the "inculcat[ion of] fundamental values necessary to the maintenance of a democratic political system."[93] And " 'the fundamental values necessary to the maintenance of a democratic political system' disfavor the use of terms of debate offensive or highly threatening to others." Therefore, the Court concludes, it is the school's prerogative as inculcator of democratic values to teach students "the boundaries of socially appropriate behavior," including the power to ban the use of profane language.[94]

The Court in *Bethel* evokes the image of democracy as a conversation between citizens. Democratic conversation, like Ciceronian and humanist *sermo*, possesses its rules of *decorum*. Citizen-interlocutors, the Court states in *Bethel*, must "take into account consideration of the sensibilities of others. . . . Even the most heated political discourse in a democratic society requires consideration for the personal sensibilities of the other participants and audiences." As an example of the civility that democratic discourse requires, the Court cites Congress's rules of debate, in which "impertinent" speech and abusive language are forbidden. But congressional debate is only a miniature version of "political discourse in a democratic society," which means, as the Court itself acknowledges, that "the habits and manners of civility" also apply to the general public. As Alexander Meiklejohn explains, the reason for limiting freedom of discussion, whether in Congress or in society, is the same. In both cases, the objective is to arrive at wise decisions, and wise decisions emerge from an environment that is rhetorically controlled. Using the metaphor of the town meeting, Meiklejohn writes:

93. *Bethel School District No. 403 v. Fraser*, 675, 681, quoting from *Ambach v. Norwick*, 441 U.S. 68, 76–77 (1979).

94. "The process of educating our youth for citizenship in public schools is not confined to books, the curriculum, and the civics class; schools must teach by example the shared values of a civilized social order. Consciously or otherwise, teachers—and indeed the older students— demonstrate the appropriate form of civil discourse and political expression by their conduct and deportment in and out of class. Inescapably, like parents, they are role models. The schools, as instruments of the state, may determine that the essential lessons of civil mature conduct cannot be conveyed in a school that tolerates lewd, indecent, or offensive speech and conduct such as that indulged in by this confused boy." *Bethel School District No. 403 v. Fraser*, 675, 683.

The [town] meeting has assembled, not primarily to talk, but primarily by means of talking to get business done. And the talking must be regulated and abridged as the doing of the business under actual conditions may require. If a speaker wanders from the point at issue, if he is abusive or in other ways threatens to defeat the purpose of the meeting, he may be and should be declared 'out of order.' He must then stop speaking, at least in that way. And if he persists in breaking the rules, he may be 'denied the floor' or, in the last resort, 'thrown out' of the meeting.[95]

Neither Meiklejohn nor the Court in *Bethel* deals with the discovery of religious truth; they are concerned with the search for political truth or practical wisdom.[96] Still, like the humanists seeking true doctrine, they take note of the rhetorical impediments to achieving their goals. Consequently, Meiklejohn concedes the possibility that some speech can be silenced, not for its ideas, but for the way it is presented. The Court, however, does not apply the logic of its argument beyond democracy's training grounds, the classroom, to the actual democratic arena.[97] Despite its talk of "consideration of the sensibilities of others," the Court is largely content to leave the marketplace of ideas to operate on its own, without imposing any rules of civility on its participants.[98]

Contemporary Applications of the Humanist Argument

Pornography and Hate Speech

Although the Supreme Court generally rejects the enforcement of minimal standards of public discourse and Meiklejohn's idea for applying such standards is only hypothetical, the case for promoting a more rational truth-seeking environment continues to be made. In this final section, I will

---

95. *Free Speech and Its Relation to Self-Government*, 23.
96. On Meiklejohn, see Baker, *Human Liberty and Freedom of Speech*, 28.
97. Meiklejohn, *Free Speech and Its Relation to Self-Government*, 24–27.
98. Robert C. Post, "Defaming Public Officials: On Doctrine and Legal History," *American Bar Foundation Research Journal*, 1987: 555–56.

analyze two different attempts to regulate the marketplace of ideas. The first advocates enforcing rhetorical sensitivity in the areas of pornography and hate speech. The second seeks to level the position of wealthy and less wealthy speakers in political speech. Both approaches, I argue, reflect the humanist concern with rhetorical *decorum*. But the second approach, I contend, is more likely to pass constitutional muster.

Those who support restricting pornography and hate speech contend that if the First Amendment is based on the marketplace of ideas, then pornographic and racist speech, which undermines the marketplace, should not be protected. I examine three justifications for restricting pornography and racist speech. The first justification focuses on how these categories of expression stigmatize their victims' speech. Proponents of this argument characterize pornography and racist speech as "linguistic abuse" and "verbal abuse on an unwilling target."[99] That racist or hate speech demeans its victims is readily apparent.[100] According to its feminist critics, however, pornography similarly debases women:

> Pornography, in the feminist view, is a form of forced sex, a practice of sexual politics, an institution of gender inequality. In this perspective, pornography is not harmless fantasy or a corrupt and confused misrepresentation of an otherwise natural and healthy sexuality. Along with the rape and prostitution in which it participates, pornography institutionalizes the sexuality of male supremacy, which fuses the erotization of dominance and submission with the social construction of male and female.[101]

99. Kenneth Lasson, "Group Libel Versus Free Speech: When Big Brother *Should* Butt In," *Duquesne Law Review* 23 (1984): 122.

100. For a discussion of the injury hate speech inflicts on its victims, see Mari J. Matsuda, "Public Response to Racist Speech: Considering the Victim's Story," *Michigan Law Review* 87 (1989): 2326–41, and Kretzmer, "Freedom of Speech and Racism," 462–67.

101. Catharine A. MacKinnon, *Feminism Unmodified: Discourses on Life and Law* (Cambridge: Harvard University Press, 1987), 148. In the words of one feminist critic, "pornography is the theory, and rape the practice." Robin Morgan, *Going Too Far: The Personal Chronicle of a Feminist* (New York: Random House, 1977), 169. Unlike obscenity law, which is based on traditional moral opposition to unbridled sexuality, the feminist critique of pornography is unconcerned with the sinfulness of sex, which it considers a male preoccupation. Rather, the feminist critique is animated by what it considers the harmful effects of male sexuality on women: "The law of obscenity, the state's primary approach to its version of the pornographic question, has literally nothing in common with this feminist critique. Their obscenity is not our pornography. . . . Men are turned on by obscenity, including its suppression, the same way they are by sin. Animated by morality from the male standpoint, in which violation—of women

Because pornography and racist speech stigmatize their victims, it is argued that these forms of speech make the words and ideas of their target-groups "less saleable in the marketplace of ideas."[102] The injury focused on here is not to the victim but to the marketplace. The marketplace ideal, like the ideal of *sermo*, is to consider ideas independent of the speaker's *ethos*. But when speech is used to devalue a person's opinions because he or she belongs to a despised minority, this ideal is undermined; the market is distorted. Good ideas lose out to bad ideas simply because the speaker's character has been demeaned.[103]

The second justification for suppressing pornography and racist speech also focuses on how these forms of expression prevent their victims' ideas from being heard. But unlike the previous justification, which emphasized the psychological effect of pornography and racist speech on the nontargeted groups, this justification highlights the speech's psychological effect on the targeted groups. Once again, the concern is not with the victim's injury per

---

and rules—is erotocized, obscenity law can be seen to proceed according to the interest of male power, robed in gender-neutral good and evil." See MacKinnon, *Feminism Unmodified*, 150. See also 151–54, 175–76, 193–94, and Donald Alexander Downs, *The New Politics of Pornography* (Chicago: University of Chicago Press, 1989), chaps. 1–2.

102. Charles R. Lawrence III, "If He Hollers Let Him Go: Regulating Racist Speech on Campus," *Duke Law Journal*, 1990:468, 470–71; MacKinnon, *Feminism Unmodified*, 129–30, 148; Robert C. Post, "Racist Speech, Democracy, and the First Amendment," *William and Mary Law Review* 32 (1991): 302–3.

103. For some radicals, pornography and racist speech ultimately derive their power from the fact that our own society is sexist and racist. We should not assume, they argue, that antisexist and antiracist views compete on an even playing field with the sexist and racist messages contained in pornography and hate speech. Speaking of pornography and the marketplace of ideas, the radical feminist Catherine MacKinnon writes: "Laissez faire might be an adequate theory of the social preconditions for knowledge in a nonhierarchical society. But in a society of gender inequality, the speech of the powerful impresses its view upon the world." The First Amendment, for MacKinnon, operates as if all views, however divergent and unorthodox, receive a fair hearing, but "it fails to notice that pornography (like the racism, in which I include anti-Semitism, of the Nazis and the Klan) is not at all divergent or unorthodox. It is the ruling ideology." *Feminism Unmodified*, 155–56. The logical conclusion of MacKinnon's argument is found in Herbert Marcuse's concept "repressive tolerance," according to which tolerance in a repressive society, like ours, functions as a repressive and not a liberating ideal. Given the unequal distribution of power in our society, Marcuse argues, the neutral toleration of all views in fact strengthens only some views—those of the "Establishment," the economic and political elite. Against the tyranny of the status quo, Marcuse supports "the systematic withdrawal of tolerance toward regressive and repressive opinions and movements." Marcuse's understanding of what constitutes regressive opinions is broad and would include not only pro-military views, but the views of those who oppose expansion of the welfare state. See Herbert Marcuse, "Repressive Tolerance," in *A Critique of Pure Tolerance*, ed. Robert Paul Wolff, Barrington Moore Jr., and Herbert Marcuse (Boston: Beacon Press, 1969), 100–101.

se, but with how that victimization undermines the marketplace of ideas. Thus, the argument is made that speech degrading women or minorities silences its victims, which decreases the amount of speech that enters the marketplace: "Women and minorities often report that they find themselves speechless in the face of discriminatory verbal attacks. . . . Fear, rage, shock, and flight all interfere with any reasoned response."[104] Like *Chaplinsky*'s fighting words, it is argued that pornography and hate speech impair rationality. The victim's impaired rationality manifests itself differently, however, in pornography and hate speech than in *Chaplinsky*'s abusive speech. *Chaplinsky* assumed that insulting words would produce anger and, possibly, violence—in short, that someone attacked would respond in kind.[105] In contrast, modern critics of pornography and racist speech maintain that, because of the powerlessness of the targeted groups, the victims will not respond.[106] This silence curtails the universe of ideas. Meiklejohn argued that "what is essential is not that everyone shall speak, but that everything worth saying shall be said."[107] The problem with expression that silences minority groups is that it keeps speech worth saying from being said.[108]

104. This inability to respond is caused by several factors. First, "the visceral emotional response to personal attack precludes speech. Attack produces an instinctive, defensive psychological reaction." A second factor is "the preemptive nature of such insults—the words by which to respond to such verbal attacks may never be forthcoming because speech is usually an inadequate response. When one is personally attacked with words that denote one's subhuman status and untouchability, there is little (if anything) that can be said to redress either the emotional or reputational injury." Finally, "the subordinated victim of fighting words also is silenced by her relatively powerless position in society. . . . In most situations, minorities correctly perceive that a violent response to fighting words will result in a risk to their own life and limb. Since minorities are likely to lose the fight, they are forced to remain silent and submissive." Lawrence, "If He Hollers Let Him Go," 452–55. See also MacKinnon, *Feminism Unmodified*, 156.

105. Similarly, the humanists counseled moderation in religious discourse, lest the audience respond intemperately.

106. Lawrence, "If He Hollers Let Him Go," 453–57.

107. *Free Speech and Its Relation to Self-Government*, 25. Because the university is especially associated with the search for truth, it is argued that the need to regulate intolerant speech is greater there. See Rodney A. Smolla, "Rethinking First Amendment Assumptions about Racist and Sexist Speech, *Washington and Lee Law Review* 47 (1990): 207, and Post, "Racist Speech," 275–77.

108. Another argument related to the previous two arguments is that certain forms of speech lack ideational content and, therefore, add nothing to the marketplace of ideas. Pornography, it is argued, is defined by "its lack of intended intellectual appeal," and is to be considered a physical rather than a mental experience; it is "non-rational, almost physical . . . material which is designed to excite sexual fantasies, largely as an aid to masturbation." Schauer, *Free*

Although the political attitudes of today's critics of pornography and racist speech are far removed from the conservative views of the Renaissance humanists, the two groups agree that rhetorical form affects the quality of discussion. Both value rational conversation as a means to discover truth, and they accept that at least certain types of incivility interfere with reaching that goal. They would concur that truth does not necessarily triumph over error. The following statement would have made perfect sense to More, Acontius, or Milton, although it is made by a contemporary legal scholar advocating regulation of racist speech: "Despite an optimism regarding the human capacity for good that can only be explained by faith, . . . I do not believe that truth will prevail in a rigged game or in a contest where the referees are on the payroll of the proponents of falsity."[109]

Finally, there is a third justification for restricting odious—particularly racist—speech that echoes the humanist defense of religious toleration: the argument from consensus. As I explained earlier, Erasmus and other humanists, harking back to the ancient rhetoricians, maintained that universal consensus is a sign of truth. For these humanists, doctrines that had achieved a universal consensus could not be debated because their veracity had already been shown. Some present-day legal thinkers make a similar argument about the "overwhelming international consensus" against racism, which is adduced to defend restrictions on racist speech.[110] "Human expe-

---

Speech, 183; Eric Barendt, *Freedom of Speech* (Oxford: Clarendon Press, 1985), 263. See also John M. Finnis, "'Reason and Passion': The Constitutional Dialectic of Free Speech and Obscenity," *University of Pennsylvania Law Review* 116 (1967): 227: "Obscenity pertains, not to the realm of ideas, reason, intellectual content and truth-seeking, but to the realm of passion, desires, cravings and titillation." For sympathetic criticism of this argument, see Post, "Cultural Heterogeneity and Law," 328–29. Similarly, racist speech is said to offer "no ideas, opinions, or proposals—nothing of substance or merit." Such speech is more properly considered "a statement of emotion" that has "no cognitive message at all, but rather conveys raw, unvarnished feeling." Lasson, "Group Libel Versus Free Speech," 122; Smolla, "Rethinking First Amendment Assumptions," 182. In contrast to the two previous arguments, this argument for restricting pornography and racist speech does not address the rhetorical effect of pornography and racist speech on the marketplace of ideas. Rather, it merely denies that these forms of speech have anything to contribute.

109. Lawrence, "If He Hollers Let Him Go," 476, n. 159.

110. Smolla, "Rethinking First Amendment Assumptions," 211; Matsuda, "Public Response to Racist Speech," 2359; Kretzmer, "Freedom of Speech and Racism," 458. A variation on the argument from consensus looks to societal, not universal, agreement to prohibit racist speech and pornography. Each society, it is implied, must uphold its own core of fundamental beliefs or values. In apparent conflict with MacKinnon's assumption that sexism and racism are American orthodoxies, this argument emphasizes our society's commitment to the ideals of social and political equality. Our commitment to equality, it is argued, is expressed in the

rience, our only source of collective knowledge," has demonstrated that racism is wrong: "We know, from our collective historical knowledge, that slavery was wrong. We know the unspeakable horror of the holocaust was wrong. We know white minority rule in South Africa is wrong. This knowledge is reflected in the universal acceptance of the wrongness of the doctrine of racial supremacy."[111] Some ideologies are found odious in certain sectors of the world. But racism finds no open support among any nation: "There is no nation left on this planet that submits as its national self-expression the view that Hitler was right."[112] Unlike the previous arguments, which prohibit racist speech because of its rhetorical effect, the present argument to exclude racist speech focuses on the content of the speech itself. Contrary to the Supreme Court's position that no idea is taboo, those who argue from the universal rejection of racism believe that some ideas are, indeed, beyond the pale and should not enter into the marketplace of ideas.

Beyond the Marketplace of Ideas

The argument from consensus and the earlier arguments for suppressing pornography and racist speech assume that freedom of speech is protected to advance knowledge of truth. Based on this assumption, these arguments exclude pornography and racist speech from First Amendment protection because these forms of expression are harmful to the marketplace of ideas or are demonstrably false. True, it is not at all clear that pornography and racist speech impede the search for truth in all the ways that have been suggested. Nevertheless, these arguments point out that protecting pornography and racist speech because of their truth-enhancing power is, at a best, a dubious

---

Fourteenth Amendment's Equal Protection Clause and in Court decisions like *Brown v. Board of Education*. This commitment to equality obligates the state to oppose racist speech. See Lawrence, "If He Hollers Let Him Go," 438–49, and Kretzmer, 456. Post cites this argument critically in "Racist Speech," 291–92. A similar argument is made by the Canadian Supreme Court upholding the suppression of pornography. In *Regina v. Butler*, 89 D.L.R. (4th) 449, 479 (1992), the Canadian High Court writes: "This court has recognized that the harm caused by the proliferation of materials which seriously offend the values fundamental to our society is a substantial concern which justifies restricting the otherwise full exercise of the freedom of expression."

111. Matsuda, "Public Response to Racist Speech," 2359. See ibid., n. 203. "The uniform rejection of racist ideology is evidence of moral truth. I suggest more than an opinion poll test. I suggest as well that the doctrine of racial supremacy is wrong, both morally and factually, and that the consensus of human opinion helps us to know this."

112. Ibid.

proposition. Pornography and racist speech, however, are not the only examples of expression left vulnerable by the argument from truth. As noted above, restrictions both on offensive speech, à la *Cohen*, and on flag burning might be justified on the grounds that such speech is inimical to the search for truth. These restrictions would be less popular with many on the political left than those recommended for pornography and racist speech.

The speech-censoring potential of the argument from truth is more apparent when the search for truth or the marketplace of ideas is placed within its broader communitarian context. The marketplace theory is communitarian, not individualistic; it looks to the discovery of truth as a good for the community. Thus, instead of protecting the speaker's right, the marketplace theory emphasizes the audience's access to information.[113] If the search for truth were not related to the communal good, however, an argument could be made that false, pernicious speech—like hate speech— should be protected, inasmuch as such speech sometimes strengthens the condition of truth. For example, John Stuart Mill observes that unless truth is challenged by error, "[truth] will, by most of those who receive it, be held in the manner of a prejudice, with little comprehension or feeling of its rational grounds. And not only this, but . . . the meaning of the doctrine itself will be in danger of being lost, or enfeebled, and deprived of its vital effect on the character and conduct."[114] But the search for truth *is* related to the communal good. And once truth is defined by its contribution to the community, it becomes difficult to maintain that false, harmful speech should be protected. Whatever gains to truth such speech might bring would be far outweighed by the dangers this speech poses to the collective social welfare, since it might be accepted by others, lead to violence, or deeply offend particular groups.[115]

If the marketplace of ideas is the dominant constitutional justification for free speech, and if this argument is so restrictive, why, then, have the courts protected so much speech? As already seen, the Supreme Court has upheld the right to wear an obscenity-emblazoned jacket in a courthouse and to

113. Dworkin, *Matter of Principle*, 385–89; Ingber, "Marketplace of Ideas," 77.

114. Mill, *On Liberty*, 258.

115. For the argument that suppressing offensive speech may be in the interest of the community, see Ronald Dworkin, review of *Make No Law: The Sullivan Case and the First Amendment*, by Anthony Lewis, *The New York Review of Books*, 11 June 1992, 58; Ingber, "Marketplace of Ideas," 4–5; Schauer, *Free Speech*, 28; Baker, *Human Liberty and Freedom of Speech*, 18–19; and Richards, *Toleration and the Constitution*, 182–83.

burn an American flag. Lower courts have also overturned an Indianapolis ordinance banning pornography, defined as "the sexually explicit subordination of women,"[116] and have defended the right of neo-Nazis to demonstrate in Skokie, a heavily Jewish suburb of Chicago with a high number of Holocaust survivors.[117] These restrictions on speech were consistent with the argument from truth, yet the courts rejected them. The reason that the courts have extended First Amendment protection beyond speech that enhances the marketplace of ideas, I believe, is because the marketplace of ideas is not the sole justification for freedom of speech. Additional justifications include, but are not limited to, the arguments that freedom of speech promotes tolerance,[118] dissent,[119] self-fulfillment,[120] and that censorship impairs the dignity and equality of the silenced speaker.[121] As is commonly recognized today, there is no single "authentic" justification for protecting free speech.[122] Rather, there are multiple rationales that, taken together, make up contemporary First Amendment doctrine. Therefore, forms of speech that would not be protected under the marketplace rationale find support in other justifications. First Amendment protection of the arts and entertainment, for example, is more plausibly justified by the argument from self-fulfillment than by the argument from truth. Consistent with freedom of speech's complex origins is an appreciation of the First Amendment's individualistic character. While the argument from truth is directed toward the public good, other rationales uphold the speaker's right, regardless of the

---

116. *American Booksellers Association Inc. v. Hudnut*, 598 F. Supp. at 1316 (S.D. Indiana) (1984); *American Booksellers Association Inc. v. Hudnut*, 771 F. 2d 323 (1985) (7th Cir.), *affirmed* 475 U.S. 1001 (1986); Downs, *New Politics of Pornography*, 114.

117. *Collin v. Smith*, 447 F. Supp. 676 (N.D. Ill.), *affirmed* 578 F. 2d 1197 (7th Cir.), *cert. denied*, 439 U.S. 916 (1978). At the time of the proposed Nazi demonstration, Skokie was estimated to have a Jewish population of 30,000 out of a total population of 70,000 inhabitants. It was also estimated to have somewhere between eight and twelve *hundred* Holocaust survivors. See Donald Alexander Downs, *Nazis in Skokie: Freedom, Community, and the First Amendment* (Notre Dame: University of Notre Dame Press, 1985), 21.

118. Bollinger, *Tolerant Society*.

119. Shiffrin, *First Amendment*.

120. Thomas Emerson, *The System of Freedom of Expression* (New York: Random House, 1970); Baker, *Human Liberty and Freedom of Speech*; Martin Redish, *Freedom of Expression: A Critical Analysis* (Charlottesville, Va.: Michie, 1984). Schauer summarizes the argument from self-expression in *Free Speech*, 52–58.

121. Dworkin, *Matter of Principle*, 386; Kent Greenawalt, *Speech, Crime, and the Uses of Language* (New York: Oxford University Press, 1989), 33–34. Schauer summarizes the argument from dignity in *Free Speech*, 61–66.

122. Schauer, *Free Speech*, 14; Greenawalt, *Speech, Crime, and the Uses of Language*, 12–14; Ronald Dworkin, *New York Review of Books*, 11 June 1992, 57.

speech's utility to the community.[123] From this individualistic, nonconsequentialist perspective, speech that would have been suppressed out of concern for the commonweal—hate speech, for example—would more likely be protected.[124]

But if the marketplace of ideas is only one among a number of rationales for freedom of speech, and if the other rationales are more protective of speech rights than the marketplace approach, what role, then, is left for the marketplace of ideas? The answer to this question has implications for the contemporary relevance of the humanist defense of toleration: if the marketplace approach is superfluous, so too are the humanists' arguments—concerned as they are with the search for truth. The argument from truth, however, is not superfluous because no free speech justification can be applied absolutely. Thus, if the argument from self-fulfillment or from dignity were applied without restraint, then more than freedom of speech would be protected. The right to freedom of speech would become a more general right to personal liberty that would protect prostitution, nude sunbathing, choice of residency, and political discourse equally. This wholesale application of an individualistic justification is unacceptable since it would give us more than we bargained for.[125] Like other free speech justifications, the argument from self-fulfillment or dignity must be applied selectively. A comprehensive discussion of when, where, and how the various rationales for free speech are applied and whether they are consistent with

---

123. Ronald Dworkin expresses this conception of individual rights when he maintains that rights "are best understood as trumps over some background justification for political decisions that states a goal for the community as a whole. If someone has a right . . . , this means that it is for some reason wrong for officials to act in violation of that right, even if they (correctly) believe that the community as a whole would be better off if they did." *Matter of Principle*, 359. See Ronald Dworkin, *Taking Rights Seriously* (Cambridge: Harvard University Press, 1978).

124. The individualistic character of the right to free speech is suggested by Justice Brandeis's opinion in *Whitney v. California*, which insists that it is not just any harm to society, but only a very grave danger that will justify limitations on free speech: "The fact that speech is likely to result in some violence or in destruction of property is not enough to justify its suppression. There must be the probability of serious injury to the State."

125. Conversely, the argument from self-fulfillment or dignity, if applied absolutely, would also be more restrictive of free speech than we would find acceptable. Speech would not merit any distinctive protection. Thus, it would not protect speech acts that cause harm to others. See also Schauer, *Free Speech*, 58. See also ibid., 64: "With respect to speech one would be justified in saying 'That's none of your business!' only if the speech can be taken as primarily self-regarding. But when words are other-regarding, . . . the ideas of dignity and insult are no more dispositive than they would be if someone claimed his dignity to be insulted by restrictions on his freedom to pollute the atmosphere, commit assault, play the saxophone in church, or practice cardiovascular surgery without a medical degree or licence."

other justifications for freedom of speech, however, exceeds the scope of this study. My concern here, though, is limited to only one rationale—the marketplace approach—because of its links to the humanist defense of toleration.

Market Reforms

The marketplace approach is not always consistent with other justifications for freedom of speech. For example, the marketplace approach is inconsistent with other justifications for freedom of speech when it is used to prohibit expression, like pornography and racist speech, that would have been protected by non-marketplace rationales. Similarly, the humanists' rhetorical regulations that enjoin irrational discourse are incompatible with the individualistic justifications for freedom of speech that emphasize the speaker's right to choose the form of expression. The marketplace theory, however, is consistent with non-marketplace rationales when it does not censor speech. Various proposals have been made and some put into effect that are intended to ensure that all, or at least more, points of view are heard in the marketplace. These proposals have been referred to collectively as market reform proposals.[126] Common to these proposals is a rejection of laissez-faire assumptions about the marketplace of ideas. The "invisible hand" of the marketplace, these proposals imply, cannot be trusted to ensure that everything that needs to be heard will be heard. The views of some people, especially the rich and the powerful, are more likely to be publicized than the views of others, like the poor, the weak, political dissenters, and so on. The reform proposals, therefore, try to level the playing field between speech producers, so that speech consumers will have a larger, more representative selection from which to choose. Although the market reform proposals differ in how they attempt to equalize the speech of the haves and have-nots, they all look to the government to facilitate speech egalitarianism. In contrast to First Amendment traditionalists, who fear governmental intrusion into the marketplace of ideas, proponents of market reform seek it. Market reformers hope that government intervention will correct the failures of an inequitable marketplace. They also believe that their proposed reforms are in line with non-marketplace justifications for freedom of speech because their reforms do not censor, but propagate speech.[127]

126. Ingber, "Marketplace of Ideas," 50–55; Baker, *Human Liberty and Freedom of Speech*, 37–40.
127. J. Skelly Wright, "Money and the Pollution of Politics: Is the First Amendment an

In many ways, the contemporary proponents of market reform appear to have little in common with the Renaissance humanists. The market reformers are primarily concerned with equalizing speech opportunities. By contrast, the humanists did not take up the problem of powerless groups communicating their message to the public-at-large. And even if they had, they, as social conservatives, would not have sanctioned state involvement in redistributing power—including the power to communicate. Nevertheless, the humanists' attempts to control the *decorum* of *sermo* foreshadow the market reform proposals. The humanists established the principle for later free speech advocates that a laissez-faire approach to speech does not work.[128] The humanists maintained that for truth to be discovered—or, in contemporary terms, for the best policy or political candidate to succeed— the optimal speech environment must be artificially constructed, quite literally fashioned by *ars* or human ingenuity. Today's proponents of market reform accept this fundamental humanist assumption. By doing so, they— wittingly or not—sustain a key element of the humanist defense of toleration, though adapting it to different circumstances. Because the market reforms are less likely to conflict with other free speech rationales, these reforms are the most practical application of the humanist argument to contemporary free speech issues.

Two well-known examples of market reforms, which have been implemented and considered by the Court, are the Fairness Doctrine and the Federal Election Campaign Act Amendments of 1974 (FECA). The Fairness Doctrine is the now-defunct Federal Communications Commission (FCC)

Obstacle to Political Equality?" *Columbia Law Review* 82 (1982): 636–39; Joel Fleischman and Pope McCorkle, "Level-Up Rather Than Level-Down: Toward a New Theory of Campaign Finance Reform," *Journal of Law & Politics* 1 (1984): 237–38.

128. Two modern free speech theorists who reject a laissez-faire approach to free speech are Zechariah Chafee and Alexander Meiklejohn. Chafee called for governmental involvement in the marketplace, as a response to private restrictions on speech: "What is the use of telling an unpopular speaker that he will incur no criminal penalties by his proposed address, so long as every hall owner in the city declines to rent him space for his meeting and there are no vacant lots available? There should be municipal auditoriums, schoolhouses out of school hours, church forums, parks in summer, all open to thresh out every question of public importance, with just as few restrictions as possible; for otherwise the subjects that most need to be discussed will be the very subjects that will be ruled out as unsuitable for discussion. We must do more than remove the discouragements to open discussion. We must exert ourselves to supply active encouragements." Zechariah Chafee Jr., *Free Speech in the United States* (Cambridge: Harvard University Press, 1967), 559. Similarly, Meiklejohn writes: "Congress is not debarred from all action upon freedom of speech. Legislation which abridges that freedom is forbidden, but not legislation to enlarge and enrich it." *Free Speech and Its Relation to Self-Government*, 16.

regulation requiring (1) that broadcasters present controversial issues of public importance; and (2) that if one side of a controversial issue is aired, the broadcast station must afford a reasonable opportunity for presenting contrasting points of view in its overall programming.[129] Despite the Fairness Doctrine's requirement that broadcasters cover controversial issues of public importance, the FCC, in practice, had left broadcast stations free to decide their own programming. Once a controversial issue of public importance was covered, however, the FCC could, and sometimes did, act to ensure that the broadcaster not restrict coverage to one viewpoint.[130] The Fairness Doctrine's objective in requiring the presentation of contrasting viewpoints was to protect the marketplace of ideas. Supporters of the Fairness Doctrine maintained that because broadcast frequencies were a scarce resource, licensed to stations by the government, there was a need to prevent broadcasters from "communicat[ing] only their own views on public issues, people and candidates"—views that, as Senator Proxmire of Wisconsin observed, were likely to coincide with the interests of the wealthy and powerful.[131] If broadcasters aired only those with whom they agreed, it was argued, the marketplace of ideas would have been impoverished. The Fairness Doctrine was designed to safeguard against this possibility. "The purpose and foundation of the Fairness Doctrine," according to the FCC, was "that of the First Amendment itself; 'to preserve an uninhibited marketplace of ideas in which truth will ultimately prevail, rather than to countenance monopolization of that market, whether it be by the Government itself or a private licensee.' "[132]

The Federal Election Campaign Act Amendments of 1974 were the most comprehensive campaign reform legislation ever passed by Congress. FECA

129. On the Fairness Doctrine, see Andrew O. Shapiro, *Media Access: Your Rights to Express Your Views on Radio and Television* (Boston: Little, Brown, 1976), 107–68, and Ford Rowan, *Broadcast Fairness: Doctrine, Practice, Prospects* (New York: Longman, 1984).

130. The reasonable opportunity for discussion of contrasting points of view, required by the FCC, did not mean that equal time must be allotted to opposing sides. Equal time is mandated by the Equal Opportunities Rule—another broadcasting regulation—which requires equal treatment of political candidates who are sold or given air time. What "reasonable opportunity" meant, according to the Fairness Doctrine, was more flexible than the equal time given to candidates. The FCC looked for a balanced presentation in its overall programming. The broadcaster could, therefore, present contrasting views at different times and on different programs. See Shapiro, *Media Access*, 50–106, 135–68; and Rowan, *Broadcast Fairness*, 6–9.

131. *Red Lion Broadcasting Co. v. FCC*; Fred W. Friendly, *The Good Guys, The Bad Guys, and the First Amendment: Free Speech vs. Fairness in Broadcasting* (New York: Vintage Books, 1977), 26.

132. Fairness Report, 48 FCC 2d 1, 6 (1974); cited in Shapiro, *Media Access*, 107.

contained restrictions in federal elections on the amounts of contributions,[133] independent expenditures on behalf of candidates,[134] personal contributions by the candidate himself and his family,[135] and total campaign expenditures.[136] The Act also provided for some public financing of primary and general elections, with major candidates receiving "full" funding, and minor and new party candidates receiving a reduced proportion of funding. An eight-member commission was created to administer and enforce the Act.

One goal of FECA was "the prevention of corruption and the appearance of corruption spawned by the real or imagined coercive influence of large financial contributions on candidates' positions and on their actions if elected to office."[137] Another of FECA's goals was to equalize the political process.[138] This equalization was intended to serve the state's interest in ending class-based discrimination in political campaigns[139] and to advance the marketplace of ideas. Thus, like the Fairness Doctrine, it was FECA's purpose to ensure a "balanced flow of differing points of view," that is, to create a marketplace in which "there is a free flow of ideas from various sources—not just from voices emanating from the affluent segment of the community."[140] Proponents of campaign finance reform legislation contend that contribution and spending limits prevent the wealthy from monopoliz-

133. The Act limited political contributions by individuals and groups to $1,000 each and by political committees to $5,000 each for any single candidate in any one election, with an annual limit of $25,000 on any individual contributor.

134. The Act limited independent expenditures "relative to a clearly identified candidate" to $1,000 per election.

135. "During any calendar year, a candidate for nomination or election to the office of President or Vice President was limited to a total expenditure of $50,000 from his, or his immediate family's, personal funds. Similarly, a $35,000 ceiling was set for senatorial candidates. Candidates to the House of Representatives were limited to $35,000 if their state was entitled to only one representative, or $25,000 if there was more than one." Marlene Arnold Nicholson, "Buckley v. Valeo: The Constitutionality of the Federal Election Campaign Act Amendments of 1974," *Wisconsin Law Review*, 1977: 324, n. 5.

136. Presidential candidates were limited to $10 million in the primary and $20 million in the general elections. Senate limitations were based on the voting age population of the state. A $70,000 limitation applied separately to primary and general House elections. See ibid., n. 6.

137. *Buckley v. Valeo*, 424 U.S. 1 (1976). See also Daniel Hays Lowenstein, "On Campaign Finance Reform: The Root of All Evil Is Deeply Rooted," *Hofstra Law Review* 2 (1989): 306–35.

138. The Act's contribution limits "serve to mute the voices of affluent persons and groups in the election process and thereby to equalize the relative ability of all citizens to affect the outcome of elections." Ibid.

139. Nicholson, "Buckley v. Valeo," 328–33.

140. "Free Speech Implications of Campaign Expenditure Ceilings," *Harvard Civil Rights—Civil Liberties Law Review* 7 (1972): 228; Nicholson, "Buckley v. Valeo," 335–36.

ing the electoral process. Unless the less affluent can afford the price of campaigning, it is argued, they will be deterred from entering political contests. It is further asserted that without ceilings on spending, wealthy candidates' excessive campaign advertising will "drown out" the voices of their financially limited opponents.[141] Elizabeth Drew, political journalist and advocate of campaign finance reform, echoes this idea when she writes: "If we . . . uncouple the idea of 'the marketplace of ideas' from the idea of 'the free market,' we can begin to get back to how the political system was supposed to work. It is one thing to establish a system that guarantees contending political factions an opportunity to express their views, and quite another to auction off the system to those factions that can afford to pay for the most time to express them."[142] In one-sided races where money dominates politics, fewer ideas are heard; "the truth-seeking process that lies at the heart of the First Amendment conception" is distorted.[143]

Unlike censorship of pornography or racist speech, the two market reforms—the Fairness Doctrine and FECA—do not ban speech. For their proponents, these market reforms promote the marketplace of ideas, without also infringing on the individual speaker's right to freedom of speech. As John Buchanan Jr., chairman of People for the American Way, states: "all that the [Fairness] Doctrine ever requires is that there be more speech . . . the Doctrine never suppresses speech, and it always promotes more, not less discussion of ideas." Similarly, Judge Skelly Wright contends that FECA is consistent with—even supports—an individualistic conception of the First Amendment as the right to self-expression.[144] Nevertheless, although neither the Fairness Doctrine nor FECA prohibits anyone from speaking, critics of these reforms view them as invasive of First Amendment rights. They argue, for example, that by requiring the broadcaster to air material that he may oppose or otherwise choose not to air, the Fairness Doctrine violates the individual's First Amendment right not to espouse

---

141. Wright, "Money and the Pollution of Politics," 631, 637; "Free Speech Implications of Campaign Expenditure Ceilings," 228; Nicholson, "Buckley v. Valeo," 336.

142. Elizabeth Drew, "Politics and Money II," *New Yorker*, 13 December 1982, 104–5.

143. Judge Skelly Wright, "Politics and the Constitution: Is Money Speech?" *The Yale Law Journal* 85 (1976): 1004.

144. U.S. Congress, House Committee on Energy and Commerce, *Broadcasters and the Fairness Doctrine, Hearings before the Subcommittee on Telecommunications and Finance of the Committee on Energy and Commerce on H.R. 315.* 101st Cong., 1st sess., 1989, 52; Wright, "Money and the Pollution of Politics," 637. For an argument, by a market reform supporter, that market reforms and individualistic rationales are in conflict, see Fiss, "Free Speech and Social Structure," 1415–16.

viewpoints with which he disagrees.[145] In addition, critics maintain that if broadcasters find the obligation to balance views costly or burdensome, they might be discouraged from airing any controversial issues. This "chilling effect," they point out, would contradict the very marketplace rationale used to justify the Fairness Doctrine.[146] Likewise, opponents of market reform argue that FECA, while not censoring political speakers outright, still sets limits on campaign contributions and spending, thus restricting the full exercise of the speaker's First Amendment rights.[147]

In 1969, the U.S. Supreme Court upheld the constitutionality of the Fairness Doctrine in *Red Lion Broadcasting Co. v. FCC*, a case involving a right-wing radio station required to offer rebuttal time to a liberal writer that the station had attacked.[148] To those claiming that the FCC regulation abridged the right to free speech, the Court answered that the Fairness Doctrine, in fact, supports the First Amendment interest in promoting the marketplace of ideas. The Court argued that because of the scarcity of broadcasting frequencies, the FCC is justified in obligating stations "to present those views and voices which are representative of the community and which would otherwise, by necessity, be barred from the airwaves."[149]

145. In *Wooley v. Maynard*, 430 U.S. 705 (1977), the Court invalidated a New Hampshire law requiring display of the state motto "Live Free or Die" on automobile license plates. The Court concluded that "the freedom of thought protected by the First Amendment [includes] both the right to speak freely and the right to refrain from speaking at all." Both rights are "complementary components of a broader concept of 'individual freedom of mind.'"

146. U.S. Congress, House Committee on Energy and Commerce, *Broadcasters and the Fairness Doctrine, Hearings before the Subcommittee on Telecommunications and Finance of the Committee on Energy and Commerce on H.R. 315.* 101st Cong., 1st sess., 1989, 100–105, 117; Rowan, *Broadcast Fairness*, 15–21, 120–23; Stephen E. Gottlieb, "In the Name of Patriotism: The Constitutionality of 'Bending' History in Public Secondary Schools," *New York University Law Review* 62 (1987): 557–58. Bill Ruder, an assistant secretary of commerce in the Kennedy years, acknowledges the possible "chilling effect" of the Fairness Doctrine when he states that it was the Democrats' strategy " 'to use the Fairness Doctrine to challenge and harrass right-wing broadcasters and hope that the challenges would be so costly to them that they would be inhibited and decide it was too expensive to continue.' " Quoted in Friendly, *The Good Guys, The Bad Guys, and the First Amendment*, 39.

147. Fleischman and McCorkle, "Level-Up Rather Than Level Down," 234–38.

148. The radio station was required to offer rebuttal time under the Personal Attack Rule, a part of the Fairness Doctrine. According to the Personal Attack Rule, "the station has a duty to notify the person or group attacked, provide a transcript or summary of the program, and offer an opportunity to respond." Rowan, *Broadcast Fairness*, 5.

149. "Nor can we say that it is inconsistent with the First Amendment goal of producing an informed public capable of conducting its own affairs to require a broadcaster to permit answers to personal attacks in the course of discussing controversial issues, or to require that the political opponents of those endorsed by the station be given a chance to communicate with the

The Court also found no validity in the claim that the Fairness Doctrine's right-of-reply regulations would force broadcasters to censor themselves and to eliminate their coverage of controversial public issues. The Court accepted the FCC argument that this supposed chilling effect "is at best speculative."

By 1974, however, the Supreme Court had adopted a different attitude toward "an enforceable right of access to the press." In *Miami Herald Publishing Co. v. Tornillo*, the Court made clear that *Red Lion*, though not overturned, had little precedential value.[150] *Tornillo* overturned a Florida statute, comparable to the Fairness Doctrine, that gave political candidates a right to reply to personal editorial attacks in newspapers. After *Tornillo*, "the *Red Lion* principle" would only apply to the broadcast media.[151] Without explicitly stating so, the Court in *Tornillo* abandoned the logic of *Red Lion*. Whereas the Court in *Red Lion* saw governmental regulation of the media as a legitimate means to bolster the marketplace of ideas, the Court in *Tornillo* held that "government-enforced right of access inescapably 'dampens the vigor and limits the variety of public debate.'" In moving from *Red Lion* to *Tornillo*, the Court exchanged its humanist view that the state is obligated to oversee discussion for a classical liberal approach that opposes government interference in free speech.[152] The FCC eventually followed the Court's lead and, in 1987, discarded the Fairness Doctrine, arguing that while it had been adopted to promote robust discussion of

---

public. Otherwise, station owners and a few networks would have unfettered power to make time available only to the highest bidders, to communicate only their own views on public issues, people and candidates, and to permit on the air only those with whom they agreed." *Red Lion Co. v. FCC*, 392.

150. *Miami Herald Publishing Co. v. Tornillo*, 418 U.S. 241 (1974).

151. Superficially, *Red Lion* and *Tornillo* can be distinguished by the physical scarcity of broadcast media—which justifies the Fairness Doctrine—and the absence of enforced scarcity in the print media. In fact, however, scarcity is as much a problem in the print media as in the broadcast media: cable television has expanded the electronic media, while the number of competitive daily newspapers continuously shrinks. See Lee C. Bollinger Jr., "Freedom of the Press and Public Access: Toward a Theory of Partial Regulation of the Mass Media," *Michigan Law Review* 75 (1976): 6–17. The Court itself, in *Tornillo*, acknowledged the argument that because newspapers are concentrated in the hands of the few, affirmative governmental action is justified: "Chains of newspapers, national newspapers, national wire and news services, and one-newspaper towns, are the dominant features of a press that has become noncompetitive and enormously powerful and influential in its capacity to manipulate popular opinion and change the course of events." The Court, however, did not explain why scarcity in print media differs from scarcity in electronic media. It did not try to reconcile *Tornillo* with *Red Lion*. Instead, the Court in *Tornillo* ignored *Red Lion*, never even mentioning the case.

152. Nicholson, "Buckley v. Valeo," 337–38.

controversial issues, enforcement of it had actually reduced, rather than enhanced, the discussion of controversial issues of public importance.[153] Thus, at present, the Fairness Doctrine is no longer in effect.

The key legal opinion on campaign reform laws is *Buckley v. Valeo*. In *Buckley*, the Supreme Court reviewed the constitutionality of FECA and sustained all the contribution limits. The Court found that the reform "Act's primary purpose—to limit the actuality and appearance of corruption resulting from large individual financial contributions—[is] . . . a constitutionally sufficient justification" for the contribution limits. The Court minimized any marginal effect these limits might have on First Amendment freedoms, concluding that "the Act's contribution limitations in themselves do not undermine to any material degree the potential for robust and effective discussion." As the Court observed, "the quantity of communication by the contributor does not increase perceptibly with the size of his contribution." In contrast to its ruling on contribution limits, the Court declared unconstitutional all but one of FECA's spending limits. The Court invalidated ceilings on independent expenditures by individuals or groups on behalf of an identified candidate. The Court also invalidated limits on campaign spending by candidates from personal or family resources, as well as limitations on candidates' overall campaign expenditures. Only the expenditure limits on presidential candidates imposed as a condition of acceptance of public funding was upheld.

Although reformers argue that spending limits promote free speech by reducing the competitive inequality between well-financed and poorly financed candidates, the Court declared the restrictions on expenditures to be unconstitutional infringements of the right to political communication: "It is clear that a primary effect of these expenditure limitations is to restrict the quantity of campaign speech by individuals, groups, and candidates. The restrictions, while neutral as to the ideas expressed, limit political expression 'at the core of our electoral process and of First Amendment freedoms.' " In arguing that expenditure limitations unconstitutionally suppress free speech, the Court, in effect, equates money with speech. According to the Court, money is not "a form of conduct related to speech—something roughly equivalent to the physical act of picketing or to the use of a soundtrack."

---

153. In 1985, the FCC concluded that the Fairness Doctrine "chilled" broadcasters' speech and may be unconstitutional. The U.S. Court of Appeals ruled in 1986 that, because the Fairness Doctrine had not been legislatively codified, the FCC had the authority to repeal the Doctrine on its own. In 1987, Congress passed legislation codifying the Doctrine, but President Reagan vetoed the measure, thus permitting the FCC to discard the Fairness Doctrine.

Rather, money is pure speech and, unlike speech-related conduct, can only be restricted in the most extreme circumstances. Why *does* the Court treat money as speech? The Court assumes that "in today's mass society" money is essential for "effective political speech." In other words, the more money spent, the greater the number of issues discussed in a campaign.[154] The Court suggests, however, that it is not primarily concerned with the listener's right to be informed, but the speaker's right to political expression. Thus, *Buckley* ignores the argument that unrestricted campaign spending drowns out the voices of the less affluent, thereby impairing the marketplace of ideas.[155] The Court is not interested here in the humanists' search for truth. For the Court, spending limits restrict the speaker's right to express political ideas to the fullest extent. In the Court's language, a ceiling on expenditures "heavily burdens core First Amendment expression." From *Buckley*'s perspective, individual self-expression cannot coexist with reasonable expenditure limitations.

Despite the difficulties encountered by the Fairness Doctrine and FECA, the drive for market reforms has not abated, although the approach taken in these reform proposals has changed. In contrast to such command-and-control restrictions as the Fairness Doctrine and the legislation invalidated in *Buckley*, characteristic of U.S. law in the 1960s and 1970s, the new reform proposals are generally more voluntary and incentive-based.[156] For example, suggested broadcasting reforms include new FCC guidelines and recommendations—technically non-binding—that promote greater diversity of view; favoring broadcasters seeking licenses who commit themselves to provide free media time for candidates and more public affairs programming; and government subsidies to fund these same goals (81–88). Similarly, new campaign finance reforms are less directly restrictive than the campaign finance laws enacted in FECA. Thus, it has been proposed that *Buckley*'s constitutional concerns may be met by linking public funding to voluntary compliance with campaign spending limits.[157] In this proposal, candidates who adhere to realistic expenditure ceilings, indexed for inflation, will

154. Wright, "Politics and the Constitution," 1005–13; Marlene Arnold Nicholson, "Campaign Financing and Equal Protection," *Stanford Law Review* 26 (1974): 844–45.

155. Nicholson, "Buckley v. Valeo," 336, 353. See also Baker, *Human Liberty and Freedom of Speech*, 297 n. 50, for the argument that the Court in *Buckley* "struck down laws restricting people's use of their money to continue speaking even after their view is 'adequately' expressed in the market place."

156. Cass R. Sunstein, *Democracy and the Problem of Free Speech* (New York: Free Press, 1993), 82–83, 99.

157. See Justice Gary S. Stein, "The First Amendment and Campaign Finance Reform: A

receive significant public funding.[158] And to encourage candidates to accept spending limits, substantial additional public funding would be provided for candidates if their nonparticipating opponents exceed prescribed spending limits. Proponents hope that these new campaign reforms will "restrain the power of money as a force in our electoral process and as a determinant of its outcomes."[159]

Although the fortunes of these particular broadcasting and campaign finance reform proposals are uncertain, the insight that motivates them—that speech is a social act—endures. Undoubtedly, some individualists will continue to focus solely on the speaker, viewing the broadcaster's proprietary rights and the candidate's right to unlimited self-expression as absolute. Nevertheless, other, more communally minded voices, will continue to point out that the speaker does not exercise his or her rights in a vacuum, but alongside other speakers, many of whom, if unaided, will lack any real opportunity to have their messages heard. It is this fact—that speech takes place within a social context—that makes the "marketplace of ideas" a misleading metaphor for free speech. This metaphor conjures up the image of disembodied ideas contending with one another. But ideas are embedded in speech, which is spoken or written by persons, and it is these persons, not the ideas, that contend. This truth—that content cannot be separated from form—is fundamental to classical rhetoric. The Renaissance humanists, as disciples of the rhetorical tradition, understood this. The humanists, therefore, spoke of *sermo*, not the marketplace, when discussing the communal search for truth. It is unlikely, however, that the terminology of the marketplace will soon be abandoned, given the contemporary dominance of the marketplace metaphor. But while the language of the marketplace may remain, the humanist perspective of civil conversation still persists. It lives on in the arguments of all those who believe that speech is too important an activity to leave to chance.

Timely Reconciliation," *Rutgers Law Review* 44 (1992): 767–93; Sunstein, *Democracy and the Problem of Free Speech*, 99–101.

158. The Court in *Buckley* and, later, in *Republican National Committee v. Federal Election Commission*, 445 U.S. 955 (1980), upheld the constitutionality of campaign spending limits imposed as a condition for public financing.

159. U.S. Congress, House, Committee on House Administration, *Entitled the "House of Representatives Campaign Spending Limit and Election Reform Act of 1991,"* H. Rpt. 102–340 (Washington, D.C.: Government Printing Office, 1991).

Selected Bibliography

Abelard, Peter. *Dialogue of a Philosopher with a Jew, and a Christian*. Translated by Piere J. Payer. Mediaeval Sources in Translation 20. Toronto: Pontifical Institute of Mediaeval Studies, 1979.

Ackerman, Bruce A. *Social Justice in the Liberal State*. New Haven: Yale University Press, 1980.

Acontius, Jacobus. *Darkness Discovered or the Devils Secret Stratagems laid open whereby He labors to make havock of the People of God, by his wicked and damnable Designs for destroying the Kingdom of Christ*. London: J. Macock, 1651. Reprint. Delmar, N.Y.: Scholars' Facsimiles & Reprints, 1978.

———. *De Methodo e Opuscoli Religiosi e Filosofici*. Edited by Giorgio Radetti. Edizione Nazionale Dei Classici Del Pensiero Italiano, vol. 6. Florence: Vallechi, 1944.

———. *Satan's Stratagems*. Edited by P. Radin. California State Library Occasional Papers. English Series, no. 5. San Francisco: California State Library, 1940.

———. *Stratagematum Satanae Libri VIII*. Edited by Giorgio Radetti. Edizione Nazionale Dei Classici Del Pensiero Italiano, vol. 7. Florence: Vallechi, 1946.

Acton, John Emerich Edward Dalberg. *Essays on Freedom and Power*. New York: Meridian, 1955.

Adams, Marilyn M. "Intuitive Cognition, Certainty, and Scepticism in William Ockham." *Traditio* 26 (1970): 389–98.

Adams, Robert H. Review of *Catholics, Anglicans, and Puritans: Seventeenth Century Essays*, by Hugh Trevor-Roper. *New York Review of Books,* 14 April 1988, 28–31.

Alan of Lille. *The Art of Preaching*. Cistercian Studies Series, no. 23. Kalamazoo: Cistercian Publications, 1981.

Allen, J. W. *English Political Thought, 1603–1660*. Vol. 1. London: Methuen, 1938.

———. *A History of Political Thought in the Sixteenth Century*. London: Methuen, 1928.

Althaus, Paul. *The Theology of Martin Luther*. Translated by Robert C. Schultz. Philadelphia: Fortress Press, 1966.

Aquinas, Thomas. *Summa theologiae*. Translated by Thomas Gilby. New York: McGraw-Hill, 1974.

Aristotle. *The Complete Works of Aristotle*. Edited by Jonathan Barnes. 2 vols. Princeton: Princeton University Press, 1984.

———. *Nichomachean Ethics*. Edited by Martin Ostwald. Indianapolis: Bobbs-Merrill, 1962.

———. *Aristotle, On Rhetoric: A Theory of Civic Discourse*. Translated by George Kennedy. New York: Oxford University Press, 1991.

Ashcraft, Richard. "Ideology and Class in Hobbes' Political Theory." *Political Theory* 6 (1978): 27–62.

———. "John Locke, Religious Dissent, and the Origins of Liberalism." Paper presented at the Folger Institute Center for the History of British Political Thought, Washington, D.C., March 1986.

———. *Revolutionary Politics and Locke's Two Treatises of Government.* Princeton: Princeton University Press, 1986.

The Attic Nights of Aulus Gellius. Translated by John C. Rolfe. 3 vols. London: William Heinemann, 1927.

Aubrey, John. *Brief Lives.* Edited by Oliver Lawson Dick. London: Secker & Warburg, 1949.

Augustijn, Cornelis. *Erasmus: His Life, Works, and Influence.* Translated by J. C. Grayson. Toronto: University of Toronto Press, 1991.

Augustine of Hippo. *Against the Academicians.* Translated by Sister Mary Patricia Garvey. Mediaeval Philosophical Texts in Translation, no. 2. Milwaukee: Marquette University Press, 1957.

———. *On Christian Doctrine.* Translated by D. W. Robertson Jr. The Library of Liberal Arts. Indianapolis: Bobbs-Merrill, 1958.

———. *On Genesis: Two books on Genesis against the Manichees; and On the Literal Interpretation of Genesis: An Unfinished Book.* Translated by Roland J. Teske, S.J. Washington, D.C.: Catholic University Press of America, 1991.

———. *Letters.* Vol. 4 of *The Fathers of the Church: A New Translation.* Translated by Sister Wilfrid Parsons. New York: Fathers of the Church, 1955.

———. *The Political Writings of St. Augustine.* Edited by Henry Paolucci. South Bend, Ind.: Regnery/Gateway, 1962.

Axtell, James L. *The Educational Writings of John Locke.* Cambridge: Cambridge University Press, 1968.

Bagehot, Walter. "The Metaphysical Basis of Toleration." In *Literary Studies,* ed. R. H. Hutton. London, 1884.

Bainton, Roland H. *Concerning Heretics.* Records of Civilization, no. 22. New York: Columbia University Press, 1935.

———. *Erasmus of Christendom.* New York: Crossroad Publishing, 1969.

———. *The Reformation of the Sixteenth Century.* Boston: Beacon Press, 1952.

———. "Sebastian Castellio and the Toleration Controversy of the Sixteenth Century." In *Persecution and Liberty: Essays in Honor of George Lincoln Burr.* New York: The Century Company, 1931.

———. *Studies on Reformation.* Boston: Beacon Press, 1963.

Baker, E. Edwin. *Human Liberty and Freedom of Speech.* New York: Oxford University Press, 1989.

———. "Scope of the First Amendment Freedom of Speech." *UCLA Law Review* 25 (1978): 964–1040.

Ball, Terrence. "Hobbes' Linguistic Turn." *Polity* 17 (1985): 739–60.

Barendt, Eric. *Freedom of Speech.* Oxford: Clarendon Press, 1985.

Bayle, Pierre. *A Philosophical Commentary on These Words of the Gospel, Luke XIV. 23. "Compel them to come in, that my House may be full."* 2 vols. London: J. Darby, 1708.

———. *Pierre Bayle's Philosophical Commentary: A Modern Translation and Critical Interpretation.* Translated by Amie Godman Tannenbaum. American University Studies, series 5: Philosophy, vol. 19. New York: Peter Lang, 1987.

Bayley, Peter. *French Pulpit Oratory: 1598–1670*. Cambridge: Cambridge University Press, 1980.

Beame, E. M. "The Limits of Toleration in Sixteenth-Century France." *Studies in the Renaissance* 13 (1966): 250–65.

Benrath, Karl. *Bernardino Ochino of Siena: A Contribution Towards the History of the Reformation*. Translated by Helen Zimmern. New York: Robert Carter & Brothers, 1877.

BeVier, Lillian R. "The First Amendment and Political Speech: An Inquiry into the Substance and Limits of Principle." *Stanford Law Review* 30 (1978): 299–358.

Black, Anthony. *Council and Commune: The Conciliar Movement and the Fifteenth-Century Heritage*. London: Burns & Oates, 1979.

Blasi, Vincent. "The First Amendment and the Ideal of Civic Courage: The Brandeis Opinion in *Whitney v. California*." *William and Mary Law Review* 29 (1988): 653–97.

Bodin, Jean. *Address to the Senate and People of Toulouse on Education of Youth in the Commonwealth*. Translated by George Albert Moore. Chevy Chase, Md.: Country Dollar Press, 1965.

———. *On Sovereignty: Four Chapters from the Six Books of the Commonwealth*. Edited and translated by Julian H. Franklin. Cambridge Texts in the History of Political Thought. Cambridge: Cambridge University Press, 1992.

———. *The Six Bookes of a Commonweale*. Translated by Richard Knolles. Edited with an Introduction by Kenneth Douglas McRae. Cambridge: Harvard University Press, 1962.

Bollinger, Lee C., Jr. "Freedom of the Press and Public Access: Toward a Theory of Partial Regulation of the Mass Media." *Michigan Law Review* 75 (1976): 1–42.

———. *The Tolerant Society: Freedom of Speech and Extremist Speech in America*. New York: Oxford University Press, 1986.

Bork, Robert. "Judge Bork Replies." *American Bar Association Journal* 70 (1984): 132.

———. "Neutral Principles and Some First Amendment Problems." *Indiana Law Journal* 47 (1971): 1–35.

Bouwsma, William J. "Changing Assumptions in Later Renaissance Culture." *Viator* 7 (1976): 421–40.

———. *The Culture of Renaissance Humanism*. Washington, D.C.: AHA Pamphlets, 1973.

———. *John Calvin. A Sixteenth-Century Portrait*. New York: Oxford University Press, 1988.

Boyle, Marjorie O'Rourke. "Erasmus and the 'Modern' Question: Was He Semi-Pelagian?" *Archiv für Reformationsgeschichte* 75 (1984): 59–77.

———. *Erasmus on Language and Method in Theology*. Toronto: University of Toronto Press, 1977.

———. *Rhetoric and Reform: Erasmus' Civil Dispute with Luther*. Harvard Historical Monographs, vol. 71. Cambridge: Harvard University Press, 1983.

———. "Weavers, farmers, tailors, travellers, masons, prostitutes, pimps, Turks, little women, and Other Theologians." *Erasmus in English: A Newsletter Published by University of Toronto Press* 3 (1971): 1–7.

Bradshaw, Brendan. "The Christian Humanism of Erasmus." *Journal of Theological Studies* 33 (1982): 411–47.

Brandt, Frithiof. *Thomas Hobbes' Mechanical Conception of Nature.* Copenhagen: Levin & Munksgaard, 1928.

Brennan, Justice William J. "The Supreme Court and the Meiklejohn Interpretation of the First Amendment." *Harvard Law Review* 79 (165): 1–20.

Briggs, E. R. "An Apostle of the Incomplete Reformation: Jacopo Aconcio (1500–1567)." *Proceedings of the Huguenot Society of London* 22 (1976): 481–95.

Bryant, Donald C. "Aspects of the Rhetorical Tradition: The Intellectual Foundation." Parts 1 and 2. *Quarterly Journal of Speech* 36 (1950): 169–76, 326–32.

Burckhardt, Jacob. *The Civilization of the Renaissance in Italy.* 2 vols. New York: Harper & Row, 1958.

Burke, Kenneth. *A Rhetoric of Motives.* Berkeley and Los Angeles: University of California Press, 1969.

Bury, J. B. *A History of Freedom of Thought.* London: Oxford University Press, 1952.

Bush, Douglas. *The Renaissance and English Humanism.* Toronto: University of Toronto Press, 1939.

Byrne, Edmund F. *Probability and Opinion: A Study in the Medieval Presuppositions of Post-Medieval Theories of Probability.* The Hague: Martinus Nijhoff, 1968.

Calvin, John. *The Institutes of the Christian Religion.* Translated by Ford L. Battles and edited by John T. McNeill. 2 vols. London, S.C.M. Press, 1960.

Canavan, Francis. *Freedom of Expression: Purpose as Limit.* Durham, N.C.: Carolina Academic Press, 1984.

Cannon, Walter B. *The Wisdom of the Body.* New York: W.W. Norton, 1939.

Cantimori, Delio. *Eretici italiani del Cinquecento: Ricerche storiche.* 1939. Reprint. Florence: Sansoni, 1967.

Caspari, Fritz. *Humanism and the Social Order in Tudor England.* Chicago: University of Chicago Press, 1954.

Cassander, George. *De officio pii ac publicae tranquillitatis vere amantis viri in hoc religionis dissidio.* 1562.

Cassirer, Ernst, Paul Oskar Kristeller, and John Herman Randall, eds. *The Renaissance Philosophy of Man.* Chicago: University of Chicago Press, 1948.

Castellio, Sebastian. *De arte dubitandi et confidendi ignorandi et sciendi.* Introduction and notes by Elisabeth Feist Hirsch. Studies in Medieval and Reformation Thought, vol. 29. Leiden: E. J. Brill, 1981.

Chafee, Zechariah, Jr. *Free Speech in the United States.* Cambridge: Harvard University Press, 1967.

Cheynell, Francis. "A Speech made at the Funerall of Mr Chillingworths mortall Booke." In *Chillingworthi Novissima: Or the Sicknesse, Heresy, Death, and Buriall of William Chillingworth.* London, 1644.

Chillingworth, William. *The Works of William Chillingworth . . . Containing His Book, Intituled, The Religion of Protestants: A Safe Way to Salvation, Together with His Nine Sermons Preached before the King . . . His Nine Additional Discourses. . . .* 9th ed. London: B. Motte, 1727.

Chomarat, Jacques. *Grammaire et rhetorique chez Erasme.* 2 vols. Paris: Société d'Edition "Les Belles Lettres," 1981.

———. "Grammar and Rhetoric in the *Paraphrases of the Gospels* by Erasmus." *Erasmus of Rotterdam Society Yearbook One* (1981).

Church, Frederic C. *The Italian Reformers: 1534–1564.* New York: Columbia University Press, 1932.

Cicero, Marcus Tullius. *Academica.* Translated by H. Rackham. Loeb Classical Library. 1979.

———. *Brutus.* Translated by G. L. Hendrickson. Loeb Classical Library. 1971.

———. *Cicero's Letters to His Friends.* Translated by D. R. Schackleton Bailey. Foreword by James E. G. Zetzel. Atlanta: Scholars Press, 1978.

———. *De finibus bonorum et malorum.* Translated by H. Rackham. Loeb Classical Library. 1983.

———. *De inventione.* Translated by H. M. Hubbell. Loeb Classical Library. 1976.

———. *De legibus.* Translated by Clinton Walker Keyes. Loeb Classical Library. 1977.

———. *De natura deorum.* Translated by H. Rackham. Loeb Classical Library. 1979.

———. *De officiis.* Translated by Walter Miller. Loeb Classical Library. 1975.

———. *De oratore.* Translated by E. W. Sutton and H. Rackham. Loeb Classical Library. 1976.

———. *De republica.* Translated by Clinton Walker Keyes. Loeb Classical Library. 1977.

———. *Letters to Atticus.* Translated by E. O. Winstedt. Loeb Classical Library. 1918.

———. *On Duties.* Edited by M. T. Griffin and E. M. Atkins. Cambridge Texts in the History of Political Thought. Cambridge: Cambridge University Press, 1991.

———. *Orator.* Translated by H. M. Hubbell. Loeb Classical Library. 1971.

———. *Partitiones oratoriae.* Translated by H. Rackham. Loeb Classical Library. 1982.

———. *Tusculan Disputations.* Translated by J. E. King. Loeb Classical Library. 1971.

Clasen, Claus-Peter. *Anabaptism: A Social History, 1525–1618.* Ithaca: Cornell University Press, 1972.

Coates, Willson H., Hayden V. White, and J. Salwyn Schapiro. *The Emergence of Liberal Humanism: An Intellectual History of Western Europe.* New York: McGraw-Hill, 1966.

Cochrane, Charles Norris. *Thucydides and the Science of History.* New York: Russell & Russell, 1965.

Cole, David. "Agon at Agora: Creative Misreadings in the First Amendment Tradition." *Yale Law Journal* 95 (1986): 857–905.

The Commonitory of Vincent of Lérins, for the Antiquity and Universality of the Catholic Faith Against the Profane Novelties of All Heresies. Translated by Rev. C. A. Heurtley. In *A Select Library of Nicene and Post-Nicene Fathers of the Christian Church.* 2d ser., vol. 11. New York: The Christian Literature Company, 1894.

Condren, Conal. "On the Rhetorical Foundations of *Leviathan.*" *History of Political Thought* 11 (1990): 703–20.

Conley, Thomas M. *Rhetoric in the European Tradition.* New York: Longman, 1990.

Connors, Robert J., Lisa S. Ede, and Andrea A. Lundsford, eds. *Essays on Classical Rhetoric and Modern Discourse.* Carbondale: Southern Illinois University Press, 1984.

Cooley, Thomas McIntyre. *A Treatise on the Constitutional Limitations which Rest Upon the Legislative Power of the States of the American Union.* Boston: 1868. Reprint. New York: Da Capo Press, 1972.

Cope, Edward Meredith. *The Rhetoric of Aristotle with a Commentary.* Revised and edited by John Edwin Sandys. 3 volumes. Cambridge: Cambridge University Press, 1877.

Curry, Thomas J. *The First Freedoms: Church and State in America to the Passage of the First Amendment.* New York: Oxford University Press, 1986.

D'Arcy, Eric. *Conscience and Its Right to Freedom.* London: Sheed & Ward, 1961.

Deane, Herbert. *The Political and Social Ideas of St. Augustine.* New York: Columbia University Press, 1963.

Dillenberger, John, ed. *Martin Luther: Selections from His Writings.* Garden City, N.Y.: Anchor Books, 1961.

Diogenes Laertius. *Lives of Eminent Philosophers.* 2 vols. Translated by R. D. Hicks. Cambridge: Harvard University Press, 1972.

Dionysius of Halicarnassus. *Critical Essays.* 2 vols. Translated by Stephen Usher. Cambridge: Harvard University Press, 1974.

Douglass, R. Bruce, Gerald M. Mara, and Henry S. Richardson, ed. *Liberalism and the Good.* New York: Routledge, 1990.

Downs, Donald Alexander. *Nazis in Skokie: Freedom, Community, and the First Amendment.* Notre Dame: University of Notre Dame Press, 1985.

———. *The New Politics of Pornography.* Chicago: University of Chicago Press, 1989.

Drew, Elizabeth. "Politics and Money II." *New Yorker,* 13 December 1982, 57–111.

Dworkin, Ronald. "Liberalism." In *Public and Private Morality,* ed. Stuart Hampshire. Cambridge: Cambridge University Press, 1978.

———. *A Matter of Principle.* Cambridge: Harvard University Press, 1985.

———. Review of *Make No Law: The Sullivan Case and the First Amendment,* by Anthony Lewis. *New York Review of Books,* 11 June 1992, 55–64.

———. *Taking Rights Seriously.* Cambridge: Harvard University Press, 1978.

———. "What Liberalism Isn't." *New York Review of Books,* 20 January 1983, 47–50.

Eisenach, Eldon J. "Hobbes on Church, State and Religion." *History of Political Thought* 3 (1982): 215–43.

————. *Two Worlds of Liberalism: Religion and Politics in Hobbes*. Chicago: University of Chicago Press, 1981.

Eisler, Riane Tennenhaus. *The Chalice and the Blade: Our History, Our Future*. Cambridge, Mass.: Harper & Row, 1987.

Ely, John Hart. *Democracy and Distrust: A Theory of Judicial Review*. Cambridge: Harvard University Press, 1980.

Emerson, Thomas. *The System of Freedom of Expression*. New York: Random House, 1970.

Erasmus, Desiderius. *Ausgewählte Werke*. Edited by Hajo Holborn with Annemarie Holborn. Munich: C. H. Beck, 1933.

————. *Collected Works of Erasmus*. Toronto: University of Toronto Press, 1974– .

————. *The Colloquies of Erasmus*. Translated by Craig R. Thompson. Chicago: University of Chicago Press, 1965.

————. *Desiderii Erasmi Roterodami Opera Omnia*. Edited by J. Clericus. 10 vols. Leiden, 1703–6.

————. *The Education of a Christian Prince*. Translated with an introduction by Lester K. Born. New York: Columbia University Press, 1936. Reprint. New York: Octagon Books, 1973.

————. *Epistolarum Des. Erasmi libri xxxi*. London, 1642.

————. *The Immense Mercy of God*. Edited by P. Radin. California State Library Occasional Papers. English Series, no. 6, part 1. San Francisco: California State Library, 1940.

————. *Inquisitio de Fide: A Colloquy by Desiderius Erasmus Roterodamus 1524*. Edited with introduction and commentary by Craig R. Thompson. Hamden, Conn.: Archon Books, 1975.

————. *Opera Omnia Desiderii Erasmi Roterodami*. Amsterdam: North Holland Publishing, 1969– .

————. *Opus Epistolarum Des. Erasmi Roterodami*. Edited by P. S. Allen, H. M. Allen, and H. W. Garrod. 12 vols. Oxford: Clarendon Press, 1906–57.

————. *Praise of Folly*. Translated by Betty Radice. Middlesex, England: Penguin Books, 1982.

Faludy, George. *Erasmus*. New York: Stein & Day, 1971.

Farber, Daniel A. "Content Regulation and the First Amendment: A Revisionist View." *Georgetown Law Journal* 68 (1980): 727–63.

Ferguson, Wallace K. "The Attitude of Erasmus Toward Toleration." In *Persecution and Liberty: Essays in Honor of George Lincoln Burr*. New York: The Century Company, 1931.

Ferguson, Wallace K., ed. *Erasmi Opuscula: A Supplement to the Opera Omnia*. The Hague: Martinius Nijoff, 1933.

Finley, John H. *Thucydides*. Cambridge: Harvard University Press, 1942.

Finnis, John M. " 'Reason and Passion': The Constitutional Dialectic of Free Speech and Obscenity." *University of Pennsylvania Law Review* 116 (1967): 222–43.

Fiss, Owen M. "Free Speech and Social Structure." *Iowa Law Review* 71 (1986): 1405–25.

Fleischman, Joel, and Pope McCorkle. "Level-Up Rather Than Level-Down: Toward a New Theory of Campaign Finance Reform." *Journal of Law & Politics* 1 (1984): 211–98.

Fletcher, Harris Francis. *The Intellectual Development of John Milton.* 2 vols. Urbana: University of Illinois Press, 1956–61.

Fortenbaugh, William W. "*Benevoletiam conciliare* and *animos permovere*: Some remarks on Cicero's *De oratore* 2.178–216." *Rhetorica: A Journal of the History of Rhetoric* 6 (1988): 259–73.

France, Peter. *Rhetoric and Truth in France: Descartes to Diderot.* Oxford: Clarendon Press, 1972.

Franklin, Julian H. *Jean Bodin and the Rise of Absolutist Theory.* Cambridge: Cambridge University Press, 1973.

———. *Jean Bodin and the Sixteenth-Century Revolution in the Methodology of Law and History.* New York: Columbia University Press, 1963.

"Free Speech Implications of Campaign Expenditure Ceilings." *Harvard Civil Rights–Civil Liberties Law Review* 7 (1972): 214–59.

Friendly, Fred W. *The Good Guys, The Bad Guys, and the First Amendment: Free Speech vs. Fairness in Broadcasting.* New York: Vintage Books, 1977.

Fumaroli, Marc. *L'Âge de l'éloquence: Rhétorique et 'res literaria' de la Renaissance au seuil de l'époque classique.* Geneva: Libraire Droz, 1980.

Funkenstein, Amos. *Theology and the Scientific Imagination from the Middle Ages to the Seventeenth Century.* Princeton: Princeton University Press, 1986.

Garnsey, Peter. "Religious Toleration in Classical Antiquity." In *Persecution and Toleration*, ed. W. J. Sheils. Oxford: Basil Blackwell, 1984.

Garver, Eugene. *Machiavelli and the History of Prudence.* Madison: University of Wisconsin Press, 1987.

Gauthier, David P. *The Logic of Leviathan.* Oxford, Clarendon Press, 1969.

Gibson, Michael T. "The Supreme Court and Freedom of Expression from 1791 to 1917." *Fordham Law Review* 45 (1986): 263–333.

Gilbert, Neal W. *Renaissance Concepts of Method.* New York: Columbia University Press, 1963.

Gilmore, Myron P. "De Modis Disputandi: The Apologetic Works of Erasmus." In *Florilegium Historiale: Essays Presented to Wallace K. Ferguson*, ed. J. G. Rowe and W. H. Stockdale. Toronto: University of Toronto Press, 1971.

Gimbutas, Marija Alseikaite. *The Gods and Goddesses of Old Europe: 7000 to 3500 B.C. Myths, Legends, and Cult Images.* Berkeley and Los Angeles: University of California Press, 1974.

Gogan, Brian. *The Common Corps of Christendom: Ecclesiological Themes in the Writings of Sir Thomas Moore.* Studies in the History of Christian Thought, vol. 26. Leiden: E. J. Brill, 1982.

Goldsmith, M. M. *Hobbes's Science of Politics.* New York: Columbia University Press, 1966.

Gottlieb, Stephen E. "In the Name of Patriotism: The Constitutionality of 'Bending' History in Public Secondary Schools." *New York University Law Review* 62 (1987): 497–578.

Gray, Hannah H. "Renaissance Humanism: The Pursuit of Eloquence." *Journal of the History of Ideas* 24 (1963): 497–514.

Green, Peter. *Alexander to Actium: The Historical Evolution of the Hellenistic Age.* Berkeley and Los Angeles: University of California Press, 1990.

Greenawalt, Kent. *Speech, Crime, and the Uses of Language.* New York: Oxford University Press, 1989.

Grimaldi, William M. A., S. J. *Aristotle, Rhetoric I: A Commentary.* New York: Fordham University Press, 1980.

———. *Studies in the Philosophy of Aristotle's Rhetoric.* In *Hermes: Zeitschrift für Klassische Philologie.* Wiesbaden: Franz Steiner, 1972.

Grube, G.M.A. *A Greek Critic: Demetrius on Style.* Toronto: University of Toronto Press, 1961.

Guggisberg, Hans R. "The Defense of Religious Toleration and Religious Liberty in Early Modern Europe: Arguments, Pressures, and Some Consequences." *History of European Ideas* 4 (1983): 35–50.

Guthrie, W.K.C. *Socrates.* Cambridge: Cambridge University Press, 1971.

———. *The Sophists.* Cambridge: Cambridge University Press, 1971.

Halevy, Yehuda. *The Kosari of R. Yehuda Haleví.* Translated, annotated, and introduced by Yehuda Even Shmuel. Tel-Aviv: Dvir Publishing, 1972.

Haller, William, ed. *Tracts on Liberty in the Puritan Revolution.* Records of Civilization: Sources and Studies, no. 18. 3 vols. New York: Columbia University Press, 1934.

Haller, William, and Godfrey Davies, eds. *The Leveller Tracts, 1647–1653.* Gloucester, Mass.: Peter Smith, 1964.

Harel, Alon. "Bigotry, Pornography, and the First Amendment: A Theory of Unprotected Speech." *Southern California Law Review* 65 (1992): 1887–1931.

Harwood, John T., ed. *The Rhetorics of Thomas Hobbes and Bernard Lamy.* Carbondale: Southern Illinois University Press, 1986.

Hassinger, Erich. *Studien zu Jacobus Acontius.* Berlin: Grünewald, 1934.

Heurtly, C. A., trans. *The Commonality of Vincent of Lerins, for the Antiquity and Universality of the Catholic Faith Against the Profane Novelties of All Heresies.* In *A Select Library of Nicene and Post-Nicene Fathers of the Christian Church.* 2d series, vol. 11. New York: The Christian Literature Company, 1894.

Himelick, Raymond. *The Enchiridion of Erasmus.* Gloucester, Mass.: Peter Smith, 1970.

Hirzel, Rudolf. *Der Dialog: Ein literarhistorischer Versuch.* 2 vols. Leipzig, 1895. Reprint. Hildesheim: Georg Olms, 1963.

Hobbes, Thomas. *De Cive or The Citizen.* Edited by Sterling P. Lamprecht. Westport, Conn.: Greenwood Press, 1982.

———. *A Dialogue between a Philosopher and a Student of the Common Laws of England.* Edited with an introduction by Joseph Cropsey. Chicago: University of Chicago Press, 1971.

———. *The Elements of Law.* Edited by Ferdinand Toennies. Cambridge: Cambridge University Press, 1928.

------. *The English Works of Thomas Hobbes of Malmesbury.* Edited by Sir William Molesworth. 11 vols. London: Bohn, 1839–45.

------. *Hobbes's Thucydides.* Edited by Richard Schlatter. New Brunswick: Rutgers University Press, 1975.

------. *Leviathan.* Edited by C. B. Macpherson. New York: Penguin Books, 1968.

Hoffmann, Manfred. "Erasmus and Religious Toleration." *Erasmus of Rotterdam Society Yearbook Two* (1982).

------. "Erasmus on Free Will: An Issue Revisited." *Erasmus of Rotterdam Society Yearbook Ten* (1990).

Hooker, Richard. *The Folger Library Edition of the Works of Richard Hooker.* Edited by W. Speed Hill. 2 vols. Cambridge: Harvard University Press, 1977.

------. *The Works of Mr. Richard Hooker . . . in Eight Books of Ecclesiastical Polity.* London: J. Best, 1662.

Horner, Winifred Byron, ed. *The Present State of Scholarship in Historical and Contemporary Rhetoric.* Columbia: University of Missouri Press, 1983.

Howell, Wilbur Samuel. *Logic and Rhetoric in England, 1500–1700.* Princeton: Princeton University Press, 1956.

Howes, Raymond F., ed. *Historical Studies of Rhetoric and Rhetoricians.* Ithaca: Cornell University Press, 1961.

Huizinga, J. *Erasmus of Rotterdam.* London: Phaidon Press, 1952.

Hunter, Howard Owen. "Problems in Search of Principles: The First Amendment in the Supreme Court from 1791–1930." *Emory Law Journal* 35 (1986): 59–137.

Hyde, Edward, earl of Clarendon. *The Life of Edward Earl of Clarendon.* Oxford: Clarendon Press, 1759.

Hyman, J. D. *William Chillingworth and the Theory of Toleration.* Cambridge: Harvard University Press, 1931.

Ijsseling, Samuel. *Rhetoric and Philosophy in Conflict: An Historical Survey.* The Hague: Martinus Nijhoff, 1976.

Ingber, Stanley. "The Marketplace of Ideas: A Legitimizing Myth." *Duke Law Journal,* 1984: 1–91.

Isocrates. *Against the Sophists.* Translated by George Norlin. Loeb Classical Library. 1982.

------. *Antidosis.* Translated by George Norlin. Loeb Classical Library. 1982.

------. *Areopagiticus.* Translated by George Norlin. Loeb Classical Library. 1982.

------. *Panegyricus.* Translated by George Norlin. Loeb Classical Library. 1980.

Jacobson, David L., ed. *The English Libertarian Heritage: From the Writings of John Trenchard and Thomas Gordon in the Independent Whig and Cato's Letters.* Indianapolis: Bobbs-Merrill, 1965.

Jardine, Lisa. "Lorenzo Valla: Academic Skepticism and the New Humanist Dialectic." In *The Skeptical Tradition,* ed. Myles Burnyeat. Berkeley and Los Angeles: University of California Press, 1983.

Jean Bodin: Actes du Colloque Interdisciplinaire d'Angers, 24 au 27 mai 1984. 2 vols. Angers: Presses de l'Université D'Angers, 1985.

Jean Bodin: Proceedings of the International Conference on Bodin in Munich. Munich: C. H. Beck, 1973.

Jebb, R. C. *The Attics Orators from Antiphon to Isaeus.* Vol. 1. London: Macmillan, 1893.

Jedin, Hubert. *Geschichte des Konzils von Trient.* 2 vols. Freiberg: Herder, 1951–57.

———. *Reformation and Counter Reformation.* Vol. 5 of *History of the Church,* ed. Hubert Jedin and John Dolan. New York: Seabury Press, 1980.

Jefferson, Thomas. *Notes on the State of Virginia.* Edited by William Peden. Chapel Hill: University on North Carolina Press, 1955.

———. *The Papers of Thomas Jefferson.* Edited by Julian P. Boyd. 2 vols. Princeton: Princeton University Press, 1950.

Jerome, Saint. *Letters of St. Jerome.* Translated by Charles Christopher Mierow. Ancient Christian Writers, no. 33. Westminster, Md.: The Newman Press, 1963.

Johnson, Nan. "Ethos and the Aims of Rhetoric." In *Essays on Classical Rhetoric and Modern Discourse,* ed. Robert J. Connors, Lisa S. Ede, and Andrea A. Lunsford. Carbondale: Southern Illinois University Press, 1984.

Johnston, David. *The Rhetoric of Leviathan: Thomas Hobbes and the Politics of Cultural Transformation.* Princeton: Princeton University Press, 1986.

Jordan, W. K. *The Development of Religious Toleration in England.* 4 vols. London: George Allen & Unwin, 1932–1940. Reprint. Gloucester, Mass.: Peter Smith, 1965.

Kahn, Victoria. "Authority and Interpretation in the Renaissance: Erasmus, Sidney, and Montaigne." Ph.D. diss., Yale University, 1979.

———. *Rhetoric, Prudence, and Skepticism in the Renaissance.* Ithaca: Cornell University Press, 1985.

Kalven, Harry, Jr. "The New York Times Case: A Note on the 'Central Meaning of the First Amendment.'" *Supreme Court Review,* 1964: 199–221.

———. *A Worthy Tradition: Freedom of Speech in America.* Edited by Jamie Kalven. New York: Harper & Row, 1988.

Kamen, Henry. *The Rise of Toleration.* London: World University Library, 1967.

Keen, Ralph, trans. *A Melancthon Reader.* New York: Peter Lang, 1988.

Kennedy, George. *The Art of Persuasion in Greece.* Princeton: Princeton University Press, 1974.

———. *The Art of Rhetoric in the Roman World.* Princeton: Princeton University Press, 1972.

———. *Classical Rhetoric and Its Christian and Secular Tradition from Ancient to Modern Times.* Chapel Hill: University of North Carolina Press, 1980.

Kerferd, G. B. "What Does the Wise Man Know?" In *The Stoics,* ed. John Rist. Berkeley and Los Angeles: University of California Press, 1978.

Kleinhans, Robert G. *"Ecclesiastes Sive De Ratione Concionandi."* In *Essays on the Works of Erasmus,* ed. Richard L. DeMolen. New Haven: Yale University Press, 1978.

———. "Erasmus' Doctrine of Preaching, A Study of *Ecclesiastes, Sive De Ratione Concionandi."* Ph.D. diss., Princeton Theological Seminary, 1968.

Klosko, George. "Rational Persuasion in Plato's Political Theory." *History of Political Thought* 7 (1986): 15–31.

Knott, Edward [Matthew Wilson, pseud.]. *Mercy and Truth, or Charity Maintained by Catholiques*. St. Omer, 1634.

Köhler, Walther. "Geistesahnen des Johannes Acontius." In *Festgabe von Fachgenossen und Freunden Karl Mueller zum Siebzigsten Geburtstag Dargebracht*. Tübingen: J.C.B. Mohr, 1922.

Kretzmann, Norman, Anthony Kenny, and Jan Pinborg, eds. *The Cambridge History of Later Medieval Philosophy*. Cambridge: Cambridge University Press, 1982.

Kretzmer, David. "Freedom of Speech and Racism." *Cardozo Law Review* 8 (1987): 445–513.

Kristeller, Paul Oskar. *Renaissance Thought: The Classic, Scholastic, and Humanist Strains*. New York: Harper & Row, 1961.

———. *Renaissance Thought and Its Sources*. Edited by Michael Mooney. New York: Columbia University Press, 1979.

Krook, Dorothea. "Thomas Hobbes's Doctrine of Meaning and Truth." *Philosophy: The Journal of the Royal Institute of Philosophy* 31 (1956): 3–22.

Kuntz, Marion Daniels. "Harmony and the Heptaplomeres of Jean Bodin." *Journal of the History of Philosophy* 12 (1974): 31–41.

Kuntz, Marion Leathers. "The Home of Coronaeus in Jean Bodin's *Colloquium Heptaplomeres*: An Example of a Venetian Academy." In *Acta Conventus Neo-Latini Bononiensis*, Proceedings of the Fourth International Congress of Neo-Latin Studies, ed. R. J. Schoeck. Bologna, 26 August to 1 September 1979.

Kuntz, Marion Leathers Daniels. *Colloquium of the Seven about Secrets of the Sublime*. Princeton: Princeton University Press, 1975.

Lanham, Richard A. *A Handlist of Rhetorical Terms: A Guide for Students of English Literature*. Berkeley and Los Angeles: University of California Press, 1968.

Lasson, Kenneth. "Group Libel Versus Free Speech: When Big Brother *Should* Butt In." *Duquesne Law Review* 23 (1984): 78–130.

Lawrence, Charles R., III. "If He Hollers Let Him Go: Regulating Racist Speech on Campus." *Duke Law Journal*, 1990: 431–83.

Lecky, William. *The History of the Rise and Influence of the Spirit of Rationalism in Europe*. Bombay: Longmans, Green, 1913.

Lecler, Joseph, S.J. "Religious Freedom: An Historical Survey," translated by Theodore L. Westow. In *Concilium: Theology in the Age of Renewal*. In *Religious Freedom, Canon Law*. Edited by Neophytos Edelby and Teodoro Jiménez-Urresti. New York: Paulist Press, 1966: 3–20.

———. *Toleration and the Reformation*. Translated by T. L. Westow. 2 vols. New York: Association Press, 1960.

Lerner, Gerda. *The Creation of Patriarchy*. New York: Oxford University Press, 1986.

Levack, Brian P. *The Witch-Hunt in Early Modern Europe*. London: Longman, 1987.

Levy, Leonard. *Emergence of a Free Press*. New York: Oxford University Press, 1985.

Libanius. *Libanii opera.* Edited by Richard Foerster. 12 vols. Leipzig: B. G. Teubner, 1903–27.

Liebeschuetz, J.H.W.G. *Continuity and Change in Roman Religion.* Oxford: Oxford University Press, 1979.

Little, David. "Roger Williams and the Separation of Church and State." In *Religion and the State: Essays in Honor of Leo Pfeffer,* ed. James E. Wood Jr. Waco, Tex.: Baylor University Press, 1985.

———. "The Western Tradition." In *Human Rights and the Conflicts of Culture: Western and Islamic Perspectives on Religious Liberty,* ed. David Little, John Kelsay, and Abdulaziz Sachedina. Columbia: University of South Carolina Press, 1988.

Locke, John. *An Early Draft of Locke's Essay.* Edited by R. I. Aaron and Jocelyn Gibb. Oxford: Clarendon Press, 1936.

———. *Epistola de Tolerantia, A Letter on Toleration.* Translated from the Latin by J. W. Gough, and edited by Raymond Klibansky. Oxford: Clarendon Press, 1968.

———. *An Essay Concerning Human Understanding.* Edited with an introduction by Peter H. Nidditch. Oxford: Clarendon Press, 1975.

———. *The Reasonableness of Christianity.* Edited by I. T. Ramsey. London: Adam and Charles Black, 1958.

———. *The Works of John Locke in Ten Volumes.* Vol. 6. 11th ed. London: T. Davison, 1812.

Lowenstein, Daniel Hays. "On Campaign Finance Reform: The Root of All Evil Is Deeply Rooted." *Hofstra Law Review* 2 (1989): 301–67.

Lowinsky, Edward E. *Secret Chromatic Art in the Netherlands Motet.* Translated by Carl Buchman. New York: Russell & Russell, 1946.

Luther, Martin. *Luther's Works.* Edited by Jaroslav Pelikan (vols. 1–30) and Helmut T. Lehmann (vols. 31–55). 55 vols. St. Louis: Concordia Press (vols. 1–30) and Philadelphia: Fortress Press (vols. 31–55), 1955–82.

———. *Martin Luther's Werke. Kritische Gesamtausgabe.* 58 vols. Weimar: Hermann Böhlaus, 1883–1908. Reprint. Graz: Akademische Druck und Verlagsanstalt. 1964– .

Lyon, T. *The Theory of Religious Liberty in England: 1603–39.* London: Cambridge University Press, 1937.

Machiavelli, Niccolò. *The Discourses of Niccolò Machiavelli.* Translated by Leslie J. Walker. London: Routledge and Kegan Paul, 1950.

MacKinnon, Catharine A. *Feminism Unmodified: Discourses on Life and Law.* Cambridge: Harvard University Press, 1987.

Mahoney, Edward P. *Philosophy and Humanism: Renaissance Essays in Honor of Paul Oskar Kristeller.* Leiden: E. J. Brill, 1976.

des Maizeaux, P. *An Historical and Critical Account of the Life of William Chillingworth.* London, 1725.

Manschreck, Clyde L. "The Role of Melancthon in the Adiaphora Controversy." *Archiv für Reformationsgeschichte* 48 (1957): 165–81.

Mansfield, Bruce E. "Erasmus in the Nineteenth Century: The Liberal Tradition." *Studies in the Renaissance* 15 (1968): 193–219.

Marcuse, Herbert. "Repressive Tolerance." In *A Critique of Pure Tolerance*, ed. Robert Paul Wolff, Barrington Moore Jr., and Herbert Marcuse. Boston: Beacon Press, 1969.

Marrou, H. I. *A History of Education in Antiquity*. Translated by George Lamb. Madison: University of Wisconsin Press, 1956.

Marsh, David. *The Quattrocento Dialogue: Classical Tradition and Humanist Innovation*. Cambridge: Harvard University Press, 1980.

Marshall, John. "The Ecclesiology of the Latitude-Men, 1660–1689: Stillingfleet, Tillotson and 'Hobbism.'" *Journal of Ecclesiastical History* 36 (1985): 407–27.

Martin, John. *Venice's Hidden Enemies: Italian Heretics in a Renaissance City*. Berkeley and Los Angeles: University of California Press, 1993.

Matsuda, Mari J. "Public Response to Racist Speech: Considering the Victim's Story." *Michigan Law Review* 87 (1989): 2320–81.

McConica, J. K. "Erasmus and the Grammar of Consent." In *Scrinium Erasmianum*, ed. J. Coppens. Vol 2. Leiden: E. J. Brill, 1969.

McCutcheon, R. R. "The *Responsio ad Lutherum*: Thomas More's Inchoate Dialogue with Heresy." *Sixteenth Century Journal* 22 (1991): 77–90.

McGrath, Alister. *The Intellectual Origins of the European Reformation*. Oxford: Basil Blackwell, 1987.

McKeon, Richard. *Rhetoric: Essays in Invention & Discovery*. Edited by Mark Backman. Woodridge, Conn.: Ox Bow Press, 1987.

McSorley, Harry J. "Erasmus and the Primacy of the Roman Pontiff: Between Concilianism and Papism." *Archiv für Reformationsgeschichte* 65 (1974): 37–54.

Meiklejohn, Alexander. "The First Amendment Is an Absolute." *Supreme Court Review*, 1961: 245–66.

———. *Free Speech and Its Relation to Self-Government*. Port Washington, N.Y.: Kennikat Press, 1972.

Melancthon, Philip. *Corpus Reformatorum*. Edited by Carolus Gottlieb Bretschneider. Halle, Germany: C. A. Schwetschke & Sons, 1846; rpt., New York, 1963.

———. *De arte concionandi forumulae, ut breves ita doctae & piae*. London: Henry Bynneman, 1570.

Menchi, Silvana Seidel. *Erasmo in Italia: 1520–1580*. Turin: Bollati Boringhieri, 1987.

Mendus, Susan, ed. *Justifying Toleration: Conceptual and Historical Perspectives*. Cambridge: Cambridge University Press, 1988.

Mensching, Gustav. *Tolerance and Truth in Religion*. Translated by Hans-J. Klimkeit. University: University of Alabama Press, 1971.

Mesnard, Pierre. "Jean Bodin à Toulouse." In *Bibliothèque d'Humanisme et Renaissance* 12 (1950): 31–59.

Meyers, Marvin, ed. *The Mind of the Founder: Sources of the Political Thought of James Madison*. Rev. ed. Hanover: University Press of New England, 1981.

Michel, Alain. *Rhetorique et philosophie chez Ciceron: Essai sur les fondements philosophique de l'art de persuader*. Paris: Presses Universitaires de France, 1960.

Mill, John Stuart. *Collected Works of John Stuart Mill*. Edited by John M. Robson and Jack Stillinger. Vol. 1. Toronto: University of Toronto Press, 1981.

———. *Collected Works of John Stuart Mill*. Edited by J. M. Robson. Vol. 18. Toronto: University of Toronto Press, 1977.

Miller, Perry. *The New England Mind: The Seventeenth Century*. Cambridge: Harvard University Press, 1982.

Milton, John. *Areopagitica*. Cambridge: Cambridge University Press, 1928.

———. *Complete Prose Works of John Milton*. 7 vols. New Haven: Yale University Press, 1953–74.

Mintz, Samuel I. *The Hunting of Leviathan*. Cambridge: Cambridge University Press, 1962.

Missner, Marshall. "Skepticism and Hobbes's Political Philosophy." *Journal of the History of Ideas* 44 (1983): 407–27.

Mitchell, W. Fraser. *English Pulpit Oratory from Andrewes to Tillotson*. London: Society for Promoting Christian Knowledge, 1932.

Monfasani, John. "Humanism and Rhetoric." In *Renaissance Humanism: Foundations, Forms, and Legacy*, ed. Albert Rabil Jr. 3 vols. Philadelphia: University of Pennsylvania Press, 1988.

Montuori, John. *John Locke on Toleration and the Unity of God*. Amsterdam: J. G. Gieben, 1983.

Mooney, Michael. *Vico in the Tradition of Rhetoric*. Princeton: Princeton University Press, 1985.

More, Thomas. *The Complete Works of St. Thomas More*. Vol. 4. Edited by Edward Surtz, S.J., and J. H. Hexter. New Haven: Yale University Press, 1965.

———. *The Complete Works of St. Thomas More*. Vol. 5, part 1. Edited by John M. Headley. New Haven: Yale University Press, 1969.

———. *The Complete Works of St. Thomas More*. Vol. 6, part 2. Edited by Thomas M. C. Lawler, Germain Marc'hadour, and Richard Marius. New Haven: Yale University Press, 1981.

———. *Utopia*. Translated by Paul Turner. Baltimore: Penguin Books, 1965.

Morgan, Edmund S. *Roger Williams: The Church and the State*. New York: Harcourt, Brace & World, 1967.

Morgan, Robin. *Going Too Far: The Personal Chronicle of a Feminist*. New York: Random House, 1977.

Murphy, James J. *Renaissance Rhetoric: A Short-Title Catalogue*. New York: Garland Publishing, 1981.

———. *Rhetoric in the Middle Ages: A History of Rhetorical Theory from St. Augustine to the Renaissance*. Berkeley and Los Angeles: University of California Press, 1974.

———, ed. *Medieval Eloquence: Studies in the Theory and Practice of Medieval Rhetoric*. Berkeley and Los Angeles: University of California Press, 1978.

———, ed. *Renaissance Eloquence: Studies in the Theory and Practice of Renaissance Rhetoric*. Berkeley and Los Angeles: University of California Press, 1983.

Murray, Robert H. *Erasmus and Luther: Their Attitude to Toleration.* New York: Burt Franklin, 1972.

Neisel, Wilhelm. *The Theology of Calvin.* Translated by Harold Knight. Philadelphia: Westminster Press, 1956.

Nelson, Ernest W. "The Theory of Persecution." In *Persecution and Liberty: Essays in Honor of George Lincoln Burr.* New York: The Century Company, 1931.

The New Cambridge Modern History. Vol. 1, *The Renaissance (1493–1520).* Edited by G. R. Elton. Cambridge: Cambridge University Press, 1957.

——. Vol. 2, *The Reformation (1520–59).* Edited by G. R. Elton. Cambridge: Cambridge University Press, 1958.

——. Vol. 3, *The Counter-Reformation and Price Revolution (1559–1610).* Edited by W. B. Wernham. Cambridge: Cambridge University Press, 1968.

——. Vol. 4, *The Decline of Spain and the Thirty Years War (1609–48/59).* Edited by J. P. Cooper. Cambridge: Cambridge University Press, 1970.

Nicholson, Marlene Arnold. "Buckley v. Valeo: The Constitutionality of the Federal Election Campaign Act Amendments of 1974." *Wisconsin Law Review,* 1977: 323–74.

——. "Campaign Financing and Equal Protection." *Stanford Law Review* 26 (1974): 815–54.

North, J. A. "Religious Toleration in Republican Rome." *Proceedings of the Cambridge Philological Society* 25 (1979): 85–103.

Nussbaum, Martha C. Review of *Socrates, Ironist and Moral Philosopher,* by Gregory Vlastos. *The New Republic,* 16 and 23 September 1991, 34–40.

Ober, Josiah. *Mass and Elite in Democratic Athens: Rhetoric, Ideology, and the Power of the People.* Princeton: Princeton University Press, 1989.

Oberman, Heiko. *The Harvest of Medieval Theology: Gabriel Biel and Late Medieval Nominalism.* Cambridge: Harvard University Press, 1967.

——. *Luther: Man between God and the Devil.* Translated by Eileen Walliser-Schwarzbart. New Haven: Yale University Press, 1989.

Ochino, Bernardino. *Dialogi XXX in duos libros.* 2 vols. Basel, 1563.

O'Donnell, Anne M. "Rhetoric and Style in Erasmus' *Enchiridion Militis Christiani.*" *Studies in Philology* 77 (1980): 26–49.

Oehler, Klaus. "Der Consensus omnium als Kriterium der Wahrheit in der antiken Philosophie und der Patristik." *Antike und Abendland* 10 (1961): 103–29.

Olin, John C., ed. *Christian Humanism and the Reformation.* Gloucester, Mass.: Peter Smith, 1973.

Olin, John C., James D. Smart, and Robert E. McNally, S.J. *Luther, Erasmus and the Reformation: A Catholic-Protestant Reappraisal.* New York: Fordham University Press, 1969.

Oltramare, André. *Les Origines de la Diatribe Romaine.* Geneva: Imprimeries Populaire, 1926.

O'Malley, Charles Donald. *Jacopo Aconcio.* Translated into Italian by Delio Cantimori. Rome: Edizioni Di Storia and Letteratura, 1955.

O'Malley, John W., S.J. "Erasmus and the History of Sacred Rhetoric: The *Ecclesiastes* of 1535." *Erasmus of Rotterdam Society Yearbook Five* (1985).

———. "Luther the Preacher." In *The Martin Luther Quincentennial*, ed. Gerhard Dünnhaupt. Detroit: Wayne State University Press, 1985.

———. *Praise and Blame in Renaissance Rome: Rhetoric, Doctrine and Reform in the Sacred Orators of the Papal Court, c. 1450–1521*. Duke Monographs in Medieval and Renaissance Studies, 3. Durham: Duke University Press, 1979.

Ong, Walter J., S.J. "Hobbes and Talon's Ramist Rhetoric in England." *Transactions of the Cambridge [England] Bibliography Society* 1 (1951): 260–69.

———. *Ramus, Method, and the Decay of Dialogue: From the Art of Discourse to the Art of Reason*. Cambridge: Harvard University Press, 1983.

Orr, Robert R. *Reason and Authority: The Thought of William Chillingworth*. Oxford: Clarendon Press, 1967.

Owen, John. *Truth and Innocence Vindicated: In a Survey of a Discourse Concerning Ecclesiastical Polity; and the Authority of the Civil Magistrate over the Consciences of Subjects in Matters of Religion*. London, 1669.

Pagden, Anthony, ed. *The Languages of Political Theory in Early-Modern Europe*. Cambridge: Cambridge University Press, 1987.

Partee, Charles. *Calvin and Classical Philosophy*. Studies in the History of Christian Thought, edited by Heiko A. Oberman, vol. 14. Leiden: E. J. Brill, 1977.

Payne, John B. *Erasmus: His Theology of Sacraments*. Richmond, Va.: John Knox Press, 1970.

Perelman, C., and L. Olbrechts-Tyteca. *The New Rhetoric: A Treatise on Argumentation*. Translated by John Wilkinson and Purcell Weaver. Notre Dame: University of Notre Dame Press, 1969.

Pérez-Ramos, Antonio. *Francis Bacon's Idea of Science and the Maker's Knowledge Tradition*. Oxford: Clarendon Press, 1988.

Perkins, William. *The Art of Prophecying or A Treatise Concerning The Sacred and Onely True Manner and Methode of Preaching*. Translated by Thomas Tuke. Vol. 2 of *Works*. London: John Legatt, 1631.

Peters, Edward, ed. *Heresy and Authority in Medieval Europe*. Philadelphia: University of Pennsylvania Press, 1980.

Pineas, Rainer. "Thomas More's Use of the Dialogue Form as a Weapon of Religious Controversy." *Studies in the Renaissance* 7 (1960): 193–206.

Plato. *The Collected Dialogues of Plato*. Edited by Edith Hamilton and Huntington Cairns. Princeton: Princeton University Press, 1985.

Pliny the Younger. *The Letters of the Younger Pliny*. Translated with an introduction by Betty Radice. Harmondsworth: Penguin Books, 1969.

Pocock, J.G.A. *The Machiavellian Moment: Florentine Political Thought and the Atlantic Republican Tradition*. Princeton: Princeton University Press, 1975.

Poliziano, Angelo. *Opera omnia Angeli Politiani*. Venice: Aldine Press, 1498.

Popkin, Richard H. *The High Road to Pyrrhonism*. Edited by Richard A. Watson and James E. Force. Studies in Hume and Scottish Philosophy, no. 2. San Diego: Austin Hill Press, 1980.

———. *The History of Scepticism from Erasmus to Spinoza*. Berkeley and Los Angeles: University of California Press, 1979.

———. "Hobbes and Scepticism." In *History of Philosophy in the Making: A*

Symposium of Essays to Honor Professor James D. Collins on his 65th Birthday by his Colleagues and Friends, ed. Linus J. Thro. Lanham, Washington, D.C.: University Press of America, 1982, pp. 133–48.

Post, Robert C. "The Constitutional Concept of Public Discourse: Outrageous Opinion, Democratic Deliberation, and *Hustler Magazine v. Falwell.*" *Harvard Law Review*, 103 (1990): 601–86.

———. "Cultural Heterogeneity and Law: Pornography, Blasphemy, and the First Amendment." *California Law Review* 76 (1988): 297–335.

———. "Defaming Public Officials: On Doctrine and Legal History." *American Bar Foundation Research Journal*, 1987: 539–57.

———. "Racist Speech, Democracy, and the First Amendment." *William and Mary Law Review* 32 (1991): 267–327.

Preus, Mary C. *Eloquence and Ignorance in Augustine's "On the Nature and Origin of the Soul."* American Academy of Religion Academy Series, ed. Carl A. Raschke, no. 51. Scholars Press: Atlanta, 1985.

Puttenham, George. *The Arte of English Poesie.* Edited by Gladys Doidge Willcock and Alice Walker. Cambridge: Cambridge University Press, 1936.

Quintilian, M. Fabius. *Institutio oratoria.* Translated by H. E. Butler. Loeb Classical Library. 1980.

Rabban, David M. "The First Amendment in Its Forgotten Years." *Yale Law Journal* 90 (1981): 514–95.

Rabil, Albert, Jr. "Desiderius Erasmus." In *Renaissance Humanism: Foundations, Forms, and Legacy*, 3 vols., ed. Albert Rabil Jr. Philadelphia: University of Pennsylvania Press, 1988.

Rahe, Paul A. *Republics Ancient and Modern: Classical Republicanism and the American Revolution.* Chapel Hill: University of North Carolina Press, 1992.

Rawls, John. *A Theory of Justice.* Cambridge: Harvard University Press, 1971.

Redish, Martin. "The Content Distinction in First Amendment Analysis." *Stanford Law Review* 34 (1981): 113–51.

———. *Freedom of Expression: A Critical Analysis.* Charlottesville, Va.: Michie, 1984.

Reik, Miriam. *The Golden Lands of Thomas Hobbes.* Detroit: Wayne State University Press, 1977.

Remer, Gary. "Dialogues of Toleration: Erasmus and Bodin." *Review of Politics* 56 (1994): 305–36.

———. "Hobbes, the Rhetorical Tradition, and Toleration." *Review of Politics* 54 (1992): 5–33.

———. "Humanism, Liberalism, and the Skeptical Case for Religious Toleration." *Polity* 25 (1992): 21–43.

———. "Rhetoric and the Erasmian Defence of Religious Toleration." *History of Political Thought* 10 (1989): 377–403.

Renaudet, Augustin. *Etudes Erasmiennes.* Paris: Libraire E. Droz, 1939.

Rhetores latini minores. Edited by Charles Halm. Leipzig: B. G. Teubner, 1863: Reprint. Frankfurt am Main: Minerva, 1964.

Rhetorica ad Herennium. Translated by Harry Caplan. Loeb Classical Library. 1954.

Richards, David A. J. *Toleration and the Constitution*. New York: Oxford University Press, 1986.

Rist, J. M. *Stoic Philosophy*. Cambridge: Cambridge University Press, 1969.

de Romilly, Jacqueline. *A Short History of Greek Literature*. Translated by Lillian Doherty. Chicago: University of Chicago Press, 1985.

Rose, Paul Lawrence. *Bodin and the Great God of Nature: The Moral and Religious Universe of a Judaiser*. Geneva: Librairie Droz, 1980.

Rousseau, Jean-Jacques. *The Social Contract and Discourse on the Origin of Inequality*. Edited with an introduction by Lester G. Crocker. New York: Washington Square Press, 1976.

Rowan, Ford. *Broadcast Fairness: Doctrine, Practice, Prospects*. New York: Longman, 1984.

Ruch, Michel. *Le Préamble dans les oeuvres philosophiques de Cicéron: Essai sur la genèse et l'art du dialogue*. Paris: Belles Lettres, 1958.

Rummel, Erika. *Erasmus and His Catholic Critics*. Bibliotheca Humanistica & Reformatorica, vol. 45. 2 vols. Nieuwkoop: De Graaf Publishers, 1989.

———, ed. *The Erasmus Reader*. Toronto: University of Toronto Press, 1990.

Rupp, E. Gordon, and Philip S. Watson, eds. *Luther and Erasmus: Free Will and Salvation*. The Library of Christian Classics: Icthus Edition. Philadelphia: Westminster Press, 1969.

Rutzick, Mark C. "Offensive Language and the Evolution of First Amendment Protection." *Harvard Civil Rights–Civil Liberties Law Review* 9 (1974): 1–28.

Ryan, Alan. "Hobbes, Toleration and the Inner Life." In *The Nature of Political Theory*, ed. David Miller and Larry Siedentop. Oxford: Clarendon Press, 1983.

Ryan, Lawrence V. "Erasmis Convivia: The Banquet Colloquies of Erasmus." *Medievalia et Humanistica: Studies in Medieval and Renaissance Culture*, n.s., 8 (1977): 201–15.

Sabine, George H. "The *Colloquium Heptaplomeres* of Jean Bodin." In *Persecution and Liberty: Essays in Honor of George Lincoln Burr*. New York: The Century Company, 1931.

Scanlon, T. M., Jr. "Freedom of Expression and Categories of Expression." *University of Pittsburgh Law Review* 40 (1979): 519–50.

Schauer, Frederick. *Free Speech: A Philosophical Inquiry*. Cambridge: Cambridge University Press, 1982.

Schmitt, Charles B. *Cicero Scepticus: A Study of the Influence of the Academica in the Renaissance*. International Archives of the History of Ideas, no. 52. The Hague: Martinus Nijhoff, 1972.

Schmitt, Charles B., and Quentin Skinner, eds. *The Cambridge History of Renaissance Philosophy*. Cambridge: Cambridge University Press, 1988.

Schochet, Gordon J. "From Persecution to 'Toleration,'" in *Liberty Secured? Britain before and after 1688*, ed. J. R. Jones. Vol. 2 of *The Making of Modern Freedom*. Stanford: Stanford University Press, 1992.

———. "John Locke and Religious Toleration." In *The Revolution of 1688–1689:*

Changing Perspectives, ed. Lois G. Schwoerer. Cambridge: Cambridge University Press, 1992.

Schoeck, Richard J. "Humanism and Jurisprudence." In *Renaissance Humanism: Foundations, Forms, and Legacy*, vol. 3, ed. Albert Rabil Jr. Philadelphia: University of Pennsylvania Press, 1988.

Schutte, Anne Jacobson. "Periodization of Sixteenth-Century Italian Religious History: The Post-Cantimori Paradigm Shift." *Journal of Modern History* 61 (1989): 269–84.

Schwartz, Bernard. *The Bill of Rights: A Documentary History*. 2 volumes. New York: Chelsea House Publishers, 1971.

Schwartz, Joel. "Hobbes & the Two Kingdoms of God." *Polity* 18 (1985): 7–24.

Seigel, Jerrold E. " 'Civic Humanism' or Ciceronian Rhetoric? The Culture of Petrarch and Bruni." *Past and Present* 34 (1966): 3–48.

———. *Rhetoric and Philosophy in Renaissance Humanism: The Union of Eloquence and Wisdom, Petrarch to Valla*. Princeton: Princeton University Press, 1968.

Sextus Empiricus. *Outlines of Pyrrhonism*. Translated by R. G. Bury. Loeb Classical Library. 1961.

Shapin, Steven, and Simon Schaffer. *Leviathan and the Air-Pump*. Princeton: Princeton University Press, 1985.

Shapiro, Andrew. *Media Access: Your Rights to Express Your Views on Radio and Television*. Boston: Little, Brown, 1976.

Shapiro, Barbara J. *Probability and Certainty in Seventeenth-Century England: A Study of the Relationships Between Natural Science, Religion, History, Law, and Literature*. Princeton: Princeton University Press, 1983.

Shapiro, Gary. "Reading and Writing in the Text of Hobbes's *Leviathan*." *Journal of the History of Philosophy* 18 (1980): 147–58.

Sharratt, Peter, ed. *French Renaissance Studies: 1540–70*. Edinburgh: Edinburgh University Press, 1976.

Shiffrin, Steven H. *The First Amendment, Democracy, and Romance*. Cambridge: Harvard University Press, 1990.

Shuger, Debora K. *Sacred Rhetoric: The Christian Grand Style in the English Renaissance*. Princeton: Princeton University Press, 1988.

Sinclair, R. K. *Democracy and Participation in Athens*. Cambridge: Cambridge University Press, 1988.

Skinner, Quentin. *The Foundations of Modern Political Thought*. 2 vols. Cambridge: Cambridge University Press, 1980.

———. "Moral Ambiguity and the Renaissance Art of Eloquence." In *Essays in Criticism* 46 (1994): 267–92.

———. "Thomas Hobbes: Rhetoric and the Construction of Morality." In *Proceedings of the British Academy* 76 (1990): 1–61.

Sloane, Thomas O. *Donne, Milton, and the End of Humanist Rhetoric*. Berkeley and Los Angeles: University of California Press, 1985.

Smolla, Rodney A. "Rethinking First Amendment Assumptions about Racist and Sexist Speech." *Washington and Lee Law Review* 47 (1990): 171–211.

Smith, Preserved. *A Key to the Colloquies of Erasmus.* Cambridge: Harvard University Press, 1927.

Spitz, Lewis W. "Luther, Humanism, and the Word." *Lutheran Theological Seminary Bulletin* 65 (1985): 3–26.

Sprat, Thomas. *History of the Royal Society.* Edited by J. I. Cope and H. W. Jones. St. Louis: Washington University Press, 1959.

Springborg, Patricia. "Leviathan and the Problem of Ecclesiastical Authority." *Political Theory* 3 (1975): 289–304.

Steadman, John M. *The Hill and the Labyrinth: Discourse and Certitude in Milton and His Near-Contemporaries.* Berkeley and Los Angeles: University of California Press, 1984.

Stein, Justice Gary S. "The First Amendment and Campaign Finance Reform: A Timely Reconciliation." *Rutgers Law Review* 44 (1992): 743–95.

Stephan, Paul B., III. "The First Amendment and Content Discrimination." *Virginia Law Review* 68 (1982): 203–51.

Stolt, Birgit. *Wortkampf: Frühneuhochdeutsche Beispiele zur Rhetorischen Praxis.* Frankfurt: Athenäum Verlag, 1974.

Stone, Geoffrey R. "Content Regulation and the First Amendment." *William and Mary Law Review* 25 (1983): 189–252.

Story, Joseph. *Commentaries on the Constitution of the United States.* 3 vols. Boston, 1833. Reprint. New York: De Capo Press, 1970.

Stough, Charlotte. *Greek Skepticism: A Study in Epistemology.* Berkeley and Los Angeles: University of California Press, 1969.

Strauss, Leo. *The Political Philosophy of Hobbes: Its Basis and Its Genesis.* Translated by Elsa M. Sinclair. Chicago: University of Chicago Press, 1952.

Struever, Nancy S. *The Language of History in the Renaissance: Rhetoric and Historical Consciousness in Florentine Humanism.* Princeton: Princeton University Press, 1970.

Stump, Eleanore. *Boethius's De topicis differentiis.* Ithaca: Cornell University Press, 1978.

———. *Boethius's In Ciceronis Topica.* Ithaca: Cornell University Press, 1988.

Sunstein, Cass R. *Democracy and the Problem of Free Speech.* New York: Free Press, 1993.

Tappert, Theodore G., trans. and ed. *The Book of Concord: The Confessions of the Evangelical Lutheran Church.* Philadelphia: Muhlenberg Press, 1959.

Thompson, Craig R. "The Humanism of More Reappraised." *Thought* 52 (1977): 231–48.

Tinder, Glenn. *Tolerance: Toward a New Civility.* Amherst: University of Massachusetts Press, 1975.

Tinkler, John F. "Humanism and Dialogue." *Parergon: Bulletin of the Australian and New Zealand Association for Medieval and Renaissance Studies* 6 (1988): 197–214.

———. "Humanism as Discourse: Studies in the Rhetorical Culture of Renaissance Humanism, Petrarch to Bacon." Ph.D. diss., Queen's University, Kingston, Ont., 1983.

————. "Renaissance Humanism and the *genera eloquentiae*." *Rhetorica: A Journal of the History of Rhetoric* 5 (1987): 279–309.

Todd, Margo. *Christian Humanism and the Puritan Social Order*. Cambridge: Cambridge University Press, 1987.

Todorov, Tzvetan. Review of *In Defence of Rhetoric*, by Brian Vickers. *New Republic*, 23 January 1989, 35–38.

Tracy, James D. "Erasmus the Humanist." In *Erasmus of Rotterdam: A Quincentennial Symposium*, ed. Richard L. DeMolen. New York: Twayne Publishers, 1971.

————. *The Politics of Erasmus: A Pacifist Intellectual and His Political Milieu*. Toronto: University of Toronto Press, 1978,

Trevor-Roper, Hugh. *Catholics, Anglicans and Puritans: Seventeenth-Century Essays*. Chicago: University of Chicago Press, 1988.

————. *Renaissance Essays*. Chicago: University of Chicago Press, 1985.

Trinkaus, Charles. *In Our Image and Likeness: Humanity and Divinity in Italian Humanist Thought*. 2 vols. Chicago: University of Chicago Press, 1970.

————. "The Religious Thought of the Italian Humanists, and the Reformers: Anticipation or Autonomy?" In *The Pursuit of Holiness in Late Medieval and Renaissance Religion*, ed. Charles Trinkaus with Heiko A. Oberman. Studies in Medieval and Reformation Thought, vol. 10. Leiden: E. J. Brill, 1974.

————. *The Scope of Renaissance Humanism*. Ann Arbor: University of Michigan Press, 1983.

Tuck, Richard. "Grotius, Carneades and Hobbes." *Grotiana* 4 (1983): 43–62.

————. "Hobbes and Locke on Toleration." In *Thomas Hobbes and Political Theory*, ed. Mary G. Dietz. Lawrence: University of Kansas Press, 1990.

————. *Natural Rights Theories: Their Origin and Development*. Cambridge: Cambridge University Press, 1979.

Tulloch, John. *Rational Theology and Christian Philosophy in England in the Seventeenth Century*. 2 vols. Edinburgh: William Blackwood, 1874.

Underhill, Edward Bean. *Tracts of Liberty of Conscience and Persecution, 1614–1661*. London: The Hanserd Knollys Society, 1646. Reprint. New York: Burt Franklin, 1966.

U.S. House. Committee on House Administration. *Entitled the "House of Representative Campaign Spending Limit and Election Reform Act of 1991"* (H. Rpt. 102–340). Washington: Government Printing Office, 1983.

Valla, Lorenzo. *On Pleasure: De voluptate*. Translated by A. Kent Hieatt and Maristella Lorch. New York: Abaris Books, 1977.

Van Leeuwen, Henry G. *The Problem of Certainty in English Thought, 1630–1690*. International Archives of the History of Ideas, no. 3. The Hague: Martinus Nijhoff, 1963.

Verkamp, Bernard J. *The Indifferent Mean: Adiaphorism in the English Reformation to 1554*. Studies in the Reformation, vol. 1. Athens, Ohio, and Detroit, Mich.: Ohio University Press and Wayne State University Press, 1977.

Vickers, Brian. *In Defence of Rhetoric*. Oxford: Clarendon Press, 1988.

————, ed. *Rhetoric Revalued: Papers from the International Society for the History of Rhetoric.* Medieval & Renaissance Texts and Studies, vol. 19. Binghamton: SUNY Binghamton, 1982.

Wallace, Ronald S. *Calvin's Doctrine of the Word and Sacrament.* Grand Rapids, Mich.: William B. Eerdmans, 1957.

Warrender, Howard. *The Political Philosophy of Hobbes: His Theory of Obligation.* Oxford: Clarendon Press, 1961.

Watkins, J.W.N. *Hobbes's System of Ideas: A Study in the Political Significance of Philosophical Theories.* London: Hutchinson University Library, 1973.

Weiss, James Michael. "*Ecclesiastes* and Erasmus: The Mirror and the Image." *Archiv für Reformationsgeschichte* 65 (1974): 83–107.

Whelan, Frederick G. "Language and Its Abuses in Hobbes' Political Philosophy." *American Political Science Review* 75 (1981): 59–75.

Williams, Roger. *The Bloudy Tenent, of Persecution, for Cause of Conscience, Discussed, in a Conference betweene Truth and Peace.* 1644.

Williams, Susan. "Content Discrimination and the First Amendment." *University of Pennsylvania Law Review* 139 (1991): 615–730.

Wilson, K. J. *Incomplete Fictions: The Formation of English Renaissance Dialogue.* Washington, D.C.: Catholic University of America Press, 1985.

Winter, Ernst F., trans. and ed. *Discourse on Free Will.* New York: Frederick K. Ungar, 1961.

Wirszubski, C. *Libertas as a Political Idea at Rome during the Late Republic and Early Principate.* Cambridge: Cambridge University Press, 1968.

Wolfe, Don M., ed. *Leveller Manifestoes of the Puritan Revolution.* Foreword by Charles A. Beard. New York: Thomas Nelson & Sons, 1944.

Wolin, Sheldon S. *Politics and Vision: Continuity and Innovation in Western Political Thought.* Boston: Little, Brown, 1960.

a'Wood, Anthony. *Athenae Oxoniensis.* London: R. Knaplock, D. Midwinter, and J. Tonson, 1721.

Woodhouse, A.S.P., ed. *Puritanism and Liberty: Being the Army Debates (1647–49) from the Clarke Manuscripts.* Introduction by A.S.P. Woodhouse. London: Dent, 1986.

Wright, Judge Skelly. "Money and the Pollution of Politics: Is the First Amendment an Obstacle to Political Equality?" *Columbia Law Review* 82 (1982): 609–45.

———. "Politics and the Constitution: Is Money Speech?" *Yale Law Journal* 85 (1976): 1001–21.

Yates, Frances E. "The Hermetic Tradition in Renaissance Science." In *Art, Science, and History in the Renaissance,* ed. Charles S. Singleton. Baltimore: Johns Hopkins University Press, 1967.

Zappen, James P. "Aristotelian and Ramist Rhetoric in Thomas Hobbes's *Leviathan*: Pathos versus Ethos and Logos." *Rhetorica* 1 (1983): 65–92.

Index

Abelard, Peter, 212n.16
Abrams v. United States, 249, 250, 253, 254
abstract thinking, 33
academic skepticism, 25–26, 37–38, 39–40;
  Augustine's rejection of, 74n.117; of Cicero, 65; of Erasmus, 57–58
academics, 38, 195
accommodation, 8–9, 41, 80–81, 231; in
  Acontius, 127, 161; in Bayle, 240; of Christ
  to audiences, 77–78; in conversation, 35–
  36; and fundamentals of faith (Chillingworth), 148, 153–62; of heretics, 99;
  objective/subjective, 161, 162; and order of
  ideas, 111; to particular circumstances,
  160–61; rejection of, by Luther, 81–84
Ackerman, Bruce, 253
Acontius, Jacobus, 3n.7, 8, 9, 11, 137, 138,
  142, 144, 147, 153, 157, 172n.12, 181,
  203, 263; accommodation in, 127, 161;
  argument from conscience in, 223–24; and
  certainty, 148–49; compared with Mill,
  132–34; forms of *sermo* in, 123–25; and
  fundamentals of faith, 158; influence on
  Chillingworth, 155; influence on Locke,
  234; as the new humanist, 112–15; and
  political order, 163–64, 165, 167; and
  practice of toleration, 134–36; and revision of humanist defense, 103–36, 228;
  theory of toleration, 129–31
Act of Toleration (1689), 237
action(s): adapted to particulars, 84; fundamentals of faith relating to, 196–98; oratory and, 31; *sermo* concerned with, 93;
  speech and, 122
Acton, John Emerich Edward Dalberg,
  106–7
adiaphora (nonessentials), 3, 169, 228;
  Church practices as, 137–38; classical view
  of, 50n.29; conversations about, 214; as
  dilemma in humanist argument for toleration, 140–41; disagreement regarding, 6,
  235; discussion of, 100–101; in Erasmus's
  theory of toleration, 49, 50–71; fundamentals of faith distinct from, 50–54;
  in Hobbes, 195; made fundamentals, by

Council of Trent, 106; open to debate, 8,
  99, 246; probability of, 234; rhetoric of,
  70–71, 85–101; skepticism regarding, 3,
  120, 122; toleration of, 156. *See also* doctrinal adiaphora
admonitory (category), 72, 75
advice/opinion (*sententiae dictio*), 93n.195
Aegidius (Pontano), 87
agon, 87, 91, 207
agonistic character of oratory, 17, 21–23, 37,
  74
Alan of Lille, 72n.107
Allen, J. W., 3–4
ambiguity, 178, 182, 184, 188
Anabaptists, 1, 84, 85n.167, 105, 136, 164
Anaxagoras, 175
ancient rhetoricians, 45–47, 75, 76
Anglican Church, 105, 137–38, 141, 186,
  235; Chillingworth and, 144
Anglicans, 139, 183
*Antica musica ridotta alla moderne prattica,
  L'* (Vicentino), 222
anti-Trinitarians, 105
Antonius, 39n.41
apathy, 36
apostates, 135
Apostles' Creed, 63–64, 116, 157
appropriateness (principle), 16
apte dicere, 14
Aquinas, Saint Thomas, 2n.5, 60n.67, 98, 99,
  133, 218, 224–25, 226
Arcesilas of Pitane, 25
Areopagitica (Milton), 12, 125, 243–44, 245
argument from accommodation, 155–56
argument from authority, 97n.202, 183; in
  Hooker, 139
argument from conscience, 141; in Bodin, 11,
  12, 223–27
argument from consensus, and marketplace
  of ideas, 263–64
argument from probability, 23–24, 239–40;
  applied to fundamentals of faith, 148–53;
  rhetorical origins of, 153n.48
argument from truth, 100; and free speech,
  249; in marketplace of ideas, 265, 266–67

argument from self-fulfillment or dignity, 266, 267–68
argument in *utramque partem*, 6, 25–26, 156; in Acontius, 123; in Aristotle, 26n90; in argument for free speech, 246; in Bodin, 206; in conversation, 38; in Erasmus, 61; in Erasmus's *Diatriba*, 96–97; in Hooker, 138; scholastic, 98
argumentation, 100n.218
Arian doctrines, 158
Aristotelean logic, 109
Aristotle, 13, 15nn.30 and 32, 16, 17, 34n.123, 53, 126, 151, 178, 184n55; argument *in utramque partem*, 26n.90; consensus in, 60, 62n.73, 65n.83; on dialectic, 30n.106; dialogues, 28, 29; on faculty of speech, 45, 46; on oratory, 19, 20, 23; on probability, 24; on rhetoric, 21–22, 36n.128
atheism, 11, 226–27
atheists: excluded from toleration, 12, 247; restrictions on, 236
Aubrey, John, 143, 177
Augsburg Confession, 105
Augustine, Saint, 21, 34n.123, 74n.117, 133n.76, 224–25; and religious coercion, 48–49
Augustinian Canons, monastery at Steyn, 44
authorities, consensus on free will, 58, 59–68
authority: appeals to, 34, 35, 36, 87; beliefs and, 128–29; of Bible, 157; Church as, 139–40; on doctrine and morality, 190; in Hooker, 139; political, 164–65; reason and, 147; of sovereign, 191–92, 198; and truth, 128
Autobiography (Mill), 245–46

baptism, 106, 113
Barbaro, Ermolao, 89–90
Bayle, Pierre, 12; and demise of humanist argument, 237–43
Beda, Noel, 51n.31
Behemoth (Hobbes), 180, 201
beliefs: and authority, 128–29; emotions in, 131; false, 246–47; fleeting, 203; open to question, 116–17, 119, 120, 121–22; reinforced through argument, 218–19; vary with time and place, 238
Bethel School District No. 403 v. Fraser, 257–58, 259
Beukels, John, 209

Bible, 196; authority of, 157; belief in, 158; divine status of, 199; interpretation of, 153–55; as source of truth, 113, 149–50. *See also* Scripture
Bill of Rights, 237n.25
Blackmun, Harry, 257
Bodin, Jean, 10–11, 12; different kind of humanist toleration, 203–30; education of, 205–7; humanist response to Hobbes, 227–30; purpose of dialogue in, 211–19
Bork, Robert, 251n.69
Borro, Girolamo, 109
Boyle, M. O., 58, 92–93, 95, 96
Bracciolini, Poggio, 87
Brandeis, Louis, 249, 250, 255, 267n.124
Brennan, William, 249n.60, 250, 253
Brief Lives (Aubrey), 143
Briefe of the Art of Rhetorique, A (Hobbes), 178, 184n.55
Bruni, Leonardo, 87
Buchanan, John, Jr., 272
Buckley v. Valeo, 275–76
Burton, Henry, 248

Calvin, John, 2, 105, 108
Calvinists, 104, 105, 106, 208
campaign reform legislation, 13, 270–73, 275–77
Campeggi, Cardinal, 84
Carneades, 25
Cary, Lucius, second viscount Falkland, 144, 145
Cassander, George, 104–5, 122, 144, 156n.58
Castellio, Sebastian, 128n.65, 144, 150n.36, 183–84, 223, 234n.11
Catholic Church. *See* Roman Catholic Church
Catholic League, 220n.40
Catholic-Lutheran colloquies, 103, 104
Catholic-Protestant reconciliation, Erasmus's dream of, 103–7
Catholics. *See* Roman Catholics
Cato's Letters (Trenchard and Gordon), 245
causa, 93. *See also* definite question
Cavendish, William, 170, 171
Celsi, Mino, 3n.7
censorship, 246, 253, 265, 266, 272
ceremonies, 161; as adiaphoral, 50–51; toleration of, 81

certainty, 22–23, 96, 119; and consensus, 60–61, 63, 65; of free will, 56–57, 68–69; in fundamentals of faith, 54, 56–57, 148–49, 153, 160, 183; human imposition and, 188; impossibility of, 25; of knowledge, 149; lack of, in history, 173; levels of, in religion, 150n.36; of principles of ethical living, 66–68; probability and, 151–52, 185; produced by science, 190; in religion, 169, 234; of religious truth, 208; skepticism and, 120, 121, 229, 239; standard of, 24; and topics of preaching, 75

Chafee, Zechariah, 269n.128

Chaplinsky v. New Hampshire, 255, 257, 262

Charles V, 103

Cheynell, Francis, 147, 158

Chicago Police Department v. Mosley, 252

Chillingworth, William, 8–9, 11, 169, 170, 173, 174, 175, 181, 183, 184, 185, 186, 203, 204; accommodation, fundamentals, and the variable standard, 153–62, 240; argument from conscience, 224; heir to a tradition, 141–48; humanist defense of religious toleration, 228; influence on Locke, 234; probability in, 239; religion versus politics in, 162–67; rhetoric and probability in, 148–53

Christ, 48, 154, 193, 218, 221; *decorum* of, 76, 77–78; imitation of, 76–79; philosophy of, 52–53. *See also* Jesus

Christendom: disintegration of, 10; Erasmus's vision of reunited, 103–5

Christian denominations/sects, 158; differences between, 241–42; toleration of, 6–7

Christian rhetoric, *decorum* in, 76–79

Christian rhetoricians, 21

Christianity, 41, 160, 186; in Bodin, 204; consensus in, 186; ethical behavior in, 52–53, 148n.33; in Hobbes, 201, 227; probability of, 151, 153; truth of, 227, 229

Chrysostom, John, 118

Church: as authority, 139-40; churches within, 105; comprehensive, 162, 163, 169, 231, 232, 241; consensus in, 62, 192; *decorum* of, 80; as religious community, 233–34; and state, 236

Church authority, and restriction of discussion, 108–9

Church Councils, 63, 64, 124–25, 128n.66, 222

Church Fathers, 59, 63, 222

Cicero, 13, 14, 15, 16, 17–18, 25, 26, 48, 72n.110, 86, 95, 96–97, 151n.40, 156, 172, 174, 213, 246; categories of oratory, 92, 93; consensus in, 64–65, 66; on conversation (*sermo*), 26–27, 28, 30–41, 87; Erasmus on, 53; on faculty of speech, 45, 46; imitation of, 76n.121; letters of discussion, 88, 89, 90; on oratory, 17–18, 19, 20–21, 22; probability in, 24; skepticism in, 153; speech effecting action in, 122; subdivision of probability, 60; *verisimile*, 152

Ciceronian dialogue, 28–29, 32, 36, 37, 86, 88, 90, 96, 97; rhetorical devices in, 29n.102

Ciceronian *sermo*, 88, 90, 94–95, 111, 123, 125, 128, 129, 139, 145

Ciceronianus (Erasmus), 76n.121

civil conversation/discourse, 95n.199, 277

civil order, 11, 255n.86

civil philosophy, 191

civil society: lack of consensus in, 242; restriction on religion and, 236

civil war(s), 11, 178, 179, 182, 183, 192, 208, 227

civility, 95; in democratic conversation, 258–59; in language, 89; rules for, 35, 36

classical genres, 74n.117; preaching distinct from, 75–76

classical rhetoric, 13–41, 245–46, 277; and argument from probability, 151–53; consensus in, 60, 62n.73; dominant characteristics, main *genera*, 16–26; and humanists' defense of toleration, 5–6; nonrational proofs in, 34–35

classical studies, 141; inherent value of, 44

clergy, Hobbes's view of, 198–99

coercion, 114–15, 164; of heretics, 225n.57; rejection of, 163, 193, 194, 199n.123, 236. *See also* physical coercion

Cohen v. California, 255–56, 257, 265

Colet, John, 91

collatio (comparison), 58, 59

Colloquium heptaplomeres de rerum sublimium arcanis abditis (Bodin), 204, 211–27; Bodin before, 205–11; as humanist response to Hobbes, 227–30

Columbia Broadcasting Co. v. Democratic Committee, 250

common people: discussion among, 93–94; excluded from debate on doctrine, 8

common prophecy, tradition of, 123–24

Commonwealth, 190, 191, 192, 196, 198; religious toleration danger to, 227; rhetoric threat to, 209–10; skepticism and, 215

communitarian context of speech, 265, 267, 277

comparison. See *collatio* (comparison)

Compassionate Samaratine, The (Walwyn), 244n.40

comprehension, 6; versus toleration, 231. *See also* Church, comprehensive

conceptual milieu of humanist toleration, 3–4

Concerning Heresy and the Punishment Thereof (Hobbes), 195–96

concrete (the)/concreteness, 17–18, 31

Condren, Conal, 182n.45

conscience: in Bayle, 238; cannot be violated, 235–36; fidelity to, 240–41; individual, 161, 238; prepolitical right to, 224. *See also* argument from conscience; right to conscience

consensus, 6, 8, 10, 12, 96, 232, 234; absence of, in philosophical debate, 32; atheism judged according to, 226; in Chillingworth, 150; of Christians, 186; and dissent, 124; on doctrinal adiaphora, 97; on doctrine, 59–68, 183–84, 186, 190; epistemological status of, 61; in Erasmus, 59–68, 140n.7, 148; regarding free will, 59–68; on fundamentals of faith, 65–66, 106, 203; lack of, 39; loss of, 237–38, 242: moral and doctrinal (Hobbes), 190; and probability, 184, 235; religious and moral, 192, 194; and restriction of discussion, 108; and truth, 113, 263–64; types of, in Erasmus, 61–63

consistency, defended by Luther, 84

consolatory (category), 72, 75

Constitution, U.S., 256

content (*res*): and form (*verba*), 14, 29–30, 171, 277; and marketplace of ideas, 262n.108

content neutrality, 252–54, 256

contentio (oratory), 26–27, 32, 37, 38, 60, 86, 96, 114; action orientation of, 31; concreteness of, 31, 72; *decorum* in, 29–30, 41; demagogic, 203; dialogue differs from, 27; genres of, 16–26, 33, 88–89, 92–93;

good, 173–74; historical contrasted with public, 174; passions in, 34; *sermo* distinct from, 87

contention, 95; rhetoric and, 183, 189

controversy, 22, 275; in sacred oratory, 74, 76

convention, and Hobbes's sovereign, 190–92. See also *nomos-physis* (convention-nature) antithesis

conversation. See *sermo* (conversation)

convivium religiosum (Erasmus), 91, 145

Convocation of 1563, 105

Council of Jerusalem, 140

Council of Trent, 105–6

covenant(s), 190–91, 192

Crantor, 36

creed(s), 158n.71, 160, 162

Crell, Johannes, 126

Cromwell, Oliver, 244

crowds, 19

Curione, Celio Secundo, 3n.7

Cynegetica (Oppian), 205

De arte dubitandi et confidendi, ignorandi et sciendi (Castellio), 150n.36

De bello turcico (Erasmus), 1n.3

De Cive (Hobbes), 179, 180, 181, 197

De conscribendis epistolis (Erasmus), 87

De doctrina christiana (Augustine), 49

De finibus (Cicero), 27, 37, 86

De inventione (Cicero), 13, 46n.11

De libero arbitrio (Valla), 90n.186

De libero arbitrio, diatribe sive collatio (Erasmus), 54, 58–59, 61, 92–97

De Methodo (Acontius), 113–14

De natura deorum (Cicero), 40, 96

De officio pii ac publicae tranquillitatis vere amantis viri in hoc religionis dissidio (Cassander), 104

De oratore (Antonius), 39n.141

De sarcienda ecclesiae concordia (Erasmus), 103

De servo arbitrio (Luther), 54, 96

De voluptate (Valla), 86, 87

debate, 37n.134, 98. *See also* discussion

decorum, 6, 50, 115, 246, 269; application to heretics, 76, 79–81; in Bodin, 204, 206–7, 212–13, 221, 228; in classical rhetoric, 13–16; consecration of classical, 76–79; in debates, 98; in democratic conversation, 258–59; in dialogue, 29–30; in *Diatriba,*

95; of doctrinal conversation, 125–29; and free speech, 243; and marketplace of ideas, 260; method of teaching and, 110; in Milton, 247–48; and political obedience, 163; of preaching, 7–8; in prudential method, 111; rules of, 14; of scholarly discussion, 88, 89; in *sermo*, 8, 10–11, 30–41, 99–101, 127–29, 163; in Supreme Court, 254–55, 257; and toleration, 79–81
definite question, 18, 31, 93; in letters, 88
deliberative genre, 23, 72–73, 74n.117, 75, 76, 87, 92–93, 94n.197, 139; *ethos* and, 96
deliberative oratory, 16, 17, 33, 172n.14; goal of, 95–96
Demetrius, 29n.104
democracy, 174–75, 179; as conversation, 258–59
demonstrative *genus*. *See* epideictic (demonstrative oratory)
Des Maizeaux, P., 143
Devotio moderna, 43
dialectic, 19n.52, 29, 32, 109–10; distinct from rhetoric, 30n.107; in Ramus, 111; *sermo* distinct from 30, 35–36
dialogic method, 37
dialogue(s), 27–29, 30; in Cicero, 28, 29, 32, 36, 37, 86, 96; *diatribē* and, 92–93; forms of, 28–29; humanist, 86–87; for nonessentials, 90–92; purpose of (Bodin), 211–19
Dialogue of a Philosopher with a Jew, and a Christian (Abelard), 212n.16
Dialogue of Giacopo Riccamati (Acontius), 112, 113, 115–18
Dialogus I (Bruni), 87
Diatriba (Erasmus) 92–97
diatribē, 92–97
Diogenes Laertius, 28, 30, 53
Dionysius of Halicarnassus, 173n.16
discourse: logically arranged and unemotional, 113–15; search for truth through reason in, 146
discussion, 100, 232; in choosing right path to salvation, 233n.8; of doctrinal essentials, 69; free, 163; matters excluded from, 243; permitted, 246–47; rhetorical form and, 263
disputatio, scholastic, 98
Disputatiuncula (Erasmus), 91
dissent: consensus and, 124; as heresy, 106;

justification of (Acontius), 112; in Luther, 84
dissenters, 6, 7, 231, 232n.2, 233n.8, 235; Hobbes's affinity for, 175; toleration of, 8, 84
divinity, speech's connection with, 47–50
Doctores Ecclesiae, 63, 64
doctrinal adiaphora: debate over, 97; in Erasmus, 51–52; free will as, 56–57, 70–71
doctrinal consensus, 59–68, 183–84, 186, 190
doctrinal conversation, *decorum* of, 125–29
doctrinal diversity, 92
doctrinal essentials, 52–53; discussion of, 69. *See also* fundamentals of faith
doctinal minimalism, in Hobbes, 195
doctrinal truths, and moral action, 73
doctrinal unity, 105
doctrine: accommodated to individual, 162; discussion of, 132n.75, 153; essentialness of, 54, 56; fundamentals of faith relating to, 196–98; genres in treatment of, 119; hierarchy of, 70n.104; knowledge of, 186; questioning, 229; restrictions on discussion of, 108–9; sovereign arbiter of, 227; unequivocal basis of, 186, 188. *See also* essential doctrine
dogma, 3, 6, 9; simplification of, 194–95; sure knowledge of, 149–50
Drew, Elizabeth, 272
Drivers Union v. Meadowmoor, 255
Dworkin, Ronald, 253, 267n.123

Ecclesiastes (Erasmus), 45, 74–75
education, and beliefs, 238–39
Elements (Euclid), 177
Elements of Law, The (Hobbes), 179, 180, 182, 184, 197
Elenchus, 37, 117n.43
elites: as audience for conversation, 33, 93; discussion limited to, 8, 40n.148, 101, 108–9, 117; educated/learned, 89, 101, 139, 213
Elizabeth, queen of England, 201
eloquence, 142n.11, 170, 206; in history, 173; Hobbes on, 180; of Thucydides, 174
Elyot, Thomas, 171
emotional appeals, 33–34, 95, 114; in Chillingworth, 147–48; in letters, 88; in preaching, 73–74; rejected, 111, 125–26

emotions: in beliefs, 131; constructive, 37; and faith, 74; incited in deliberative oratory, 95–96; negative impact of, 35–36; oratory appeals to, 17, 19–21; role of, in religious persuasion, 115; role of, in search for truth, 99
encomiastic letters, 87
England, 2n.7; religious diversity, 237
"Englands New Chains Discovered" (tract), 244–45
English Civil War, 1, 6, 147–48, 163, 164, 165, 174, 201, 203, 208, 210n.13; Hobbes and, 178, 179, 180; Leveller tracts in, 244–45
English Licensing Order of 1643, 243, 247
enharmonic *genus*, 221–22
Enlightenment, 3–4
enthymeme, 24, 184n.55
Established Church, 6
essential doctrine: free will as, 70–71; rejection of accommodation in, 81. *See also* fundamentals of faith
Epictetus, 53
Epicureans, Epicureanism, 37, 39n.143, 221
Epicurus, 53
epideictic (demonstrative) oratory, 16, 17, 21, 27n.91, 33, 72, 88, 93
Equal Opportunities Rule, 270n.130
Erasmus, Desiderius, 9, 10, 11, 29n.104, 41, 112, 113, 116, 118, 119, 120, 122, 131, 137, 153, 171, 203, 205; accommodation in, 154, 161; Acontius differs from, 121; argument from consensus in, 150, 151; aversion to force in, 45–50; consensus in, 263; and divinity of speech, 47–50; education of, 43–44; on ethics, 183n.53, 184; on free will, 54–59; and fundamentals of faith, 158; humanist defense after, 103–7; humanist defense of religious toleration, 4n.12, 7–8, 129, 134, 228, 229; influence of, 140, 144, 155, 234n.11; paradigm of humanist toleration, 43–101; persuasion in, 193; and political order, 163–64, 165, 167; on protection of non-Christians, 1n.3; *sermo* in, 123, 124, 125, 145; successors of, 103–5
error(s), 41, 119, 120, 128, 133, 159; evidence of, 130; learning from, 91; punishment for, 225; response to, 129; sincere, 224, 225; toleration of, 121

ethical behavior: certainty regarding principles of, 66–68, 69; Christianity as, 148n.33; as fundamental of faith, 52–53
ethics, 3, 4, 6
ethos, 20, 34, 36, 95–96, 125, 261; in Acontius, 128–29; attacks on, 133; in Chillingworth, 146, 152; of heretics, 130; in religious controversy, 139
Euclid, 177, 178
excommunication, 84, 117, 121, 135–36, 155
exhortative (category), 72, 75
expediency, 16, 97n.207, 121; arguments arranged according to, 110; of Christ, 78; as end in oratory, 17; heretics tolerated for reasons of, 85; in *sermo*, 94

facts, 172–73
Fairness Doctrine, 12–13, 269–70, 271, 272, 273–75, 276
faith, 107, 217; cannot be compelled, 1n.3, 49, 80, 223, 225n.57; doctrinal requirements of, 148; emotions and, 74; persuasion and, 121; and salvation, 54–55, 113, 197; variable standard of, 159–60
Fall (the), 119
familiar letters, 88
Federal Communications Commission (FCC), 269–70, 273–74, 276
Federal Election Campaign Act Amendments of 1974 (FECA), 269, 270–73, 275, 276
Ferguson, Robert, 232n.2
fictive speeches, 172n.14
"fighting words," 255, 257, 262
First Amendment, 12, 237, 248–49, 250, 251, 252, 253, 255, 257–58, 260, 261n.103, 264, 266, 268, 270, 272–73, 275, 276
First Continental Congress, 245
Fisher, John, 143
flag burning, 253, 257, 265, 266
force: advocated by churchmen, 48; imposing religious unity through, 3; opposed by Acontius, 130–31; opposed by Erasmus, 84–85; rhetorical predisposition to persuasion over (Erasmus), 45–50. *See also* coercion
forensic genre, 87
form (*verba*), content (*res*) and, 14, 29–30, 171, 277

France, 211
Frankfurter, Felix, 255
Franklin, Julian, 207
free will, 92–93, 97, 108, 195; doctrinal consensus, 59–68; in Erasmus, 54-59; reality of, 93–94; rhetorical choices, 68–71
freedom of religion, 237n.25, 222
freedom of speech, 12–13, 40n.148, 100; justifications for protecting, 266, 268; and marketplace of ideas, 266–67, 277; move from religious toleration to, 242–48; restrictions on, 247, 248; right to, 242, 243–59, 267–68, 272–73
French Wars of Religion, 1, 208, 210n.13
Fundamental Constitutions of Carolina, 236n.21, 248
fundamental doctrines, in preaching, 75
fundamentals of faith, 3, 6, 10, 169, 229, 231, 234; accommodation and (Chillingworth), 153–62; in Acontius, 120–22, 131; agreement on, 11, 156–57; amorphousness of concept of, 163; argument from probability applied to, 148–53; in Cassander, 104–5; certainty in, 54, 56–57, 148–49, 153, 160, 183; consensus regarding, 65–66, 106, 203; debate on, forbidden, 246; defining, 157–62; denial of, 99, 135–36; destroyed by Bayle, 238, 240–41; discussion of, in Bodin, 214–15; distinct from nonessentials, 50–54; duty to obey sovereign as, 196; in Erasmus's theory of toleration, 8, 49, 50–71; in Hobbes, 9, 192–93, 196–97, 227, 230; individual's understanding of, 159–60; loss of consensus regarding, 237; minimal, 155–56, 160–61, 162, 193, 194–95; non-Christians and, 204; probability standard, 9, 235; rational investigation of, 138; rhetoric of, 71–85; and seventeenth-century humanism, 144; *sermo* and, 117; sincere error on, 225; skepticism regarding, 120–22; variable standard of, 153–62, 224

Galen, 92
Garnsey, Peter, 47n.18
Gemeinschaft, 10
General Council of the English Army, 244
Geneva Catechism, 105
geometry, 9, 178, 189, 191
Gerhardt, Paul, 106n.10

Germany, 209
Gertz v. Robert Welch, Inc., 250
Gesellschaft, 10
God, 159, 162, 195; accommodation to humanity, 154–55, 160, 235, 240; belief in, 226; and conversion, 82–83
Godly directives, 50n.30
"Godly Feast, The" (Erasmus), 53–54
Gordon, Thomas, 245
Gorgias (Plato), 16, 19n.52, 181
Gorgias, 23
government intervention in marketplace, and speech egalitarianism, 268–77
grace, 55, 106
grammar, 5
Gray, Hanna H., 5
Great Tew, 144–45
Grindal, Archbishop, 136n.84
Grotius, Hugo, 144, 150n.36, 156n.58
Guicciardini, Francesco, 172n.12

Haemstade, Adrian, 136n.84
Hale, Sir Matthew, 231n.1
Hales, John, 144
Hammond, Henry, 144
Hand, Learned, 250
Harlan, John, 256
hate speech, 12, 259–64, 266, 268, 272
Hellenistic philosophies, 40, 41
Henry of Navarre (King Henry IV), 220n.40
heresy, 3, 49, 132n.75; Council of Trent and, 106; in Erasmus, 66, 67–68; Hobbes on, 195–96; and search for truth, 133, 218
heretics, 66, 127, 154–55, 160; application of *decorum* to, 76, 79–81; capital punishment for, 85, 133; errors of, 218, 219; excommunication of, 121; fidelity to conscience and, 240; Luther on, 83; persecution of, 1–2, 49; punishment of, 225; scholastics' view of, 99; toleration of, 6, 7–8, 85, 134–35; treatment of, 104, 130–31, 136; use of compulsion against, 199n.123
Herodotus, 176
historical knowledge, is probable, 172–73
history, 5, 178; in Hobbes, 179n.33, 184; and rhetoric, 171–72, 173–74
history of ideas, 6
History of Oxford Writers (a'Wood), 142–43

History of the Peloponnesian War (Thucydides), 170–76, 177, 178, 179, 184
Hobbes, Thomas, 144, 167, 169–201, 210, 211, 235, 238, 239; "break" debate, 177–79, 181; critique of humanism, 9–11, 208; education of, 170–71; humanism of, 169–76, 203–5; humanist response to, in Bodin, 227–30; versus the humanists, 192–201; as scientist, 169, 177–92
Holmes, Oliver Wendell, 249, 250, 253, 254
Holy Office of the Inquisition, 2n.7
Holy Spirit, 82, 83, 97, 113, 119, 121; and scriptural interpretation, 108; in search for truth, 125–26
homeostasis, 127
Homer, 24n.77, 178
honor (*honestum*), 17, 94
Hooker, Richard, 137–41, 142, 144, 161, 169, 195
Huguenots, 208, 210n.13
human nature, 119–20; common, 176
humanism: aftermath of, 231–77; of Bodin, 205–7; of Hobbes, 170–76, 177–78, 179, 181, 203–5; internal tensions of, 169–70; legacy of, 12–13; liberalism and, 231–36; and religious toleration, 4–5; and scholasticism, 98; in seventeenth century, 137–67; turned against itself, 169–201. *See also* Renaissance humanists
humanist defense of religious toleration, 8–9, 13, 263; Acontius and revision of, 103–36; argument from truth in, 249; in Bodin, 203–30; Bayle and demise of, 237–43; characteristics of, 3; contemporary relevance of, 259–77; continuity and changes in, 112, 115–34; conversation in, 27–41; decline of, 162–63; dilemma in, 140–41; Erasmus paradigm of, 7–8, 43–101; extended to secular realm, 242, 243–48, 252; forms of, 7–8; fundamentals of faith in, 3; Hobbes's critique of, 208, 227; humanism used to undermine (Hobbes), 169–70, 178–79, 194–99; intellectual roots of, 13; liberals and, 232–33; neutralizing (Hobbes), 192–99; rejected by Bayle, 241–42
Hyde, Edward, earl of Clarendon, 144–45
Hymn to Hermes (Homer), 24n.77
Hyperaspistes diatribae adversus servum arbitrium (Erasmus), 54, 58, 61n.71

Iliad (Homer), 178
imitatio Dei, 76–79
imitation, 76
Immaculate Conception, doctrine of, 52, 154
Incarnation (doctrine), 224
indefinite question, 32, 93
Index, 106
individual freedom, and political obedience, 163–67
individual rights, 12, 224, 267n.123
individualism, 4, 11, 12; of Hobbes's social contract theory, 10; in Reformation, 107; in protection of speech, 267, 268, 277; of Protestantism, 112
induction, 151, 173
Inquisitio de fide (Erasmus), 64, 91, 116
Institutio oratoria (Quintilian), 13
Institutio Religionis Christianae (Calvin), 105
instruction, as function of preaching, 71, 79
instructive (category), 72n.108
intellectual changes, 107–11
Interim of Augsburg, 103–4
International Brotherhood of Electrical Workers v. Labor Board, 250
interlocutors, relationship between, 36–37
inviolability of conscience (principle), 6
irrational discourse/speech, 248, 252, 255, 268
Isocrates, 45–46
Italian Academicians, 112
Italy, 2–3n.7

Jefferson, Thomas, 232, 233n.6, 237
Jerome, Saint, 117
Jesus, 47, 77; belief in, 194–95, 235
Jews, 81, 139–40, 193, 201, 223, 238; expulsion of, 84; Jesus and, 77; toleration of, 1
Johnson, Nan, 34n.123
Johnston, David, 178, 179n.33
Jordan, W. K., 4, 107
judgment, classes of, 62n.73
judicial (forensic) oratory, 16, 17, 23, 26, 33, 38–39, 74n.117, 93, 139
judicial letters, 87
juries, 18–19
jurisprudence, humanist, 206
justice, 17, 46
justification, doctrine of, 106
justification by works, 128, 136
Justinian, 206n.6

kairos, 14

Knott, Edward (Matthew Wilson), 145, 151, 153, 158–59

knowledge: denial of, 22 (*see also* skepticism); individual level of, 159, 160; kinds of, 149; probable, 183, 194; probability as standard of, 175, 184; religious and civil, 243–44; unequivocal theory of, 188–89; univocal, 188–89

Kristeller, Paul Oskar, 5, 44, 98

Kuntz, Marion, 214, 219, 221

language: immoderate/inflammatory, 83; for scholarly discussion, 89

Latitudinarians, 231n.1

laudatory (category), 72, 75

law of nature, 196

Lecky, W. E. H., 107

Lecler, Joseph, 214

legal humanism, 208–11

letter(s), 29; classes of, 87–91; Erasmus on, 87–91

Letter Concerning Toleration (Locke), 226, 232, 233

"Letter to Boniface" (Augustine), 49

letters of discussion, 88–90

Leveller tracts, 244–45

Leviathan (Hobbes), 178, 180, 181, 184, 185, 187, 189, 190, 197, 200, 208

liberalism, liberals, 3–4, 224; and belief in consensus, 237; and humanism, 231–36; and religious liberty, 231–43

liberty of discussion, and truth, 132–34

Life of Plato (Diogenes Laertius), 28

limited toleration, 1n.3, 85, 219

linguistic theory, of Hobbes, 186–88

Locke, John, 204, 224, 226, 231–32, 237, 238, 242, 243, 247; humanism of, 241; on right to conscience, 12, 248

logic, 24; Aristotelean, 109; reform of traditional, 109–11, 114

logical explanation, 20, 21, 24

logical speech, 113–15

logos, 97n.208, 125, 126

Lucian, 172, 173n.16

Luther, Martin, 2, 63n.76, 66, 80, 94, 106, 128, 155, 229n.64; Erasmus's debate with, 68–71, 92, 95, 96, 97n.207; and free will, 54–59; as heretic, 67–68; rejection of accommodation, 81–84; and scriptural interpretation, 107–8; view of preaching, 71, 72n.107

Lutheran church, 105, 106

Lutherans, 68, 79, 80, 164; attempts to reconcile with Catholics, 103–4, 116; toleration of, 84

Lyon, Thomas, 4

Machiavelli, Niccolò, 172n.12

MacKinnon, Catherine, 261n.103

Madison, James, 232, 233n.6, 237

Madruzzo, Cardinal, 112

magistrate(s), 163; duty of, 134–35

Manichaeus, 59

Marcuse, Herbert, 261n.103

market reforms, 268–77

marketplace of ideas, 12–13, 100, 118, 243, 248–59; beyond, 264–68; conceptual roots of, 250–52; distinct from economic marketplace, 127–28; regulation of, 260–77

Marshall, John, 252

Meiklejohn, Alexander, 251n.69, 258–59, 262, 269n.128

Melancthon, Philip, 70n.104, 72n.108

Mercy and Truth (Wilson), 145

metaphor, 114, 182–83

metaphysical certainty, 149–51

method, 109–11, 112; in Acontius, 113–15; in Thucydides, 171

Miami Herald Publishing Co. v. Tornillo, 274

Middle Ages, 13; philosophy of, 98

Mill, John Stuart, 100, 217, 245–46, 248n.54, 265; Acontius compared with, 132–34; and marketplace of ideas, 250–52

Milton, John, 12, 100, 125, 126, 142n.10, 243–44, 246–47, 263; *decorum* in, 247–48; and marketplace of ideas, 250–52

moderation, 7–8, 95n.201, 96

modernity, 10, 11

monarchy, Hobbes supported, 171, 174–75, 179

moral certainty, 149–51, 173

moral epithets/language, 191–92, 196; in Hobbes, 186–88, 189

moral philosophy, 5

moral principles, in preaching, 75

moral truths, consensus regarding, 183–84

morality: certainty on principles of, 66–68,

69; and consensus, 186, 190, 191; sovereign's authority over, 191–92
More, Thomas, 50n.30, 63n.76, 126, 263
mos gallicus, 206
mos italicus, 206n.6
musical genera, 221–22
mutual toleration, 105

natural law, 67, 222
nature: elements of, 219, 220, 221; and Hobbes's sovereign, 190–92; see also *nomos-physis* (convention-nature) antithesis
Negotium, 32
neutrality, principle of, 12, 253–54, 257
New Academy, 37
New Rhetoric, The (Perelman and Olbrechts-Tyteca), 14, 100
New Testament, 57, 97n.206
Nichol, Thomas, 170
nomos, 176
nomos-physis (convention-nature) antithesis, 176, 188–89
non-Christian religions, toleration of, 229, 247
non-Christians, 135n.80, 183, 204, 219; limited toleration of, 1n.3; right to conscience, 236; salvation for, 161; toleration of, 7n.18, 11, 12
nonessentials. *See* adiaphora (nonessentials)
nullity of the will (doctrine), 82

obligation to obey, 196–98
obscenity law, 260n.101
Ochino, Bernardino, 3n.7, 115n.40, 144
Odyssey (Homer), 178
Of the Laws of Ecclesiastical Polity (Hooker), 137–38
officia oratoris, 17n.43
Olbrechts-Tyteca, Lucie, 14, 100
Old Testament, 57
On Liberty (Mill), 132, 245
On Style (Demetrius), 29n.104
Ong, Walter J., 109
Oppian, 205
Oratio de instituenda in republica in juventute ad Senatum Populumque Tolosatem (Bodin), 206, 207
orator(s): metaphors for, 22; reliance on consensus, 60; responsibility of, 14, 15–16
oratory. See *contentio* (oratory)

original sin, 106, 241n.35
Otium (leisure), 32, 33, 36
Outlines of Pyrrhonism (Sextus Empiricus), 25n.86
Owen, John, 232n.2

pagans, 1, 53–54, 81, 118, 241
Pantotheca, 213
parable of the tares, 81, 134, 199
paradiastole, 182
Paraphrases (Erasmus), 45
passionate discourse, 142n.12
passions, the, 34–35, 37; appeal to, 171, 181 (*see also* emotional appeals); and conversation, 125, 126, 127–28, 129; exploited by Satan, 119–20; and free discussion, 133; manipulation of, in rhetoric, 180, 181, 182; negative, 74, 173; pacification of, entailed by rule of reason, 146; proponents of method and, 110–11; rhetoric free of, 142n.12
pathos, 20, 21, 34–35, 114, 125, 127; in Chillingworth, 146, 152; and reason, 73–74
Paul, Saint, 78, 79, 82, 193
Peace of Augsburg, 84
People v. Ruggles, 237n.25
Perelman, Chaim, 14, 100
Peripatetics, the, 26n.90, 221
Perkins, William, 114–15
persecution, 163, 197; Acontius on, 113; of heretics, 134; justification of, 48–49, 225; Mill on, 132; Protestant/Catholic theories of, 107n.11. *See also* religious persecution
Personal Attack Rule, 273n.148
persuasion, 3, 5, 7; in Augustine, 49; based on reason, 146–47; and Christian unity, 241–42; by clergy, 198–99; emotional appeals in, 20–21; and faith, 121; as function of preaching, 71, 72–73, 75–76; with heretics, 80; in Hobbes, 183, 193–94; logical speech in, 114–15; modes of, 20; probable arguments in, 152–53; rhetorical predisposition to, over force (Erasmus), 45–50, 85; *sermo* as tool of, 119; and skepticism, 76
persuasive (category), 72
persuasive letters, 88–89
persuasiveness, of writings of Erasmus, 44–45
Petrarch, 57n.50, 86, 87

Pflug, Julius, 103–4
Phaedrus (Plato), 15–16
philosopher king, 46–47
Philosophical Commentary, A (Bayle), 238
philosophical debate, 32, 38–39, 40, 41
philosophical dialogue(s): of Cicero, 88, 90, 93, 145; *diatribē* as popularization of, 92
philosophical subject matter of conversation, 31–32, 33
philosophy, 171; conversation suited to, 32–33; and rhetoric, 32; speech for, 89
philosophy of Christ, 52–53, 74
physical coercion: effect on truth, 130, 132; against heretics, 85; in preaching, 83; rejected by Acontius, 135
physis, 176
Pico della Mirandola, Count Giovanni, 89n.180
Plato, 15–16, 19n.52, 33, 34n.123, 37, 89, 151, 181, 182; philosopher king, 46–47; improbability in, 23–24; Socratic dialogues of, 28; twofold division of rhetoric, 27n.91
Pliny the Younger, 88, 90
Plutarch, 92, 172
poetry, 5, 218
points of view: heard in marketplace, 268–69, 270, 273; systematization of, 240n.30
political assembly(ies), 16, 18–19, 93, 139; Athenian, 173
political authority, right to conscience and, 232
political discourse, 96, 179; limits on freedom of, 258–59; toleration of, 244
political obedience, 9, 194; individual freedom and, 163–67; necessity of (Hobbes), 196–99
political obligation, 167, 190
political order, 163; and religious liberty, 169, 175; threatened by religious disputation, 208–10, 211
political process, equalization of, 271–72
political speech, 21, 273; in humanist defense of toleration, 242, 244–45; protection of, 251–52; wealth and, 260, 268, 271–72, 275–77
political stability, 211; effect of skepticism on, 215–16; religious discussion and, 211, 227–28
political theory: of Bodin, 210n.13; of

Hobbes, 9, 169–70, 174–75, 176, 188, 191, 196, 210n.13
political truth, 244–45; free speech in, 255, 259
politics, religion versus, 162–67
Politiques, the, 211
Poliziano, Angelo, 88–90
Pontano, Giovanni, 87
popular audience(s), 17, 18–19, 93; preaching addressed to, 73–74
pornography, 12, 259–64, 266, 268, 272; justification for rejecting, 260–64
Postel, Guillaume, 229
Powell, Lewis, 250
preacher(s), 7, 48; Anglican, 142n.11; Presbyterian, 179–80, 198–99, 203; role of, 71, 82
preaching (genre), 7–8, 93, 96, 100, 112, 119; categories of, 72, 75; in Erasmus's theory of toleration, 49–50, 71–76; functions of, 71; Luther's view of, 82–83; moral reformation through, 147; as rhetorical genre of essential doctrines, 118–19; topics of, 75, 76
predestination, 127n.61, 154, 195
Presbyterian preachers, in English Civil War, 179–80, 198–99, 203
priesthood of all believers, 109
private worship, 200–201
probabilism, 12
probability, 6, 8–9, 96, 190, 231, 243; in Bayle, 238, 239–40; and certainty, 185; Cicero's subdivision of, 60; consensus as evidence of, 60–61, 63, 65, 184; in conversation, 38, 39; of free will, 57–58, 59–68; of historical knowledge, 172–73; in Hobbes, 170, 172–73; in Hooker, 138, 139; in Locke, 234–35; rhetoric and, 148–53; as standard of knowledge, 23–24, 25
probable knowledge, epistemological legitimacy of, 151–53
proof(s): emotional appeals as, 20–21, 23; kinds of, 150n.36; nonrational, 34–35
proposition (*propositum*), 18, 92–93
propriety, 30; adaptation to, 14, 16
Protestant Churches, fundamentals of faith in, 106–7
Protestantism, 112; of Acontius, 113, 115, 120, 136; of Chillingworth, 143, 145–48; subdivision of, 105

Protestants: adiophoral debates among, 156–57; differences among, 241n.35; dissenting, 235; fundamentals of faith for, 163; intolerance of, 155; and political authority, 165–66

Proxmire, William, 270

prudence, 146; in Bodin, 210–11; of Christ, 76, 77, 78; in Hobbes, 184–85, 188, 189

prudential argument for toleration, 199–201

prudential knowledge, in rules of rhetoric, 15

prudential method, 110–11

public, identification of rhetoric with the, 19n.52. See also common people

public assemblies, 174

public discourse, 259; Supreme Court and, 257–59

public disorder, rhetoric and, 173, 174

public law, 208–11

public worship, 200

Puritans, 114, 137, 138, 139, 140–41, 161, 166, 169, 181, 193, 210n.13; right to rebel, 194, 195

Putney Debates, 244

Puttenham, George, 182n.47

Pyrrho of Ellis, 25n.86

Pyrrhonian skepticism, 25

Pythagoreans, 34, 96, 195

Quattrocento humanists, 90, 91–92

Quintilian, 13, 15n.30, 16, 17, 18, 27n.91, 34n.123, 45, 93, 95–96, 172, 182, 246; Erasmus's attraction to, 44; on oratory, 19–20, 21, 22, 23; probability in, 24

Ramus, Peter, 109–10, 111, 113, 114, 115, 142

rational discussion, 12–13, 248, 252, 263; and marketplace of ideas, 254–55, 256, 263; and religious truth, 204

rationalism, 4, 142; of method, 112; in Reformation, 107; and rejection of decorum, 111

rationality, pornography/hate speech and, 262

Rawls, John, 232, 233n.6, 237, 253

reason, 20, 99; appeals to, 114, 125–26; in conversation, 125–26, 127; emotional appeals and, 73; and external authority, 147; and faith, 107; proponents of method and,

110–11; science and, 142n.12; search for truth through, 146, 164

Red Lion Broadcasting Co. v. FCC, 250, 273–74

Reformation. 2, 6, 68n.99, 90, 104, 107–9, 112, 155

Rehnquist, William, 257

Reik, Miriam, 178, 179n.33

relativism, 254; of Chillingworth, 158, 159

religion(s), 190, 242; and certainty, 150n.36, 234; duty to protect and foster, 134, 135; education and, 238–39; in Erasmus, 45; feeling, 218; in Hobbes, 169, 199; versus politics, 162–67; as private activity, 232–33; is probable, 148–51, 162, 183; restrictions on, 236; representing aspects of truth, 11, 212, 219, 220, 221–22, 223, 226, 228, 229; sovereign's authority over, 191; uncertainty in, 185–86, 216–17

Religion of Protestants, The (Chillingworth), 145–48, 158–59, 165, 240

religious belief/action distinction, 141n.9

religious beliefs, rational investigation of, 138. See also beliefs

religious community, right to conscience and, 232, 233

religious conflict, 183; pernicious effect of, 208–9

religious debate/discussion, 169; and civil war, 227; dangers of, 208–9, 210, 211, 215–17; futility of, 214; between members of different religious, 215–18; and political stability, 227–28; reinforcing beliefs through, 218; and the state, 204

religious dissenters. See dissenters

religious diversity, 10, 66, 163; in Bodin, 210–11, 220, 221–22; Catholic Church and, 143; growth of, 237–38; toleration of, 92, 226

religious doctrine. See doctrine

religious intolerance, 1–2, 80, 83–84, 99

religious liberty, 11, 12, 131, 135; in Hobbes, 200–201; liberalism and, 231–43; limits on, 141; and political order, 169, 175; theory of, 224; toleration distinct from, 7

religious oratory, threat to political stability, 209–10

religious persecution, 2, 47, 99; condemned by Erasmus, 79–80; and search for truth, 129 religious pluralism, 9, 85

religious rhetoric, disruptive power of, 203

religious toleration: Acontius and practice of, 134–36; in Bodin, 230; Cicero and, 40–41; *decorum* and, 79–81; in Erasmus, 67, 100–101, 106; forms of, 6–7; as grant or privilege, 7; of heretics, 6, 7–8, 85, 134–35; in Hobbes, 169–70, 175, 179, 199; Hobbes versus the humanists, 192–201; humanist, 1–13 (*see also* humanist defense of religious toleration); limits of, 84–85; in Luther, 81–82, 83–84; minimal form of, 6, 7; move to freedom of speech, 243–48; precondition to conversation, 129–31; prudential argument for, 199–201; of public imperfections, 80–81; rational discussion in, 107; rhetoric and, 115–34; *sermo* and, 97–101; types of, 71

religious truth: certainty of, 208; nature of (Bodin), 219–23. *See also* truth

religious unity, 210–11

Renaissance, 1, 4, 13, 98, 141; revival of *studia humanitatis*, 5

Renaissance humanists, 2–13, 156, 263, 269, 277; dialogue in, 86–87; Hobbes versus, 192–201; opposition to scholastics, 97–98

"repressive toleration," 261n.103

Republic (Plato), 33, 46–47

Reynolds v. U.S., 141n.9

rhetoric, 5–6, 29, 109–10; in Acontius, 136; civilizing power of, 210; and contention, 189; in curriculum, 206; *decorum* feature of, 29–30; dialectic distinct from, 30n.107; in Erasmus, 44–45; of fundamentals, 71–85; genres of, 93; history and, 171–72, 173–74; Hobbes and, 170–71, 178, 179–88; improper, as threat to discussion, 133–34; method and, 111; of nonessentials, 85–101; origin of humanist defense of religious toleration in, 7–8; philosophy and, 32; predisposition to persuasion over force (Erasmus), 45–50; and probability, 148–53; public disorder and, 173, 174; rules of, 15; science and, 189–90; in seventeenth century, 142; threat to civil order, 209–10: and toleration, 115–34. *See also* classical rhetoric

Rhetoric (Aristotle), 13, 19, 21–22, 126, 178, 184n.55

Rhetoric and Reform (Boyle), 92–93

Rhetorica ad Caius Herennium, 13

rhetorical devices, 182–83

rhetorical epistemology, Hobbes's rejection of, 190

rhetorical form, and quality of discussion, 263, 268

rhetorical principles, implications of, 148

rhetorical setting, proper, 163–64

rhetorical strategies, regarding free will, 68–71

rhetorical style, and freedom of speech, 256–57, 259

right to conscience, 4, 12, 223, 224; of atheists, 226, 227; in Locke, 248; in theory of religious liberty, 231, 232, 233–34, 236

rites and rituals, as adiaphoral, 50–51

Roellenbleck, Georg, 213

Roman Catholic Church, 116; authoritarianism of, 146; Chillingworth and, 143, 144, 165; claim to be sole judge of truth, 147; decrees of, 59; doctrinal unity in, 105–6; fundamentals of faith in, 155; Hooker on, 137–38; as interpreter of Bible, 153; legal powers of, 198; persecution of doctrinally deviant, 1–2; proscription of, 246–47; Reformation and, 107; rites and rituals of, 50–51

Roman Catholics, 140, 183; attempts at reconciliation with Lutherans, 103–4, 116; expulsion of, 84; and fundamentals of faith, 135–36; penal laws against, 231n.1; political dangers posed by, 12, 241n.33; rejection of truth by, 118; restrictions on, 236; salvation for, 161; and sovereign, 195; and variable standard of faith, 159

Roman religion, 40–41, 47n.18

Rousseau, Jean-Jacques, 227–28

Royal Society, 142n.12

Rummel, Erika, 96n.202

Ryan, Alan, 198, 199n.123

sacraments, 52, 106, 113

salvation, 161, 228; beliefs necessary to, 9, 157, 158, 159, 195, 225 (*see also* fundamentals of faith); conscience and, 224; doctrinal standard for, 64; essentials of, must be accommodated to individual, 162; through faith alone, 113; free will in, 54–

55; of non-Christians, 229; requirements for, 196, 197; right to conscience in, 233; solely through Christ, 136; truths necessary to, 234

Satan, 119–20, 123, 126, 130, 132

Satan's Stratagems (Acontius), 112–13, 118, 119, 129–30, 132, 135, 155, 181

Savonarola, Girolamo, 209

schism/schismatics, 49, 67–68, 81

scholastic discussion/debate, 97, 98–99

scholarly elite. *See* elite(s)

scholastics/scholasticism, 53, 59, 97–99; Erasmus as, 53n.38

science, 9; of Hobbes, 169, 176, 177–92; promise of, 188–92; and reason, 142n.12

scientific method, in Hobbes, 176

scriptura sola, 107–8

scriptural interpretation, individual, 107–9, 113

Scripture, 59, 64, 70, 197; authority in, 247; divine origin of, 57, 58; infallibility of, 151; interpretation of, 62, 63, 193; study of, 66, 117. *See also* Bible

Secretum (Petrarch), 87

secular humanism, 5

secular realm: humanist defense of toleration in, 242, 243–48; toleration in, 134–35; use of force in, 48

sedition, 67–68, 164n.85, 174, 179

Seneca, 92

sense experience, 185, 190; knowledge from, 149, 150

separation of church and state, 236

sermo (conversation), 7, 8–9, 26–41, 93, 94n.197, 100, 156, 173, 174, 221, 231, 255, 258, 261, 269, 277; in Acontius, 115–18, 123–25, 133; in Bodin, 10–11, 204, 207, 212–13, 217, 228, 229; characteristics of, 87; in Chillingworth, 142–43; Ciceronian model of, 88, 90, 94–95, 111, 123, 125, 128, 129, 139, 145; civil, 12, 277; classical, 89; *decorum* of, 127–29, 163; democracy as, 258–59; in *Diatriba,* 96; disagreements in, 37–39; in Erasmus's theory of toleration, 49–50; expansion of, 112; forms of, 123–25; as genre of doctrinal adiaphora, 118–19; in Great Tew meetings, 145; grounded on principle of *decorum,* 99; ideal of, 10; in Milton, 247;

as primary model of toleration, 112, 115–18, 119; in rhetoric of nonessentials, 85–92; rules of civility for, 35, 36; skepticism and *decorum* in, 99–101; source of conversation genre, 85–86; threat to civil order in, 11; and toleration, 97–101; toleration precondition to, 129–31; and truth, 97n.208, 138–39, 246

Sextus Empiricus, 25n.86

Sextus Turpilius, 29n.104

Sheldon, Gilbert, 144

Six livres de la république (Bodin), 207–11, 226

skeptical inquiry, 122, 123

skeptical tolerance, 87; of divergent opinions, 92

skepticism, 10, 11, 25–26, 96, 149, 169; in Bayle, 12, 239–40, 242; in Bodin, 215–16, 217; and certainty, 229, 239; characteristic of classical rhetoric, 17, 22–23; in Cicero, 37–38, 153; and consensus, 61; in *contentio,* 38; and controversy, 74; of Erasmus, 56–57, 59; and loss of consensus, 238; in nonessentials, 3, 5–6, 54, 56–57; persuasion and, 76; rhetoric and, 26; in scholastics, 98, 99; in *sermo,* 38–39, 99–101; in Supreme Court, 253–54; theology of, 118–22. *See also* academic skepticism

skeptics, 47n.18

Skinner, Quentin, 182, 214

social context of religion, 233

social context of speech, 277

social contract, 232, 233n.6

social contract theory (Hobbes), 10

social convention as threat to open discussion, 132

social order, 163; atheists danger to, 226; in Hobbes, 190

society: atomistic, 10; multireligious, 242

Socinians, 157

Socinus, Faustus, 144, 234n.11

Socrates, 32, 53, 175, 213; *elenchus,* 37; Erasmus on, 53–54; negative dialectic in, 38

Socratic dialogues, 28

Sophists, 176, 181, 188

sovereign(s), 175; control over religion, 12, 169, 227; duty to obey, as fundamental of faith, 196–99; in Hobbes, 169, 190–92, 194, 195, 196; and moral authority, 195,

196; and orators, 210; and religious unity, 203; right to coercion, 10, 163–64; and toleration, 9, 199–201; and state religion, 210–11

sovereignty, undivided and absolute, 194, 210n.13

Sozzini, Lelio, 3n.7

"speaking picture," 171n.9

speech: adapted to particulars, 84; categories of, 16–26; content of, 252–54, 255–57; as essential characteristic of humanity and godliness, 45–50; ethical value of, 47–50; false, 265; in humanist defense of toleration, 242, 245–48; logical, 113–15; money equated with, 275–76; order of, 110; protection of, 251–52, 255, 256, 257–59, 265–67, 272–73; restrictions on, 265, 266; silencing, 259; as social act, 277; standards for good, 89

speech egalitarianism, 268–77

speech of victims, stigmatized, 260–61

spiritual realm, toleration in, 134, 135–36

Sprat, Thomas, 142n.12

state: church and, 236; granting toleration, 7; in Hobbes, 10; limiting religious liberty, 141; multireligious, 209, 211; and principle of neutrality, 253–54; and religious discourse, 204; religious persecution by, 49; responsibility of, to foster discovery of truth, 12–13; role in religion, 130–31, 200–201; unity of religion in, 84, 200, 203–4, 210–11

state intervention in religion, Luther and, 83

Stillingfleet, Edward, 231n.1

Stoics, 36, 37, 65, 89, 221

Strauss, Leo, 177, 179n.33

studia humanitatis, 5, 44, 141–42

Summa theologiae (Aquinas), 98

Summary of the Christian Religion (Acontius), 113

syllogism, 24, 30, 151, 184n.55

Sylvest, Edward, 142

Talon, Omer, 109

teaching, 44; method of, 110–11, 114n.37

Tenison, Thomas, 231n.1

Texas v. Johnson, 253, 257

Thirty-nine Articles, 105, 144, 157

Thirty Years' War, 1

Thucydides, 170–76, 177, 178, 179, 184

Tillotson, John, 231n.1

Tisias, 23

to prepon, 14

toleration. See religious toleration

Toleration Act of 1689, 231n.1

tradition, 150–51

tranquility, 169; in conversation, 36–37; political obedience and, 163–64

tranquility of the Church, disturbed by heresy, 66, 67–68

Trenchard, John, 245

Trinity, the, 75, 158, 195; doctrine of, 51–52

tropes, 182

truth, 171; ability to know, 242; ability to triumph over error, 117–18, 126, 132, 133, 164, 263; absence of controversy as quality of, 189–90; appeal to, 224; authority and, 128; consensus as criterion of, 59, 60, 113, 184, 226, 263–64; in conversation, 97n.208, 130; devotion to, in Luther, 84; emerges from discussion of ideas, 98, 100, 237; as goal of scholarly letter, 89–90; hindered by restraints on discussion, 132–34; and honor, 94n.198; inborn, 65; necessary for salvation, 234 (see also fundamentals of faith); passions obscuring, 173; pluralistic conception of, in Bodin, 212, 219–23, 226, 228–29; probability as criterion of, 151, 152, 240; questioning, 120; religions representing aspects of, 11, 212, 219, 220, 221–22, 223, 226, 228, 229; rhetoric masks, 180–81; right to free speech and, 249, 252, 253–54, 257; scientific, 189; sermo in attaining knowledge of, 37, 117–18; sermo-based tolerance and, 212; and toleration, 133–34, 229. See also political truth; religious truth

truth, discovery of, 8, 10, 96; role of state in, 12–13

truth, search for, 94–95, 96, 163; Church and, 233–34; in conversation, 37, 38, 123, 127–29, 138–39; in decorum, 100; emotions in, 99; and free speech, 247–48; freedom of debate in, 246; heresy and, 218; hindered by intemperate discussion, 248n.54; by individual(s), 125–26; and marketplace of ideas, 254, 255, 257, 259, 263, 264–65, 267, 269, 276, 277; no longer limited to religion, 242, 244; rational

discussion in, 204; through reason, 146; tranquil environment required for, 163
Truth of the Christian Religion (Grotius), 150n.36
Tusculan Disputations (Cicero), 92, 96, 156

uncertainty, 22; in Acontius, 131; in letters of discussion, 90; in religion and morals, 185–86, 216–17
Unitarians, 231n.1
United States, religious diversity in, 237
U.S. Supreme Court, 12, 141n.9, 243, 249–59, 264, 265–66, 269, 273–76
unity, Christian, 4, 7, 10, 241–42
univocality, 176, 190–91
"Unlawfulness of Resisting the Lawful Prince" (Chillingworth), 166
Utopia (More), 126

Valla, Lorenzo, 59, 86, 87, 90n.186
variable standard of fundamentals of faith, 153–62, 224
Varro, 40–41
Venice, 213, 223
verbal abuse, 130, 163, 260
verbal coercion, 80, 135
verbal discord, as natural state, 188
verisimile, 152
Via regia, sive de controversis religionis capitibus conciliandis sententia (Witzel), 104

Vicentino, Nicolo, 222
victimization, and free speech, 260–62
Victor, C. Julius, 27n.91, 34

Walwyn, William, 244n.40
war(s), justification of, 33, 46
wars of religion, 208
"watchword of the faith," 122, 131
Watkins, J. W. N., 198
wealth, in/and political speech, 260, 268, 271–72, 275–77
Western culture, 10
Whitney v. California, 250, 267n.124
Wilkins, John, 231n.1
Wilson, Matthew (Edward Knott), 145, 151, 153, 158–59
witch-hunting, 1
Witzel, George, 104
word, divinity of the, 47–50
words, logical ordering of, 189
Wood, Anthony a', 142–43
works, justification by, 128, 136
Wright, Skelly, 272
Wycliffe, John, 59, 79

Zeno the Stoic, 29n.103
Zwingli, Huldreich, 2
Zwinglian (church), 105
Zwinglians, 84, 104, 106